Southern Heritage

Cookbook

. . . compilation of directions for cooking some delightful dishes from the Muscle Shoals section of northwest Alabama, southwest Tennessee and northwest Mississippi.

Compiled By
Mildred Ballinger Anderson
Florence, Alabama

Published by: The House of Collectibles, Inc.
                Orlando Central Park
                1900 Premier Row
                Orlando, FL 32809
                Phone: (305) 857-9095

Printed in the United States of America

ISBN: 0-87637-120-9

Contents

Love Creates Good Cooking

There is a tendency to think of gourmet dishes, whatever"gourmet dishes"are, as creations of chefs in the huge kitchens of fine restaurants.

I do not agree!

Delightful food may be reproduced in great restaurants by accomplished chefs, but I think these palatable productions originate elsewhere.

Good and great food preparation is the result of hungry people rather than a catering to pampered palates. Great dishes are originated by loving hands for people who have earned the right of being fed and who are loved by the originators.

Here again, necessity has been the mother of invention.

The first strudel had to be prepared by a Germanic mother or wife to reward an Alpine shepherd or one who had labored hard in the potato fields. The many variations of cheese could only be the result of a loving housekeeper trying to reward one who had spent many lonely weeks following the sheep, his only companionship a faithful dog and his only food simple bread and cheese.

The highly seasoned and savory dishes of Mexico were created by those who had to take the beans, tough beef and coarse meal, day after day, and vary its taste with available peppers and other spices for those who worked the arid fields to produce the ingredients.

The same is true in this area of the South. The hundreds, possibly thousands, of dishes which have been created from locally available products originated out of necessity and love.

Appetizers

Vegetable Appetizers

Prepare these vegetables ahead, wrap in foil and refrigerate. Serve beautifully cold and crisp with one of the tasty dips.

Carrots—scrape and cut lengthwise in strips, then crosswise in 3-to-4-inch lengths.

Cauliflower—Separate flowers and trim the stalks a bit to make them easy to handle when dunking.

Celery—Trim tender stalks; cut lengthwise in ½-inch strips, then crosswise in finger lengths.

Radishes—Remove root ends and trim off all leaves except a few center ones; make several cuts from root end toward stem end and drop into ice-cold water to make radish roses.

Belgian Endive—Cut in lengthwise strips or separate into leaves.

Cucumbers—Peel, cut in half lengthwise and remove center if seeds are large; then cut in strips and, if cucumbers are long, cut strips crosswise.

Zucchini—Use small ones, cut in half lengthwise, then in strips.

Cherry Tomatoes—Wash, leave blossom end on.

Fennel—Remove outside tough stalks. Trim feathery tops, leaving just the tenderest, greenest portion. Cut the whole bulb-like end right up through the stalks.

Fruit Appetizers

Suitable fruits are apples, pears, canteloupes, bananas and pineapple and firm, not too juicy, orange sections. Cut fruit into wedges or spears leaving skin on. Dip in lemon juice; arrange on serving dish, cover with foil, and chill in refrigerator until needed. They will stay fresh without discoloring about 6 hours. Place a bowl of curry—or Roquefort—flavored dip in center. Garnish with firm grapes, whole strawberries with hulls on, bing cherries...any colorful fruit in season.

Broiled Mushrooms

Select medium-size fresh mushrooms, or use drained canned mushroom caps. Chop stems with a small amount of onion. Sauté in butter, adding salt and pepper to taste. Sauté chicken livers, chop and season well, adding the sauteed stems, or use liverwurst or chopped cooked ham. Fill caps. Cover with foil refrigerate. Before serving, remove cover, brown under broiler 6 to 8 minutes.

Curry Dip

1 pint mayonnaise
1 tablespoon curry powder
1 tablespoon Worcestershire
   sauce
3 tablespoons chili sauce

1 tablespoon finely grated onion,
   pulp and juice
1 teaspoon salt
¼ teaspoon white pepper
Small clove garlic, crushed

Mix all ingredients together. Cover tightly and store in refrigerator.
Good served with celery sticks, cucumber slices, raw or parboiled carrot sticks, cauliflower and cooked artichokes.

Beulah Phillips
Lexington

Deviled Ham Dip

1 8-ounce package cream cheese
¼ teaspoon Tabasco
¼ cup mayonnaise
2 tablespoons prepared mustard

2 4½-ounce cans deviled ham
1 teaspoon minced onion
2 tablespoons chopped stuffed olive

Combine cream cheese, Tabasco, mayonnaise. Then stir in mustard, deviled ham, onion, and olives. Refrigerate until serving time. Makes about 2¼ cups.

Mrs. Linda J. McDougal
Killen

Peppered Cheddar Dip

1½ cups dairy sour cream
1 cup shredded cheddar cheese
   (about 4 ounces)
¼ cup finely chopped onion

3 tablespoons minced green
   pepper
¼ teaspoon salt
⅛ teaspoon red pepper sauce
1 tablespoon milk

Mix all ingredients. If necessary, add another tablespoon milk to make a good dipping consistency. Cover; refrigerate at least 1 hour. Makes 2 cups.

Mrs. Jerry Turbyfill
Florence

Oyster Dip

Chop 1 4-ounce can fresh oysters
Salt, pepper and paprika to taste
½ teaspoon seafood seasoning

½ teaspoon dried onion
½ teaspoon Worcestershire sauce

Chop into half pint dairy sour cream.

Mrs. Flanagan Simpson
Florence

Shrimp Dip

Softened cream cheese
Tomato ketchup, only a little

Onions, chopped finely
Mayonnaise, a little

Blend all these ingredients together. Then add drained canned shrimp or fresh boiled shrimp. Mix well.

2

Three Cheese Dip

1 package (8 ounce) cream
  cheese
1½ cups grated cheddar cheese
5 ounces cheese spread

1 teaspoon Worcestershire sauce
½ teaspoon dry mustard
½ teaspoon salt

Let all cheeses reach room temperature. Beat with electic mixer until smooth. Add remaining ingredients. Place in serving dish and chill.

Mrs. Edward Mullen
Florence

Brown Derby Cottage Cheese And Avocado Dip

1 small ripe avocado
8 ounces cottage cheese
2 ounces soft butter

¼ teaspoon celery salt
1 tablespoon chopped chives
Dash of salt

Remove skin and seed from ripe avocado. Put the pulp and cheese through a fine sieve. Place in mixing bowl, add ingredients, beat slowly until smooth. Serve in bowl surrounded by potato chips.

Donna M. Hayes
Florence

Roquefort And Cottage Cheese Dip

2 (1¼ ounces) portions Roquefort
  Cheese
1 (8 ounce) container cottage cheese

½ teaspoon onion juice
6 tablespoons sour cream

Crumble Roquefort cheese and add to cottage cheese. Mix well. Stir in onion juice. Add enough sour cream to give good dipping consistency.

Donna M. Hayes
Florence

Philly Dip

2 (3 ounce) packages cream cheese
1 triangle Roquefort cheese
1 tablespoon chopped parsley

2 tablespoons finely chopped onion
2 tablespoons finely chopped celery

Allow cheese to soften at room temperature. Blend in parsley, onion, celery, and mix.

Donna M. Hayes
Florence

Copenhagen Dip

⅓ cup crumbled Danablue cheese,
  at room temperature
1 pint dairy sour cream
½ teaspoon seasoned salt

1 clove garlic, crushed
¼ cup minced green onion
¼ teaspoon Worcestershire sauce

In medium-size mixing bowl, mash blue cheese with a fork. Add remaining ingredients and blend thoroughly. Refrigerate 1 hour. Makes 2½ cups dip.

Mildred Anderson

3

Danish Dip

½ cup sliced (unblanched) almonds

⅓ cup Danish blue cheese, crumbled

2 cups dairy sour cream

½ cup whipping cream, whipped

Spread almonds in shallow pan. Toast at 350 degrees for 5 minutes or until light gold in color. Cool. Reserve 1 to 2 tablespoons for garnish. Crush remainder under rolling pin. Mix crushed almonds, sour cream and blue cheese; fold in whipped cream; turn into bowl. Sprinkle with reserved sliced almonds. Serve with strawberries, apple or pear wedges, cubes of melon, assorted crackers or raw vegetables. Makes 4 cups dip.

Curried Cheese Dip

2 teaspoons butter or margarine

½ cup chopped walnuts or almonds

¼-½ teaspoon curry powder

1 cup grated sharp natural cheddar cheese

¾ cup grated muenster cheese

2 tablespoons crumbled blue cheese

½ cup sour cream

¼ teaspoon salt

¼-½ teaspoon mustard

¼ teaspoon paprika

½ cup half-and-half or milk

Crisp, raw vegetables

Preheat oven to 300°. Put butter in shallow baking pan. Add nuts and curry powder to butter and toss until well mixed. Toast nuts in oven for 15 minutes, stirring once, until very lightly browned. Cool. In medium bowl with electric mixer, beat cheeses together with sour cream, salt, mustard and paprika until thoroughly blended. Gradually add half-and-half and beat until smooth. Clean beaters. Stir in nuts, scraping in curry butter. Serve with crisp, raw vegetables, such as carrot and celery sticks, cucumber and zucchini slices, cauliflowerets, raw mushrooms and cherry tomatoes.

Makes 2 cups dip

Chili Con Queso
(Cheese Dip)

2 pound box cheese

1 can tomatoes

Heat together very slowly until cheese melts. Stir and keep warm while serving in a chafing dish or fondue pot. Serve with potato chips.

Mrs. Don White
Florence

Tybo Dip

1 cup grated Danish Tybo cheese, at room temperature

1 package (3-ounces) cream cheese, softened

¼ cup tomato ketchup

3 tablespoons chopped pimiento peppers

½ teaspoon Worcestershire sauce

Milk to moisten

Blend all ingredients together and if not moist enough, add a bit of milk. Makes 1¼ cups dip.

4

Hot Shrimp Dip

½ stick butter
1 8 ounce package cream cheese
1 can small shrimp
3 drops of Tabasco sauce

Small amount of lemon juice
1 or 2 tablespoons chopped
  green onions

Melt butter with cream cheese in top of double boiler. Add can of shrimp and 1 or 2 tablespoons of liquid from can, Tabasco sauce, lemon juice and green onions. Serve warm with chips.

Sherry McKenzie
Florence

Ann's Curry Dip

1 pint mayonnaise
3 tablespoons catsup
3 teaspoons curry

1 tablespoon Worcestershire sauce
1 tablespoon grated onion
Salt and pepper to taste

Blend together well. This makes an excellent dip for raw vegetables, particularly cauliflower.

Curry Dip

1 teaspoon horseradish
1 teaspoon tarragon vinegar
1 teaspoon grated onion

1 cup mayonnaise
1 teaspoon curry powder
1 teaspoon garlic salt

Mix all together in a bowl. Cover and chill overnight in refrigerator. Serve with chilled raw vegetables—carrot sticks, celery, green pepper, cauliflower and sliced raw mushrooms. Note: Be sure to use dry measuring cup for mayonnaise.

Mrs. John Formby, Jr.
Florence

Vegetable Dip

½ pint of sour cream
Juice of ½ lemon
1 tablespoon wine vinegar
1 tablespoon horseradish
1½ teaspoons salt

1 teaspoon dry mustard
½ teaspoon paprika
1 teaspoon onion juice
Cayenne pepper to taste

Mix all ingredients and serve as a dip with carrots, radishes, cucumbers, cauliflower, or cherry tomatoes.

Mrs. Pat Peck
Florence

Dandy Dip For Vegetables

1 package (8 ounces) cream
  cheese, softened
1 envelope seasoning mix for
  Sloppy Joes

½ cup milk
Cut up raw vegetables such as
  radishes, carrots, cucumber,
  zucchini, celery

Combine cream cheese, contents of seasoning mix envelope and milk; blend well and chill. Serve with cut-up raw vegetables or create whimsical characters from vegetable pieces held together with food picks. Makes about 1½ cups dip.

Elizabeth Medaris

Clam Dip

2 (8 ounce) packages cream
   cheese
2 small cans drained, minced
   clams
½ small onion, chopped

2 tablespoons lemon juice
1½ tablespoons Worcestershire
   sauce
Salt
Hot sauce

Drain clams; save juice. Mix all ingredients; thin with clam juice. Salt and add hot sauce to taste.

Mrs. Gene Hamby, Jr.
Sheffield

Clam Dip

2 packages (3 ounces each) cream
   cheese
2 teaspoons fresh lemon juice
1 teaspoon Worcestershire sauce

¼ teaspoon salt
Cayenne pepper
½ cup minced clams
1 tablespoon clam broth

Blend cream cheese, lemon juice, Worcestershire sauce, salt, dash cayenne pepper, clams and broth. Place in dish on a tray and garnish with chives. Surround with crisp potato chips. Makes 1¼ cups dip.

Mildred Anderson
Florence

Mushroom Dip

½ pound mushrooms
2 tablespoons butter
1 teaspoon corn flake crumbs

½ cup heavy cream
Salt, pepper, and nutmeg

Melt butter and add finely chopped mushrooms. Cook 5 minutes and sprinkle with corn flake crumbs. Stir and add heavy cream. Cook until thick. Season with salt, pepper, and nutmeg. Serve hot with toast or crackers or serve in a chafing dish or electric saucepan. Use as the filling for rolled sandwiches. Toast just before serving.

Donna M. Hayes
Florence

Smoked Oyster Dip

1 can smoked oysters, drained
2 (8 ounce) packages cream cheese
1 teaspoon Worcestershire sauce

2 teaspoons lemon juice
1 cup sour cream
Salt to taste

Blend oysters and cheese thoroughly with fork or mixer. Add other ingredients and mix well. Serve with corn or potato chips. Serves 12 to 14.

Mrs. Pat Peck
Florence

Tuna-Anchovy Dip

1 can (6½ or 7-ounce size) tuna
1 can (2 ounces) anchovy fillets
½ pint dairy sour cream

2 tablespoons mayonnaise
1 hard-cooked egg, sliced
1 tablespoon freeze-dried chives

Drain oil from tuna and anchovy fillets and place in blender. Blend until smooth. Empty into a bowl.

Blend in sour cream and mayonnaise. Put in a glass bowl. Garnish top with sieved egg yolk and finely chopped egg whites.

Top with a sprinkling of chives. Makes 1½ cups dip.

Lou's Cheese Roll

5 ounces Roquefort cheese
2 packages (3 ounces each or 1
   8-ounce) cream cheese
5 ounces cheddar cheese

1 onion, finely grated
1 teaspoon Worcestershire sauce
½ pound pecans, chopped fine

Soften the cheeses; add onion, Worcestershire sauce and one-half of the pecans. Mix well. Shape into desired form. Chill for a while. Before serving coat or roll cheese ball in rest of pecans.

Mildred Anderson
Florence

Roquefort Balls

6 ounces Roquefort cheese
2 4-ounce jars sharp cheese
12 ounces cream cheese
6 tablespoon Worcestershire
   sauce

1 teaspoon monosodium
   glutamate
2 tablespoons grated onion
¼ cup minced parsley
½ cup ground nuts

The day before, leave cheeses at room temperature to soften. Then combine and blend with Worcestershire sauce, monosodium glutamate and onion. Refrigarate for 24 hours. Next day, form into 1 large ball or 2 small balls, roll in parsley mixed with nuts.

Christine Harrison
Killen

Sausage Cheese Balls

3½ cups biscuit mix
1 pound sausage

10 ounces sharp cheddar
   cheese, grated

Mix sausage with biscuit mix: melt cheese in top of double-boiler, add cheese to sausage mixture, stir to make even blend of ingredients. Form into small balls, freeze, thaw when ready to use. Bake on ungreased cookie sheet at 400 degrees for 10 minutes.

Mrs. Robert Walther
Tuscumbia

Cheese And Sausage Puffs

1 pound sausage
3 cups Bisquick

8 ounces medium sharp
   cheese (grated)

Work Bisquick into sausage, 1 cup at a time, add grated cheese into mix. Roll in ball about size of large marble. Bake at 350 degrees for about 15 minutes on ungreased cookie sheet.

Mrs. Tracy Gargis
Sheffield

Cheese Straws

3 cups plain flour
1 pound grated (soft) New York
  sharp cheese
2 sticks margarine (soft)
1 teaspoon salt
1 teaspoon red pepper

Blend last 4 ingredients, then slowly add flour. Place in pastry tube and lay out on cookie sheet. Preheat oven to 350 degrees. Bake until very light brown. Makes 2 pounds.

Mrs. John Gargis
Leighton

Cheese Straws

1 pound New York State sharp
  cheddar cheese
2 cups plain flour
1½ sticks margarine (less 3 pats)
1 teaspoon baking powder
1 teaspoon cayenne pepper (if desired
½ teaspoon cayenne pepper and
red pepper mixed may be added)

Grate cheese, allow cheese and margarine to become room temperature. Sift flour, add baking powder and pepper and mix. Mix cheese and margarine well, add flour mixture. Place dough in cookie press and press on greased cookie sheet which has been greased with 3 pats margarine. Bake in preheated oven at approximately 300 degrees until color changes slightly. Must be watched closely. Be careful not to overcook. May be frozen after cooking.

Clifford Delony
Tuscumbia

Cheese Sticks

1¾ cups unsifted flour
2 teaspoons baking powder
½ teaspoon salt
½ cup shortening
1 cup shredded sharp
  cheddar cheese
¾ cup milk
Paprika

With pastry blender, combine first four ingredients until mealy. Stir in cheese and enough milk for a soft but not sticky dough. Turn onto floured board; knead until smooth. Roll pieces of dough between palms to ½ inch in diameter and 4 inches long. Bake in an ungreased baking pan at 450 degrees for 10 minutes. Sprinkle with paprika. Cool and serve. Yields: 20 to 24 sticks.

Lou Ware
Tuscumbia

Chili Cheese Rounds

½ cup butter or margarine
2 cups grated cheddar cheese
2 cups sifted flour
1 tablespoon chili powder
1 teaspoon salt

Cream softened butter and cheese. Blend in sifted dry ingredients. Shape into two rolls 1½ inches in diameter. Chill for two hours. Thinly slice and place on an ungreased baking sheet. Bake at 350 degrees for 8-10 minutes, or until lightly browned. Serve hot or cold with soup, salad or beverage. Yield: 4 dozen.

Gladys Hickman
Florence

8

Party Cheese Drops

1 pound grated sharp cheese
2 sticks margarine
2 teaspoons salt
½ or 1 teaspoon red pepper
3 cups plain flour
1 cup pecans chopped fine

Have cheese and margarine room temperature. Cream together in mixer. Add salt, pepper, and flour one cup at a time. Add nuts. Drop by ½ teaspoon on cookie sheet. Bake in 300-325 degree oven for 15 minutes.

Mrs. Gladys Russell
Cherokee

Cheese Rings

1 pound sharp cheese
1 pound butter or margarine
1 pound plain flour (4 cups)
1 teaspoon salt
1 teaspoon cayenne pepper

Grate cheese and mix well with butter. Gradually add flour to which salt and cayenne pepper have been added. Press through cookie press using star disk. Shape into rings. Bake at 425 degrees for 10 to 12 minutes.

Mrs. Craig H. Groce
Muscle Shoals

Cheese Olives

25 ripe olives
2 or 3 minced green onions
½ cup flour
¼ teaspoon salt
⅛ teaspoon dry mustard
4 ounces sharp cheddar cheese
3 tablespoons butter, melted and
   cooled slightly
1 tablespoon milk
2 drops Tabasco

Stuff olives with onions. Blend flour with salt, mustard and shredded cheese. Stir into mixture: butter, milk and Tabasco. Using 1 teaspoon per olive, wrap around olives and place on baking sheet. Bake at 400 degrees for 10-12 minutes. Yields 25 canapes which can be frozen.

Mrs. Evie Boyles
Russellville

Olive Appetizers

Completely cover large stuffed olives with cream cheese. Roll in chopped almonds (salted). Spear with toothpicks.

Evie Boyles
Russellville

Pickle Fans

For each pickle fan use a gherkin (small pickle). Make four lengthwise cuts from one end to the other; spread gently to form a little fan.

Mrs. Jerry L. Turbyfill
Florence

9

Cheese Ball

1 package (8 ounce) cream cheese,
at room temperature
1 package (4 ounce) sharp cheese,
at room temperature
1 clove garlic, crushed

¾ teaspoon Worcestershire
sauce
¾ teaspoon dry mustard
Red pepper and cayenne pepper
to taste

Blend cream cheese and sharp cheese. Add remaining ingredients. Refrigerate. Before serving, shape into ball and roll in chopped pecans and parsley.

Mrs. Judy McKelvey
Tuscumbia

Chili Cheese Ball

2 pounds Velveeta cheese
1 8-ounce package cream cheese
1 cup chopped nuts

¼ teaspoon garlic powder
Dash of salt
Chili powder

Place cheeses in large bowl; let come to room temperature. Mix cheeses well. Add nuts, garlic powder and salt; mix well. Shape into ball; roll in chili powder. Wrap in foil; chill until firm.

Mrs. Joan Pugh
Florence

Little Links In Oriental Sauce

1 cup brown sugar, firmly packed
3 tablespoons all-purpose flour
2 teaspoons dry mustard
1 cup pineapple juice
½ cup vinegar
1½ teaspoons soy sauce

2 (1 pound) packages little wieners
2 (1 pound) packages cocktail
smoked sausages (can use
regular sausage rolled into
balls)

Combine brown sugar, flour and mustard in saucepan. Add pineapple juice, vinegar and soy sauce. Heat to boiling, stirring constantly. Boil 1 minute. Stir in wieners and sausages. Cook slowly for 5 minutes or until heated through. Keep warm over low heat in chafing dish. Use wooden picks for serving. Yield: 64 appetizers.

Mrs. Claire S. Pitts
Sheffield

Vienna Spread

2 cans Vienna, mashed well
1 small tomato, diced fine
4 boiled eggs, diced fine

½ cup mayonnaise
Dash of salt
Dash of hot sauce

Mix well. Spread on plain or toasted bread. Serve with lettuce and pickle if desired.

Mrs. G.K. Counts
Florence

Pickled Shrimp by Mary Olga

2½ pounds cooked shrimp
2 large onions, thinly
  sliced
7-8 bay leaves
1¼ cups salad oil

¾ cup vinegar
1½ teaspoons salt
2½ teaspoons celery seed
2½ tablespoons capers and juice
Tabasco dash

Make alternate layers shrimp and onions. Add bay leaves. Mix remaining ingredients and pour over shrimp. Let stand at least 24 hours.

Chicken Hor D'Oeuvres

1 (3 ounce) package cream
  cheese, softened
1 (5 ounce) can chicken spread
⅓ cup chopped apple
¼ cup chopped walnuts

2 tablespoons chopped parsley
½ teaspoon Worcestershire
  sauce
Dash of cayenne pepper
Toasted wheat germ

Stir cream cheese in bowl until smooth; blend in remaining ingredients except wheat germ. Chill. Shape into 38 balls; roll in wheat germ. Place on serving platter.

Mrs. Joan Pugh
Florence

Martha's Guacamole

This avocado dip contains crunchy bits of bacon. Cook pieces ahead and refrigerate. Crisp a few seconds before adding to the dip. To help keep this dip from darkening, add lemon or lime juice.

6 slices bacon, optional
1 ripe avocado, mashed
¼ cup mayonnaise
1 tablespoon lemon juice

1 teaspoon minced onion
½ teaspoon garlic salt
¼ teaspoon chili powder
¼ teaspoon salt

Cook bacon until crisp; drain and crumble. Blend avocado with mayonnaise, lemon juice, onion and seasonings. Stir in crumbled bacon. Chill thoroughly. Serve with tortilla chips (totopas). Makes 1 cup.

Cocktail Cheese Popovers

1 cup boiling water
½ cup butter
½ cup sifted flour
½ cup Parmesan cheese

Few grains salt
Few grains nutmeg
2 eggs

Put the water in a saucepan; when it boils, melt the butter in it. Stir in the flour, cheese and seasonings all at once. Beat very hard, slipping pan on and off a very low flame. Let the mixture cool. Half an hour before serving popovers, beat in the eggs, one at a time. Beat well; grease and flour a cookie sheet and drop 30 little tablespoons of mixture on the sheet. Bake 15 minutes at 375 degrees and 15 minutes at 350 degrees. Serve immediately.

Gladys Hickman
Florence

Mary Olga's Antipasto

½ head cauliflower, cut and
   sliced
2 carrots, peeled and cut in 2-
   inch slices
2 stalks celery, cut in 1
   inch pieces
1 green pepper, cut in 1 inch
   strips
1 4 ounce jar pimientoes, drained
   and cut in strips

2 small cans button mushrooms
1 4-ounce jar pitted olives
1 can artichoke hearts
¾ can wine vinegar
¼ cup salad oil
2 tablespoons sugar
1 teaspoon salt
½ teaspoon pepper
Dash or two of Tabasco Sauce

In large skillet, combine all ingredients with ¼ cup water. Bring to a boil, stirring occasionally. Reduce heat. Simmer 5 minutes. Refrigerate 24 hours Drain well before serving.

Savory Party Mix

3 cups small pretzels
2 cups shoestring potatoes
2 cups Spanish peanuts
1½ cups seasoned croutons

1 can (3½ ounces) French-
   fried onions
½ cup squeeze margarine
½ cup grated Parmesan cheese

Combine pretzels, potatoes, peanuts, croutons, and onions. Pour margarine over combined ingredients. Sprinkle with cheese. Spread mixture on ungreased 15½ by 10½-inch jelly roll pan. Bake at 250 degrees for 1 hour, stirring mixture twice during baking. Makes 10 cups.

Ethel Rutherford
Cherokee

Loretta's Hot Beef Dip

1 8-ounce softened cream cheese
2 tablespoons milk
1 package dried beef, finely
   cut
1 small onion, cut

3 tablespoons green pepper, cut
½ cup sour cream
⅛ teaspoon pepper
¼ cup chopped walnuts

Blend cheese and milk; stir in onion, green pepper, salt and pepper and beef. Put into shallow pan. Sprinkle walnuts on top. Bake 350 degrees for 15 to 20 minutes. Serve hot with crackers.

Bertha's Crab Dip

2 cans crab meat
3 jars cheese and chives
   or use 4 small ones
1½ sticks butter

1 package onion soup (Put
   in strainer and shake only
   seasoning into dip)
About 2 tablespoons sherry

Heat and serve over very low heat.

12

Italian Artichoke Hearts

2 or 3 cans of imported artichoke hearts. Drain off liquid. In shallow baking dish stack artichoke hearts; fill the whole bottom.

Use imported olive oil and pour over the top of artichoke hearts until there is ¼ to ½ inch in the dish.

Take a tablespoon of Italian bread crumbs and sprinkle over each individual heart. Make a tent of aluminum foil or use covered dish and bake at 350 degrees for 25 minutes so that hearts are well steamed. Then remove tent or top, turn oven up to brown quickly. Do not dry out.

Mrs. John A. (Daryl) Thompson
Florence

Glema's Tenderloin

Have meat at room temperature. Brush with Kitchen Bouquet and Worcestershire. Coat with seasoned salt and pepper. Let dry. Pour Italian dressing over meat and let stand. Place tenderloins in pan so they touch. Cover again with salt and pepper. Let stand 3-4 hours. Heat oven to 450 degrees. Cook 20 minutes. Cool and slice very thin. Glema figures ⅛ pound per person for parties.

Ham Fritters

1 cup flour	2 eggs
1 teaspoon baking powder	¼ cup milk
1 teaspoon salt	1 cup finely chopped ham (cooked)
	Oil for deep frying

Sift flour, salt and baking powder into a bowl. Beat eggs, add milk and ham. Combine mixtures and stir until just mixed. Drop by teaspoons into hot oil (365) degrees. Fry until brown. Drain on paper towels.

Mrs. Walter Shaff
Florence

Easy Sausage Pinwheels

1 can biscuits   1 pound hot sausage

On floured board roll each biscuit out thin. Cover with raw sausage and roll up. Chill before cutting in thin slices. Place on ungreased cookie sheet and bake in preheated oven at 375 degrees until brown. Yields: 5 to 6 dozen.

Evie Boyles
Russellville

Mexican Relish

½ pound soft American cheese	½ teaspoon sugar
2 tablespoons butter	Speck Cayenne
1 seeded green pepper	1 cup kidney beans
1 red pepper	2 tablespoons catsup
½ teaspoon salt	Buttered toast
⅛ teaspoon paprika	

Slice the cheese and melt over a slow heat in the fat, stirring constantly. Add peppers which have been finely minced and seasonings. Add beans and catsup, beat thoroughly and serve on hot buttered toast. Serves six.

Mrs. Joan Pugh
Florence

Shrimp Mold

10 ounces tomato juice
1 large package cream cheese
  (softened)
1 envelope gelatin
½ cup mayonnaise

Chopped celery to taste (¼ to
  ½ cups)
¼ cup minced onion
Salt and pepper to taste
Dash or cayenne

Fresh or frozen shrimp (save liquid), cooked and coarsely ground (any amount will do), 1 or 1½ cups.

Soak gelatin in ¼ cup shrimp liquid. Heat tomato juice to boiling and add it to softened cream cheese, a little at a time. Blend well in top of double boiler. Add gelatin. Cool. Add mayonnaise, celery, onions, seasonings, and shrimp. Chill until mixture thickens a bit, then pour into greased fish mold. Olives may be used for fishes' eyes and pimiento for fins after unmolded.

Mrs. Robert T. Ervin, III
Florence

Crab Canapes

⅓ cup mayonnaise
2 tablespoons grated Parmesan
  cheese
1 tablespoon lemon juice

1 7½-ounce can crab meat,
  flaked
20 melba toast rounds
Parsley sprigs

Twenty minutes before serving; preheat broiler 10 minutes. In medium bowl, combine mayonnaise with cheese, lemon juice, and crabmeat. Spread each toast round with crab mixture up to edges. Place on cookie sheet and broil until bubbly. Garnish each with parsley sprig. Yield: 20 canapes or 6 appetizer courses.

Mrs. Horace Mitchell
Florence

Quick Quiche Lorraine Tarts

1 package pie crust mix
1 tablespoon poppy seed
1⅓ cup coarsely shredded
  Swiss cheese
⅔ cup chopped salami
⅓ cup sliced green onion

4 eggs, slightly beaten
1⅓ cups dairy sour cream
1 teaspoon salt
1 tablespoon Worcestershire
  sauce

Heat oven to 375 degrees. Prepare pastry as directed on package except stir in poppy seed before mixing. Roll pastry 1/16 inch thick on lightly floured board, cut into 3 inch rounds. Fit rounds into muffin pans. Combine cheese, salami and onion, spoon into pastry-lined tins. Stir together eggs, sour cream, salt and Worcestershire sauce. Pour a bit of sour cream mixture into muffin pans. Bake 20 to 25 minutes or until lightly browned. Cool in pans 5 minutes. Makes 36.

Glacé Walnuts

¼ cup margarine
½ cup sugar
¼ cup light corn syrup

½ teaspoon vanilla
3 cups walnuts

In 2-quart saucepan melt margarine. Stir in sugar and corn syrup. Bring to boil over medium heat stirring constantly. Boil without stirring 5 minutes. Remove from heat; stir in vanilla. Place nuts in 13x9x2-inch pan. Pour syrup over nuts, stirring constantly to coat evenly. Bake in 250 degree oven 1 hour, stirring several times. Remove from pan immediately. Cool. Store in tightly covered container. Makes 3 cups.

Deviled Eggs With Cheese

6 hard boiled eggs
¼ cup grated sharp cheese
1 dill pickle, finely chopped

1 tablespoon grated onion
5 tablespoons mayonnaise
2 tablespoons prepared mustard

Cut eggs in half, remove yolks and place in small bowl. Mash egg yolks and blend with cheese, pickle, onion, mayonnaise, and mustard. Stuff egg whites with mixture. Garnish with paprika.

Mrs. J.P. Poe
Florence

Confetti Eggs

2 eggs
1 tablespoon sugar
2 tablespoons vinegar
1 teaspoon butter
1 pimiento, chopped fine

1 small green pepper, chopped fine
2 3-ounce packages cream cheese
1 small onion, chopped fine
Tabasco sauce to taste
Salt to taste

Combine eggs, sugar, and vinegar. Cook over hot water, stirring constantly until mixture thickens. Add butter and cream cheese. Beat until smooth. Add onions, pimiento, green pepper, salt and Tabasco sauce. Serve with crackers.

Mrs. C.R. Malone
Austin, Texas

Crispy Chicken Puffs

1 cup finely chopped cooked chicken
½ cup finely chopped onion
¼ cup chopped parsley
⅓ cup cornflake crumbs

½ teaspoon poultry seasoning
1 egg, slightly beaten
½ cup cornflake crumbs

Preheat oven to 450: in medium bowl, combine chicken, onion, parsley, one-third cup cornflake crumbs, poultry seasoning, 1 egg , and chunky blue cheese dressing. Shape into 1-inch puffs. Dip each puff into remaining egg, then into remaining cornflake crumbs. Place on ungreased baking sheet; bake 10 minutes. Serve hot. Makes about 2 dozen appetizer puffs.

15

Make-Ahead Meatballs

Everyone is on the search for do-ahead foods. Meatball lovers will be happy to know that a quantity of party meatballs will freeze well. Store in oven cooking bags and cook in the same bag in a roasting pan or heavy oven casserole as needed. If serving is delayed, hold the meatballs in the bag to keep them from drying out. Meatballs will keep safely in freezer storage in the plastic bags. For longer storage, overwrap them with heavy duty aluminum foil and tag with day of storage.

2 pounds ground beef
¼ cup finely chopped onion
2 teaspoons salt
⅛ teaspoon pepper
½ teaspoon sage
½ teaspoon dry mustard
4 eggs, beaten
4 slices soft bread, broken
  in small pieces

2 teaspoons Worcestershire
  sauce
1 package (1½ ounces) dry
  spaghetti sauce mix
1 can (8 ounces) tomato
  sauce
1½ cups water

Combine ground beef, onion, salt, pepper, sage and dry mustard. Mix eggs, bread and Worcestershire sauce together. Add to beef mixture. Shape 1 tablespoon of meat mixture into ball. Place in plastic open cooking bag and continue with remaining mixture. Combine spaghetti sauce mix, water and tomato sauce. Pour over meatballs. Close bag with twist tie. Freeze. For prolonged storage, overwrap with heavy duty aluminum foil. When ready to cook, remove bag from freezer and preheat oven to 350 degrees. Place in oven bag in two-inch deep roasting pan. Make six half-inch slits in top of bag. Cook for one hour. Makes 6 dozen meatballs.

Chinese Sausage Bits

1 pound bulk pork sausage
1 slightly beaten egg
½ cup bread cubes
4 tablespoons butter
¾ cup chili sauce

¼ teaspoon garlic salt
¼ cup brown sugar
2 tablespoons vinegar
2 tablespoons soy sauce

In a bowl combine sausage, egg and bread cubes. Use a teaspoon to form small balls. Melt butter in frying pan. Cook balls evenly until brown; drain on absorbent paper. In a pot, mix the remaining ingredients. Cook slowly for 20 minutes, stirring occasionally. Place balls in a serving bowl; cover with sauce. Serve with toothpicks. Yield: 20 to 25 appetizers.

Dilly Almonds

1 cup whole natural
  (unblanched) almonds
1 cup whole blanched almonds

2 teaspoons butter
¾ teaspoon dill weed
½ teaspoon seasoned salt

Spread almonds in shallow baking pan. Bake at 300 degrees for 25 minutes. Melt butter in skillet. Add almonds, dill weed and salt; stir over medium heat just until almonds are well-coated. Turn onto paper towels to cool thoroughly. Store in tightly-closed container in refrigerator. Makes 2 cups.

Almond-Coated Cheese

Spread roasted diced almonds on waxed paper or plastic wrap; place a block of natural Danish cream cheese with orange or other fruit flavor in center. Bring up sides of paper to help coat cheese with almonds, then turn cheese over and, with fingers, pat almonds onto any areas of cheese that have not been covered. Slice and serve with assorted crackers or rounds of raw zucchini or carrots.

Nuts, Bolts and Screws

1 pound pecans
1 large box cheerios
1 medium box stick pretzels
1 tablespoon Worcestershire

1 box Wheat Chex
2 tablespoons salt
1 tablespoon garlic salt
1 pound oleo

Melt butter in large roaster; pour in all cereals, nuts and pretzels, and seasonings. Set oven at 200 degrees. Stir every 15 minutes for one hour.

Mrs. Ruth Butler

Spread For Stuffing Celery Or Spreading Sandwiches

¼ cup chopped nuts
3 hard boiled eggs, grated

¼ cup grated cheese
1 tablespoon pimiento

Mix all together with enough mayonnaise to spread evenly. Stuff into prepared celery or spread on sandwiches.

Mrs. Howard Kirkpatrick
Florence

Stuffed Mushrooms

Remove stems from one pound small mushrooms and finely chop stems. Cook one and one-half cups chopped stems with two tablespoons finely chopped onion in two tablespoons butter or margarine until tender. Finely roll 24 bacon flavored crackers; reserve one and one-half tablespoons crumbs. Toss remainder with mushroom mixture, two tablespoons chopped parsley and dash ground black pepper. Sprinkle insides of mushroom caps with salt; fill with stuffing. Brush mushrooms with one and one-half tablespoons melted butter or margarine. Place in shallow baking dish and sprinkle with remaining crumbs. Bake in preheated moderate oven (350 degrees) about 20 minutes or until tender. Insert wooden picks diagonally into mushrooms. Serve warm. Makes about three dozen.

Cheese Dollars
(4 dozen)

½ pound natural mild Cheddar, in small pieces	1 cup sifted flour
½ cup butter	⅛ teaspoon salt
	Generous grating of pepper

Let cheese stand at room temperature until soft. Cream butter; add cheese and whip with electric mixer until well blended. Add flour sifted with salt and pepper. Mix thoroughly. Chill until firm, then form into 3 rolls about 1 inch in diameter. Wrap each roll in foil and chill or freeze. To serve: Thaw frozen rolls briefly, cut in ¼-inch slices, and arrange ½ inch apart on foil-covered cookie sheet. Bake in 425 degree oven 8 to 10 minutes, until very lightly browned. Serve hot or cold.

Harvarti-Olive Dip

1 cup coarsely shredded Danish Havarti cheese	½ cup finely chopped stuffed olives
½ cup dairy sour cream	Cayenne pepper
	Seasoned salt

Blend Havarti cheese, sour cream together. Add olives, a dash of cayenne and just enough salt to flavor. Makes 1½ cups dip.

Dill Dip

1 cup mayonnaise	1½ teaspoons dill weed
1 cup sour cream	1½ teaspoons season salt

Mix together well and serve as a vegetable dip.

Beverages

Peggy's Tea Toddy

1 quart freshly drawn cold water
1 teaspoon lemon rind
8 whole cloves
6 teaspoons instant tea, 6 teabags
 or 6 teaspoons loose tea

2 tablespoons brown sugar
Rum or rum flavoring to taste
6 thin slices clove-studded lemon

Combine water, lemon rind and cloves in a saucepan. Bring to a full rolling boil. Pour over tea. Cover and let stand 5 minutes. Stir and strain. Add brown sugar and rum or rum flavoring. Serve with clove-studded lemon slices.

Makes 6 servings.

Hot Spiced Cranberry Tea

3 cups boiling water
½ cup sweetened lemon-flavored
 ice tea mix

3 cups cranberry juice cocktail
Whole cloves
Cinnamon sticks

Combine water, tea mix, and cranberry juice. Heat thoroughly. Serve hot in mugs or cups with a lemon slice decorated with cloves. Stir with cinnamon sticks. Yields 6 cups.

Ethel Rutherford
Cherokee

Cranberry Tea

3 quarts water
1 pound cranberries
3 cups sugar
1 cup cinnamon red hot candies

12 whole cloves
Juice of 3 oranges
Juice of 3 lemons
1 46-ounce can pineapple juice

Combine 1½ quarts water with cranberries; boil and strain. Combine remaining 1½ quarts water, sugar, cinnamon candies and cloves; strain and add to cranberry mixture. Add remaining ingredients. Serve hot or cold. NOTE: May be stored in refrigerator for an indefinite time. Yield: 1 gallon.

Mrs. Roy Burgess
Florence

Perfect Hot Tea

1. Rinse teapot with hot water to warm it.
2. Bring freshly drawn cold water to a full rolling boil.
3. Use one teabag, one teaspoon of instant tea or one teaspoon loose tea for each cup (about 5½ ounces) of water.
4. Pour the boiling water over the tea and let it stand for 3 to 5 minutes.
Note: If using instant tea, there's no need to brew. Just stir and serve.

Hot Tea Lemonade

3 cups boiling water
4 orange spice flavored tea bags
2 cups cranberry juice cocktail

½ cup orange juice
¼ cup sugar
Halved orange slices

Pour boiling water over tea bags in saucepan and steep 5 minutes. Remove tea bags; add cranberry juice, orange juice, and sugar. Stir and heat to serving temperature. Pour into mugs and garnish with half a slice of orange. Makes 1½ quarts.

Mrs. Myron Barnett
Sheffield

Instant Holiday Spiced Tea

2 cups sugar
1 cup instant tea
2 cups Tang

2 packages instant lemonade mix
2 teaspoons ground   cinnamon
2 teaspoons cloves

Mix together thoroughly and when serving, use about 2 teaspoons to a cup of hot water.

Mrs. Marty Nunnelly
Florence

Russian Tea

6 tea bags
1 gallon boiling water
1 stick cinnamon
4 teaspoons whole cloves

1 cup sugar
Juice of 3 lemons
Juice of 4 oranges

Bring first three ingredients (tea, cinnamon, cloves) to a boil; add the last three (sugar, lemon, oranges). Serves about 20 cups of hot tea.

Honeyed Tea

1 quart strong hot tea
2 tablespoons non-dairy creamer

2 tablespoons honey
½ teaspoon lemon extract

In medium heat-proof pitcher, combine ingredients; blend well. Serve piping hot.

Ethel Rutherford
Cherokee

Viennese Coffee

4 tablespoons instant coffee
2 cups boiling water
½ cup heavy cream, whipped and
  sweetened

Nutmeg
¼ cup orange-rind pieces, optional

Combine coffee and water in coffee server. Pour into small cups. Top each with a spoonful of whipped cream and sprinkle with a little nutmeg. Serve with a twist of orange rind, if desired. Makes 4 servings.

Trisha Chesnut
Greeneville, Tennessee

Spiced Coffee

2 cups water
1 tablespoon brown sugar
2 three-inch cinnamon sticks

Peel of 1 orange
¼ teaspoon whole allspice
1 tablespoon instant coffee

Combine all ingredients except coffee in saucepan; heat to boiling. Strain mixture; pour liquid over coffee in heat-proof container and stir until coffee is dissolved. If desired, serve with twist of lemon peel or a cinnamon stick. Makes six ⅓ cup servings.

Mrs. Jerry L. Turbyfill
Florence

Coffee Roses

Warm stemmed goblets by rinsing with hot water. Dry. Pour 1½ ounces whiskey into each. Add strong, hot coffee to within ½ inch of rim of goblet. Sweeten to taste. Top with crown of whipped cream.

Instant Spiced Tea

1 1-pound jar Tang
1 package lemonade mix
¾ cup instant tea

2 cups sugar
1 teaspoon ground cloves
2 teaspoons ground cinnamon

Mix all ingredients well. Place in jar; cover tightly. Place 2 teaspoons in cup of boiling water to serve. Yield: 30 servings.

Hot Chocolate Mix

1 box (8 quart size) instant milk
1 jar (16 ounces) non-dairy
  creamer

1 jar (16 ounces) quick chocolate
  mix
1 pound box powdered sugar

Mix ingredients together. For each cup of chocolate, place ⅓ cup of mix in cup and pour hot water over it.

Mrs. J. G. Sesler
Florence

The Welcome Bowl

Say "welcome" to your relatives and friends who stop by with gifts...to the neighborhood children who serenade you with carols...to anyone who drops 'round during this holiday season. The easiest way to do this is to have a brimming bowl of refreshing fruit punch on the table, ready for anyone to help himself.

3 tablespoons instant tea
1 quart bottle cranberry-apple juice
1 quart can apricot nectar

1 (6 ounce) can frozen daiquiri mix, thawed

Combine all ingredients in a punch bowl or serving pitcher. Stir well to mix. Add ice cubes or ice block. Makes 15-20 punch cup servings. Recipe may be doubled.

Punch

1 package gelatin (lime or strawberry)
1 can lemon juice, frozen
2 cups hot water

1½ quarts cold water
1 quart pineapple juice
1 quart giner ale

Dissolve gelatin in hot water; add lemon juice, cold water and pineapple juice, sweeten to taste with syrup. Chill. Add ginger ale when ready to serve. Sherbet may be added.

Alice Marshall
Tuscumbia

Jello Punch
Serves 32

2 packages lime jello
Juice of 6 lemons
1 quart water

1½ cups sugar
1 quart pineapple juice
1 quart ginger ale

Mix jello as directed. Dissolve sugar in 1½ cups water. Mix all ingredients. Add ginger ale just before serving.

Evelyn Pless
Cherokee

Real Good Punch

2½ pounds sugar
6 quarts water
1 large can pineapple juice

3 cups bottled lemon juice
2 large cans orange juice
3 quarts ginger ale

Mix sugar and water well. Add other ingredients except ginger ale. To one gallon punch, add 1 quart gingerale. Pour over block of ice. Stir and serve. Yield 3 gallons.

Evie Boyles
Russellville

Holiday Eggnog

¼ cup sugar
6 egg yolks, beaten
4 cups milk, scalded
¼ teaspoon salt
6 egg whites

¼ cup sugar
2 cups heavy whipped cream
2 teaspoons vanilla
Nutmeg

Beat ¼ cup sugar into egg yolk; stir in milk slowly. Cook over hot water until mixture coats spoon, stirring constantly. Chill. Add salt to egg whites and beat until stiff, but not dry. Continue to beat, adding remaining ¼ cup sugar gradually. Fold egg whites and whipped cream into mixture separately. Add vanilla. Chill for several hours. Pour into cups and sprinkle with nutmeg. Makes about 20 half cup portions.

Mrs. Tracy Gargis
Sheffield

Froth Eggnog Punch

12 egg whites
12 egg yolks
1 cup sugar
1 quart rich milk

1 tablespoon sherry or rum flavor
6 7-ounce bottles lemon-lime
  beverage (Seven-Up)

Beat egg whites to soft peaks and set aside. Beat egg yolks; gradually beat in sugar. Slowly add milk and mix until well blended. Add sherry or rum flavoring. Fold yolk mixture into egg whites. Pour mixture into punch bowl. Float scoopfuls of ice cream on top. Slowly pour in chilled lemon-lime carbonated beverage and sprinkle top with nutmeg. Makes about 25 servings.

Mrs. Joan Allen
Florence

Cream Sherry Eggnog

4 eggs, separated
1 cup sugar, divided
2 quarts milk

1 bottle cream sherry (Oloroso
  type)
Grated nutmeg

Beat egg yolks until thick and lemon-colored. Beat in ¾ cup sugar slowly. Continue beating until sugar is dissolved. Add milk and sherry; chill. Beat egg whites until stiff; beat in remaining sugar. Add sherry mixture. Spoon into wine glasses. Sprinkle with nutmeg. Makes about 15 to 18 servings.

Holiday Eggnog

6 eggs
1 cup sugar
½ teaspoon salt

1 cup golden rum or 1 to 2
  tablespoons   rum flavoring
1 quart light cream (20 percent)
Nutmeg

In large bowl, beat eggs until light and foamy. Add sugar and salt, beating until thick and lemon colored. Stir in rum and cream. Chill at least three hours. Just before serving, sprinkle with nutmeg. Makes 12 one-half cup servings.

Mrs. Jerry L. Turbyfill
Florence

Peachy Champagne Punch

1 package frozen peaches
1 bottle peach brandy
4 bottles champagne
4 quarts club soda
Ice cubes

Place frozen peaches in large punch bowl. Pour in remaining ingredients; mix and serve. Garnish with maraschino cherries. Yields 50 servings.

Mrs. G.E. Smith
Leighton

Blushing Champagne Punch

4 6-ounce cans frozen orange
  juice concentrate, thawed,
  undiluted
6 cups cold water
1 cup sugar
1½ cups grenadine
¼ teaspoon salt
2 fifth bottles champagne,
  chilled

Combine all ingredients except champagne and chill. Pour over ice in punch bowl. Add champagne. If desired, garnish with mint sprigs. Approximately 30 ½-cup servings.

Ruby Punch

6 ounces fresh lime juice
10 ounces cranberry juice,
  chilled
1 fifth vodka, chilled
2 quarts club soda, chilled
Mint for garnish

Combine all ingredients except club soda. Stir well; pour over large block of ice in punch bowl. Add club soda and stir gently. This can be served in punch cups or in tall glasses over ice, garnished with mint sprigs and lime shells. Makes 12 servings.

Red Rum Punch

1 pint lime juice
1 quart orange juice
1 quart pineapple juice
2 fifths white rum
6 ounces Grenadine
2 quarts club soda
Fruits for garnish

Mix together first five ingredients, stirring vigorously. Chill; or add a large block of ice to punch bowl. Just before serving, add chilled club soda. Stir gently. Decorate with fruit slices. About 50 servings.

Gelatin Party Punch

12 cups sugar
3 pints water
6 3-ounce packages flavored
  gelatin
12 cups hot water
3 small cans frozen orange juice
3 small cans frozen lemon juice
3 quarts pineapple juice
1 2-ounce bottle almond extract

Boil sugar and the 3 pints water for a few minutes. Dissolve gelatin in boiling water; add to sugar solution. When ready to serve, add fruit juices, extract and 2 gallons cold water. Serve over ice cubes. Yield: 150 servings.

Mrs. Hayes Bartley
Red Bay

Apple Cider Punch

6 cups apple cider
½ cup dark brown sugar, packed
12 cloves
2 1-inch cinnamon sticks
½ teaspoon nutmeg
½ teaspoon ginger
2 oranges, thinly sliced
1 lemon, thinly sliced

Simmer in large saucepan, stir occasionally. Do not boil. Keep warm. Serve in mugs or glasses.

Mrs. J.H. Mitchell
Florence

Fruit Punch

2 large cans grapefruit juice
2 large cans orange juice
2 large cans pineapple juice
3 or 4 bottles concentrated lemon
juice
2 quarts gingerale
4 pounds sugar dissolved in ½ gallon of water

Mix all ingredients together except gingerale. Just before serving add gingerale. Can be made without orange juice for variation. Serves about 75.

Lela Hall
Leighton

Cranberry Lemon Punch

2 cups ice water
½ cup sugar
⅓ cup lemon juice
1 pint cranberry juice, chilled
1 pint ginger ale, chilled
1 pint lemon sherbet

Combine water, sugar, lemon juice, cranberry and sherbet in a punch bowl. Slowly pour in ginger ale. Makes 14 cups.

Addie Carl Montgomery
Tuscumbia

Hot Cider Punch

4 cups water
4 cups apple cider
⅔ cup orange flavored instant
breakfast drink
¼ teaspoon cinnamon
⅛ teaspoon nutmeg
⅛ teaspoon ground cloves

Combine all ingredients in a saucepan; blend well and bring just to a boil. Serve hot in punch cups or mugs. Makes about 2 quarts or 16 servings using punch cups, or 8 servings using mugs.

Orange Brandy Punch

3 cups orange juice
½ cup sugar
½ cup lime juice
¾ cup cognac
½ cup curacao
1 fifth cahmpagne, chilled

Combine orange juice, sugar, lime juice, cognac and curacao. Stir until sugar dissolves. Chill. Pour into punch bowl over ice. Add champagne. Approximately 18 ½-cup servings.

25

Christmas Punch

1 large can frozen orange juice	2 packages red soft drink mix
2 small cans frozen lemonade	2 cups sugar
1 No. 2 can pineapple juice	2 cups water

Mix all ingredients in a gallon jug. Fill remainder of jug with water. Serves 50.

Pat Gatlin
Leighton

Hot Christmas Punch

2 cups sugar	1 can frozen lemonade, diluted with
2 cups water	3 cans water
1 pint cranberry juice	Juice from 1 bottle Maraschino
1 quart apple cider	cherries
1 can orange juice, diluted with	Maraschino cherries
2 cans water	

Combine sugar and water. Boil until syrupy. Add cranberry juice, cider, orange juice and lemonade. Heat slightly. Add cherry juice. Place one cherry in each cup. Yields 12 servings.

Mrs. Walter Shaff
Florence

Cranberry Christmas Punch

1 3-ounce package cherry gelatin	3 cups cold water
1 cup boiling water	1 quart cranberry juice cocktail
1 6-ounce can frozen lemonade	1 quart chilled giner ale
concentrate	

Dissolve cherry gelatin in boiling water. Stir in lemonade concentrate. Add cold water and cranberry juice cocktail. Place two trays of ice cubes or a molded ice ring in a large punch bowl. Pour punch over ice. Pour in chilled ginger ale.

Mrs. Brenda Heupel
Florence

Christmas Punch

6 tea bags	1 pint boiling water
1 pint water	2 small cans frozen lemon juice
1½ cups sugar	2 large cans frozen orange juice
2 packages lemon kool aid	1 large can pineapple juice
2 packages orange kool aid	4 cans cranberry juice
1 small jar red cherries	2 bottles ginger ale

Prepare the two flavors of Kool aid, using only half the amount of water called for on package. Mix sugar with the pint of water. Then mix the tea bags in 1 pint of boiling water. Then mix all ingredients together except cherries and ginger ale. Add them before serving. Serves 50.

Mrs. Roisell Miller
Tuscumbia

Christmas Wreath Punch

2 6-ounce cans frozen limeade
concentrate
2 6-ounce cans frozen lemonade
concentrate
2 1-pound 4-ounce cans unsweetened
grapefruit juice

2 1-pound 4-ounce cans
pineapple juice
3 1-quart bottles ginger ale, chilled
1 quart water
3 quarts chopped ice
Christmas wreath

In punch bowl, blend undiluted limeade and lemonade, grapefruit, and pineapple juices. Just before serving stir in ginger ale, water, ice. Then unmold Christmas wreath on top of punch. Makes about 50 punch cups.

Christmas Wreath

Wash excess color from 13 red and 13 green maraschino cherries. Arrange cherries, alternating colors in bottom of 1¼ quart ring mold. Pour just enough boiling water to cover cherries; freeze solid. Fill to top with cold boiled water, freeze solid. Unmold.

Mrs. Linda J. McDougal
Killen

Christmas Cranberry Drink

2½ cups boiling water
2 tablespoons tea leaves or 6 bags
¼ teaspoon allspice

¼ teaspoon cinnamon
¼ teaspoon nutmeg

Pour boiling water over tea and spices. Steep five minutes. Strain.

¾ cup sugar
1 pint cranberry juice

1½ cups water
½ cup orange juice

Add sugar and other ingredients. Heat just to boiling. Serve with peppermint canes as stirrers.

Evelyn Pless
Cherokee

Holiday Fruit Punch

2 quarts boiling water
¼ cup loose tea
2 cups lemon juice
4 cups orange juice
2 cups sugar

1½ quarts cranberry juice
1 quart water
1 quart ginger ale
1 lemon sliced and 2 limes sliced
Whole maraschino cherries

Bring 2 quarts or water to a full rolling boil. Immediately pour the tea. Brew 5 minutes. Strain.. Set aside to cool at room temperature. Combine with fruit juices and one quart water. Chill. Just before serving, pour over large piece of ice or ice cubes, then add giner ale. Garnish with lemon and lime slices and cherries.

Mrs. Joan Allen
Florence

27

All Purpose Punch

1 quart can apple juice
1 quart can pineapple juice
1 small can frozen lemon juice
1 quart gingerale

Mix all ingredients together and pour over crushed ice to serve.

Lela Hall
Leighton

Tomato Punch

4 quarts tomato juice
1 quart canned beef consommé

Season to taste with lemon juice. Chill and pour into a bowl that has been rubbed with garlic.

Lemon-Grape Punch

1 quart grape juice
4 scoops lemonade flavor drink mix
1 quart lemon-lime carbonated beverage

Combine grape juice and soft drink mix in a punch bowl; stir to dissolve and chill. Just before serving, add carbonated beverage; then add Frozen Ring Mold (recipe follows). Makes 8 cups or 16 servings.

Frozen Ring Mold

Pour ¼ cup water into a 4-cup ring mold; freeze. Arrange a layer of thin lemon slices and green maraschino cherries on ice and freeze about 15 minutes, until fruit is frozen. Add cold water to fill mold. Freeze until firm. Unmold and float in punch.

Purple Cow

1½ cups cold milk
3 tablespoons frozen grape juice concentrate
2 scoops vanilla ice cream (about ⅔ cup)
Vanilla ice cream

Blend milk, grape juice concentrate and 2 scoops ice cream in blender until smooth. Pour into two 12-ounce glasses. Top with scoops of vanilla ice cream. Serve immediately.

Amy Chesnut
Greeneville, Tennessee

Williamsburg Wine Cooler

¾ cup lemonade
¼ cup claret
Mint sprig and cherry for garnish (optional)

Pour lemonade over ice cubes or crushed ice in glass. Carefully pour in claret, which will float on top. Garnish with mint and cherry if desired. Makes one serving.

Veranda Froth

4 scoops lemonade flavor drink mix
1 quart lime sherbet, softened
1 bottle (28 fluid ounces) club soda
½ cup orange liqueur or orange juice
Crushed ice

Combine drink mix and sherbet in a bowl and blend until smooth. Gradually add club soda and liqueur; mix well. Serve over ice and garnish with mint leaves, if desired. Makes 2 quarts or 16 servings.

Vintage Grape Drink

1 bottle (4-5 quart) sauterne
1 pint raspberries, fresh or frozen
1 quart club soda

3 cups concord grape drink
1 can (6 ounces) frozen concord
  grape juice concentrate,
  thawed

Pour grape drink into ice cube trays. Freeze until firm. Just before serving, pour reconstituted grape juice and wine over raspberries in large pitcher. Add club soda and grape ice cubes.

Wibby Medaris
Florence

New Orleans Gin Fizz

¾ ounce lemon juice
¼ ounce lime juice
¼ ounce simple syrup (1
  teaspoon sugar)

White of 1 egg
1 ounce cream
1¼ ounce gin

Shake thoroughly or blend on slow speed for 20 seconds. Serve in chilled 8 ounce glass.

Christmas Morning Beverage

1 quart boiling water

½ cup flavored instant breakfast

Dissolve instant breakfast drink in boiling water. Serve hot. Makes 1 quart or 6 servings.

Chilly Cocktail

Have you tried consomme on the rocks? For a cooling first course, mix equal parts of consomme and apple juice and serve over ice cubes. The melting cubes will dilute to desired potency.

Cherry Danish

1½ ounces cherry kijafa
1 ounce aquavit

Juice of ⅛ lime

fill glass with ice and soda.

Cherry Split

1 part cherry kijafa

1 part white creme de cocoa

Pour over ice cubes in low ball glass.

29

Hot Mulled Cider

2 quarts fresh or canned apple cider
Peel of 1 lemon
1 1-inch stick cinnamon
Honey
1 orange, sliced
6 Maraschino cherries, sliced
6 whole cloves

Combine cider, lemon peel, cinnamon and honey; simmer 20 minutes. Top each drink with orange and cherry slices. Float a whole clove in each.

Mrs. John Hopkins
Haleyville

Apple-Grape Bounce

⅓ cup chilled unsweetened
  grape juice
⅓ cup chilled ginger ale
Increase quantity as needed.
½ cup chilled apple juice

Stir together all the ingredients. (Measure ginger ale after foam has subsided.). Serve at once. Makes a little over 1 cup—1 or 2 servings.

Hot Orange Nog

1 package (3¼ ounce) vanilla
  pudding and pie filling
1 quart milk
3 tablespoons orange flavored
  instant breakfast drink

Empty pudding mix into saucepan. Add milk, stirring to blend. Cook and stir over medium heat until mixture just comes to a boil. Stir in instant breakfast drink; blend well. Serve warm in punch cups. Makes about 4½ cups or 9 servings.

Note: Mixture may be prepared in advance. Heat gently over low heat; do not boil.

Wake-Up Orange Nog

1 can (6 ounces) frozen orange
  juice concentrate
2½ cups milk
½ cup egg substitute
¼ teaspoon cinnamon

Combine orange juice and milk and egg substitute in a blender. Mix for 1 minute. Makes 1 quart.

Addie C. Montgomery
Tuscumbia

Orange Bliss

1 6-ounce can frozen orange juice
  concentrate
1½ cups cold water
4 large marshmallows
1 cup ice cream (vanilla)
15 ice cubes

Pour into blender orange juice and water, blend approximately five seconds or until the mixture is liquid. Add ice cream, marshmallows and enough ice cubes so that when they are finely crushed the mixture will be thick like a milk shake. Since ice cubes vary in size you may have to add or delete a few. Pour into serving glasses and garnish with an orange slice or marshmallow and cherry.

Martha Mosakowski
Killen

Strawberry Delight For Dieters

1 cup milk
1 pint fresh strawberries

4 teaspoons sugar
1 cup quick-frozen strawberries

Place milk in a blender container. Add other ingredients. Add one cup of finely cracked ice. Put cover on the container, turn on mixer and run until contents are thoroughly blended, 15 seconds to 2 minutes. One-half cup of ice cream added makes a richer drink.

Donna M. Hayes
Florence

Golden Orange For Dieters

1 cup milk
½ cup orange juice
1 orange, peeled and quartered

3 tablespoons sugar
Cracked ice (optional)

Place milk in a blender container. Add other ingredients. Put cover on the container and mix until contents are thoroughly blended, one to two minutes. One-half cup of ice cream added to recipe makes a richer drink.

Donna M. Hayes
Florence

Banana Milk Shake For Dieters

1 cup milk
1 medium-sized ripe banana

1 teaspoon vanilla
1 cup cracked ice

Place milk in the blender container. Add other ingredients. Put cover on the container. Mix until contents are thoroughly blended, one to two minutes. One-half cup of ice cream makes a richer drink.

Donna M. Hayes
Florence

Mocha Milk Shake For Dieters

1½ cups milk
1 cup strong coffee

⅛ teaspoon nutmeg
½ pint chocolate ice cream

Place all ingredients in blender, replace top and turn to high speed. Blend thoroughly, about 30 seconds—if solid fruit is added, slightly longer.

Donna M. Hayes
Florence

Soups

Black Bean Soup

1 pound black beans
1 pound ham or hambone
4 pods garlic
1 teaspoon sugar

2 cloves
3 bay leaves
2 onions

Wash beans well. Place beans and all other ingredients in large pot. Cover with water until beans are thoroughly done, adding water as required. Remove two cups cooked beans and blend in blender with some water from bean pot. Place contents of blender back in the bean pot (this is used to thicken soup); salt to taste. Heat and serve. Small amount of rice and chopped red onions may be added to top in serving dish.

Mrs. John E. Higginbotham
Florence

Onion And Toast Soup

2 cups chopped onions
3 cups boiling water
3 cups milk
1½ tablespoons butter

½ cup grated cheese
½ teaspoon salt
¼ teaspoon black pepper
6 slices toast

Peel and chop onions and cook in boiling water until tender; add milk and simmer 10 minutes; add butter and seasoning. Place a slice of toast in a large soup bowl, cover with cheese and pour soup over it. (Serves six).

Split Pea Soup

2 cups dried split peas
2 quarts water
1 ham bone
1 cup minced celery

1 medium onion, finely chopped
(about ½ cup)
1 sprig parsley
¼ teaspoon pepper

Heat peas and water to boiling; boil gently 2 minutes. Remove from heat; cover and let stand 1 hour.

Add remaining ingredients. Heat to boiling. Reduce heat and simmer 2½ to 3 hours or until peas are very soft.

Remove bone; trim meat from bone and add to soup. If desired, thin with milk or water. Season to taste. Makes six 1 cup servings.

Mrs. Jerry Turbyfill
Florence

Brennan's Onion Soup

1½ cups butter
4 cups white onions, sliced
1¾ cups all-purpose flour
12 cups beef stock
1½ teaspoons salt
½ teaspoon cayenne pepper

1 egg yolk
2 tablespoons cream
Croutons or toasted bread rounds
Parmesan cheese
Buttered bread crumbs

Melt butter in a 6 quart soup kettle. Add onion, reduce heat to very low and cook until onions are transparent but not browned. Add flour and cook 5 to 10 minutes longer, stirring occasionally. Blend in beef stock, salt and cayenne pepper; bring to a boil. Reduce heat and simmer about 15 minutes. Remove kettle from heat. Beat egg yolks and cream together; add a little of the soup and mix quickly; add to soup in kettle. Serve in soup cups with croutons. Sprinkle with Parmesan cheese and bread crumbs. Brown under broiler and serve hot. Yield: 3 quarts.

Mrs. Claire Pitts
Sheffield

Cream of Spinach Soup

2 tablespoons butter or margarine
1 leek, chopped or 6 to 8 green
    onions cut in 1-inch pieces
1 clove garlic, cut in half
1 can (13¾ ounces) chicken
    broth
2 packages (10 ounces each) fresh
    spinach, cleaned

1 medium potato, shredded
3 cups milk
1 teaspoon salt
⅛ teaspoon nutmeg
Pepper
Dairy sour cream

In a 5-quart dutch oven melt butter over medium heat; sauté leek and garlic until tender, but not browned. Add ½ cup of the chicken broth, spinach and potato. Simmer, covered, over medium heat, stirring occasionally, about 15 minutes. In bowl of food processor place chopping blade; add spinach mixture. Process just until blended. Carefully return spinach mixture to dutch oven. Add remaining chicken broth, milk, salt and nutmeg; stir until blended. Cook, covered, over medium heat for 15 minutes or until hot. Season with salt and pepper as desired. Garnish with dollop of sour cream. Makes 8 (1 cup) servings.

Note: May be served hot or cold.

Betty Ballinger
Madisonville, Kentucky

New England Clam Chowder

2 dozen large chowder clams or 2
  cans (10½ ounces each)
  minced clams
1 quart water
¼ pound salt pork, diced
1 cup chopped onion (1 large)
3 large potatoes, pared and diced

¼ teaspoon leaf thyme, crumbled
½ teaspoon salt
⅛ teaspoon pepper
2 cups milk
2 cups light cream
2 tablespoons butter or margarine

If using fresh clams, scrub them well under running water. Put into deep kettle; add water; cover. Steam 8 minutes or until shells open. Discard any that do not open. Remove clams from shells with small knife, working over a bowl so you catch all juice. Remove and discard dark parts of clams. Chop clams coarsely. Strain broth from kettle into bowl containing clam juice. Add water, if needed, to make 4 cups of liquid. If using canned clams, drain them; measure juice. Add water to make 4 cups.

Cook salt pork in heavy kettle 5 minutes or until bits are crisp and golden. Remove with slotted spoon. Drain on paper towels. Cook onion in fat left in pan until soft. Add clam broth and water mixture, salt pork bits, potatoes, thyme, salt and pepper. Cover. Simmer 10 minutes or until potatoes are tender but not soft. Add clams. Stir in milk and cream slowly. Add butter or margarine. Bring just to boiling, but do not boil. Makes 8 servings.

M.B. Anderson

Corn And Frank Chowder

½ cup diced salt pork
1 green pepper, seeded and diced
1 cup diced onion (1 large)
1 cup sliced celery
3 tablespoons flour
1 can (13¾ ounces) chicken broth
1 cup water
1 cup diced, pared potatoes

¼ teaspoon ground thyme
1 bay leaf
1 teaspoon salt
Dash of pepper
1 can (12 ounces) whole-kernel corn
1 pound frankfurters, sliced
3 cups light cream or half-and-half,
  scalded

Cook salt pork in large heavy saucepan until crisp and brown. Remove; reserve. Add green pepper, onion and celery to fat left in pan. Cook until soft, stirring occasionally. Sprinkle with flour. Stir until fat is absorbed. Add chicken broth and water. Bring to boiling, stirring constantly. Add potatoes, thyme, bay leaf, salt and pepper. Simmer 7 minutes or until potatoes are tender. Remove bay leaf. Add remaining ingredients. Heat through. Makes 8 servings.

Golden Cheese Chowder

3 cups water
4 medium-size potatoes, pared and diced
1 cup sliced celery
1 cup pared, sliced carrots
½ cup diced onion (1 medium)
2 teaspoons salt
¼ teaspoon pepper
½ cup butter or margarine
½ cup all-purpose flour
1 quart milk
1 pound sharp Cheddar cheese, shredded (4 cups)
2 cups cubed, cooked ham (about 1 pound)
Hot-pepper sauce to taste

Bring water to boiling in kettle. Add potatoes, celery, carrots, onion, salt and pepper. Cover. Simmer 10 minutes or until vegetables are tender.

Melt butter or margarine in large saucepan. Blend in flour. Stir in milk gradually. Cook over medium heat, stirring constantly, until the mixture comes to boiling; boil 1 minute. Stir in cheese until melted. Add to vegetables; add ham. Heat, but do not boil. Add pepper sauce. Makes 12 ser-

Cream Of Almond Soup

½ cup sliced natural almonds
¼ cup butter or margarine
¼ cup flour
1 can (10¾-ounce) condensed chicken broth
2 cups half-and-half
2 teaspoons instant minced onion
⅛ teaspoon salt
1 tablespoon dry sherry
Minced parsley
Sliced almonds for garnish

With rolling pin, finely crush ½ cup almonds. Stir-cook with butter in saucepan over medium heat until light golden and fragrant; stir in flour, then broth (undiluted), half-and-half, onion and salt. Cook, stirring, until soup comes to boil; stir in sherry. Serve garnished with parsley and almonds. Makes 5½ cups.

Trilla Anderson

Chicken Noodle Soup

2 to 3 pound broiler-fryer chicken
Salt
1½ cups fine noodles
1 tablespoon chopped onion
⅛ teaspoon pepper
1 bay leaf

Wash chicken but do not cut up. Cover chicken with water. Add ½ teaspoon salt per pound of chicken and the pepper. Heat to boiling. Reduce heat; cover and simmer 1½ hours or until chicken is tender. Remove chicken from broth; remove meat from bones and cut into small pieces. Skim fat from broth, measure broth into medium saucepan. Add chicken meat and remaining ingredients. Heat to boiling. Reduce heat and simmer until noodles are tender, 10 to 15 minutes. Remove bay leaf before serving. Makes six to eight 1 cup servings.

Mrs. Jerry L. Turbyfill
Florence

Muscle Shoals Soul Soup

4 cups water
1 package frozen okra
3 chicken or beef bouillon cubes
1 purple onion, cut in strips
¼ head purple cabbage, shredded
1 pound can stewed tomatoes
15 ounce can tomato sauce with bits
1 can tomato paste
2 8-ounce cans tomato sauce
½ bell pepper, cut in thin strips
1 can water chestnuts, sliced (for
  crunch)
6 scallions, sliced
 To Taste:
Salt
Coarse black pepper
Worcestershire sauce
Minced garlic

2 cups diced celery
1 cup cooked and shredded chicken
  (or any leftover meat)
1 pound cooked carrots
16-ounce can French-style green
  beans, drained
2 15-ounce cans Irish potatoes,
  drained and cubed
8-ounce can very small English
  peas, drained
2½ ounces sliced mushrooms
1 17-ounce can creamed yellow corn
3-4 tablespoons bacon drippings

Minced onion
Celery salt
Italian seasoning
Bay leaf

Boil water and dissolve bouillon cubes (leftover gravy may be substituted). Stir. Add meat, onion, cabbage, bell pepper, stewed tomatoes, tomato sauce, green beans, celery, okra and seasonings. Simmer slowly for 1 hour, stirring occasionally. Add potatoes, English peas, carrots, mushrooms and water chestnuts. Simmer 1-2 hours, stirring frequently. Add creamed corn (optional, but good) and tomato paste and heat thoroughly. Taste for seasoning, and serve. Refrigeration or freezing only improves the taste.

If the soup gets too thick, add an 8-ounce can of tomato sauce or tomato juice until soup is the desired consistency.

David Hood
Muscle Shoals

John's Oyster Stew

¼ cup butter
1½ cups sliced fresh mushrooms
½ cup chopped onion
¼ cup all-purpose flour
1 tablespoon salt
¼ teaspoon white pepper

1 teaspoon Worcestershire sauce
1 pint shucked oysters
1 quart milk
1 pint half and half
Chopped fresh parsley

In a 3-quart saucepan, melt butter. Sauté mushrooms and onion until tender, 3 to 5 minutes. Stir in flour, salt, pepper and Worcestershire sauce; cook until bubbly. Stir in oysters and their liquid. Add milk. Cook until simmering and oyster edges curl. Stir in cream. Remove from heat. Sprinkle with chopped parsley. Serve hot.

Mrs. John Ballinger
Madisonville, Kentucky

Norwegian Fruit Soup

1 quart water
12 prunes
½ cup raisins

1½ tablespoons cornstarch
3 tablespoons water
sugar

Cook dried fruits in water until soft, then mix starch with a little water and add gradually while stirring. Add as much sugar as desired and sprinkle a little on top. Serve hot or cold with a little whipped cream, some cookies, or just plain.

Variation: Use cherries, diced, cored apples, pineapple chunks, canned peaches, or any of your favorite fruit.

Bente Erlien
Oslo, Norway

Fruit Soup

6 whole cloves
3 cups orange juice
2 cups pineapple juice

⅓ cup water
3 tablespoons cornstarch
¾ cup lemon juice

Heat cloves, orange juice, pineapple juice, sugar and cornstarch. Cook until thick and clear, stirring. Cook thoroughly. Add lemon juice, mix well. Chill and serve cold.

Mrs. W.M. Barnett
Sheffield

Georgia Peanut Soup

¼ cup margarine
¼ cup finely chopped onion
¼ cup finely chopped celery
1 cup peanut butter
1 tablespoon flour

4 cups beef bouillon
2 teaspoons lemon juice
Unsweetened whipped cream
½ cup chopped cocktail peanuts

In a large heavy saucepan, melt margarine. Add onion and celery; sauté until tender. Stir in peanut butter and flour; blend well. Gradually stir in beef bouillon and lemon juice until smooth. Cook over medium heat for 20 minutes, stirring occasionally. To serve, garnish with unsweetened whipped cream and chopped cocktail peanuts.

Elizabeth Medaris

Avila, Spain Tuna Soup

1 can tuna fish (which has been
rinsed with boiling water)
2 cloves of garlic or garlic juice
½ onion, finely chopped
2 tablespoons oil
1 can tomatoes

1 bell pepper, cut in strips
Red hot peppers to taste
2 potatoes, peeled and cubed
Salt, pepper
Small amount of water

Sauté chopped onion and garlic in oil until golden brown. Transfer to a soup kettle and add tuna fish, peppers, tomatoes and potatoes. Add enough water to make 2 servings. Season to taste and simmer slowly until vegetables are cooked but not mushy. If the soup is too thick, add more water. Soup should be cooked in 20 minutes.

Mrs. R.A. Fonseca
Florence

37

Black Bean Soup From France

2 cups black beans
3 quarts water
1 bay leaf
1 ham bone
1 grapefruit
1 beef bouillon cube

1 small green pepper, minced
1 garlic clove, crushed
2 oz. (¼ cup) dry sherry
1 cup fluffy buttered rice
½ cup finely-chopped onion

Wash beans; cover with cold water; soak overnight; drain. Add 3 quarts water, bay leaf and ham bone. Boil gently until the beans are completely soft and the liquid fairly thick, adding more water from time to time if necessary. Add the pulp from the grapefruit, the bouillon cube, green pepper, garlic and sherry. Simmer ½ hour longer. Let each dinner guest garnish his soup with rice and chopped onion. Makes 8 servings.

Chicken-Olive Soup

¼ cup butter or margarine
½ teaspoon paprika
¼ cup flour
4 cups homemade or canned
  chicken broth
1 can (5 or 6 ounces) pitted
black olives, chopped

1 cup slivered cooked chicken
  (optional)
Salt and pepper
Lemon or lime slices

Melt butter in 2-quart saucepan. Add paprika and flour and blend until smooth. Gradually add broth and cook, stirring, until smooth and thickened. Simmer 3 to 4 minutes. Add olives, and chicken, if desired. Heat and add salt and pepper to taste. Serve with a lemon slice in each bowl. Makes about 5 cups.

Mrs. Robert E. Brown
Madisonville, Kentucky

Montreal Cheese Soup

2 cups milk
1 cup chicken broth or stock
½ cup American or cheddar cheese,
  cubed
¼ cup sliced carrots
¼ cup sliced celery

1 sliced onion
2 tablespoons flour
½ teaspoon salt
6 peppercorns
¼ teaspoon nutmeg

Chop all ingredients in a blender for 30 seconds. Turn into saucepan and heat and stir until smooth and thickened. Makes 1 quart.

This recipe has been an easy, quick and satisfying change for those who want nutrition when the holidays call for a lighter touch before big family meals. It can also be used as a fondue dip.

Marcia McCalpin
Spruce Pine

Salads

Meaty Potato Salad

Combine and mix well:

3 cups cubed, cooked potatoes
½ cup diced celery
⅓ cup chopped onion
¼ cup bottled French dressing

½ cup mayonnaise
Salt and pepper to taste
1 can (12 ounce) luncheon meat,
  thinly sliced

Mix well. Chill thoroughly. Serve. Makes 4-5 servings.

Mrs. Ruby Allison
Muscle Shoals

Cheese Potato Salad

1 cup diced cheese
1½ cups cooked, cooled,
* diced potatoes*
1½ cups coarsely chopped
* hard-boiled eggs*

1½ teaspoon chopped onion
½ teaspoon salt
¼ cup salad dressing
⅛ cup sweet pickle liquid
1 cup ham
½ cup celery, chopped

Begin by combining salad dressing and pickle liquid. Set aside and combine all other ingredients in a large bowl. Add salad dressing and stir well. Chill thoroughly to blend flavors. Serves 4.

Sandra Hollis
Florence

Cucumber Salad

3 ounces lime gelatin
¾ cup hot water
1 teaspoon onion juice

¼ cup lemon juice
1 cup sour cream
1 cup grated cucumber (unpeeled)

Dissolve gelatin in hot water. Add juices and sour cream and mix well. Chill until set. Fold in grated cucumber. Refrigerate. Serves 8.

Mrs. Jesse A. Keller
Florence

Cucumbers In Sour Cream

2 medium cucumbers, sliced
2 teaspoons salt

1 tablespoon minced onion, optional
2 tablespoons vinegar

Peel and slice cucumbers, cover with ice water, add salt, let stand about 20 minutes. Drain and rinse well. Mix cucumbers with sour cream, add onions and vinegar. Chill well before serving.

Evelyn Pless
Cherokee

Green Pea Salad

1 can English peas
1 cup chopped celery
1 cup chopped cabbage
1 cup grated carrots
¼ cup chopped pimiento

¼ cup chopped, stuffed olives
½ cup sweet pickle relish
2 hard boiled eggs, chopped
2 tablespoons chopped onion
1½ cups mayonnaise

Heat English peas, drain and set aside. Add remaining ingredients and mix. Serve cold.

Mrs. Donald E. Holt
Florence

The Salad

1 (10-inch) bowl with good depth,
   flat bottom
5 or 6 carrots
2 tablespoons sugar
1 head lettuce

1 large onion
1½ cups celery, chopped
1 pint mayonnaise
12 slices crisp bacon, crumbled

Grate carrot, add chopped lettuce, a layer chopped, thin-sliced onion, and a layer of chopped celery. Cover the entire top with the carrots. Mask top with mayonnaise and refrigerate for several hours. Before serving, sprinkle with bacon. Make at dawn; serve at dusk.

Mrs. Gorman Jones, Jr.
Sheffield

Cranberry Horseradish Salad

2 cups cranberries
2 cups sugar
1½ cups boiling water
2 packages lemon gelatin
1½ cups celery, diced

½ cup nuts, chopped
1 or 2 tablespoons horseradish,
   (it should not be
   sweet or hot)

Grind up cranberries to make 4 cups. Mix with sugar and let stand until sugar is dissolved. Add boiling water to gelatin and stir until dissolved; add to cranberry-sugar mixture. Add celery, nuts and horseradish. Pour into a mold and stir a few times until chilled and firm.

Mrs. Leonard Burt
Sheffield

Avocado Bacon Boats

12 slices bacon, crisp-cooked
   and crumbled
½ cup sour cream
2 tomatoes, peeled, seeded and
   chopped

2 tablespoons sliced green onion
1 tablespoon lemon juice
¼ teaspoon salt
3 avocados, halved and pitted

In bowl, combine crumbled bacon, sour cream, tomatoes, onion, lemon juice and salt. Carefully scoop out avocado meat, leaving a firm shell. Dice the meat. Fold into bacon mixture. Spoon into shells and serve immediately.

Mrs. Robert Burdine
Florence

Shrimp Salad

1 cup cooked cleaned shrimp
½ cup diced celery
½ cup diced cucumber
2 tablespoons diced onion
1 bell pepper, diced

1 tablespoon lemon juice
3 tablespoons mayonnaise
Salt and pepper to taste
Crisp lettuce
1 lemon quartered

Chop shrimp; combine with celery, cucumber, onion, and bell pepper. Sprinkle with lemon juice. Add mayonnaise, salt, and pepper; toss lightly. Chill in covered bowl in refrigerator. Serve on lettuce leaves with quartered lemon as garnish. Yield: 4 servings.

Mrs. Preston White
Rogersville

Shrimp Tomato Stars

1 can (10¾ ounces) Condensed
  Cream of Chicken Soup
⅓ cup mayonnaise
½ teaspoon salt
⅛ teaspoon tarragon leaves
1 pound frozen cleaned raw shrimp,
  cooked and cut up (about
  2 cups)

2 hard-cooked eggs, chopped
½ cup celery
½ cup chopped green pepper
2 tablespoons thinly sliced green onion
6 medium tomatoes,
Salad greens

In bowl, blend soup, mayonnaise, salt, and tarragon. Stir in shrimp, eggs, celery, green pepper, and green onion; chill. Place tomatoes stem end down. Cut almost to stem, but not quite through, making 6 wedges; arrange on greens. Spoon shrimp mixture into tomatoes. Garnish with parsley if desired. Makes about 4 cups.

Shrimp Salad Mold

2 small cans shrimp,
  chopped and drained
1 cup mayonnaise
Juice of one lemon (or one tablespoon
  bottled lemon juice)

½ large onion, grated
2 tablespoons catsup
1 envelope unflavored gelatin

Dissolve gelatin in ¼ cup water in top of double boiler. Add all other ingredients; mix and refrigerate.

Mrs. Don Wassner
Muscle Shoals

Salmon Salad

1 can red salmon, boned and minced
2 hard cooked eggs, diced
2 small onions, minced
2 stalks celery, diced
2 boiled potatoes, diced

1 teaspoon dry mustard
2 apples, peeled and diced
2 teaspoons sugar
1 cup vinegar
Salt and pepper to taste

Mix, chill, and serve on lettuce leaves.

Mrs. Tracy Gargis
Sheffield

Tuna Salad

Two six-ounce cans tuna
½ cup salad dressing
One 8-ounce package sour cream
¼ teaspoon celery salt

1 tablespoon pimiento, chopped
1 small onion, chopped
2 tablespoons chopped green pepper
2 eggs, boiled and chopped

Combine all ingredients and chill thoroughly before serving.

Apple-Tuna Salad

1 package (3 ounce) gelatin—lemon
   or lime
½ teaspoon salt
1 cup boiling water
¾ cup cold water

1-2 teaspoons lemon juice
dash of pepper
1 cup diced peeled tart apples
1 can (7 ounce) flaked, drained tuna
½ cup chopped celery

Dissolve gelatin and salt in boiling water; add cold water, lemon juice, pepper. Chill until very thick. Fold in apples, tuna, and celery. Pour into a one quart mold or individual molds. Chill until set but not firm. Prepare 1 package lemon-lime gelatin as directed on package. Chill until very thick. Whip with rotary beater until mixture is fluffy and thick. Spoon into mold, 6 servings.

Mrs. J.P. Poe
Florence

Tuna Salad

1 cup cooked shell macaroni
1 small can tuna fish
1 or 2 green onions, sliced
1 stalk celery, sliced

1 teaspoon salad seasoning
¼ to ½ cup mayonnaise
Salt and pepper to taste

Mix all ingredients and chill.

Mrs. Edward Mullen
Florence

Spinach Molded Salad

1 small package lemon jello
1½ tablespoons vinegar
½ cup mayonnaise
¼ teaspoon salt
⅓ cup chopped celery

1 tablespoon minced onion
1 cup chopped frozen spinach
   (thawed and drained)
¾ cup cottage cheese

Dissolve jello in ¾ cup boiling water. Add 1 cup cold water. Add vinegar, mayonnaise, and salt. Put in freezer tray and chill until firm 1 inch around sides of tray. Turn into bowl and beat until fluffy. Add celery, onion, spinach and cottage cheese. Place in 1 quart mold and chill in refrigerator until firm.

Best made a day ahead of serving date to allow for better flavor. Serves six.

Green Bean Salad

1 large can sliced French green
  beans, drained
1 can English peas, drained
1 onion, chopped
Dressing:
¼ cup olive oil
½ cup cooking oil
1¼ cups sugar

1 cup celery, chopped
1 small can pimiento
2 large carrots, grated

1 cup vinegar
1 tablespoon water
1 garlic bulb

Blend dressing well and pour over vegetables. Let stand 24 hours. Remove garlic bulb and drain before serving. Note: dressing can be used again.

Virginia Daily

Green Bean Salad

1 large can green beans, drained
1 large can English peas, drained
2 large onions
4 stalks celery
1 jar pimiento peppers

¾ cup vinegar
1 cup sugar
1 teaspoon salt
1 teaspoon paprika
½ cup cooking oil

Mix all ingredients together and let sit in refrigerator overnight. Drain.

Mrs. Marshall Pennington
Tuscumbia

Overnight Vegetable Salad

1 medium onion, diced
1 one-pound can English peas
1 one-pound can French cut
  green beans
1 one-pound can whole kernel corn

1 cup celery, diced
½ cup green pepper, diced
1 two-ounce jar pimiento, cut fine
Salt to taste

Drain all canned vegetables and mix vegetables, pimiento, celery and salt. Combine:

1½ cups white sugar
1 cup vinegar
½ cup salad oil

2 tablespoons water
½ teaspoon paprika

Mix until sugar is dissolved and pour over vegetables. Chill for 24 hours. Keeps well several days in refrigerator.

Billy Townsend
Florence

Hot Lettuce

1 head of lettuce
6 slices bacon
2 tablespoons bacon fat

¼ cup vinegar
1 teaspoon sugar
1 tablespoon chopped onions

Fry bacon, drain and crumble. Put 2 tablespoons of fat in pan and heat. Add vinegar and sugar. Sprinkle onions over lettuce in a bowl, pour dressing over lettuce and sprinkle with bacon. Cover for about 5 minutes and serve. (Serves 4.)

Celery Salad

1 tablespoon sugar
½ teaspoon salt
¼ teaspoon paprika
⅛ teaspoon black pepper
2 tablespoons salad oil

1 tablespoon vinegar
⅓ cup dairy sour cream
3 cups chopped celery
½ cup shredded carrot

Combine sugar, salt, paprika, pepper, oil and vinegar. Slowly stir into sour cream. Add to celery and carrot. Toss lightly. 6 servings.

Addie Montgomery
Barton

Spinach Salad

1 pound spinach
1 can water chestnuts. sliced

1 can bean sprouts

Wash spinach and add water chestnuts and bean sprouts. Crisp spinach by putting in the refrigerator.

Dressing

1 red onion
⅛ cup catsup
½ cup vinegar

6 cups oil
⅔ cup sugar
Boiled eggs and bacon

Shake dressing so as to mix well before pouring over salad. Top with boiled eggs and bacon.

Mrs. J.E. Tease
Florence

Dutch Spinach Salad

3 cups of fresh spinach
 cut into bite-size pieces)
5 slices crisp bacon crumbled
1 medium carrot, shredded

1 tablespoon minced onion
¼ cup bottled Italian dressing
⅛ teaspoon dry mustard
Dash of pepper

Combine spinach, bacon, carrots and onion in medium bowl. Heat Italian dressing with mustard and pepper in a small saucepan, pour over spinach and toss. Serves 4.

Mrs. E.H. Moore
Florence

German Potato Salad

7 slices bacon, diced
¾ cup chopped onion
2 tablespoons flour
1½ tablespoons sugar
2 teaspoons salt

¼ teaspoon pepper
¾ cups water
½ cup vinegar
6 cups sliced cooked potatoes

Cook bacon until lightly browned. Add onion. Cook until tender. Add flour. Stir until smooth combine water, vinegar, sugar, salt and pepper. Add slowly to bacon mixture. Add sliced potatoes. Mix lightly. Cover and simmer 20 minutes.

Mrs. J.P. Poe
Florence

Refrigerator Slaw

1 large head cabbage
2 small onions
Bring to a boil:
1 cup vinegar
1 cup sugar
1 teaspoon white mustard seed

3 or 4 stems celery
1 bell pepper

1 teaspoon tumeric
Dash salt and pepper

Pour over chopped vegetables. Let sit in refrigerator overnight.

Virginia Daily
Florence

Refrigerator Cole Slaw

1 large head of cabbage
1 or 2 small onions
3 or 4 stalks of celery
1 bell pepper
Salt

Pepper
1 cup sugar
1 cup vinegar
1 teaspoon white mustard seeds
1 teaspoon tumeric

Chop cabbage, onions, celery, and pepper. Add salt and pepper to taste. Bring sugar, vinegar, mustard seed and tumeric to boiling. Remove from heat and pour over grated cabbage mixture. Cover and place in refrigerator. This mixture will keep several weeks in the refrigerator.

Pearlene Creasy
Florence

Slaw

Chop:
1 medium head cabbage
1 green pepper
Bring to boil:
1 cup sugar
1 cup white vinegar
1 teaspoon tumeric

1 large onion

1 teaspoon dry mustard
1 teaspoon salt

Pour over cabbage, pepper and onion while still hot. Put in refrigerator. Keeps for days.

Pat Gatlin
Leighton

Vegetable Slaw

2 cups shredded green cabbage
½ cup shredded red cabbage
¼ cup shredded carrots
¼ cup chopped green pepper
¼ cup chopped onion

2 teaspoons vinegar
½ teaspoon salt
⅛ teaspoon dry mustard
¾ cup dairy sour cream
1 teaspoon sugar

Combine green cabbage, red cabbage, carrots, green pepper, and onion. Chill. Mix vinegar, sugar, salt, and dry mustard together. Fold into sour cream. Chill. Just before serving, pour sour cream dressing over vegetables. Toss lightly.

Mrs. Christine F. Moss
Russellville

Cabbage Slaw

1½ cups vinegar
¾ cup sugar
1 tablespoon mustard
1 teaspoon salt

½ cup salad oil
1 medium cabbage head
2 medium onions

Chop cabbage and onion, set aside. Boil together vinegar, sugar, mustard and salt for one minute. Remove from heat. Stir in oil and pour over cabbage and onion. Set in refrigerator overnight. The slaw can be kept in the refrigerator for several days.

Addie C. Montgomery
Tuscumbia

Creamy Corn Slaw

¼ cup sour cream
¼ cup mayonnaise
1 tablespoon prepared mustard
2 teaspoons white vinegar
1 teaspoon sugar
¼ teaspoon salt
⅛ teaspoon pepper

1 17-ounce can whole kernel
  corn, drained
2 carrots, peeled and coarsely
  grated
1 green pepper, diced
½ cup diced red onion

Mix sour cream, mayonnaise, mustard, vinegar, sugar, salt and pepper. Add remaining ingredients and toss to blend. Cover and refrigerate for one hour or longer. Makes 3 cups or 4 servings. Good with fried chicken and mashed turnips.

Mrs. Tracy Gargis
Sheffield

24-Hour Slaw

1 medium cabbage, shredded
½ cup sugar
1 medium onion, chopped
1 green pepper, chopped
6 olives, chopped (optional)
1 cup white vinegar

1 teaspoon celery seed
1 teaspoon black pepper
1 teaspoon salt
1 teaspoon prepared mustard
½ cup salad oil
1 tablespoon tumeric

Boil together for three minutes, vinegar, celery seed, black pepper, salt, prepared mustard, salad oil and tumeric. Pour over cabbage mixture and let stand for 24 hours. Slaw may be frozen.

Mrs. Preston White
Rogersville

Peanut Salad

2 cups shredded cabbage
1 cup pineapple, well drained

⅔ cup salted peanuts
½ cup mayonnaise or salad dressing

Salt and pepper to taste. Add peanuts just before serving. Serve on lettuce leaf is desired.

Mrs. Ruby Allison
Muscle Shoals

Thousand Island Dressing

⅔ cup mayonnaise
1 tablespoon catsup

1 boiled egg, chopped
1 tablespoon sweet pickle relish

Combine all ingredients.

Mrs. Judy McKelvey
Tuscumbia

Papa's Italian Dressing

¾ cup vinegar
½ teaspoon onion salt
1 heaping tablespoon
   salad supreme

1 cup salad oil
1 heaping tablespoon instant
   minced onion
1 package "Italian Good Seasons"

Put ingredients in vinegar. Stir and let soak for 5 minutes. Add the oil. Stir and mix well. Recipe makes a generous amount so you may store it in the refrigerator.

Mrs. R.A. Fonseca
Florence

Salad Sweet Fruit Dressing

½ cup sugar
1 teaspoon paprika
1 teaspoon celery salt
1 teaspoon dry mustard

1 teaspoon salt
1 cup vegetable oil
¼ cup vinegar

Mix dry ingredients. Add oil and vinegar in small amounts, vinegar being the last addition. Use on lettuce, mandarin orange sections, avocado slices, raisins, pineapple.

Mozelle Carter
Cherokee

Fruit Salad Dressing

½ cup honey
2 tablespoons lemon or lime juice

⅛ teaspoon hot sauce

Combine ingredients. Serve over fresh fruit salads. Yield: About ½ cup.

Donna M. Hayes
Florence

Hidden Valley Salad Dressing

1½ teaspoon garlic salt
1½ teaspoon onion salt
1 teaspoon parsley flakes
½ teaspoon Accent

1 pint mayonnaise
1 cup buttermilk
1 small container sour cream

Mix all ingredients together. Use on baked potatoes, or as a dip.
Only 1 teaspoon of garlic and onion salt can be used.

Mrs. Ken Hewlett
Muscle Shoals

Roquefort Cheese Dressing

⅓ pound imported Roquefort
  cheese, mashed fine
1 tablespoon powdered mustard
¼ teaspoon cayenne pepper
1 teaspoon salt
1 pod garlic, chopped very fine

Juice of 1½ lemons
3 cups oil
½ cup vinegar
2 hard boiled eggs, chopped
  fine

Mix all ingredients except eggs thoroughly. Then add eggs. Will keep for several weeks.

Mrs. Leonard Burt
Sheffield

Oilless French Dressing

1 teaspoon unflavored gelatin
1 tablespoon cold water
¼ cup hot water
3 tablespoons sugar (or equivalent
  non-caloric sweetener)

½ teaspoon salt (Garlic or celery may
  be used)
⅛ teaspoon dry mustard
½ teaspoon paprika
½ cup lemon juice

Soak gelatin in cold water. Dissolve in hot. Add seasonings. When cool, add lemon juice. Chill.

Mrs. James. A. Gafford
Florence

Lemon Honey Dressing

1 cup sour cream
3 tablespoons fresh lemon juice
½ teaspoon salt

3 tablespoons honey
½ teaspoon grated lemon rind

Combine all ingredients and chill 30 minutes or longer to blend flavors.

Mrs. James A. Gafford
Florence

Lime Honey Dressing

¼ cup lime juice
3 tablespoons lemon juice
6 tablespoons honey

1 tablespoon Worcestershire sauce
⅛ teaspoon salt
1 cup salad oil

Blend all ingredients thoroughly. Refrigerate.

Mrs. James A. Gafford
Florence

Shrimp Luncheon Salad For Diabetics

1 small head lettuce	½ cup thinly sliced mushrooms
3 to 4 cups torn spinach	½ cup chopped green peppers
2 cups (12 ounce package) fresh	½ cup sliced celery
or frozen shrimp, cooked	½ cup sliced cucumber
and chilled	½ cup sliced green onion

In a large bowl, combine all salad ingredients. Just before serving, toss with shrimp sauce; serve immediately. Makes 6 (2 cup) servings. 1 serving equals 2 meat exchanges and 135 calories.

Low Calorie Salad Dressing

2 cups tomato juice	Pinch of dry mustard
1 tablespoon lemon juice	¼ teaspoon garlic or celery salt
½ teaspoon salt	1 tablespoon chopped green onion

Blend all ingredients well. Chill before serving.

Mrs. James A. Gafford
Slorence

Creamy Low-Calorie Dressing

½ cup buttermilk	1 tablespoon vinegar
2 tablespoons prepared yellow	1 tablespoon oil
mustard	¼ teaspoon salt

Combine all ingredients, stirring until well blended. Serve as dressing with lettuce. Makes ¾ cup dressing.

Low Calorie Salad

1 small can crushed pineapple	1 package whipped topping mix
1 package lime gelatin (small)	½ pint cottage cheese
1 cup cold water	

Heat undrained pineapple in a two-quart saucepan. Add gelatin and dissolve; add water. Cool mixture. Prepare whipped topping according to package directions and fold into other mixture. Fold in cottage cheese. Chill thoroughly before serving. Yield: 8 servings.

Evelyn Pless
Cherokee

Low Calorie French Dressing

1 cup tomato soup	1 teaspoon salt (garlic salt if
1 cup vinegar	preferred)
1 tablespoon dry mustard	1 ground onion
2 tablespoons Worcestershire sauce	Artificial sweetener

Mix thoroughly. Sweeten to taste. Store in jar in refrigerator.

Evelyn Pless
Cherokee

Chicken Salad

1 cup diced celery
3 cups cubed cooked chicken
¼ cup whipping cream, whipped
½ cup small seedless grapes
½ cup toasted pecans, coarsely
   chopped

¼ cup flaked coconut
¾ cup salad dressing or mayonnaise
¼ teaspoon salt
Few grains pepper

In a large bowl, combine first five ingredients, tossing together lightly with a fork. Gradually blend the salad dressing and seasonings into whipped cream. Pour over salad ingredients in bowl, fork-toss to mix lightly but thoroughly. Cover and chill thoroughly. Serve on chilled, crisp greens, or use to fill center of a tomato aspic ring or halves of fresh pineapple. 6 servings.

Mable Allison
Tuscumbia

Chicken Salad With Fruit

1½ cups diced cooked chicken
¾ cup diced celery
½ cup white grape halves

1 cup diced apple, unpeeled
Mayonnaise

Mix well, serve on lettuce with garnish of avocado slices, ripe olives or tomato wedges.

Mrs. R.W. Weaver
Florence

Chinese Chicken Salad

2 cups cooked chicken, chopped
1 can mushroom soup
1 cup celery, chopped
1 medium onion, chopped
1 small jar pimiento, chopped

¾ cup mayonnaise
1 can mushrooms, sliced
1 medium can Chow Mein noodles
1 can water chestnuts, sliced

Mix all ingredients together. Save ¼ of noodles to sprinkle on top of the casserole. Bake at 350 degrees for 30 to 45 minutes.

Mrs. Pat Peck
Florence

Hot Buttons and Bows Salad

1 8-ounce package bow-tie egg noodles
1 8-ounce jar pasteurized process cheese spread
¼ cup milk

6 hard boiled eggs, coarsely chopped
½ cup thinly sliced sweet pickle
¼ cup chopped onion
¼ cup chopped celery
2 tablespoons chopped pimiento

About 45 minutes before serving, prepare bow ties as label directs; drain and set aside. In same saucepan over medium heat, stir cheese spread and milk until hot and smooth; stir in bow ties and remaining ingredients and heat thoroughly, stirring to prevent sticking. Yield: 6 servings.

Mrs. E.N. Rutherford
Cherokee

Pimiento Cheese Mold

1 package lime gelatin
1 cup hot water
1 small can crushed pineapple
2 cups marshmallows
2 cups nuts

Juice of 1 lemon
1 teaspoon vinegar
Pinch of salt
½ pint whipped cream
1 jar pimiento cheese spread

Dissolve gelatin in hot water; cool, add pineapple, marshmallows, nuts, lemon juice, vinegar and salt. Combine whipped cream and cheese spread; blend with gelatin mixture. Refrigerate for eight hours.

Mrs. Roisell Miller
Tuscumbia

Waldorf Salad

2 or 3 apples, cubed
½ cup pecans, broken up
½ cup grapes, break in half, remove seeds

½ to 1 cup chopped celery
½ cup marshmallow sauce

Mix ingredients, tossing lightly. If marshmallow sauce is too thick, add a couple of tablespoons of water and, if desired, a teaspoon of lemon juice.

Lucille Prince
Sheffield

Jellied Waldorf Salad

1½ cups boiling water
2 3-ounce packages lemon gelatin
½ cup raisins
½ cup grated raw carrots
½ cup dried, unpared apples

½ cup coarsely chopped walnuts
1 teaspoon salt
Salad greens
Mayonnaise or cooked dressing

Pour boiling water over gelatin in medium bowl; stir to dissolve gelatin. Add 1½ cups cold water. Set bowl in pan of ice; leave in ice, stirring occasionally until mixture is consistency of unbeaten egg whites (about 30 minutes). Let raisins stand 10 minutes in boiling water to cover; drain. Stir raisins, carrots, apple and walnuts into gelatin mixture. Pour into mold. Refrigerate one hour. Makes 6-8 servings.

Mrs. Tracy Gargis
Sheffield

Copenhagen Salad

1 pound fresh peas, hulled
(1 cup)
1 cup diced celery
¾ cup diced creamy Havarti
cheese
½ cup whole natural (unblanched)
almonds, chopped and roasted

½ cup dairy sour cream
1 tablespoon lemon juice
1 tablespoon minced onion
¼ teaspoon prepared mustard
⅛ teaspoon salt
2 medium tomatoes, cut in wedges
Watercress or parsley

Cook peas in lightly salted boiling water until barely tender, about 1 to 2 minutes; drain thoroughly. Combine peas, celery, cheese, almonds, sour cream, lemon juice, onion, mustard and salt. Toss lightly to mix. Spoon into 4 individual glasses or bowls or one serving bowl. Garnish with tomatoes and watercress. Makes 4 servings (3 cups).

Mom's Tomato Aspic

2 envelopes (2 tablespoons)
unflavored gelatin
4 cups tomato juice
⅓ cup chopped onion
¼ cup chopped celery leaves
2 tablespoons brown sugar
1 teaspoon salt

2 small bay leaves
4 whole cloves
3 tablespoons lemon juice
½ to 1 cup finely chopped celery
(optional)
2 tablespoons chopped green
pepper

Soften gelatin in 1 cup cold tomato juice. Combine 2 cups of the tomato juice and the onion, celery leaves, sugar, salt, bay leaves, and cloves. Simmer uncovered 5 minutes; strain. Dissolve the softened gelatin in the hot tomato mixture. Add remaining tomato juice and the lemon juice. Chill till partially set. Stir in celery and green pepper. Pour into a 5½-cup mold. Chill firm, 5 to 6 hours or overnight. Unmold on chilled platter. Makes 6 to 8 servings.

Betty Ballinger

Rice Salad

3 cups ready cooked rice
½ cup mayonnaise
4 hard-boiled eggs
½ cup chopped pickles

½ pound bacon
½ cup chopped celery
2 tablespoons French dressing
½ cup chopped onions

Fry bacon crisp. Crumble bacon and add eggs, chopped and seasoned. Mix with cooked rice. Add chopped pickles, celery, onions, stir in mayonnaise and French dressing. Mix well. Serves 6 or 8 people.

Donna M. Hayes
Florence

Macaroni Salad

Cook 2 cups macaroni with salt and black pepper. Drain off water, let cool. Chop one apple, one small pimiento, one small cucumber, and a boiled egg. Mix together with oil.

Hannah J. Phillips
Bear Creek

Chilled Macaroni Supper Salad

2 cups cooked elbow macaroni
¼ cup Italian salad dressing
1 cup mayonnaise
8½ ounce can green peas, drained
1 can pimento, diced

12 ounce can luncheon meat
2 tablespoons cider vinegar
1 teaspoon salt
⅛ teaspoon pepper
1 can asparagus spears, drained

Turn macaroni into large bowl, add Italian dressing and toss lightly. Set aside, cut thin strips of luncheon meat to alternate with asparagus, dice remainder and set aside. In a small bowl, mix mayonnaise with vinegar and a blend of salt and pepper. Add to macaroni. Blend in diced luncheon meat, peas, and pimento. Toss. Turn salad mixture into a shallow 2 qt. dish, alternating the luncheon meat strips and asparagus spears lengthwise on salad mixture. Brush meat and asparagus generously with additional Italian salad dressing. Chill. About 6 servings

Mrs. J.H. Mitchell
Florence

Buffet Taco Salad

1 pound ground chuck
1 package taco seasoning mix
1 pound velveeta cheese
1 can rotelle chilies
 Cooked rice
Chopped lettuce

Chopped green pepper
Chopped onion
Corn chips
Chopped tomato
Chopped cucumber

Brown ground chuck and add taco seasoning mix. Melt cheese and add rotelle chilie in the top of a double boiler.

Set everything on a buffet table and let each person build his or her own meal starting with corn chips. Add rice, various vegetables and top with plenty of cheese sauce.

Mrs. Billy Heupel
Florence

Frozen Fruit Salad

⅔ ounce cream cheese
1 cup heavy whipped cream
½ cup green cherries, quartered
2½ cups diced marshmallows

1 cup mayonnaise
½ cup red cherries, quartered
1 No. 2 can crushed pineapple, drained

Combine cheese and mayonnaise, blend until smooth. Fold in whipped cream, fruit and marshmallows. Freeze.

Mrs. Rufus Sherrod
Cumberland City, Tennessee

Cottage Cheese Fruit Salad

2 cups cottage cheese
1 cup grated carrots
1 cup chopped apples

¼ cup minced celery
1 cup mayonnaise

Toss together the cheese, carrots, apples, and celery until well mixed. Gradually add salad dressing (mayonnaise). Serve on crisp lettuce heart.

Mrs. Ernest Moore
Florence

Heavenly Fruit Hash

1 can fruit cocktail
½ cup whipped cream
2 tablespoons sugar

2 teaspoons lemon juice
6 finely chopped marshmallows
1 banana

Drain fruit cocktail. Mix whipped cream, sugar and lemon juice. Fold in fruit cocktail, sliced banana and chopped marshmallows. Chill an hour or longer before serving.

Mozelle Carter
Cherokee

Magnolia Salad

½ teaspoon mustard
1 teaspoon flour
1½ teaspoons vinegar
3 eggs yolks
½ cup sweet milk

1 cup pineapple
1 cup chopped nuts
½ pound miniature marshmallows
½ pint whipping cream

Combine mustard, flour, vinegar, egg yolks, and sweet milk and cook until thick. Add pineapple, nuts, marshmallows. Beat cream until thick and add to mixture. Place in refrigerator overnight.

Mrs. Larry W. Hester
Muscle Shoals

Sour Cream Salad

1 large can fruit cocktail
  (drained well)
1 can coconut

1 package miniature marshmallows
1 cup sour cream

Mix well. Chill overnight. For best results refrigerate items before mixing. Variation: Pink pineapple, drained; mandarin oranges, mixed with coconut, marshmallows and sour cream.

Mrs. F.A. Wallace
Killen

Sprinkle Salad

1 large can sliced pineapple,
  diced and drained
1 can mandarin oranges, diced
  and drained

1 one-pound carton cottage
  cheese
1 large container refrigerated
  whipped topping

Mix together. Sprinkle one box orange gelatin on top. Stir again. "Ready to eat." (Flavor of gelatin can be changed when another color is desired).

Pat Gatlin
Leighton

Heavenly Hash Salad

8 ounce package cream
  cheese
1 large can tidbits pineapple
1 small box whipping cream

1 package miniature marshmallows
3 tablespoons sugar
Nuts, if desired

Cream cheese with juice from pineapple. Blend in sugar. Mix rest of ingredients and chill overnight.

Mrs. J.P. Stephens
Dennis, Mississippi

Paradise Salad

1 small can crushed pineapple
½ cup sugar
2 packages cream cheese
1 envelope gelatin

½ pint whipping cream
Juice of 1 lemon
1 small bottle maraschino
  cherries

Dissolve gelatin in half cup of cold water. Combine pineapple, sugar and lemon juice and bring to a boil. Remove from heat and stir into dissolved gelatin; let cool. Mix cream cheese with cherry juice, using a fork. Add finely chopped cherries and pineapple mixture. Fold in whipped cream and pour into mold and chill until set.

Virginia Daily
Florence

Angel Flake Salad

2 cans flaked coconut
1 No. 2 can fruit cocktail
1 No. 2 can crushed pineapple
1 container sour cream

1 container cottage cheese
1 6¼ ounce package miniature
  marshmallows

Combine and let stand overnight. Do not drain fruit.

Virginia Daily
Florence

Easy Summer Salad

1 8½ ounce can crushed
  pineapple
1 ounce package mixed
  fruit flavor gelatin

1 envelope whipped topping mix
1 12 ounce box cottage cheese

Cook pineapple 2 minutes. Add gelatin and cook 2 minutes longer. Set aside to cool. Prepare whipped topping according to package directions. Add cottage cheese and stir well. Add to gelatin mixture. Pour into mold or shallow dish and chill until firm. Serves 8.

Donna M. Hayes
Florence

Salad

1 can cherry pie filling
1 can fruit cocktail, drained
1 small can crushed pineapple

2 double handfuls of miniature
  marshmallows
1 large carton whipped topping
Pecans

Mix pie filling, fruit cocktail, pineapple, and marshmallows the night before serving. Refrigerate. The next day, add whipped topping and pecans.

Mrs. George Barnett
Florence

Dry Gelatin Salad

1 package gelatin, any flavor
1 small can crushed pineapple,
  drained
1 small carton cottage cheese

½ cup nuts
1 cup marshmallows
1 small container refrigerated
  whipped topping

Sprinkle dry gelatin over cottage cheese and mix well. Blend in other ingredients and fold in whipped topping last. Let set in refrigerator about 15 minutes before serving.

Dianne Austin
Sheffield

Ribbon Salad

1 3-ounce package lemon
    gelatin
1 envelope unflavored gelatin
¼ cup cold water
1 pound can fruit cocktail, drained,
    reserve syrup

½ cup syrup from fruit cocktail
1 pint creamed cottage cheese
1 3-ounce package cherry gelatin

Lightly oil a two quart gelatin mold. Prepare lemon gelatin by directions on package. Pour into pan, chill until firm. Soften unflavored gelatin in cold water. Bring fruit cocktail syrup to a boil. Remove from heat and dissolve unflavored gelatin in hot syrup. Stir into cottage cheese. Add fruit cocktail. Spread evenly over lemon gelatin. Chill until firm. Prepare cherry gelatin by directions on package. Chill until thick and syrupy. Pour over cheese layer. Chill until firm. Unmold on platter.

Lula Hyde
Florence

Green Salad

1 package lime-flavored gelatin
1 cup boiling water
1 small can crushed pineapple
1 package (8 ounce) cream cheese

2 tablespoons mayonnaise
1 dozen marshmallows
1 cup chopped celery
1 cup chopped nuts

Pour boiling water over gelatin and marshmallows and stir until dissolved. Cool. Mix cream cheese with mayonnaise and combine with pineapple, celery and nuts. Add to first mixture and put in refrigerator until congealed.

Mrs. Walter Shaff
Florence

Sunshine Salad

1 cup grated carrot
1 package lemon gelatin

¼ cup sugar
1 can crushed pineapple

Make gelatin as directed, add sugar to gelatin; then add other ingredients. Mix well and chill. Serve on lettuce leaf.

Addie Montgomery
Barton

Frozen Gingerale Salad

1 tablespoon gelatin
¼ cup orange juice
2 tablespoons lemon juice
¼ cup sugar
½ cup crushed pineapple

½ cup diced pears
½ cup crushed strawberries
1 cup gingerale
¾ cup mayonnaise
1 cup whipping cream

Soak gelatin in orange juice 5 minutes. Add lemon juice; place pan in hot water and stir until dissolved. Add sugar and gingerale and stir until sugar is dissolved. Add fruit and cool until slightly thickened. Fold in mayonnaise and whipping cream beaten stiff. Freeze.

Donna M. Hayes
Florence

Pineapple-Lime Salad

1 package lemon gelatin
1 package lime gelatin
3 cups boiling water
24 large marshmallows (10
  miniature equal 1
  regular size)

1 can (No. 202) crushed pineapple,
  drained
2 small packages cream cheese
1½ cups chopped, toasted pecans

Mix and chill first 4 ingredients until slightly set. Add softened cream cheese with gelatin mixture and beat with mixer until cheese is blended. Fold in well drained pineapple and nuts. Return to refrigerator. Serves 10 to 12.

Mrs. Jesse A. Keller
Florence

Pineapple Salad

1 can crushed pineapple
  (432 grams)
1 boxed mixed fruit gelatin (3
  ounce size)

1 large carton whipped topping
1 (12 ounce) carton cottage
  cheese
½ cup pecans (approximately)

Bring pineapple to boil and stir in mixed fruit gelatin and stir for 2 minutes. Take off stove and allow to cool completely. Mix whipped topping and cottage cheese together. Then stir in pineapple and pecans. Put in 9x13-inch pyrex dish and chill. Will keep 2 weeks.

Mrs. John D. Clement, Jr.
Muscle Shoals

Jellied Pineapple Salad

2 cups boiling water
2 cups miniature marshmallows

1 package orange gelatin

Mix well and cool. Mix one package cream cheese with four tablespoons milk; add one can crushed pineapple, drained. Pour in mold or tray. Chill.

Alpha H. Jeffreys
Town Creek

Congealed Salad

1 carton cottage cheese
1 small can crushed pineapple,
  drained
½ box gelatin, any flavor

1 cup small marshmallows
½ cup chopped nuts
1 small carton whipped topping
  or ½ large carton

Mix gelatin with cottage cheese; then mix all ingredients together and chill.

Mrs. Frances M. Holt
Florence

Buttermilk Salad

1 large box peach or apricot
  gelatin
2 cups boiling water
1 large can crushed unsweetened
  pineapple

2 cups buttermilk
1 large container frozen whipped
  topping

Dissolve gelatin in boiling water and add pineapple. Let mixture cool. Add buttermilk and fold in whipped topping and let set.

Myra T. Crowe
Florence

Summer Salad

1 (8½ ounce) can crushed pineapple
1 (3 ounce) package mixed-fruit
  flavor gelatin
1 envelope whipped topping mix

1 (12 ounce) carton cottage cheese
¾ cup carrots chopped in blender
  or grated

Cook pineapple 2 minutes. Add gelatin and cook 2 minutes longer. Set aside to cool. Prepare whipped topping according to package directions. Add cottage cheese and stir well. Add gelatin mixture. Pour into mold or shallow dish and chill until firm. Serves 8 or 10.

Donna M. Hayes
Florence

Pink Gelatin Salad

1 3-ounce package cherry gelatin   1 cup hot water

Dissolve gelatin in water and set aside. Mix and bring to boil one small can crushed pineapple and ¾ cup sugar. Stir into gelatin. Refrigerate mixture until almost set. Whip one-half pint whipping cream. Grate one cup longhorn cheese. Take whipping cream, cheese, ¼ cup chopped nuts and one cup miniature marshmallows and fold into set gelatin. Refrigerate and cut into squares to serve.

Mrs. Carl Rickard
Florence

Cola Congealed Salad

2 small colas
1 package cherry gelatin
1 package strawberry gelatin
1 large can crushed pineapple,
  drained

1 can Bing cherries, drained
1 cup chopped nuts
1 package (8 ounces) cream
  cheese

Use juice from pineapple and cherries and bring to a boil and pour over gelatin. Stir and cool. Fold in cheese, nuts, pineapple and cherries. Add cola; stir often until jelled.

Mrs. John Ballinger
Madisonville, Kentucky

Gelatin Salad

1 large package peach gelatin
1 8-ounce carton cottage cheese

1 pint peaches, cut up, without
  juice

Mix dry gelatin with cottage cheese; then mix in peaches. Mix large carton refrigerated whipped topping and spread on top of mixture. Garnish with halved red and green cherries.

Mrs. Emma Bendall
Leighton

Lime Gelatin Salad

2 packages lime gelatin
1 large can crushed pineapple
  including juice
¾ cup cottage cheese

1 cup mayonnaise
1 cup nuts
1 cup celery (optional)

Dissolve the gelatin in two cups hot water. After gelatin has cooled, add pineapple and cottage cheese which has been mixed with mayonnaise. Add chopped nuts and celery if desired. Refrigerate.

Mres. Ellis Moore
Cloverdale

Lime Salad

1 package lime gelatin
2 cups pecans, chopped
Small can of crushed pineapple,
  drained

Small box of cottage cheese
1 cup hot water
1 cup mayonnaise

Mix hot water with gelatin. Then mix all other ingredients. Chill until set.

Mrs. Kelly Moore
Red Bay

Lime Congealed Salad

1 cup pecans
1 box lime gelatin
1 box lemon gelatin
2 cups boiling water
1 can sweetened condensed milk

¼ cup mayonnaise
1 small can crushed pineapple,
  drained
1 package (12 ounces) cottage
  cheese

Melt lemon and lime gelatin with boiling water. Put in refrigerator until syrupy, then add sweetened condensed milk, mayonnaise, cottage cheese, pineapple, and nuts. Let congeal.

Gertrude Snider
Sheffield

Lemon Salad

1 No. 2 can crushed pineapple
1 box cottage cheese
½ cup mayonnaise

2 packages lemon gelatin
1 cup nuts
Pinch of salt

Mix and chill gelatin until partially set. Stir in pineapple, cottage cheese, mayonnaise, and nuts. Top with cherries.

Addie Carl Montgomery
Barton

Seven-Up Salad

1 large or 2 small boxes lemon gelatin
2 cups hot water
2 small bottles cold Seven-Up

2 or 3 bananas, diced
1½ cups miniature marshmallows
1 medium can crushed drained pineapple

Mix gelatin with hot water and Seven-Up. Add bananas, marshmallows and pineapple. Chill until firm.

Topping

½ cup sugar
3 tablespoons (level) flour
2 tablespoons butter

1 cup pineapple juice
2 eggs
1 package topping mix

Mix first 5 ingredients; cook until thick. Cool. Add topping mix to mixture; pour on top of salad.

Mrs. Joe L. Puckett Sr.
Muscle Shoals

Alaskan Salad

1 large carton frozen whipped
   topping
1 box (3 ounces) orange gelatin
1 can (11 ounces) mandarin
   oranges

1 can (11 ounces) crushed pineapple
1 small carton cottage cheese
½ cup nuts, optional

Drain oranges and pineapple. Mix dry gelatin and whipped topping. Mix well. Add drained pineapple, orange slices, cottage cheese and nuts and mix again. Salad can be served immediately or kept in the refrigerator for several days. Makes eight to 10 servings.

Ethel Rutherford
Cherokee

Strawberry-Nut Salad

1 package (6 ounces) strawberry
    gelatin
1 cup boiling water
2 packages (10 ounces each)
    frozen sliced strawberries

1 can (1 pound, four ounces)
    crushed pineapple, drained
3 medium bananas, mashed
1 cup coarsely chopped walnuts
    or pecans
1 cup miniature marshmallows

Combine gelatin and water in a large bowl, stirring until gelatin is dissolved. Fold in strawberries with juice, drained pineapple, bananas, nuts, and marshmallows all at once. Turn into mold and refrigerate until firm. Best if made day before serving. This will serve a gang or half will serve four to six.

Mrs. Everett Vickery
Russellville

Cherry Salad

2 cups boiling water
1 large package cherry gelatin

1 one-pound can cherry pie
    pie filling
Small can crushed pineapple

Dissolve gelatin in 2 cups boiling water. Add pineapple and pie filling. Pour in 13 x 9 pan and chill until firm.

Topping

1 8-ounce package cream cheese,
    softened
1 8-ounce carton sour cream

1 cup pecans, chopped
¾ cup sugar

Combine all ingredients for topping and beat with mixer until smooth. Spread on top of cherry mixture. Serves 12 to 16.

Mrs. Carl Richard
Florence

Raspberry Salad

1 small package raspberry
    gelatin
1 small can applesauce

1 small can crushed pineapple,
    drained
½ cup chopped nuts
1 cup hot water

Add hot water to gelatin and mix until dissolved. Add applesauce and pineapple. Mix and add chopped nuts. Chill until firm.

Donna M. Hayes
Florence

Sunset Salad

1 3-ounce package orange gelatin
½ teaspoon salt
1 cup boiling water
1 8-ounce can crushed pineapple
    in juice

1 tablespoon lemon juice or
    vinegar
1 cup grated carrot

Dissolve gelatin and salt in boiling water. Add pineapple with juice and lemon or vinegar. Mix well. Add carrots; mix again. Pour into individual dishes. Chill until set, one hour or more. Makes six servings.

Addie C. Montgomery

Marshmallow Fruit Salad

2 packages strawberry gelatin
1 package large marshmallows
1 cup whipped cream
1 cup chopped pecans

1 small jar maraschino cherries,
  chopped
1 small jar crushed pineapple

Dissolve gelatin according to directions on package. Add marshmallows while gelatin is hot and stir until dissolved. Refrigerate until gelatin starts to congeal. Add other ingredients to mixture and chill until firm.

Frosted Salad

1 large or 2 small pineapple gelatin
  Prepare as directed on package.
1 (20 ounce) crushed
  pineapple

2 large bananas, diced
1 cup small marshmallows

Chill gelatin until partly set. Fold in bananas, pineapple (well drained) and marshmallows. Save juice.

Topping

¾ cup sugar
2 tablespoons flour
1 cup pineapple juice
1 egg, beaten

2 tablespoons butter
1 cup whipping cream
Grated cheese to cover all salad

Combine sugar and flour well. Beat egg and add juice and butter. Cook until thick and clear. Set it in cold water to cool. Whip cream. Add to cooled mixture. Spread over gelatin and chill several hours or overnight. Takes large, long pan for this.

Mrs. G.K. Counts
Florence

Fresh Cranberry Salad

1 pound ground fresh cranberries
1 ground whole orange
1 cup sugar
1 cup chopped pecans or walnuts

1 package red gelatin, plus
  one envelope plain,
  unflavored gelatin
1 can crushed pineapple

Let cranberries, orange and sugar stand for one hour. Prepare gelatin according to instructions on box. Mix.

Viola T. Holder
Florence

Blueberry Salad

1 (15 ounce) can blueberries
1 (8½ ounce) can crushed pineapple
2 (3 ounce) packages black
   raspberry gelatin
1 cup boiling water

1 (8 ounce) package softened
   cream cheese
1 (8 ounce) package sour cream
½ cup sugar
1 cup chopped pecans
1 teaspoon vanilla

Drain blueberries and pineapple, save liquid. Dissolve gelatin in boiling water; add fruit juices and water to make 1¾ cups; add to dissolved gelatin. When slightly set, add fruit. Chill until firm; combine cream cheese, sour cream, sugar and vanilla. Beat well and spread over gelatin. Sprinkle with pecans.

Mrs Ken Hewlett
Muscle Shoals

Easy Bavarian

1 cup boiling water
1 (3 ounce) package red gelatin
   (or any flavor)
¼ cup sugar

1 cup cold water
⅓ cup thawed dairy whipped
   topping

Dissolve gelatin and sugar in boiling water. Add cold water. Chill until slightly thickened. Blend whipped topping into gelatin. Chill in 1 quart or 6 to 8 individual molds until firm. Unmold and garnish with additional topping. Variations: Drained fruit cocktail may be added when topping is.

Paula Doggett
Florence

Orange Sherbet Salad

2 (3 ounce) packages orange-
   flavored gelatin
1 cup boiling water
1 pint orange sherbet
1 (8¼ ounce) can crushed pineapple
1 cup miniature marshmallows

1 (11 ounce) can mandarin orange
   sections, drained
½ pint whipping cream, whipped
   or 2 cups non-dairy dessert
   topping

Dissolve gelatin in boiling water. Add orange sherbet. When partially set, add other ingredients, folding in whipped cream last. Chill until firm. Yield: 12 servings.

Mrs. Donald E. Holt
Florence

Sherbet Salad

1 package orange gelatin
1 cup hot water
1 cup orange sherbet

1 medium can crushed pineapple
1 cup chopped pecans
1 can mandarin orange segments

Dissolve gelatin in hot water, add sherbet and mix well. Chill until slightly set. Remove from refrigerator and add pineapple (well drained), nuts, and orange segments. Return to refrigerator. Serves 6.

Mrs. Jesse A. Keller
Florence

Sawdust Salad

1 package lemon gelatin
1 package orange or orange-
  pineapple gelatin
½ cup sugar (optional)
2 cups boiling water
1½ cups cold water
1 medium can crushed pineapple
1 can apricots, mashed
2 or 3 diced bananas
Grated cheddar cheese

2 cups miniature marshmallows
½ cup apricot syrup
½ cup pineapple syrup
¾ cup white sugar
1 whole egg, beaten
2 tablespoons flour
1 package whipped cream
1 8 ounce package creamed
  cheese, softened

Mix both packages of gelatin and sugar with hot water. Add cold water and let set until thickened. Drain and reserve syrup from pineapple and apricots. When gelatin thickens, add the drained pineapple and apricots (mashed), 2 or 3 diced bananas, 2 cups marshmallows; mix all together and chill until well set. Cook until thick pineapple and apricot syrup, sugar, egg, flour. When this mixture is cold, spread it on the gelatin mixture. Take one package whipped cream and beat according to package directions, add cream cheese (softened). Beat until smooth. Spread on top of mixture. Sprinkle top with grated cheddar cheese.

Margaret Dennis
Florence

Holiday Salad

2 packages of red or green gelatin
1 cup boiling water
1 No. 2 can crushed pineapple
1 carton cottage cheese

¾ cup condensed milk
½ cup mayonnaise
1 cup chopped pecans

Dissolve gelatin in boiling water. Add pineapple, cottage cheese, milk, mayonnaise and pecans. Pour into a mold or long pan. Chill.

Pearlene Creasy
Florence

Yuletide Salad

1 package lime gelatin
2 cups boiling water
1 bottle maraschino cherries
1 cup cottage cheese

1 cup crushed pineapple
¼ cup chopped nuts
¼ teaspoon salt

Dissolve gelatin in boiling water; cool. Reserve eight whole cherries; chop remaining cherries. Add cottage cheese, pineapple, nuts, chopped cherries and salt to gelatin mixture. Place a whole cherry in bottom of cone paper cup; add gelatin mixture. When unmolded, cherry will be at top of "tree." Serve on lettuce leaf with dressing. Yield: 8 servings.

Gladys Hickman
Florence

Breads

Saturday Bread Baking Is Back

Many of us have fond memories related to homemade bread. Perhaps it was your mother's or grandmother's kitchen—or the smell of bread baking at your best friend's home—or the aroma in the street as you passed the baker's shop.

Some may recall the delightful smell of bubbling, growing yeast proofing in a big old-fashioned bread bowl; hanging around the kitchen counter watching mother knead the huge mound of pliable dough; then the way the kitchen smelled as the bread baked; and when it was done, peeking under the tea towel at the tawny loaves and dozens of buns lined up in neat rows. And finally—when the bread was barely cool—slicing off the heel and spreading it with butter and raspberry jam. Those were the days!

And it looks as though those days are coming back for lots of folks. During and after World War II homemade bread almost became a thing of the past when many housewives put away their aprons to work in factories and offices. Now, thirty years later, almost half of the women of America have jobs away from home. But more and more women—and now, men—are going back to baking bread. Some women never stopped. Job or no job.

WHAT TYPE BREAD BAKER ARE YOU?

There are two basic types of bread bakers. Those that make the most home-made bread are the women who never stopped baking. Every Saturday they make a batch of bread to last the week. Bread for school lunch boxes, for husband's lunch pails, for breakfast toast and the family dinner table. Making good bread, for them is simply standard procedure.

The other type of bread baker is the adventurer—the gal that makes bread once or twice a month for the fun of doing it. Often it's a new recipe for a pretty coffee cake, a fancy holiday bread with a foreign flavor or an unusual bread using different grains. It is from this group that new converts to bread baking come. And the ranks are growing daily with concern over increased costs for many basic needs, with the energy crisis keeping more folks home, with a whole new interest in the craft—the art, if you will—of making bread.

BREAD AND NUTRITION

Bread justly earns its place on our tables. Bread and cereals form one of the basic food groups that everybody should eat every day to stay healthy. Although we're convinced man does not live by bread alone we know that he cannot live without it. Enriched breads and cereals give us carbohydrates for energy; protein for growth and repair of body tissues; iron to help build rich red blood cells; thiamin (Vitamin B1) for normal appetite and digestion, a healthy nervous system and to help change sugar and starches into energy; riboflavin (Vitamin B2) to help us use oxygen and to help keep mouth and eyes healthy; and niacin, another of the B vitamins, is needed to help us use the energy in food.

Versa-Dough

5½ to 6½ cups unsifted flour
⅓ cup sugar
1 teaspoon salt
2 packages active dry yeast

1½ cups milk
½ cup (1 stick) margarine
2 eggs (at room temperature)

In a large bowl thoroughly mix one and one-half cups flour, sugar, salt and undissolved active dry yeast.

Combine milk and margarine in saucepan. Heat over low heat until liquid is very warm (120-130 degrees). Margarine does not need to melt. Gradually add to dry ingredients and heat two minutes at medium speed of electric mixer, scraping bowl occasionally. Add eggs and one cup flour. Beat on high speed two minutes, scraping bowl occasionally. Stir in enough additional flour to make a soft dough. Turn out on lightly floured board; knead until smooth and elastic, eight to 10 minutes. Place in greased bowl, turning to grease top. Cover; let rise in warm place, free from draft, until doubled in bulk, about one hour.

Punch dough down; turn out onto lightly floured board. Divide dough into three equal pieces then proceed according to directions for desired variation.

Cloverleaf Rolls: Divide one piece of dough into 12 equal pieces. Form each piece into three small balls; place three in each section of greased muffin pans, two and one-half by one and one-fourth inches. Cover; let rise in warm place, free from draft, until more than doubled in bulk, about one hour 15 minutes. Bake at 375 degrees 12 minutes.

Butterscotch Pecan Buns: Melt one-fourth cup (one-half stick) margarine. Stir in one-half cup firmly packed dark brown sugar and one-fourth cup dark corn syrup. Heat, stirring, until sugar is dissolved. Pour into a nine-inch square rectangle. Brush with one tablespoon melted margarine; then sprinkle with three tablespoons sugar combined with one-fourth teaspoon ground cinnamon. Roll up from long end as for jelly roll. Pinch seam to seal. Cut into nine one-inch slices. Arrange cut side up in prepared pan. Cover; let rise in warm place, free from draft, until doubled in bulk, about one hour. Bake at 375 degrees for 20 to 25 minutes or until done. Cool for five minues. Invert rolls onto wire rack over waxed paper to cool.

Hamburger Buns: Divide one piece of dough into eight equal pieces. Form each piece into a smooth round ball. Place on greased baking sheets about two inches apart; press to flatten. Brush each with slightly beaten egg white and sprinkle each with one-fourth teaspoon sesame seeds. Cover; let rise in warm place, free from draft, until doubled in bulk, about one hour. Bake at 375 degrees 13 to 15 minutes, or until done. Remove from baking sheets and cool on wire racks.

Sourdough experts say that the best onion sourdough is found in San Francisco. Then ask a San Franciscan why: it is due to "something in the air," they would immediately reply. There is no valid explanation to this answer, but onion sourdough lovers from everywhere say it is true.

The onion sourdough is easily made after the starter is prepared. For the mod baker use the Rapidmix method to combine the ingredients. Add your liquids to your dry yeast and some of the dry ingredients. In this way the dough rises faster and creates a more even-textured bread.

If you would like to compare the onion sourdough baked in your oven to the one made in San Francisco, find a friend who is returning home from the San Francisco airport. They sell the sourdough right at the airport for people who want to try the best or for sourdough lovers.

Almost everyone knows that bread is one of the Basic Four nutrients that is needed by the body each day along with the other groups: milk, vegetables and fruits, and meats. Each one of them is essential for daily good health.

Sourdough Starter

3½ cups unsifted strong,
bread-type flour
1 tablespoons sugar

1 package active dry yeast
2 cups warm water

Combine flour, sugar and undissolved active dry yeast in a large bowl. Gradually add warm water to dry ingredients and beat until smooth. Cover with transparent wrap; let stand in warm place for two days.

To use in recipe: Measure out amount called for in recipe and use as directed.

To replenish starter: To remaining starter add one and one-half cups strong bread-type flour and one cup warm water. Beat until smooth. Store covered in warm place. Stir before using. If not used in one week, remove one and one-half cups starter and follow directions for replenishing.

Monkey Bread

2 packages yeast
1 cup lukewarm water
1 cup shortening
¾ cup sugar
1½ teaspoons salt

1 cup boiling water
2 beaten eggs
6 cups plain flour
2 sticks melted margarine

In a bowl dissolve yeast in the lukewarm water. In a second bowl, mix shortening, sugar and salt. Add the boiling water and mix well. Add eggs and stir. Add flour and yeast mixture alternately to shortening mixture. Let this rise until it doubles in size. Punch it down. Add enough flour so that dough can be rolled on to floured board about a half inch or a quarter inch in thickness. Cut this into various shapes. Dip the shapes into melted margarine and lay the pieces in layers in two loaf pans until each pan is half full. Let this rise to the tops of the pans. Bake at 350 degrees until brown, or approximately 45 minutes. Makes two large loaves. (Dough can be refrigerated after it is punched down.)

Viola T. Holder
Florence

Onion Sourdough Bread

1½ cups Sourdough Starter
3¾ cups (about) unsifted
  strong, bread-type flour
3 tablespoons sugar
2½ teaspoons salt
1 package active dry yeast
1 cup milk

2 tablespoons margarine
Cornmeal
Egg white, beaten
1 tablespoon water
⅔ cup finely chopped onion
  Caraway seed

Prepare Sourdough Starter.

Combine one cup flour, sugar, salt and undissolved active dry yeast in a large bowl.

Combine milk and margarine in a saucepan. Heat over low heat until liquid is very warm (120 to 130 degrees). Margarine does not need to melt. Gradually add to dry ingredients and beat two minutes at medium speed of electric mixer, scraping bowl occasionally. Add one and one-half cups starter and one-fourth cup flour. Beat at high speed two minutes, scraping bowl occasionally. Stir in enough additional flour to make a soft dough. Turn out onto lightly floured board; knead until smooth and elastic, about eight to 10 minutes. Place in greased bowl, turning to grease top. Cover; let rise in warm place, free from draft, until doubled in bulk, about one hour.

Punch dough down; turn out onto lightly floured board. Divide in half. Cover; let rest 15 minutes. Shape as desired (below).

Place on greased baking sheets which have been sprinkled with cornmeal where dough is to be placed. Cover; let rise in warm place, free from draft, until doubled in bulk, about one hour.

Combine egg white and water. Brush mixture generously over loaves. Top loaves with chopped onion and sprinkle with caraway seed.

Bake at 400 degrees about 25 minutes, or until done. Remove from baking sheets and cool on wire racks. Makes two large long loaves or four small round loaves.

Large, long loaves: Roll each half of dough into an oblong, 12x8 inches. Tightly roll from 12-inch side; pinch seam to seal. Pinch ends and fold underneath.

Small round loaves: Divide each half of dough in half again. Form each piece into a round ball; flatten slightly.

To Make Tea Sandwiches:

Slice bread thin; remove crusts (save crusts—they make a delicious bread pudding). Spread half the slices with pineapple cream cheese spread; put together with remaining slices to make sandwiches. Cut each sandwich into "fingers" or squares.

Casserole Rye Batter Bread

Batter breads are so easy to make. Instead of kneading, the batter is beaten. They need to rise just once. The result is a tender, open-textured bread with old-fashioned home-baked flavor, ready for the table and enjoyment in a very short time.

1 cup milk, scalded
¼ cup brown sugar, packed
2 teaspoons salt
¼ cup butter or margarine
2 packages active dry yeast

1 cup warm water
2 tablespoons caraway seed
3 cups all-purpose flour
2 cups rye flour

In the large bowl of electric mixer, pour scalded milk over brown sugar, salt and butter; cool to lukewarm. Dissolve yeast in warm water; add to milk mixture. Add caraway seed and about half of each flour; beat at medium speed for 2 minutes, or until smooth. Add remaining flour and beat until well blended, 1 to 1½ minutes. Cover bowl and set to rise in a warm place until double in bulk, about 45 minutes. Stir batter vigorously for ½ minute. Turn into a well-buttered 2-quart casserole or straight-sided soufflé dish. Brush the top with milk and sprinkle with caraway seed. Bake in moderate oven (350 degrees) 45 to 50 minutes. Turn out on a rack to cool.

Cheese Casserole Bread

4 to 5 cups unsifted all-purpose flour
3 tablespoons sugar
1 tablespoon salt
2 packages dry yeast
2 cups hot water (120 degrees
   to 130 degrees)
⅓ cup instant nonfat dry milk

2 tablespoons shortening,
   room temperature
1½ cups grated sharp
   cheddar cheese
1 egg, room temperature
   and beaten

In a large bowl, combine 2 cups flour, sugar, salt and yeast. In a saucepan, combine water, instant dry skim milk and shortening. Gradually add to dry ingredients and beat mixture for 4 minutes. Stir in additional flour, about 2 cups, to make a stiff but manageable batter. Cover and put in a warm place (80 degrees to 85 degrees) until batter doubles in bulk.

Meanwhile, preheat oven to 375 degrees. Grease 2 (1-quart) casseroles or similar-sized baking pans. Stir down batter and beat vigorously about 30 seconds. Divide between prepared casseroles. Bake until brown and crusty. Turn out of pans onto rack to cool. Makes 2 loaves.

French Onion Bread

2 loaves French bread
1 cup melted butter
2 tablespoons parsley flakes

¾ cup finely chopped
   green onions

Slice bread lengthwise almost through loaf, leaving one side like a hinge. Combine butter, parsley, and onion. Spread mixture inside loaves; wrap in heavy-duty foil. Place on grill until well heated. Serves 8.

Sherry McKenzie
Florence

Bishop's Bread

2½ cups sifted enriched flour
1 tablespoon baking powder
1 teaspoon salt
4 ounces German sweet
   chocolate
2 cups finely chopped pecans
1 cup chopped dates
1 cup chopped Maraschino
   cherries, well drained
4 eggs
1¼ cup sugar

Sift flour, baking powder and salt together. Cut chocolate into small pieces. Add chocolate, pecans, dates and cherries to flour mixture Stir to coat pieces with flour. Beat eggs until foamy. Add sugar gradually and continue beating until eggs are thick and light. Add flour mixture. Mix thoroughly. Turn into greased 5¼ x 9½ inch loaf pan. Bake in 325 degree oven for 1 hour, 35 minutes. Cool and slice.

Mrs. J.P. Poe
Florence

Swedish Bread

2 packages active dry yeast
1 teaspoon sugar
4½ cups warm (not hot) water
7 to 8 cups sifted white flour
1½ tablespoons salt
1 cup dark brown sugar
5 tablespoons dark molasses,
   heated
A pinch of soda added to
   heated molasses
5 tablespoons shortening,
   melted
1½ cups rye flour
1½ cups whole wheat flour
Grated rind of 1 orange
1 teaspoon caraway seed
   (optional)

Dissolve yeast and sugar in ½ cup of the water. Add remaining water and enough white flour (about 4 cups) to make a soft sponge. Let stand in a warm place until it becomes bubbly. Add remaining ingredients, in the order given, beating well. Add enough of remaining white flour to make dough stiff enough to knead. Put in greased bowl and set in a warm place to rise. When double in bulk, knead and let rise again. Then shape into 4 loaves. Place in greased loaf pans and let rise. Or shape into round loaves. Bake in a moderate oven, 375 degrees, about 40 minutes.

It's delightful bread, almost a dessert by itself.

Mildred Anderson
Florence

Fluffy Pancakes

1 cup flour
½ teaspoon salt
1 egg
2 tablespoons sugar
2 tablespoons baking powder
¾ cup melted shortening

Mix and beat all ingredients until smooth. Bake on ungreased griddle.

Mrs. Leonard Burt
Sheffield

Spoon Bread

1 packet dry yeast
  dissolved in 2 cups lukewarm
  water

¾ cup shortening
1 egg
4 cups self-rising flour
¼ cup sugar

Pour water and yeast mixture over flour mixture and stir well. Bake for 20 minutes at 450 degrees in greased muffin tins. May be stored in refrigerator 1-2 weeks.

Mrs. John Ballinger
Madisonville, Kentucky

Southern Spoon Bread

2 cups skim milk
½ cup yellow corn meal
3 tablespoons margarine

1 teaspoon baking powder
¼ teaspoon salt
½ cup cholesterol-free egg substitute

Scald 1½ cups milk. Mix remaining ½ cup milk with corn meal; stir into scalded milk. Cook, stirring, over medium heat until mixture thickens and comes to a boil. Remove from heat. Stir in 3 tablespoons margarine, baking powder and salt. Gradually add egg substitute, stirring until thoroughly blended. Pour into well-greased 1-quart casserole.

Bake at 350 degrees 40 to 45 minutes, until puffed and golden brown. Serve hot with margarine. Makes 6 servings.

Old South Spoon Bread

1 cup yellow or white cornmeal
1½ teaspoons salt
2 tablespoons butter
2 cups boiling water
2 whole eggs
2 eggs, separated

½ cup milk
½ cup flour
4 teaspoons baking powder
2 whole canned pimientos,
  chopped

Stir cornmeal, salt and butter into boiling water. Stir over low heat until smooth and thick. Remove from heat; cool to room temperature. Blend in whole eggs and egg yolks beaten with milk. Sift flour and baking powder together; stir into mixture. Whip egg whites until stiff. Fold into cornmeal mixture until all white disappears. Pour into a buttered 2-quart baking dish. Bake 30 minutes in 375 degree oven. Makes 6 to 8 servings.

Mrs. Ron Chesnut
Greenville, Tennessee

Old Family Recipe Sally Lunn

1 cake of yeast
1 cup warm milk
½ cup butter
⅓ cup sugar

3 eggs, well beaten
4 cups flour
1 teaspoon salt

Dissolve yeast in the warm milk. Cream butter and sugar together until fluffy. Add the well-beaten eggs and mix throughly. Sift flour. Measure. Add salt. Sift in the flour and salt alternately with the milk-yeast mixture. Beat vigorously by hand. Place in a warm place. Brush the top with melted butter. Cover with a cloth. Let rise about 2 hours. During this time the dough should be practically double in bulk. Punch down, then beat vigorously again. Pour—because this dough is thinner than a bread dough, rather like a very thick cake batter—into a well-buttered tube pan. Brush the top again with melted butter and set in a warm place to rise again. Allow to rise until it comes just short of the top of the pan. Bake in a 350-degree oven for approximately 1 hour. Slip out of the pan, slice and serve.

Vickers Family
Semiway, Kentucky

White Bread

2 cups milk
¾ cup sugar
8 teaspoons salt

¾ cup (1½ sticks) margarine
6 cups warm water (105-115 degrees)
24 cups unsifted flour (about)

Scald milk; stir in sugar, salt and margarine. Cool to lukewarm. Measure warm water into large warm bowl. Sprinkle in active dry yeast; stir until dissolved. Add lukewarm milk mixture and 12 cups flour; beat until smooth. Add enough additional flour to make a stiff dough. Turn out onto lightly floured board; knead until smooth and elastic, about 10 to 12 minutes. Place in greased bowl, turning to grease top. Cover; let rise in warm place, free from draft, until doubled in bulk, about one hour.

Punch dough down. Cover; let rest 15 minutes. Divide dough into 6 equal pieces. Roll each piece to a 14x9-inch rectangle. Shape into loaves. Place in six greased 9x5x3-inch loaf pans.

Cover; let as many as will fit in oven rise in warm place, free from draft, until doubled in bulk, about one hour. Cover remaining loaves; put in cooler place, free from draft, until doubled in bulk, about one and one-half hours.

Bake at 400 degrees about 30 minutes, or until done. Remove from pans and cool on wire racks. Makes six loaves.

Maria's Cuban Bread

1½ packages active dry yeast
1 tablespoon sugar
2 cups warm water (100 degrees
*   to 115 degrees)*
1 tablespoon salt
5 to 6 cups unsifted
*   all-purpose flour*

3 tablespoons yellow cornmeal
1 tablespoon egg white,
*   mixed with 1 tablespoon*
*   cold water*

Combine yeast with sugar and warm water in a large bowl; stir to dissolve. Mix salt with the flour and add to the yeast mixture, a cup at a time, until dough is stiff. Remove to a lightly floured board and knead about 10 minutes, adding flour as necessary. Place dough in greased bowl and turn to grease all sides. Cover; let rise in a warm place until doubled in bulk, 1½ to 2 hours.

Punch down; shape into two long loaves. Place on cornmeal-sprinkled baking sheet. Slash the top of loaves on the diagonal with a razor and brush with egg-white wash. Place in cold oven, set temperature at 400 degrees, and bake 35 minutes or until well browned. Makes 2 loaves.

Milly's Easter Bread

6½ to 7¼ cups unsifted flour
1 cup sugar
1 teaspoon salt
2 packages active dry yeast
1 cup milk

¼ cup water
¼ cup (½ stick) margarine
3 eggs (at room temperature)
8 hard-cooked eggs

In large bowl thoroughly mix 2 cups flour, sugar, salt and undissolved active dry yeast.

Combine milk, water and margarine in a saucepan. Heat over low heat until liquids are very warm (120 degrees-130 degrees). Margarine does not need to melt. Gradually add to dry ingredients and beat 2 minutes at medium speed of electric mixer, scraping bowl occasionally. Add 3 eggs and ¾ cup flour. Beat at high speed 2 minutes, scraping bowl occasionally. Stir in enough additional flour to make a soft dough. Turn out onto lightly floured board; knead until smooth and elastic, about 8 to 10 minutes. Place in greased bowl, turning to grease top. Cover; let rise in warm place, free from draft, until doubled in bulk, about 1 hour.

Punch dough down; turn out onto lightly floured board. Divide dough into 8 equal pieces. Take about ¼ of each piece and set aside. Shape larger pieces into round balls. On greased baking sheets, press large pieces of dough down into circles about ½-inch thick. Place a hard-cooked egg in center of each. Divide each of the remaining 8 pieces of dough in half. Shape each into a 6-inch rope. Using 2 ropes, cross in an "X" over each egg and seal ends underneath dough. Cover; let rise in warm place, free from draft, until doubled in bulk, about 1 hour.

Bake at 350 degrees 20 to 25 minutes, or until done. Remove from baking sheets and cool on wire racks. Makes 8 individual breads.

Angel Biscuits

5 cups self-rising flour
¼ cup sugar
2 tablespoons water
1 package yeast

1 cup oil
2 cups buttermilk
1 egg

Sift dry ingredients together. Dissolve yeast in warm water, add buttermilk. Put oil into dry ingredients. Stir buttermilk and yeast into flour mixture. Add egg and mix well. If needed, add more flour to make a soft dough. Roll ¼ inch thick. Cut with biscuit cutter. Fold biscuits in half, dip in butter. Let rise 1 hour. Bake at 400 degrees for 15 minutes. Use dough as needed. Will keep in refrigerator about 7 days.

Lavonne Brown
Hixson, Tennessee

Wibby's Biscuits

1 cup sifted flour
1½ teaspoons baking powder
½ teaspoon salt

2 tablespoons plus 2
   teaspoons shortening
¼ cup plus 2 tablespoons
   sweet milk

Mix flour, baking powder and salt in bowl. Cut in shortening. Add milk. Stir with fork. Knead 10 times. Cut out biscuits. Place on ungreased cooking sheet. Bake for 10 minutes at 450 degrees.

Elizabeth A. Medaris
Villagio della Pace
Vicenza, Italy

Sesame Cheese Biscuits

1 can unbaked biscuits
¼ cup (½ stick) melted butter
   or margarine

¾ cup grated Parmesan chese
3 tablespoons toasted sesame seed

Method: Pre-heat oven to 500 degrees. Dip biscuits in melted butter. Mix cheese and toasted seeds in shallow pan. Dip each biscuit in mix, coating both sides. Bake on ungreased baking sheet about 8 minutes.

Mrs. J.R. Prater Sr.
Florence

75

Ice Box Rolls

1 packet yeast
1 cup sugar
¾ cup shortening

1 tablespoon salt
2 cups boiling water
5 cups flour

Add shortening, sugar and salt to water; let cool. Dissolve yeast in ¼ cup lukewarm water. Then add flour and yeast when water is cool. Put in refrigerator and let rise about four hours or overnight. Pour out on floured board and knead. Cut out and let rise, then put in cold oven and heat to 400 degrees. Bake until golden brown.

Deedy Harrison
Florence

Old Time Rolls

1 package yeast
1 cup warm water
3 tablespoons sugar,
  heaping

3 tablespoons shortening,
  slightly rounded
1 teaspoon salt
1 egg
3 cups flour, unsifted

In large bowl, dissolve yeast in warm water. Add sugar, shortening, salt, egg and one cup flour. Beat for two minutes. Add remaining two cups flour; beat. Cover with wet towel and let rise in warm place for one hour or until double in bulk. Punch down. Pour onto floured board and knead until easy to handle. Shape as desired. Place in pan and let rise for one hour. Bake at 400 degrees until brown.

Opalene Litral

Patsy's Refrigerator Rolls

2 cups warm water
½ cup sugar
1½ teaspoons salt
2 packages of yeast

1 egg
¼ cup shortening
6½ to 7 cups all-purpose flour

Mix water with yeast. Mix sugar, salt, egg and shortening together. Then mix with dissolved yeast. Mix in flour and stir. After all the flour has been added, knead dough well. Cover with a towel and let rise for 1 hour. Tear apart and make rolls, coffee cake or doughnuts, let rise again. Then bake or refrigerate until ready to bake.

Mrs. Patsy Indelicat
Florence

Martha's Ice Box Rolls

2 cups lukewarm water
2 eggs, beaten
7 cups sifted flour
½ cup sugar

4 teaspoons melted shortening
  or oil
1½ teaspoon salt
1 package yeast, or 1 yeast cake

Combine sugar and salt in bowl. Add yeast, water and beaten eggs. Add ½ flour and stir well. Add shortening and mix well. Add remainder of flour. Allow to double in bulk, then punch down and shape into rolls. Allow to rise for 2 hours. Bake 8 minutes at 425 degrees.

Refrigerator Rolls

½ cup melted shortening
½ cup boiling water
½ cup cold water.
1 egg, beaten
⅓ cup sugar

1 teaspoon salt
3½ cups plain flour
1 packaged yeast, dissolved
    in ¼ cup lukewarm water

Add shortening to sugar and salt, then add boiling water, then cold water. Set aside and cool completely. Then add beaten egg, yeast, flour and place in the refrigerator all day or overnight. Roll out and let stand 2 hours or more. Top with melted butter.

Mrs. Troy Trousdale
Sheffield

Grandmother's Ice Box Rolls

1 pint sweet milk
½ cup sugar
½ cup shortening
1 tablespoon salt

1 yeast cake
1 teaspoon baking powder
8 cups flour

Heat milk; add sugar, shortening and salt. Cool to lukewarm. Add yeast. Add enough flour to make dough like cake batter. Let rise until doubled (about 1 hour). Then add enough flour to make batter like biscuit dough or stiff dough. In this flour add soda and baking powder. This helps keep batter. Let rise again until double. Knead. Make into rolls. Store batter in closely covered container in refrigerator as many days as you like. Always make out rolls 1 hour before ready to bake. These rolls do better when put into a cold oven and baked until 400 degrees is reached; not too hot an oven.

Mrs. Robert M. Hill Jr.
Florence

Grandmother's Whole Wheat Rolls

1 egg
3 cups white flour, sifted
2 cups whole wheat flour, sifted
1 cup graham cracker crumbs
½ cup sugar
½ cup shortening

1½ teaspoons salt
1 cup boiling water
1 cup tepid water
1 tablespoon sugar
1 package dry yeast

Place ½ cup sugar, shortening, and salt in large bowl and pour boiling water over it and let dissolve. In another bowl, put tepid water, 1 tablespoon sugar, and dry yeast and place in warm spot until yeast begins to rise (looks bubbly). Do not put on stove eye. When first mixture cools, add yeast mixture to it. Then, add egg, white flour, whole wheat flour and graham cracker crumbs. Cover dough and let stand 1 to 2 hours until double in bulk. Work down, cover and put in refrigerator over night. Make out for rolls, dipping half the circle in melted butter and graham cracker crumbs; fold in half. Let rise 1 to 2 hours. Bake slowly in 350 to 375 degree oven for about 15 minutes on a greased baking sheet. Dough will keep in refrigerator for a week.

Mrs. Donald Patterson
Florence

Steamed Cornbread

Mrs. Jessie Clements' Steamed Cornbread is good—really good. She's had a lot of practice since she began making it in 1898.

Mrs. Clements, now 93, learned the recipe from one of her father's tenants when the family lived in Knoxville, Tenn. "The woman gave me the recipe and I tried it on my father. It didn't kill him, so I kept using it."

The unique point of the recipe is that the batter is cooked in tin cans—"five Number-Two vegetable cans, those cans of beans you use all the time," Mrs. Clements said.

When she began making the cornbread at the age of 14, she used Rumford Baking Powder cans. "The cans were the right size and they had lids." With the demise of the lidded baking powder cans, she began using vegetable cans. To seal the cans, aluminum foil secured with a band is convenient.

The recipe which the family has enjoyed for so many years is:

3 cups corn meal (plain)
1 cup flour (plain)
1 tablespoon soda
1 tablespoon salt

1 egg
½ cup molasses
2 cups sweet milk
1 cup buttermilk

Beat egg and molasses. Slowly add the sweet milk and buttermilk. Mix the meal, flour, soda and salt; then sift into the liquid. Use 5 well-greased No. 2 vegetable cans. Fill ⅔ full, cover with aluminum foil and fasten foil down with a rubber band. Set cans down in three inches of slowly boiling water and cover kettle. Steam for three hours. Serve hot.

Mrs. Jesse Clements
Tuscumbia

Cornmeal Sponge

1 cup corn meal
¼ cup flour
2 teaspoons baking powder
1 teaspoon chili powder
½ teaspoon salt
1 egg, slightly beaten
1 cup milk

¼ cup (2-ounce can)
  deviled ham
2 tablespoons chopped onion
1½ cups shredded cheddar
  cheese
½ cup shredded cheddar
  cheese

Mix together: corn meal, flour, baking powder, chili powder and salt. Stir egg and milk into dry ingredients. Blend in ham, onion and Cheddar cheese. Turn into a buttered 8 or 9-inch skillet. Bake in 400 degree oven for 20 to 25 minutes. Sprinkle cheese on top a few minutes before removing from oven. Serves 8.

Trisha Chesnut
Greeneville, Tennessee

"Hot" Corn Bread

2 cups self-rising corn meal
½ cup self-rising flour
½ cup finely chopped onions
1 egg, slightly beaten
1 small can creamed corn
¼ teaspoon red ground pepper
¼ cup finely chopped bell pepper
½ cup finely chopped hot
  green pepper
¼ cup cooking oil
½ cup milk

Set oven temperature at 350 degrees. Mix all ingredients in a large mixing bowl. Mix well and pour mixture either in a muffin pan or your favorite corn bread pan or skillet. Cook from 35 to 45 minutes at 350 degrees. Serves approximately eight.

Miss Debbie Joy Carter
Leighton

Mexican Bread

1 cup oil
1½ cups self-rising corn meal
1 small onion, chopped
1 cup buttermilk
1 can cream style corn
2 chili jalepeno peppers, chopped
  fine
1 pound grated cheese
2 eggs, well beaten
Small amount of pimiento can be
  added for color

Mix above ingredients. Bake in heavy skillet at 350 degrees for one hour.

Evelyn Pless
Cherokee

Hush Puppies

¼ cup self-rising pre-sifted flour
1 scant cup self-rising meal
1 medium onion, chopped
¼ teaspoon garlic salt
1 egg
½ cup sweet milk
Fat for deep frying

Into mixing bowl, add flour, meal, onion, and garlic salt. Mix. Add egg and milk. Stir until well mixed. Drop by heaping tablespoons into hot deep fat and fry until golden and crisp on both sides. Drain on absorbent paper. Serve hot.

Mrs. Wallace Aycock
Spruce Pine

Hush Puppies

1½ cups self-rising corn meal
½ cup self-rising flour
½ teaspoon salt
1 medium onion, finely chopped
1 cup milk
1 egg, well beaten

Sift together corn meal, flour and salt in a large bowl. Mix in onion. Stir in milk and egg. Let mixture stand about 3 minutes. Drop from teaspoon, a few at a time into deep fat (360 degrees). Fry to a golden brown on both sides. This takes about 3 minutes. Drain on absorbent paper.

Evelyn Pless
Cherokee

Nut Bread

1½ cups flour
1 cup sugar
3½ teaspoons baking powder
1 teaspoon salt
1 teaspoon plus one teaspoon
    grated orange peel

3 teaspoons salad oil
½ cup milk
¾ cup orange juice
1 egg
1 cup finely chopped nuts
1 cup finely cut up dried apricots

Heat oven to 350 degrees and flour loaf pan 9x5x3 inches (or two loaf pans 8½ x 4½ x 2½ inches). Measure all ingredients into large mixing bowl. Beat on medium speed one minute. Pour into pans. Bake 55-65 minutes or until wooden pick inserted in center comes out clean. Remove from pan. Cool thoroughly before slicing.

Mrs. Evelena Thompson
Florence

Cranberry Fruit Nut Bread

2 cups all purpose flour,
    sifted
1 cup sugar
1½ teaspoons double acting
    baking powder
½ teaspoon soda
1 teaspoon salt

¼ cup shortening
¾ cup orange juice
1 tablespoon grated orange rind
1 egg, well beaten
½ cup chopped nuts
2 cups fresh or frozen cranberries,
    chopped

Sift together flour, sugar, baking powder, soda and salt. Cut in shortening until mixture resembles coarse corn meal. Combine orange juice and grated rind with well beaten egg. Pour all at once into dry ingredients, mixing just enough to dampen. Carefully fold in chopped nuts and cranberries (if frozen cranberries are used, put through food chopper in frozen state). Spoon into greased loaf pan (9 by 5 by 3). Spread corner and sides slightly higher than center. Bake in a 350 degree oven for about 2 hours, until crust is golden brown and toothpick inserted comes out clean. Remove it from pan, cool. Store overnight for easy slicing.

Donna M. Hayes
Florence

Banana Nut Bread

Cream one-half cup shortening and one cup sugar. Mix in two whole eggs and three or four ripe bananas, mashed fine.

Combine two cups flour, one teaspoon soda, one-fourth teaspoon salt. Mix well and sift three times. Stir the flour mixture into the first mixture.

Add one-half cup nut meats mixed in a little flour.

Place in greased loaf pan and bake for one hour in a 250 degree oven.

Mrs. John Ballinger
Madisonville, Kentucky

Banana Bread

1 cup shortening
2 cups sugar
3 cups cake flour (sifted)
2 eggs
2 cups ripe mashed bananas
1 cup chopped pecans
1 teaspoon salt
1 teaspoon soda
¼ cup buttermilk
1 teaspoon vanilla

Cream shortening and sugar by hand or use a mixer. Add sugar slowly and beat until light. Add unbeaten eggs one at a time, then mashed bananas. Next sift salt and flour together. Stir the soda in the buttermilk and alternately add flour and buttermilk mixtures. Finally, add nuts and vanilla. Bake in one or two loaf pans. Grease only the bottoms of the pans. Bake at 350 degrees for one hour.

Mrs. E.R. Dallas
Somerville

Walnut Bread Plus Carrots

1½ cups finely grated raw carrots
1 cup firmly packed light brown
  sugar
1 teaspoon grated fresh
  orange peel
1 tablespoon vegetable oil
1 cup boiling water
2 eggs, beaten
1⅓ cups unsifted
  all-purpose flour
1 cup unsifted whole
  wheat flour
2½ teaspoons baking
  powder
1 teaspoon baking soda
1 teaspoon salt
1 cup chopped walnuts

Combine carrots, brown sugar, grated orange peel, oil and boiling water in large bowl; mix well; set aside to cool. Stir eggs into carrot mixture. Mix and sift flours, baking powder, baking soda and salt; blend into carrot mixture. Stir in walnuts. Turn into well-greased 9x5x3-inch loaf pan. Let stand 5 minutes. Bake at 350 degrees 50-60 minutes, until cake tester inserted in center of bread comes out clean. Remove from pan; cool on wire rack. Wrap in foil or plastic wrap; let stand overnight at room temperature before slicing.

Pumpkin Bread

3 cups sugar
1 cup salad oil
4 eggs, beaten
2 cups cooked pumpkin or
  1 can (16 ounces)
3½ cups all purpose flour
1 teaspoon baking powder
2 teaspoons salt
1 teaspoon round cloves
1 teaspoon each of cinnamon, nutmeg,
  and allspice
1½ cups chopped nuts

Combine sugar, oil and eggs, beat until light. Combine and sift together all dry ingredients. Stir into pumpkin mixture. Add nuts and stir well. Spoon batter into 2 well greased 9¼ by 5¼ by 2¾ inch loaf pans. Bake at 325 degrees for one hour and 10 minutes.

Mrs. Jack Thomason
Muscle Shoals

Apple Bread

½ cup shortening
1 cup sugar
2 eggs
2 cups all-purpose flour
1 teaspoon salt
1 teaspoon soda
1 teaspoon baking powder
1 teaspoon vanilla extract
2 tablespoons buttermilk
2 cups peeled, diced apples

Cream shortening and sugar until light and fluffy. Add eggs and beat well. Combine flour, salt, soda, and baking powder; add to creamed mixture, blending well. Stir in vanilla, buttermilk and apples. Spoon batter into a greased 8½ x 4½ x 2⅝-inch loaf pan. Bake at 350 degrees for one hour. Makes 1 loaf.

Sherry McKenzie
Florence

Fresh Apple Bread

2 cups sifted flour
1 teaspoon baking powder
½ teaspoon salt
⅓ cup shortening
1 cup sugar
1 egg
⅓ cup orange juice
¾ cup raisins
1 cup finely chopped apples
¼ cup nuts, chopped
1 tablespoon grated orange peel

Sift together flour, baking powder, soda and salt. Cream shortening and add sugar gradually; add egg and beat thoroughly. Add dry ingredients and orange to creamed mixture and blend well. Add remaining ingredients and mix. Pour into three well-greased 1 pound cans. Bake in 350 degree oven for 45 minutes. Makes three loaves.

Mary Ellen Priest
Tuscumbia

Pennsylvania Applesauce Bread

2 cups flour
1 teaspoon baking powder
1 teaspoon salt
1 teaspoon soda
1 teaspoon cinnamon
½ teaspoon nutmeg
½ cup butter or shortenin.
¾ cup butter or shortening
¾ cup sugar
1 teaspoon vanilla
2 eggs
1 cup applesauce
½ cup walnuts

Sift together flour, baking powder, salt, soda, cinnamon and nutmeg. Cream butter; add sugar gradually, creaming well. Blend in dry ingredients gradually; mix thoroughly. Add applesauce and chopped nuts; mix only until blended. Pour into well-greased loaf pan. Push batter up into corners of pan, leaving the center slightly hollowed. For well-rounded loaf, allow to stand 20 minutes before baking. Bake at 350 degrees for 55-60 minutes. Cool thoroughly before slicing. Makes 1 loaf.

Mrs. Joan Pugh
Florence

Easy Cheese Crescents

1 can (8 ounces) refrigerated
   crescent rolls

4 slices American cheese, halved
   diagonally
1 egg, well beaten

Separate rolls into 8 triangles. Preheat oven to 375 degrees. On top of each dough triangle, place ½ slice of cheese. Roll up, starting at the shortest end of the triangle. Place rolls, point side down, on ungreased cookie sheet, curve into crescent shape. Brush with egg. Bake 12 to 15 minutes. Serve hot.

Ethel Rutherford
Cherokee

Peanut Butter Muffins

2 tablespoons crunchy peanut butter
3 tablespoons butter
2 tablespoons sugar
1 egg

1 cup flour
½ teaspoon salt
1 teaspoon baking powder
½ cup milk

Cream together peanut butter, butter and sugar. Add egg. Sift together flour, salt, and baking powder. Add dry ingredients alternately with milk. Bake at 400 degrees for 25 minutes. Very good at breakfast with bacon and eggs.

Mrs. Leonard Burt
Sheffield

Cottage Cheese Muffins

⅓ cup sugar
3 tablespoons margarine
½ cup cream style cottage cheese
1 teaspoon grated lemon peel

1 egg
1¾ cups biscuit mix
½ cup milk

Cream sugar and oleo, beat in cottage cheese and lemon peel. Add egg and beat well. Stir in biscuit mix and milk, just until moistened. Bake in greased muffin tins at 400 degrees for 20 minutes. Makes a great breakfast treat.

Mrs. E.R. Dallas
Somerville

Sweet Muffins

1 egg
½ cup milk
¼ cup salad oil
1½ cups all-purpose flour

½ cup sugar
2 teaspoons baking powder
½ teaspoon salt

Heat oven to 400 degrees. Grease the bottoms of 12 medium muffin cups. Beat egg; stir in milk and oil. Mix in remaining ingredients just until flour is moistened. Batter should be lumpy.

Fill muffin cups ⅔ full. Bake 20 to 25 minutes or until golden brown. Immediately remove from pan.

Mrs. Jerry Turbyfill
Florence

Bacon Muffins

2 cups flour
2 tablespoons sugar
2½ teaspoons baking powder
½ teaspoon salt

3 tablespoons bacon fat
1 egg, beaten
1 cup milk
½ cup crumbled crisp bacon

Sift dry ingredients into a bowl. Make a hollow in the center and in bacon fat blended with egg and milk. Stir lightly, mixture should be lumpy. Add crumbled crisp bacon to mixture. Fill muffin tins ⅔ full and bake at 400 degrees until golden brown (20-25 minutes). Makes 12 muffins.

Mrs. Joan Pugh
Florence

Bran Muffin Mix

15-ounce box raisin bran cereal
2 cups sugar
5 cups plain flour
5 teaspoons soda

1 teaspoon salt
4 beaten eggs
1 cup oil
1 quart buttermilk

Mix dry ingredients well and add remaining ingredients; mix well. Lightly grease muffin tins. Bake 15-20 minutes at 400 degrees. Keeps in refrigerator tightly covered for six weeks.

Dollie Lawson
Tuscumbia

Coffee Cake

1 box yellow cake mix
1 box instant vanilla pudding
¾ cup vegetable oil
¾ cup cold water

1 teaspoon vanilla
1 teaspoon butter flavoring
4 eggs

Mix all together and add eggs, one at a time. Grease and flour tube pan; sprinkle ½ cup pecans on bottom of pan.

Topping

½ cup pecans
⅓ cup sugar

2½ tablespoons cinnamon

Pour one-third of cake batter in tube pan; sprinkle one-half of mixture over batter; repeat.

Icing

2 cups confectioners' sugar
1 teaspoon butter flavoring
1 teaspoon vanilla flavoring

5 tablespoons sweet milk,
or more if needed.

Mix thoroughly and spread on cake.

Deedy Harrison
Florence

84

Maple-Nut Sticky Rolls

1 envelope active dry yeast
1½ cups very warm water
¼ cup maple syrup

5 cups sifted all-purpose flour
1 teaspoon salt
¼ cup (½ stick) butter, softened

Topping:

½ cup chopped nuts
½ cup shredded coconut

¼ cup (½ stick) butter
½ cup maple syrup

Sprinkle yeast over very warm water in a 2-cup measure ("very warm water" should feel comfortably warm when dropped on wrist). Stir in 2 teaspoons of the syrup. Let stand 10 minutes until bubbly.

Place 3 cups of the flour in large bowl. Stir in yeast mixture and remaining syrup, salt and butter. Beat at medium speed with electric mixer until smooth. Cover and let rise 1 hour.

Stir in remaining flour to make a soft dough. Turn dough out onto lightly floured surface. Knead 8 to 10 minutes, or until smooth and elastic.

Place in a medium-size buttered bowl, turning to bring buttered side up. Let rise in a warm place, away from draft, 1 hour or until double in volume.

Punch dough down and divide in half. Roll each half to a 9-inch circle, ½-inch thick. Using a 2-inch biscuit cutter, make 14 rolls from each circle.

Butter two 8 by 1½ inch layer pans. Sprinkle half the nuts, coconut and butter in each pan. Place syrup in shallow dish; dip each roll in syrup, then place syrup side down in pan. Repeat with all rolls. Cover and let rise about 15 minutes or until light and almost double in volume.

Bake in a moderate oven (350 degrees) for 30 minutes until golden brown. Turn upside down onto serving plate.

Mark McClellan
Florence

Sour Cream Coffee Cake

2 sticks butter
1½ cups sugar
1 cup sour cream
2 eggs, well beaten
1 teaspoon vanilla
2 cups all-purpose flour

1 teaspoon baking powder
¼ teaspoon salt
½ teaspoon soda
1 cup finely chopped nuts
1½ teaspoons sugar
2½ teaspoons cinnamon

Cream butter, sugar and sour cream; add eggs, vanilla and beat well. Combine dry ingredients and add to creamed mixture. Beat well. Thoroughly grease a ten-inch tube pan. Make topping by combining chopped nuts, 1½ teaspoons sugar and cinnamon. In bottom of the tube pan, put a third of topping mixture and alternate layer of batter and topping ending with batter. Bake at 350 degrees for 45 minutes.

Mrs. J.P. Poe
Florence

85

Williamsburg Tea Brings Fond Memories

The pleasant custom of afternoon tea was first introduced to the New World by the good burghers of New Amsterdam in the middle of the seventeenth century.

In New England, British governors and their Tory friends helped to give a note of elegance to teatime manners. By the turn of the century when tea became more plentiful and less costly, tea drinking was enjoying an extraordinary vogue and the ladies of the day collected with pride special silver, pewter or china tea services.

The recipes here are adaptations of these early Colonial favorites. Today's homemaker can make them quickly and easily, using convenient ready-to-use jams, jellies and preserves for bright color and fresh fruit flavor.

Orange Marmalade Bread

3 cups all-purpose flour
1 tablespoon baking powder
½ teaspoon salt
½ cup sugar
1 cup coarsely broken
   walnuts
1 tablespoon grated
   orange rind

1 cup orange marmalade
2 eggs
1 cup orange juice
   or milk
2 tablespoons melted
   butter or oil

Sift flour, baking powder, salt and sugar into a large bowl. Add walnuts and orange rind; stir to coat evenly. In a separate bowl, beat marmalade, eggs, orange juice and melted butter until blended. Add to dry ingredients and mix until thoroughly moistened. Bake in a well greased 9x5x3-inch loaf pan in a preheated moderate oven (350 degrees) for 1 hour or until cake tests done. Cool on a rack for 10 minutes before removing from pan. Cool thoroughly before cutting. Serve in thin slices with cream cheese whipped with additional orange marmalade. Makes 1 9x5x3-inch loaf.

Macaroon Jam Tarts

1½ cups all-purpose flour
2 tablespoons sugar
Grated rind of 1 lemon
½ cup butter or margarine
3 egg yolks
1 tablespoon lemon juice
3 egg whites

1⅓ cups confectioners' sugar
2 cans (8¾ ounces each) blanched
   almonds, grated in a
   nut grater
2½ cups assorted jams or preserves—
   strawberry, grape, apricot
   and peach

Mix together flour, sugar and lemon rind. Cut in butter until particles are like coarse cornmeal. Stir in egg yolks and lemon juice. Knead a few times on floured board until smooth. Shape into a ball, wrap with foil or plastic wrap and chill for at least 1 hour. Roll out a small amount of dough at a time to ⅛-inch thickness on a floured board. Cut into 2-inch rounds and place 2 inches apart on ungreased cookie sheets. Beat egg whites until stiff. Gradually beat in confectioner's sugar until stiff and glossy. Fold in grated almonds. Using a pastry bag or spoon, place mixture around edge of each cookie, making a border about ½-inch wide. Bake in a preheated moderate oven (350 degrees) for 12 to 15 minutes or until lightly browned. Cool on a rack. Before serving, fill centers with assorted jams or preserves, selecting them for variety in color as well as flavor. Makes about 36 2-inch tarts.

Poultry

Chicken Curry

3 tablespoons butter or margarine
1½ cups chopped onion
1 cup chopped celery
1 cup chopped green pepper
1½ cups chicken broth

1 tablespoon curry powder
1½ teaspoons salt
2 tablespoons cornstarch
¼ cup water
6 whole chicken legs

Melt butter in a large skillet. Add onion, celery and green pepper and sauté over low heat about 10 minutes. Remove from heat and puree vegetable mixture in a blender. Return mixture to skillet; stir in chicken broth, curry powder and salt. Combine cornstarch and water; add to vegetable mixture. Cook over medium heat, stirring until mixture boils.

Meanwhile, cut chicken thighs and drumsticks apart. Remove skin from chicken; add chicken to sauce. Cover skillet and simmer, stirring occasionally until chicken is tender, about 45 minutes. Serve with Fruited Rice. Makes six servings.

Billy Townsend
Florence

Chicken Stew

1 whole chicken
1 large onion, chopped
1 can tomato soup
1 can (14-15 ounce) stewed tomatoes, chopped in blender
4 potatoes, peeled and chopped
1 can (14-15 ounce) cream corn

1 can (14-15 ounce) baby lima beans
½ cup macaroni (chopped dry in blender)
1 teaspoon oregano
Salt, black pepper to taste.

Cook chicken; let cool. Pull chicken apart into small pieces. Cook onions and potatoes, tomato soup and stewed tomatoes in chicken broth for about 20 minutes. Add corn, lima beans, salt, pepper and oregano. Cook for about one hour. Add macaroni; let thicken.

Bobby Trousdale
Tuscumbia

Alabama Barbecue Chicken

1½ teaspoons salt	⅔ cup tomato juice
4 teaspoons sugar	¼ cup butter
⅔ cup catsup	1½ teaspoons paprika
½ cup freshly squeezed lemon juice	1 teaspoon Worcestershire sauce
1 teaspoon black pepper	1⅓ cups water
½ teaspoon garlic salt	2 small onions, minced

For 4 or 5 broiler size chickens, cut in halves. Combine all ingredients in a large saucepan. Bring to boiling (full, rolling), then remove from heat. Cool; put in a glass container, cover and allow to stand in refrigerator overnight for flavor to blend. Heat to boiling and baste chicken the last 30 minutes of cooking time on the grill. 8 to 10 servings.

Mrs. J.R. Gobbell
Florence

Charred Grilled Chicken

Place parts of chicken on grill only after coals have turned completely white all over. Immediately salt and pepper to taste and when browned on one side, turn over and salt and pepper that side. A covered grill is best. Lid is shut when chicken is cooking. Melt one stick of margarine and baste frequently. It takes about 30 minutes, if coals are hot enough, for chicken to reach doneness.

Roger Moore
Cherokee

Barbecue Chicken

For each serving:

½ broiling chicken, cut in pieces	Pinch black pepper
½ clove garlic, crushed	½ teaspoon onion or chives, finely chopped
1 teaspoon olive oil	¼ teaspoon parsley, finely chopped
½ teaspoon poultry seasoning	Pinch dry mustard
¼ teaspoon salt	

Prepare fire for direct heat cooking. Rub chicken with garlic and then olie oil. Combine remaining ingredients and rub into chicken with fingertips. Place on cooking grid and cook 15-20 minutes per side with lid closed.

Anthony Haid
Muscle Shoals

Barbecued Broiled Chicken I
(Basic Directions for Broiling Indoors)

Wash broiler-fryer halves or quarters and dry on absorbent paper. Arrange, skin side down, on rack on broiler pan. Brush chicken with preferred barbecue sauce and put in preheated broiler 7" or 8" from heat. Broil, brushing occasionally with sauce, 30 minutes. Turn, brush again with sauce and broil 15 to 30 minutes longer, depending on size of chicken.

Caution: High-sugar sauces, such as those made with molasses, honey, catsup or chili sauce, have a tendency to burn easily, so partially broil chicken before brushing with sauce.

Barbecued Broiled Chicken II
(Basic Directions For Broiling On Grill Outdoors)

Wash broiler-fryer halves or quarters and dry on absorbent paper. Arrange, skin side up, on grate set 3" to 6" from heat (set 6" from heat if high-sugar sauce is used from brushing). Brush chicken with preferred barbecue sauce and cook, turning and brushing occasionally, 45 minutes to 1¼ hours, or until tender (time depends on weight and distance from heat).

Barbecue Sauces For Chicken

Spicy Barbecue Sauce

Heat ½ cup butter or margarine, 1 teaspoon salt, 2 tablespoons vinegar, 1 teaspoon sugar, 1 tablespoon Worcestershire, 1 teaspoon onion salt, ¼ teaspoon pepper and ½ cup water until butter is melted. Makes 1 cup.

Curry Barbecue Sauce

Mix ½ cup butter or margarine (melted), 2 tablespoons curry powder, 1½ teaspoons garlic salt, 1 tablespoon dry mustard, 2 tablespoons steak sauce and ⅔ cup wine vinegar. Makes about 1¼ cups.

Herb Barbecue Sauce

Mix 1 cup catsup; ½ cup water; 3 tablespoons tarragon vinegar; 1 tablespoon steak sauce; dash of garlic salt; and ¼ teaspoon each ground marjoram, oregano and thyme. Makes about 1⅔ cups.

Sherry Barbecue Sauce

Mix 1 cup sherry; ½ cup vegetable oil; 2 tablespoons Worcestershire; 1 tablespoon each onion powder, dry mustard and brown sugar; 1 teaspoon garlic salt; and ½ teaspoon each salt and pepper. Makes 1½ cups.

Barbados Barbecue Sauce

Mix ½ cup molasses, ⅓ cup prepared mustard, ½ cup vinegar, 2 tablespoons Worcestershire, ½ teaspoon hot pepper sauce and 1 cup catsup. Makes about 2⅓ cups.

Southern Fried Chicken Breast

Cut breasts in halves. Coat well with flour, then dip in milk with two eggs. Sprinkle well with seasoned salt. Brown in Dutch oven in shortening. Turn often until well browned. Turn heat low, put lid on and simmer for twenty minutes, drain on paper towels.

Mrs. C.E. James
Barton

Baked Chicken Breast

6 chicken breasts
4 crumbled bay leaves
Juice of ½ lemon

Salt
Freshly ground black pepper
½ cup water

Salt and pepper bottom of 10 x 12 inch pan. Arrange chicken breasts on pan, salt and pepper chicken. Squeeze lemon juice over top, sprinkle bay leaves around pan, add water, cover pan with foil. Bake at 300 degrees for 1 hour, or until tender. Turn once. Spoon broth over breasts and set aside to cool. (Remove any bones remaining.)

Mrs. W.M. Barnett
Sheffield

Ruth's Chicken Breasts With Supreme Sauce

Cook 10 to 12 chicken breast halves in brown-in-bag for nearly one hour at 325 degrees. Follow directions for bag cooking. Save chicken stock for sauce.

Supreme Sauce

½ pint milk
½ pint whipping cream
1½ stick butter
½ cup flour

¼ teaspoon white pepper
½ teaspoon salt
1 pint chicken stock
Almonds

Melt butter; add flour and stir until smooth. Add salt and pepper. Heat chicken stock, milk and cream separately. Pour heated stock into above mixture and stir until smooth. Add milk and cream, heated, and cook over low flame. Serve very hot over chicken breasts in bed of fluffy rice.

Ruth Gobbell
Florence

Chicken Breasts Stuffed With Ham And Cheese

4 whole chicken breasts (boned)
4 small slices ham
4 small slices cheese (Cheddar or
  Swiss)

2 eggs, beaten
Bread crumbs

Flatten chicken breast with meat mallet. Place a slice of ham and one of cheese in center of chicken breast. Fold into a packet and secure with toothpicks. Dip in egg, then bread crumbs. Place in roasting pan, dot with oleo and cook in moderate oven for an hour or until done. Can be made a day ahead.

Claire S. Pitts
Sheffield

Chicken Kiev

6 chicken breasts, boned
and skinned
Salt and pepper
½ cup finely chopped onion
½ cup finely chopped parsley
Butter

2 eggs, beaten
Flour
2 cups cracker crumbs
Cooking oil
½ cup light cream

Salt and pepper chicken breasts; pound flat. Place a ½-inch piece of cold butter, rounded tablespoon parsley, rounded tablespoon onion in center of each breast. Roll as for jelly roll, tucking in sides of meat and pressing to seal well. Fasten with toothpick. Dust chicken with flour. Dip in egg mixture, then roll in cracker crumbs. Chicken rolls may be chilled 1 hour. Brown chicken rolls in hot fat. Bake in a 325 degree oven for 1 hour or until tender. Baste with butter while baking.

Mrs. Orville O. Sharp
Florence

Chicken Crunch

1 can mushroom soup
¾ cup water
1 tablespoon finely chopped onion
1 tablespoon finely chopped parsley
2 pounds chicken parts

1 cup finely crushed herb-seasoned
stuffing
2 tablespoons melted butter
or margarine

Mix one-third cup soup, ¼ cup water, onion, and parsley. Dip chicken in soup mixture; then roll in stuffing. Place in shallow baking dish (12x8x2). Drizzle butter on chicken. Bake at 400 degrees Farenheit for 1 hour. Meanwhile, combine remaining soup and water. Heat; stir now and then. Serve over chicken. Makes four servings.

Note: You may add part of the soup in the baking dish before baking and add some extra soup mixture before the 1 hour is up. Do not heat a glassbaking dish at 400 degrees.

Mrs. Orville O. Sharp
Florence

Chicken In A Skillet

2 tablespoons butter
2 tablespoons shortening
2½ pounds frying chicken pieces
3 tablespoons flour
1 can (10½ ounces) condensed cream
chicken soup

½ cup chopped celery
1 cup undiluted evaporated milk
¼ teaspoon poultry seasoning
6 to 8 small peeled white onions
6 to 8 carrots
2 tablespoons chopped parsley

Melt butter and shortening in 10-inch frying pan. Roll chicken in flour. Brown in frying pan. Remove extra fat from pan. Mix chicken soup, celery, milk and poultry seasoning; blend well. Pour over chicken. Cut carrots in half lengthwise. Partially cook carrots and onions in small amount of salted boiling water. Place vegetables around chicken. Heat to boiling, then reduce heat to low. Cover and simmer until chicken and vegetables are tender (35-45 minutes). Top with parsley; serve with cooked rice.

Mrs. Sandra Hollis
Florence

91

Chicken Casserole

1 chicken
1 can cream of mushroom soup
1 can cream of chicken soup
1 soup can of milk

2 packages herb seasoning stuffing mix
1 or 2 eggs
1 stick of butter, melted

Cook chicken and take meat off bones. Put in bottom of a casserole dish. Mix cream of mushroom soup, cream of chicken soup and milk together and pour over chicken. Mix stuffing mix wih eggs and melted butter; pour over chicken. Bake at 350 degrees until brown.

Mrs. J.G. Sesler
Florence

Easy Chicken Casserole

5 chicken breasts
Salt and pepper
1 stick oleo, cut up
Juice of one lemon

4 tablespoons Worcestershire sauce
1 small garlic clove

Bake in slow oven 350 degrees for three hours. Serves five.

Evelyn Pless
Cherokee

Chicken Casserole

2 5-ounce cans chicken
½ teaspoon salt
½ teaspoon pepper
½ cup minced celery
½ cup mayonnaise

2 tablespoons minced onion
3 hard-boiled eggs, chopped
1 can chicken soup
2 cups crushed potato chips

Mix all ingredients except potato chips. Place in casserole dish. Sprinkle potato chips on top and bake for 30 minutes at 350 degrees.

Barbara D. Ayers
Phil Campbell

Chicken Breast Casserole

1 small package spaghetti
4 chicken breasts
2 cups grated American cheese
1 medium onion

1 can cream of chicken soup
½ bell pepper
1 can cream of celery soup

Cook spaghetti according to package directions and set aside. Cook chicken and bone, set aside. Sauté onion and bell pepper. Place a layer of spaghetti in a casserole dish. Then place a layer of pepper and onion, cheese, then another layer of spaghetti and more cheese. Have chicken cut in chunks. Place chicken on top. Mix together the celery soup and mushroom soup. Pour over the layers. Cook in a hot oven until bubbly. Serves eight to ten people.

Evelyn Pless
Cherokee

Chicken And Rice Casserole

6 chicken breasts, boneless
1 can cream of chicken soup
1 can cream of mushroom soup
1 can cream of celery soup
1 cup chopped onions
1½ cups rice (long grain, no "quick" rice)

Butter casserole dish and pour rice in bottom. Lay breasts of chicken on top of rice. Mix the three soups plus onions and pour over top of chicken. Add ½ cup water. Bake in 300 degree oven for 2 hours.

James Coburn
Florence

Crunchy Chicken Casserole

3 cups cooked chicken, chopped
1 cup celery, chopped
1 hard cooked egg, chopped
1 can cream of chicken soup
1 tablespoon Worcestershire sauce
½ cup mayonnaise
1 teaspoon grated onion
Potato chips

Mix all ingredients together except potato chips. Bake in a greased casserole dish for 30 minutes at 350 degrees. Top with potato chips the last 10 minutes of cooking.

Donna M. Hayes
Florence

Hot Chicken Salad Deluxe Casserole

½ cup sliced almonds
1 tablespoon margarine
2 cups diced cooked chicken
1 cup diced celery
½ teaspoon salt
½ cup crushed potato chips
½ teaspoon flavor enhancer
2 teaspoons grated onion
½ cup mayonnaise
½ cup cream of mushroom soup, undiluted
½ cup shredded cheese

Sauté almonds in margarine; drain. Combine all ingredients except the potato chips. Spoon into a lightly greased casserole (one quart size), sprinkle with potato chips. Bake at 425 for 20 minutes.

Mrs. E.R. Dallas
Somerville

Chicken Breast Supreme

2 chicken breasts
½ can condensed cream of mushroom soup
3 tablespoons dry onion soup mix

Place each chicken breast on a square of heavy duty foil. Combine soup and soup mix; spread half on each chicken breast. Wrap foil securely. Bake at 350 degrees for 1 hour.

Ethel Rutherford
Cherokee

93

Moo Goo (Mushroom) Gai Pai (Chicken)

Bone a chicken. Mix in a bowl with the mat:

Soy sauce
Cooking wine
Salt
Sugar

Cornstarch
Sememi oil
Vinegar

Brown in vegetable oil in the wok. Mix together:

Mushrooms
Chinese cabbage
Green pepper

Carrot
Bamboo shoots
Water chestnuts

Combine with chicken mixture, and return to wok for about 1 minute. Serve over rice.

Sun-See Hsu
Florence

Chicken, Italian Style

1 broiler, fryer, about 3 pounds, cut up
Salt and pepper
Flour
¼ cup olive oil
¼ pound prosciutto, thinly sliced
4 or 5 small onions

1 green pepper, minced
1 canned pimiento, chopped
1 clove garlic, crushed
1 cup chicken broth
1 can (1 pound) tomatoes
1 cup or 1 can (3 ounces) sliced mushrooms

Season chicken with salt and pepper and dredge lightly with flour. Brown on all sides in the olive oil in large skillet. Add all ingredients, except mushrooms, bring to boil and simmer, covered, 1 hour. Add fresh or undrained canned mushrooms and simmer 15 minutes longer. Good with spaghetti. Makes 4 servings.

Wibby A. Medaris

Italian Style Chicken Livers With Herb Rice

7-ounce package herb flavored rice
10½ ounce can chicken consommé
¼ cup water
1 small onion, minced

1 clove garlic, crushed
1 teaspoon salt (diabetic)
1 pound chicken livers, chopped
½ pound mushrooms, sliced
2 cups olive oil

Combine rice, consomme, water, onion, garlic and salt. Bring to a boil. Lower heat, cover and barely simmer until all liquid is absorbed. Meanwhile, sauté the livers and mushrooms in olive oil until livers taste done. Add livers, mushrooms and pan juices to rice mixture and stir thoroughly. Serves 5. For diabetics, one serving equals 3 meat exchanges, 2 bread exchanges and 1 B-vegetable exchange. (This recipe may be prepared and frozen. Thaw and heat to serve.)

Mrs. Paul Buettner
Florence

94

Persian Chicken

1 cup converted rice
Broiler-fryer chicken (about 3
   pounds), cut up
½ cup butter or margarine
1 cup finely chopped onion
10-ounce package frozen large
   (Fordhook) lima beans

¼ teaspoon nutmeg
2 to 4 tablespoons finely chopped fresh
   mint
½ cup dark or light (golden) raisins
¼ cup finely chopped fresh dill

Cook rice according to package directions for firm rice.

Sprinkle chicken with salt. In a 12-inch skillet in 2 tablespoons of the butter, gently cook onion until wilted; with a slotted spoon, remove onion and reserve. To the skillet add 2 more tablespoons of the butter and heat; add chicken and cook uncovered, turning as necessary and adjusting heat, until browned and tender—33 to 45 minutes.

Cook lima beans according to package directions, adding nutmeg; drain, reserving liquid. Rapidly boil liquid, uncovered, until reduced to about 2 tablespoons; stir in the mint; reserve.

In a 3 to 4-quart saucepot or rangetop casserole, melt 2 more tablespoons of the butter. Add one-half the rice, all the chicken, one-half the onion, one-half the raisins, one-half the lima beans and one-half the dill. Add one-half of the remaining rice and all the remaining onion, raisins, lima beans and dill. Top with remaining rice. Gently heat the remaining 2 tablespoons butter with the bean liquid and mint until butter melts; spoon over rice. Place a clean towel over the top of the pot; cover and cook over medium-low heat about 40 minutes; there should be a golden-brown crust at the bottom. But even if you don't achieve the crust, simmering the cooked ingredients—rice, chicken, onion and lima beans—with the raisins, mint and dill results in a delicious blending of flavors.

Makes 4 generous servings of chicken with a plentitude of rice. On serving, the rice will mingle with the lima beans and raisins; any of the mixture left over will be delicious reheated in a double boiler.

Betty Tarant
Nashville, Tennessee

Brashford Manor Salad

1½ pounds chicken breasts,
   cubed
½ quart green goddess
   dressing
2 heads iceberg lettuce,
   chopped

⅔ pound bibb lettuce
¼ cup French dressing
½ pound crisp bacon
½ quart cherry tomatoes
6 deviled eggs
3 ounces caviar

Mix iceberg lettuce with green goddess dressing, add shrimp, tomatoes and chicken and mold in the center of large serving platter. Halve deviled eggs and arrange on top of bibb lettuce around salad. Ladle caviar on eggs and top with French dressing. Serves about 10 persons.

Chicken Normandy

2 broiler-fryers, about 3 pounds
  each, cut up (omit
  necks and backs)
½ cup butter or margarine
¼ cup brandy
Seasoned salt and pepper
1 medium onion, thinly sliced
¾ cup thinly sliced celery

2 tart medium apples, peeled
  and diced (if not
  tart, sprinkle with lemon
  juice)
2 tablespoons chopped parsley
¼ teaspoon marjoram leaves
⅓ cup sherry
⅓ cup heavy cream

Sauté chicken pieces in the butter in skillet until browned. Transfer to large casserole. Reserve drippings in skillet. Heat brandy in small saucepan, ignite and pour over chicken. Sprinkle with seasoned salt and pepper. Add next 4 ingredients to drippings in skillet and cook, stirring frequently, 2 to 3 minutes. Sprinkle with seasoned salt and pepper. Add marjoram and sherry and pour over chicken. Cover and bake in moderate oven (350 degrees) about 2 hours. Add cream to gravy, stir to mix and spoon over chicken. Or remove chicken to serving dish, stir cream into gravy and pour over chicken. Makes 6 servings.

Pam West
Memphis, Tennessee

Israeli Chicken

1 large roasting chicken (5-6 pounds)
4 tablespoons chicken fat (or
  butter)
⅔ cup raw rice
2 tablespoons chopped pecans
2 tablespoons chopped dates
1 teaspoon salt
Dash each (¼ teaspoon each):
  pepper, paprika, ginger,
  cinnamon

1 tablespoon chopped, fresh
  parsley
1 cup white cooking wine
1 cup tomato juice
1 large onion, chopped coarsely
1 tablespoon dehydrated chicken soup
Water as needed (See directions)

Sprinkle chicken with salt and rub inside and out with chicken fat or butter. Mix stuffing of rice, pecans, dates, dehydrated soup (mash with spoon first) and salt. Add pepper, paprika, ginger, cinnamon and parsley to stuffing. Stuff chicken and sew. Roast chicken in tomato juice, wine and onions in 350 degree oven for 1½ hours, basting frequently. Add small amount of water if sauce evaporates. Serve sauce over stuffing and chicken and with a salad and garlic bread. Serves 4.

Mrs. Robert W. Mullaly
Florence

Chicken Mornay On Broccoli

1 package (10 ounces) frozen
broccoli (cut or
spears)
¼ cup butter or margarine
¼ cup flour
1 cup chicken broth
½ cup heavy cream

½ cup dry white wine
Salt and pepper to taste
⅛ teaspoon Worcestershire
Grated Parmesan cheese
2 cups diced cooked chicken
Chopped parsley

Cook broccoli until barely tender, drain and arrange in shallow 1½ quart baking dish. Melt butter and stir in flour. Add chicken broth and cream. Cook, stirring, until thickened. Stir in wine, salt and pepper, Worcestershire and ⅓ cup cheese. Arrange chicken on broccoli, pour sauce over top and sprinkle with 2 tablespoons cheese. Bake in hot ove (425 degrees) 15 minutes, or until bubbly. Sprinkle with parsley. Makes 4 to 6 servings.

Chicken Livers With Rice

2 tablespoons margarine
5 teaspoons minced onion
¾ cup pre-cooked rice
½ pound chicken livers cut
into 1-inch pieces

Seasoned flour
½ can cream of chicken soup,
undiluted
¼ cup milk
Chopped parsley

Melt half margarine in saucepan, add onions and cook until tender. Add to rice which has been cooked according to package directions. Roll chicken livers lightly in flour; saute in remaining margarine in a skillet until browned. In a 1½ quart casserole, combine livers, rice, soup and remaining ingredients. Bake at 375 degrees for 30 minutes.

Ethel Rutherford
Cherokee

Hashed Brown Omelet

4 slices bacon
2 cups shredded cooked potatoes
¼ cup chopped onion
¼ cup chopped green pepper
4 eggs

¼ cup milk
½ teaspoon salt
1 cup shredded sharp process cheese
Dash pepper

In 10 or 12-inch skillet, cook bacon until crisp. Leave drippings in skillet, remove bacon and crumble. Mix potatoes, onion, and green pepper and pat into skillet. Cook over low heat until the underside is crisp and brown. Blend eggs, milk, salt and pepper and pour over potatoes. Top with cheese and bacon. Cover and cook over low heat. When egg is done, loosen omelet and fold. Yield: 4 servings.

Mrs. Gene B. Mance
Muscle Shoals

A La Golden Rod

4 tablespoons butter or margarine
4 tablespoons flour
½ teaspoon salt
¼ teaspoon pepper

2 cups milk
4 hard boiled eggs
8 slices toast

Melt butter in saucepan over low heat. Blend in flour, salt and pepper. Cook over low heat, stirring until mixture is smooth and bubbly. Remove from heat and slowly stir in milk. Heat to boiling, stirring constantly. Boil and stir one minute.

Cut white of hard boiled eggs into small slices and stir into white sauce. Pour over toast. Crumble egg yolks over top and serve. Goes good with bacon and/or cantaloupe.

Mrs. Danny W. DeLano
Russellville

Ruth's Chicken Tetrazzini

Butter or margarine
½ cup flour
1 cup hot milk
1 cup hot chicken broth
½ teaspoon salt
½ teaspoon pepper
⅛ teaspoon nutmeg
¼ cup dry sherry
¾ cup heavy cream

1 pound thin spaghetti
½ pound mushrooms, sliced,
   or 2 cans (4 ounces
   each) mushrooms,
   drained
2 to 3 cups diced cooked
   chicken
½ cup grated Parmesan or
   Romano cheese

Heat ½ cup butter and stir in flour. Combine milk and chicken broth and stir into flour mixture. Cook, stirring, until sauce is smooth and thickened. Blend in next 4 ingredients. Stir in cream and remove from heat. Cook and drain spaghetti. Saute mushrooms in 2 tablespoons butter 5 minutes. Mix half the sauce with spaghetti and mushrooms. Place in buttered shallow baking dish. Make well in center of spaghetti mixture. Mix remaining sauce with chicken and place in well. Sprinkle with cheese. Bake in hot oven (400 degrees) 20 minutes. Serves 6 to 8.

Betty Ballinger
Madisonville, Kentucky

Mom's Chicken Broth

3 pounds chicken necks and
   backs
Salt
10 whole white peppercorns

½ lemon
Few parsley sprigs or celery
   tops
1 medium onion, sliced

Put chicken in kettle or Dutch oven and add cold water to cover. Bring to rapid boil and skim. Add about 2 teaspoons salt for each quart water added above, and remaining ingredients. Bring again to boil, cover and reduce heat. Simmer very slowly 1½ to 2 hours. Strain, chill and skim off fat. Makes about 4 cups. Broth can be frozen.

Rotisserie Duckling For Two

1 (4-5 pounds) frozen duckling,
  thawed
2 tablespoons lemon juice

3 tablespoons coarse salt
Cumberland Glaze (recipe
  follows)

Squeeze lemon juice over ducklin. Sprinkle with coarse salt, inside and out. Place in refrigerator at least 4 hours or overnight. With paper towels rub off salt; do not rinse. Preheat open hearth broiler-rotisseries. Inset spit through duckling so that both pronged forks are tightly inserted; tighten screws. Balance duckling on spit. Place spit on spit supports. Adjust supports so duckling is as close as possible to heating element without touching it. Attach motor and turn on. Cook two hours. Brush duckling with Cumberland Glaze and continue cooking for 15 minutes, brushing frequently with glaze.

Note: If glaze is not desired, cook duckling 2 hours and 15 minutes and serve with Fruited Gravy.

Cumberland Glaze

¾ cup red currant jelly
¾ cup orange juice
¼ cup lemon juice
¼ teaspoon ground ginger

Dash cayenne
2 tablespoons corn starch
2 tablespoons water

In small saucepan heat jelly over medium heat until melted. Gradually stir in orange and lemon juices. Add ginger and cayenne. Mix corn starch and water. Gradually stir into jelly mixture. Stirring constantly, bring to boil over medium heat and boil 1 minute. Brush on duckling during last 15 minutes of cooking time. Makes 1½ cups.

Fruited Gravy

2 tablespoons duckling pan
  drippings
2 tablespoons corn starch

2 cups chicken bouillon
¼ cup orange marmalade

Measure pan drippings into saucepan. Sprinkle corn starch into pan. Stir and cook over medium heat just until smooth; remove from heat. Gradually stir in bouillon until smooth. Stirring constantly, bring to boil over medium heat and boil 1 minute. Stir in marmalade. Heat until melted. Makes 2 cups.

Roast Dove Or Quail

10 or 12 birds
Salt and pepper to taste
2 sticks butter
Juice of 3 lemons

1 tablespoon cooking sherry
  for each bird
½ cup water

Clean and dry each bird, then salt and pepper them. Sear in generous amount of butter in a heavy iron skillet. Remove brids and place them breast-side-down in roaster. Pour lemon juice and butter and water over them. Add sherry, cover and bake at 250 degrees for about three hours, basting occasionally.

Outdoor Grilled Turkey

About one hour before cooking, start your fire. A large turkey will require more charcoal briquets than smaller meats.

While the briquets burn down, remove giblets of fresh or thawed turkey, rinse, tie legs together and secure wings to body. Rub the turkey with oil and sprinkle the outside and cavities with salt, pepper and flavor enhancer. Do not stuff turkey. Arrange hot briquets around a drip pan centered in fire bed. Place bird, breast side up, on center of greased cooking grill directly above drip pan. Roast covered for 13-15 minutes per pound.

Cover barbecue with lid or foil cover to maintain a roasting temperature of 325 degrees. To construct a cover, you will need the wire from six or seven coat hangers and a pair of pliers. Form the wire into a firm circle or rectangle to fit the grill. Attach half circles of wire to this base as if spokes of an umbrella. Completely cover the wire dome with heavy duty aluminum foil, leaving a small opening for draft.

To spit roast a small turkey (6-12 pounds), insert spit rod under legs and through the center of the bird. Tighten spit forks at both ends and test for balance, re-adjusting until satisfactory. Roast about 30 minutes per pound.

Add briquets to the fire every hour to keep temperature constant. Brush the bird with oil or melted butter during the cooking. After grilling, allow turkey to rest for about 30 minutes before serving.

Internal temperature should be 180-185 degrees. Use a meat thermometer inserted into the thickest part of thigh, not touching a bone.

For party perfect partners, serve a variety of Danish Cheeses and fresh fruits. Plan on one-half pound of each of four cheeses for 12 guests.

Grilled Turkey Drumsticks

1 cup brown sugar	5 tablespoons minced onion
½ cup vegetable oil	5 tablespoons soy sauce
½ cup catsup	1 teaspoon flavor enhancer
½ cup white vinegar	12 turkey drumsticks
⅓ cup pineapple juice	

In a bowl, mix together, brown sugar, vegetable oil, catsup, vinegar, pineapple juice, onion, soy sauce and flavor enhancer. Place drumsticks in a large plastic bowl. Cover with sauce and marinate 2 to 3 hours at room temperature or overnight in refrigerator. Drain turkey drumsticks and cook on grill over medium hot coals, 1 to 1¼ hours or until done. Baste often with sauce. Makes 12 servings.

Kentucky Hot Brown Sandwiches

12 slices turkey breast
12 slices bread
12 slices bacon
12 to 36 mushroom caps

1 cup grated Parmesan cheese
1 can cream of chicken soup
⅓ cup light cream
1 teaspoon lemon juice

Add cream, Parmesan cheese and lemon juice to cream of chicken soup and heat (do not boil). Wrap mushrooms in tin foil and heat in 350-degree oven. Cook bacon until crisp and drain bacon on bread slices and toast on one side. Place bread in large baking dishes and top with turkey slices, cheese sauce and salt and pepper to taste. Cover and heat in 350-degree oven until turkey is slightly brown. Remove and add bacon slices and other condiments if desired. Serves 12 persons.

Dana DeVoss
Florence

Lucky Seven Sandwich With Dressing

4 slices rye bread
4 slices Swiss cheese
8 slices tomato
8 crisp lettuce leaves

8 slices crisp bacon
4-8 slices cooked breast of
  turkey
Thousand Island Dressing

For each sandwich, place 1 slice rye bread on a luncheon plate. Top with 1 slice Swiss cheese, 2 tomato slices, 2 lettuce leaves, 2 strips bacon, 1 or 2 turkey slices. Top each sandwich with a generous portion of Thousand Island Dressing and serve extra dressing as needed. Makes 4 sandwiches.

Favorite Thousand Island Dressing

2 cups salad oil
1½ cups catsup
1 small can pimento, finely
  chopped
1 small onion, finely grated
½ cup sweet pickle relish,
  drained

2 eggs
½ teaspoon mustard
¼ teaspoon salt
3 tablespoons sugar
2 tablespoons vinegar
Dash paprika
Dash red pepper

Beat eggs until thick; add mustard, salt, sugar, vinegar, paprika and red pepper. Gradually add salad oil, (almost drop by drop at first) beating constantly until oil is used and dressing is thick. Gradually add catsup. Stir pimento, onion and pickle relish into dressing. Store in covered jar in refrigerator for several hours before using. Makes 1 quart.

Meats

Lemon 'N Spice Beef Steaks

1 or 2 beef blade steaks, cut
   ½ to ¾ inch thick
⅔ cup lemon juice
½ cup water
1 tablespoon oil
1 tablespoon sugar

1½ teaspoons salt
1 teaspoon thyme
¼ teaspoon garlic powder
Citrus Prune Kabobs (recipe
   below)

Combine lemon juice, water, oil, sugar, salt, thyme and garlic powder in a small saucepan and cook slowly 5 minutes. Cool. Place steaks in utility dish or plastic bag and pour marinade over them, turning to coat. Cover dish or tie bag securely and marinate in refrigerator 6 hours or overnight, turning at least once. Remove steaks from marinade and place on grill so surface of meat is 4 inches from heat. Broil at moderate temperature 7 to 10 minutes on each side, depending upon degree of doneness desired (rare or medium). Brush steaks with marinade occasionally while broiling. Makes 3 to 6 servings.

Citrus Prune Kabobs

16 pitted prunes
1 lemon, cut in wedges

2 oranges, halved and cut in
   wedges

Alternately thread prunes and wedges of citrus fruit on skewers. Brush with marinade and broil 8 to 10 minutes, turning and brushing with steak marinade frequently. Serve with Lemon 'N Spice Beef Steaks.

Coffee Citrus Round Steak

2 or 3 beef top round steaks,
   cut 1¼ inches thick
4 teaspoons freeze-dried or
   instant coffee
⅓ cup hot water
1 can (6 ounces) frozen orange
   juice concentrate, defrosted

2 tablespoons instant minced
   onion
1 tablespoon salt
1 tablespoon lemon juice
⅛ teaspoon cloves
⅛ teaspoon hot sauce

Dissolve coffee in water. Add orange juice concentrate, onion, salt, lemon juice, cloves and hot sauce. Place steaks in plastic bag, add marinade, press out air and tie securely. Marinate in refrigerator 6 to 8 hours (or overnight), turning at least once. Place steaks on grill top so surface of meat is 4 to 5 inches from heat and broil at moderate temperature to rare or medium (25 to 35 minutes), turning and brushing with marinade occasionally. Serves 16 to 20.

Steak In A Nest

2 pounds round steak, cut ½
   to ¾ inch thick
¼ cup flour
2 teaspoons salt
¼ teaspoon paprika
⅓ teaspoon pepper
1 can (10¾ ounces) frozen
   mixed vegetables, defrosted

1 10¾-ounce can condensed
   cream of mushroom soup
⅓ cup milk
¼ teaspoon leaf thyme
¼ teaspoon basil leaves

Cut round steak in 6 serving size pieces. Combine flour, salt, paprika and pepper; dredge pieces of meat on both sides and pound in seasoned flour. Combine soup, vegetables, milk, thyme and basil. Prepare 6 double-thick 12x12-inch pieces of heavy duty aluminum foil; place a piece of steak in center of each. Top pieces of meat with vegetable mixture. To close packets, bring two opposite edges of foil together over meat and vegetables (allowing air space) and fold edges over 2 or 3 times, pressing crease in tightly each time. Flatten foil at ends close to meat and crease edges of each end to form a triangle; fold ends several times toward packet, pressing tightly to seal. Place packets on grill 4 to 5 inches from heat and cook at a low to moderate temperature for 1½ hours or until meat is tender. Serve in opened packets.

Maverick Steak

1 cup mayonnaise
¼ cup red wine vinegar
1 tablespoon finely chopped onion
1 teaspoon salt
1 6 ounce can tomato paste

3 tablespoons Worcestershire
   sauce
1 tablespoon horseradish
1 or 1½ pounds round steak

Cut up beef and place in baking dish with 1 tablespoon lemon juice for one hour. Combine other ingredients and mix well. Score meat and top with sauce. Place under broiler until tender, basting from time to time.

Mrs. Donna M. Hayes
Florence

Marinated Black Pepper Steak

Place a sirloin steak, cut 1½ to 2 inches thick, in a shallow pan. Cover with steak marinade and leave several hours or overnight. Remove from the marinade and press coarsely ground peppercorns into both sides of steak. Grill about 4 inches from coats about 15 min. Turn only once. Cut steak in diagonal thin slices.

Steak Marinade

1 cup red wine vinegar
½ cup wesson oil
⅓ cup brown sugar
Few drops Tabasco sauce
¼ teaspoon salt

¼ teaspoon marjoram
¼ teaspoon rosemary
¾ cup chopped onion
1 clove garlic

Shake ingredients in a jar to blend.

Mrs. John H. Carter
Waterloo

103

Shishkabobs For Two

Shishkabobs

1 pound filet mignon (8 ounces per person)
2 small tomatoes

2 small bell peppers
2 small onions
3 or 4 small baked potatoes

Sauce

1 tablespoon lemon juice
1 teaspoon tenderizer
1 teaspoon coarse pepper
1 teaspoon garlic salt

1 teaspoon steak sauce
½ teaspoon liquid hickory smoke
2 tablespoons bacon grease

Shishkabobs: Wedge each of the ingredients and put on 2 separate skewers.

Sauce: Combine all ingredients for sauce and beat until well blended. Baste meat and vegetables which were put on skewers earlier. Grill until done.

Mrs. John E. Higginbotham
Florence

Steak Strip Kabobs

2 pounds beef round steak, cut 1 to 1½ inches thick
½ cup salad oil
¼ cup lemon juice
2 teaspoons salt

2 teaspoons dry mustard
2 teaspoon sugar
¼ teaspoon hot sauce
1 medium onion, finely chopped
1 clove garlic, finely chopped
Cherry tomatoes, if desired

Cut steak into thin slices (¼ inch thick or less) and place in plastic bag or utility dish. Combine salad oil, lemon juice, salt, dry mustard, sugar and hot sauce. Stir in onion and garlic and pour over meat, mixing to coat strips. Tie bag securely or cover dish and marinate in refrigerator 4 to 6 hours (or overnight), turning at least once while marinating. Pour off marinade and reserve. Thread strips of beef on metal skewers (weaving back and forth). Thread cherry tomatoes on skewers, if desired. Place kabobs on grill and broil at moderate temperature 3 minutes, brushing with marinade occasionally. Turn and broil to desired doneness (3 to 4 minutes), brushing with marinade. Makes 4 to 6 servings.

Jere Medaris

Hidden Treasure Kabobs

1 tablespoon finely chopped chives
2 teaspoons salt
⅛ teaspoon pepper

2 pounds ground beef
18 mushrooms (¾ to 1 inch diameter)
3 to 4 ounces blue cheese

Remove caps of mushrooms and stuff each with a piece of cheese. Chop mushroom stems and lightly but thoroughly combine with ground beef, chives, salt and pepper; divide into 18 portions. Shape each portion into a small patty and place a stuffed mushroom cap in the center of each patty. Press mixture around mushrooms to form balls. Carefully thread balls on skewers, place on grill and broil at low to moderate temperature 20 to 25 minutes or until done, turning occasionally. Serves 6.

Stuffed Beef Round

2 pounds round steak, cut ½
   inch thick
1 cup (4 ounces) cheddar cheese,
   shredded
½ cup chopped onion
½ cup chopped celery
¼ cup snipped parsley
1 teaspoon salt
½ teaspoon pepper
2 tablespoons cooking oil
1 (10 ounce) can condensed
   beef broth
½ teaspoon dry mustard
2 tablespoons plain flour
¼ cup water

Cut steak into 6 serving pieces; pound to ¼ inch thick. Combine cheese, onion, celery, and parsley. Place ¼ cup of cheese mixture in center of each piece of steak. Reserve remaining cheese mixture. Roll each piece of steak up, jelly roll fashion. Secure with wooden toothpicks. Combine ¼ cup flour, salt and pepper. Roll meat rolls in flour mixture to coat. Slowly brown meat in 2 tablespoons cooking oil. Drain excess fat. Combine beef broth and mustard. Pour over steak rolls. Cover and simmer 45 minutes. Add reserved cheese mixture and simmer 15 to 20 minutes longer or until meat is tender. Remove meat to platter. Skim excess fat from skillet. Blend together 2 tablespoons flour and water; stir into pan juice. Cook, stirring constantly until sauce thickens. Pour over meat rolls. Serves 6.

Mrs. Robert Burdine
Florence

Round Steak Rosea

3 to 3½ pounds round steak,
   cubed
½ cup flour
1½ teaspoons salt
¼ teaspoon pepper
¼ cup cooking oil
2 cups Rosea wine
1 cup water
½ package onion soup mix
1 can tomato paste mix
½ cup water
2 tablespoons brown sugar
1 cup sharp cheddar cheese,
   shredded
8 ounces fresh mushrooms

Cube steak. Combine salt, flour, pepper and sprinkle over meat. Brown in large skillet. Combine wine and 1 cup water and onion soup mix. Add to meat, cover tightly and cook slowly 45 minutes. Combine tomato paste, ½ cup water and brown sugar and add to meat mixture. Continue cooking 20 minutes or until meat is tender, stirring occasionally. Add cheese and mushrooms; cook slowly 10 minutes more. Serve with rice or noodles.

Evelyn Pless
Cherokee

Zuricher Geschnetzeltes
"Ute's Dish"

2 pounds round steak cut into
  1-inch cubes
Salt and pepper to taste
Margarine

½ pint whipping cream
Small jar chopped mushrooms
Flour and water
Parsley (fresh or omit)

Brown steak slowly in margarine. Add salt and pepper to taste. Make a flour and water paste and add slowly to browned steak. Simmer (about 10 minutes). Add whipping cream to mixture from carton and simmer slowly again. About five minutes, or until warmed, before serving add chopped mushrooms and parsley.

Serve over rice or the real German way with hash brown potatoes. Serves four to six.

Mrs. Everett Vickery
Russellville

Cheeseburger Round Steak

2 tablespoons all-purpose flour
¼ teaspoon salt
1 pound beef round steak, cut
  ½-inch thick
2 tablespoons cooking oil

½ cup water
1 teaspoon instant minced onion
2 slices process American cheese,
  halved

Preheat oven at 325 degrees. Combine flour and salt in small bowl. Pound meat to ¼-inch thickness with meat mallet. Cut meat into 4 pieces. Carefully heat oil in skillet. Brown the meat slowly in hot oil. Add water and onion. Cover skillet; bake in oven for 1 hour. Add more water, if needed. Top with cheese; heat, covered, to melt cheese.

Shelia Ann Bown
Killen

Minute Steaks

6 medium size minute steaks
1 can (8 ounces) tomato sauce

1 can water
1 medium onion

Salt, pepper and flour steaks and quick brown on both sides in a little shortening. After browning, drain any excess shortening. At this point you might need to wash skillet since it will probably have scorched flour in it. Add tomato sauce, water and sliced onion. Cover and simmer on very low heat about an hour.

This can also be used for pork chops, chicken breasts or frying chickens.

Mrs. Orville O. Sharp
Florence

Chuck Steak Teriyaki

| 1 4½ to 5 pound chuck | top round 2 inches |
| boneless steak or | thick |

Pierce surface of steak and put in 12x8x2 inch baking pan.
Mix:
1 4-5 ounce package instant marinade, oil, vinegar and water as directed on package.

Add to this:

2-3 cups cold water	2 tablespoon soy sauce
½ teaspoon ginger	2 tablespoons molasses
½ teaspoon dry mustard	1 clove garlic

Pour sauce over steak and marinate 15 minutes to one hour, turning steak occasionally. Drain. Bake uncovered at 400 degrees for one hour, basting occasionally with marinarde.

Mrs. W.M. Barnett
Sheffield

Oriental Stir-Fried Steak

2 to 3 pounds beef flank steak	½ cup soy sauce
(or top round steak,	2 cloves garlic, minced
cut ¾ to 1 inch thick)	4 medium green peppers
2 tablespoons cornstarch	4 small tomatoes
1 teaspoon sugar	Cooking fat
½ teaspoon ginger	Water

Partially freeze steaks to firm and slice diagonally across the grain into very thin strips. Combine cornstarch, sugar and ginger; stir in soy sauce and garlic. Pour mixture over meat and stir. Cut green peppers into thin strips and cut tomatoes into wedges. For each serving, place desired amount of marinated beef strips in 1 tablespoon hot fat and quickly brown. Remove from pan. Reduce heat; add green pepper and 1 tablespoon water to pan and cook until green is tender-crisp, 5 to 6 minutes. Stir in meat and tomatoes and heat through. Serves 4 to 5.

Hawaiian Meat Sticks

½ cup soy sauce	1 clove garlic, crushed
¼ cup green onions and tops,	¼ teaspoon ground ginger
chopped	2½ pounds beef sirloin steak,
2 tablespoons sugar	boned and trimmed
1 tablespoon salad oil	of fat
1½ teaspoons cornstarch	

In the morning, blend all but beef in saucepan; simmer, stirring constantly until thickened, about 1 minute. Cool, cover and keep at room temperature. Slice meat into ½ inch thick strips, 1 inch wide and 4 inches long. Thread 1 piece of meat on bamboo or metal skewers. Wrap in plastic wrap and refrigerate. About 30 minutes before serving, brush skewered meat on both sides with sauce. Arrange on serving tray. Cook meat sticks on charcoal hibachi or grill. Makes about 5 dozen appetizers.

Mrs. Claire Pitts
Sheffield

Pot Roast

2 or 3 pounds brisket roast
3 tablespoons rye flour

1 teaspoon salt
3 tablespoons hot fat

Roll the roast in flour and salt. Brown on both sides in the hot fat, put in pressure cooker and cook 30 minutes at 10 pounds pressure with a cup of water. Let the pressure go down and then add following ingredients.

1 cup English peas
8 or 10 small potatoes
2 small onions
8 or 10 carrots

6 or 8 pieces of celery
1 teaspoon paprika
½ teaspoon garlic salt
Salt and pepper to taste

Cover and bring pressure up to 10 pounds. Pressure and cook 30 minutes longer.

Donna M. Hayes
Florence

Pot Roast

1 to 2 or 3 pound beef roast
Salt and pepper
1 can cream of mushroom soup

1 soup can of water
1 package dry onion soup mix

Salt and pepper roast to taste. Flour and brown in oil in skillet, pour off excess oil. Mix together soup, water, and onion soup mix and pour over roast. Cover and cook on medium heat for 1 hour or until tender.

Mrs. Jimmy Black
Sheffield

Beef Tip Roast

3½ to 8-pound beef tip roast

Place roast, fat side up, on rack in open roasting pan. Insert meat thermometer so bulb is centered in the thickest part. Do not add water. Do not cover. Roast in a slow oven (325 degrees F.) to desired degree of doneness: 140 degrees for rare; 160 degrees for medium. For a 3½ to 5-pound roast, allow 35 to 40 minutes per pound, depending on desired doneness. For a 5 to 8-pound roast, allow 30 to 35 minutes per pound.

For easier carving, allow roast to "set" in a warm place 15 to 20 minutes after removal from oven. Since roast usually continues to cook after removal from oven, it is best to remove it about 5 degrees below the temperature desired.

Beef Pot Roast With Dumplings

4 pound beef pot roast (chuck   Salt
   or arm)   Pepper

Brown in hot fat. Add:

½ cup water   3 onions, sliced
1 (8 ounce can) tomato sauce   2 cloves garlic, minced

Cover and cook over low heat for 2 hours. Add:

2 tablespoons brown sugar   ¼ cup catsup
¼ teaspoon paprika   ¼ cup vinegar
½ teaspoon dry mustard   1 tablespoon Worcestershire
¼ cup lemon juice   sauce

Cover and continue cooking until meat is tender. Serve with cornmeal or plain dumplings.

Cornmeal Drumplings

¾ cup cornmeal   ½ teaspoon salt
½ cup flour   1½ teaspoons baking powder

Add 1 egg beaten with ½ cup milk and blend. Add 2 tablespoons melted shortening or margarine. Drop 1 tablespoon batter in sauce of pot roast, cover pan tightly. Simmer 15 minutes.

Mrs. Robert M. Metcalfe
Madisonville, Kentucky

Pastel De Choclo
From Chile

2 onions   ½ pound olives
2 tablespoons lard   2 hard-boiled eggs
2 pounds chuck   8 ears of corn, grated or ground
½ cup meat stock   2 tablespoons butter
Salt, red pepper, marjoram,   1 cup milk
   cumin seed to taste   2 beaten eggs
½ cup seedless raisins

Chop the meat and brown in the lard. Add stock, salt, pepper and spices. Simmer for 30 minutes. Add chopped onions and when cooked, thicken the gravy with 1 tablespoon flour, dissolved in a little water. Pieces of cooked chicken may be added.

Place the mixture in a baking dish. Scatter raisins, olives and pieces of sliced hard-boiled eggs over it. Cover with the following mixture: Cook the corn with the butter and milk, stirring constantly. Add a little sweet basil, salt and sugar to taste, then add the egg yolks and the whites, beaten stiff. Pour over meat. Sprinkle sugar and brown in oven.

Mrs. Marina Sanchez
Florence

American Style Pot Roast

¼ cup corn oil
1 (4-pound) chuck roast
1 cup chopped onion
1 cup sliced celery
2 cloves garlic, minced
3 cups beef broth

¼ cup catsup
½ teaspoon dried thyme leaves
1 teaspoon salt
¼ teaspoon black pepper
¼ cup corn starch
¼ cup water

In Dutch oven or large kettle heat corn oil over medium heat. Add meat. Brown on all sides. Add onion, celery, garlic, broth, catsup, thyme, salt and pepper. Cover; bring to boil. Reduce heat and simmer two and one-half hours or until meat is tender. Remove meat to platter. Stir cornstarch and water until smooth. Add to liquid in Dutch oven. Bring to boil over medium heat, stirring constantly, and boil one minute. Serve gravy with pot roast. If desired, arrange boiled potatoes, carrots and green beans around roast. Makes six to eight servings.

Note: Vegetables may be cooked with roast in Dutch oven. After roast has simmered two hours, add six medium potatoes peeled and quartered, and four carrots, peeled and cut into two-inch pieces. Cover and simmer one-half hour. Add one-half pound whole green beans and simmer an additional 10 minutes or until vegetables are tender.

Mrs. Pearl Moore
Calhoun, Kentucky

Barbecued Chuck Roast

1 (3 to 4 pound) roast
4 cloves garlic, minced
¼ cup olive oil
1 teaspoon rosemary
½ teaspoon dry mustard
2 teaspoons soy sauce

⅓ cup wine vinegar
¼ cup sherry (optional)
2 tablespoons catsup
½ teaspoon Worcestershire sauce
1½ teaspoons steak sauce

Select U.S. Choice chuck roast, 2½ to 3 inches thick. Sauté garlic in olive oil; add rosemary, mustard and soy sauce. Remove from heat and add vinegar and sherry, if desired. Place roast in a bowl and cover with marinade. Cover and place in refirgerator for 24 hours, turning meat occasionally in marinade.

Remove meat from marinade. Add catsup, Worcestershire sauce, and steak sauce to marinade. Place meat on grill, 3 to 5 inches from coals which have burned to a gray ash. Brush marinade over roast as it cooks; cooking time is about 40 minutes, with roast rare in center and browned on the outside. Yield; 6 servings.

Jack McWilliams
Cherokee

Hamburger Harvest

1½ pounds hamburger meat
1 can tomatoes
1 large onion, sliced thin
2 potatoes, peeled and thinly
   sliced

1 can of corn
1 can of butter beans
1 green sweet pepper
½ cup flour
Grated cheese

Mix together hamburger meat, tomatoes and onion. Place in a casserole dish. Layer in order the potatoes, corn, butter beans and sweet pepper. Sprinkle flour over each layer. Sprinkle grated cheese on top and cook for 1 hour in a 350-degree oven.

Emma Bendall
Leighton

Cheeseburger Casserole

1 pound ground beef
¼ cup chopped onion
¾ teaspoon salt
⅛ teaspoon pepper
¼ cup catsup

1 can (8 ounces) tomato
   sauce
8 ounces cheese
1 can biscuits

Combine beef and onion in a skillet; cook until beef is lightly browned. Drain and add salt and pepper. Stir in catsup and tomato sauce, heat thoroughly. Turn into an 8-inch square pan. Cut cheese into thin strips and spread over beef mixture. Top with biscuits. Bake at 425 degrees for 20 to 25 minutes or until biscuits are golden brown.

Anita Pilkilton
Tuscumbia

Ground Beef Casserole

1 pound ground beef
½ cup celery
½ cup onion
½ cup sweet pepper
1 can cream of mushroom soup
1 can cream of celery soup or
   chicken noodle soup

1 cup grated cheese
1 tablespoon Worcestershire
   sauce
½ cup water
¾ cup rice
Salt and pepper to taste

Cook meat, pepper, onion and celery until nearly done. Mix other ingredients with meat and pour into tightly-covered casserole dish with buttered bread crumbs on top. Bake 1½ hours at 300 degrees.

James Coburn
Florence

Indoor-Outdoor Browned Sirloin Tip Roast

Sirloin tip roast
Salt and pepper to taste

Meat tenderizer
½ cup Dale's Steak Sauce

Place roast in iron skillet on top of the stove over extremely low heat. Sprinkle with salt and pepper and a little meat tenderizer; add steak sauce. Cover very loosely and cook two to three hours. (This is a combination simmer and marinade—mixture should not boil) Place skillet, uncovered, on grill and cook another 45 minutes to one hour, basting frequently with gravy.

Bob Morrow
Florence

Yams 'N Sprouts Pot Roast Dinner

4 to 4½ pounds (bottom round)
  pot roast
2 tablespoons salad oil
1 can (15 ounces) tomato sauce
1 can (10½ ounces) beef broth
1 cup red Burgundy wine
  (or water)
½ teaspoon thyme leaves,
  crushed
1 teaspoon onion salt
1 teaspoon salt
¼ teaspoon pepper

½ cup water
¼ cup flour
6 medium yams, cooked,
  peeled and quartered
  or 3 cans (16 ounces
  each) yams, drained
  and quartered
1 pound small white onions,
  peeled
3 packages (10 ounces each)
  frozen Brussels sprouts

Brown pot roast on all sides in hot oil in large pot; remove meat and drain off fat. Mix tomato sauce, beef broth, wine and seasonings in pot; add meat and simmer covered about 2½ hours or until meat is tender.

Boil cooking liquid in pot until about 3 cups remain; skim off fat. To thicken liquid: gradually blend ½ cup water into flour; stir into cooking liquid. Bring to a boil, stirring constantly; simmer 1 minute. Add meat, Brussels sprouts and onions. Return to boil; cover and simmer 15 minutes. Add yams and cook just until heated through. Remove meat and vegetables to serving platter and serve with gravy. Makes 6 to 8 servings.

Pearl Moore
Calhoun, Kentucky

Swiss Steak

2 pounds round steak
½ cup flour
2 teaspoons salt
½ teaspoon pepper

3 tablespoons shortening
1 chopped onion
1 can tomatoes

Mix flour, salt and pepper thoroughly, beat into steak. Brown meat in hot shortening. Add onions and tomatoes. Cover, let cook over low heat or in oven at 350 degrees for 1½ hrs.

Evelyn Pless
Cherokee

Slow-Cooker Swiss Steak

2 pound round steak, tenderized
Salt and pepper to taste
1 large onion, thinly sliced
1 medium green pepper,
cut in narrow strips
1 1-pound can tomatoes

Cut round steak into serving pieces; season with salt and pepper. Flour both sides of meat and brown in small amount of hot oil. Drain off excess oil and place meat in slow cooker. Top with onion, green pepper and tomatoes. Cover and set to High for one hour, then turn to Low for 8-10 hours.

Billy Townsend
Florence

Cabbage And Beef Rollups

1 pound ground beef
1½ cups corn flake crumbs
⅓ cup chopped onion
1 teaspoon Worcestershire sauce
1 teaspoon salt
¼ teaspoon pepper
1 teaspoon paprika
1 can (8 ounces) tomato
sauce, divided
8 cabbage leaves
¼ cup water

Mix together ground beef, corn flake crumbs, onion, Worcestershire sauce, salt, pepper, paprika and ½ cup tomato sauce.

Blanch cabbage leaves in boiling water for four minutes; drain. Place equal portions of meat mixture in center of each cabbage leaf; fold ends over, roll up and fasten with a toothpick. Combine ½ cup tomato sauce and ½ cup water. Pour over cabbage rolls. Simmer covered for 30 minutes.

Mrs. J.H. Mitchell
Florence

Meat-N-Potato Loaf

2 pounds ground beef
¾ cup instant mashed potato
flakes
½ cup finely chopped onion
⅛ teaspoon pepper
2½ teaspoons salt
1 teaspoon leaf basil
1 teaspoon dry mustard
1 tall can (13 ounce) evaporated
milk (1⅔ cups)
1 can (8 ounce) tomato sauce

In large mixing bowl, blend beef, instant potatoes, onion, seasoning and evaporated milk lightly but thoroughly. Press lightly into large loaf pan..

Bake in pre-heated moderate oven (350 degrees) one hour and 15 minutes. Remove from oven. Spoon tomato sauce over top. Return to oven and bake 5 to 10 minutes longer. Cool five minutes in pan before slicing and serving. Garnish top with onion rings if desired. Makes 8 servings.

Mrs. Walter Shaff
Florence

Stuffed Peppers

6 green peppers
1 egg
1½ teaspoon salt
⅛ teaspoon pepper
3 tablespoons minced onions

1 cup drained canned tomatoes
½ cup soft bread crumbs
1 pound ground beef
2 teaspoons aromatic bitters

Wash and dry peppers. Cut small slice from each side of pepper, removing seeds and membranes. Leave stem end intact. Beat egg slightly; add salt, pepper, onion, tomatoes, and bread crumbs. Let stand a few minutes till bread crumbs are soft. Add ground beef and bitters and mix well. Fill green peppers with meat mixture. Arrange in greased baking dish, stuffed side up. Sprinkle open tops with dry bread crumbs and dot with butter. Bake in moderate oven (375 degrees) for fifty minutes. Yield 6 servings.

Mrs. Malcolm R. Turberville
Cherokee

Stuffed Green Peppers

4 green peppers cut in halves
¾ pound ground beef
½ cup cooked rice
1 teaspoon salt
Dash pepper

1 egg
¼ cup onions, chopped
1 10½-ounce tomato soup
¾ cup water

Remove seeds and wash peppers. Par boil 3 minutes. Stuff peppers lightly. Add tomato soup and water. Cook for 35 minutes at 400 degrees.

Mrs. Bernice Bump
Sheffield

Meat Mixture

2 to 4 tablespoons instant minced
    onion
½ cup molasses
¼ cup catsup

1 to 2 pounds ground beef
2 cans (1 pound each) pork
    and beans

In large skillet, brown beef. Drain. Add beans, onion, molasses and catsup. Mix well. Bring to a boil. Set aside and keep warm.

Mrs. J.P. Poe
Florence

Dublin Short Ribs

3 to 4 pounds beef short ribs
1 quart water
2 teaspoons salt
¼ teaspoon pepper
2 parsley sprigs

Leaves from 2 celery stalks
1 pound small white onions,
    peeled
1 pound young carrots, pared
    and halved

Place short ribs in heavy stew pot. Add water, salt, pepper, parsley and celery. Cover and simmer until almost tender, about 1½ hours. Add onions and carrots; simmer until desired doneness, about 20 minutes. Season to taste with salt and pepper. Serve with Creamy Horseradish Sauce.

Skillet Macaroni & Beef

2 tablespoons vegetable oil
¼ cup chopped onion
¼ chopped bell pepper
1 pound ground beef
2 cups cooked elbow
  macaroni

1 teaspoon prepared mustard
1 can (10 ounces) condensed
  tomato soup
½ cup sour cream

Heat oil in a large skillet over moderate high heat. Add onions and pepper, cook until light brown, stir in ground beef and brown meat lightly, stirring frequently. Drain off fat. Stir in macaroni, mustard, tomato soup and sour cream. Blend well. Add salt to taste. Heat mixture to a serving temperature.

Sharon Isom
Tuscumbia

Meat 'N Macaroni Supper

2 medium onions, chopped (½ cup)
2 tablespoons butter or margarine,
  melted
1 can condensed cream of celery
  soup
1 8-ounce can tomatoes, chopped
  (1 cup)
¼ teaspoon thyme

Dash pepper
1 cup elbow macaroni, cooked
  and drained
1 12-ounce can luncheon meat,
  cut in 1x½ inch strips
¼ cup chopped green pepper
¼ cup shredded process cheese

In medium skillet, cook onion in butter until tender, but not brown. Stir in the soup, tomatoes, thyme, and pepper. Add the cooked macaroni, luncheon meat, and green pepper. Spoon into 1½ quart casserole. Top with cheese. Bake, uncovered in moderate oven (350 degrees) for 35-40 minutes or until heated through. Yield 4-6 servings.

Mrs. Gene Mance
Muscle Shoals

Beef Oriental

3 onions, finely chopped
1 cup celery
3 tablespoons butter
½ cup regular rice, uncooked,
1 pound ground beef
1 can cream of chicken soup

1 can mushroom soup
1 cup water
½ cup soy sauce
¼ teaspoon pepper
1 can bean sprouts
1 can Chinese noodles

Brown onions and celery in butter. Brown rice and round beef. Put aside. In buttered 2 quart casserole, combine soups, water, soy sauce, and pepper (salt to taste). Add browned onions, celery, ground beef, and rice. Stir in bean sprouts lightly. Bake, covered, in moderate oven (350) or 30 minutes. Uncover and bake 30 minutes longer. Serve with warm noodles.

Mrs. Malcolm R. Turberville
Cherokee

Roast Beef Casserole

2 cups left-over roast beef (cut
    into bite size pieces)
½ cup chopped onion
½ cup chopped celery
½ cup chopped green pepper
2 tablespoons butter

2 tablespoons soy sauce
2 cans cream of chicken soup,
    undiluted
1 can water
⅛ teaspoon Tabasco sauce

Preheat oven to 325 degrees. In skillet, cook onion, pepper and celery in butter until limp (about 10 minutes). Do not brown. Remove vegetables from skillet, then cook beef until brown. Mix all ingredients. Pour in 2 quart casserole. Cover and bake 30 minutes. Remove cover and bake 10 minutes longer. Serve over rice, or sprinkle top with chow mein noodles for last 10 minutes of baking time. This casserole freezes well. Yield: 6 to 8 servings.

Mrs. John E. Higginbotham
Florence

Meatball Casserole

Combine:
1 pound ground beef
¼ pound pork sausage
½ cup dry bread crumbs

⅓ cup evaporated milk
2 tablespoons chopped onions
1 teaspoon chili powder
⅛ teaspoon pepper

Mix well. Mix in balls, brown lightly. Combine one can cream of mushroom soup, one can celery soup, one cup evaporated milk, and half cup water. Heat until steaming. Pour over meatballs. Top with biscuits. Sift 1⅓ cups flour, 3 teaspoons baking powder, ½ teaspoon chili powder, and ¼ teaspoon salt. Cut in ⅓ cup shorting until particles are fine. Combine 1 unbeaten egg with ⅓ cup evaporated milk. Add to ingredients stirring until dough clings together. Knead on floured board. Roll out to 12 inch square, sprinkle with 1½ cups cheese, 1 tablespoon dried parsley. Roll up like jelly roll and cut into 16 slices. Place on top of meatballs and bake until biscuits are done.

Mrs. Virgie Greer
Killen

Papa's Sicilian Supper

1 pound ground beef
½ cup chopped onion
1 (6-ounce) can of tomato
    paste
¾ cup water
½ cup parmesan cheese
½ cup chopped green pepper

2 cups egg noodles, cooked
1½ teaspoons salt
¼ teaspoon pepper
¾ cup milk
1 (8-ounce) package cream
    cheese, cubed
½ teaspoon garlic salt

Borwn meat, add onion, cook until tender. Add tomato paste, water, salt and pepper. Simmer 5 minutes. In same pan heat milk and cream cheese, blend well, stir in ¼ cup parmesan cheese, garlic salt, green pepper. In casserole dish alternate layers of noodles and meatsauce. Bake at 375 degrees for 20 minutes. Sprinkle on remaining cheese and serve. Makes 6 servings.

Jane's Beef Goulash

2 pounds lean beef for stew,
  cubed
4 tablespoons cooking oil
1 cup sliced celery
2 (8-ounce) cans tomato
  sauce
4 tablespoons chopped parsley

½ cup water
1½ teaspoon paprika
1 teaspoon salt
1 package (8-ounce) noodles
  (cooked)
2 teaspoons sugar

Brown meat in oil. Add celery, onion; cook until tender. Blend next six ingredients; pour over meat. Cover. Simmer 2 hours. Serve goulash over hot cooked noodles tossed with parsley. Makes 6 servings.

From Las Cruces, New Mexico

Roast Beef Casserole

1½ cups leftover roast beef,
  cut up
1 small onion, finely chopped
1 small green pepper, finely
  chopped

1 cup cooked rice
1 can (No. 303) tomatoes
1 teaspoon salt
¼ teaspoon black pepper
2 tablespoons butter

Combine all ingredients except butter in a greased casserole dish. Dot with butter. Cook at 300 degrees for 45 minutes. Yields 6 servings.

Mrs. Joan Pugh
Florence

Grill-Top Garden Pot-Roast

3 to 4-pound beef blade
  roast or 7-bone pot-roast
1 package (0.6 ounce) Italian
salad dressing mix
¼ cup flour
1 teaspoon salt

½ teaspoon paprika
⅛ teaspoon pepper
2 cups thinly sliced carrots
2 cups sliced zucchini, cut
  ¾ inch thick
½ teaspoon salt

Combine salad dressing mix, flour, 1 teaspoon salt, paprika and pepper; thoroughly dredge meat on both sides. Place meat in center of a double thick rectangle of heavy duty aluminum foil (twice the circumference and 8 inches longer than roast.) Sprinkle any remaining flour mixture over meat. Bring 2 opposite edges of foil together over top of meat. Fold edges over 3 or 4 times, pressing crease in tightly each time. (Allow some air space.) Flatten foil at one end, crease to form triangle and fold edge over several times toward package, pressing tightly to seal. Repeat procedure on other end. Place on grill and cook at low to moderate temperature 1½ hours, turning after 1 hour. Remove foil packet from grill; open carefully and add carrots and zucchini. Sprinkle ½ teaspoon salt on vegetables. Close foil, sealing securely. Place on grill (vegetable side up) and continue cooking 30 minutes or until meat and vegetables are done.

117

Beefy Corn Pie

1 pound lean ground beef
¼ cup fine dry bread crumbs
¼ cup ketchup
2 tablespoons minced onion
1 teaspoon chili powder
1 teaspoon salt
½ teaspoon pepper
1 egg
½ cup milk

1 8½-ounce can golden cream
  style corn
1 7-ounce can vacuum packed golden
  whole kernel corn,
  drained
1 2½-ounce jar sliced mushrooms,
  drained
⅓ cup chopped green pepper
¾ cup shredded cheddar cheese

Combine ground beef, bread crumbs, ketchup, onion, chili powder, salt and pepper. Pat the meat mixture evenly over the bottom and sides of a seven by eleven or nine by nine-inch baking pan. Combine eggs, milk, corn, mushrooms and green pepper; pour over hamburger. Bake in a preheated 375 degree oven for 35 minutes. Sprinkle cheese over the top and bake an additional five minutes. Serves four to six.

Mom's Italiano Meat Pie

1 pound lean ground beef
⅓ cup green pepper,
  chopped
¾ cup water
6 ounce can tomato paste
1½ ounce package spaghetti
  sauce mix

1 package deep dish
  pie crust shell
⅓ cup parmesan cheese, grated
1½ cups Mozzarella cheese,
  grated

Preheat oven to 400 degrees. Brown beef in skillet. Drain. Add green pepper and cook 2 minutes. Stir in water, tomato paste and spaghetti sauce mix. Cover and simmer 10 minutes. Sprinkle half of the parmesan cheese over bottom of frozen pie shell. Spread half meat mixture in pie shell. Sprinkle 1 cup of the Mozzarella cheese over meat. Layer remaining meat and Parmesan cheese. Bake on cookie sheet 15 minutes. Sprinkle top with remaining Mozzarella cheese. Return to oven until cheese melts. Serves 6.

Elizabeth Medaris
Vicenzia, Italy

Betty's Burritos

Filling:
Left over roast
1 small onion
1 small can hot sauce

1 small can tomato sauce
½ cup water
½ teaspoon salt
Tortillas (flour)

Chop meat and onion into small pieces, add hot sauce, tomato sauce and salt, and water. Simmer until juice is almost gone. Heat tortilla, put 2 tablespoons of ingredients into tortilla and roll. Makes 1½ dozen. Chopped ham, or pork roast, or cheese could also be used.

Las Cruces, New Mexico

Beef Fondue
(6 to 8)

1⅜ pounds of beef tenderloin   Salad oil
cut in cubes

Pour salad oil into fondue pot to depth of about 2 inches. Heat to 425 degrees, just below smoking point. Have beef cubes at room temperature in serving bowls. Set out small bowls or individual cups of sauces. Each guest spears a beef cube with a fork or skewer and holds it in hot oil until meat is done, about 1 to 2 minutes. He then dips meat in sauce and with another fork removes the meat from skewer and eats it.

Accompanying sauces such as
Sweet and Sour Sauce,
Barbecue Sauce, Blue
Cheese Sauce, Mustard
Sauce; Horseradish
Sauce.

Sweet And Sour Sauce

½ cup butter or margarine   ¼ cup prepared mustard

Whip butter until light and creamy. Blend in mustard.

Blue Cheese Sauce

½ cup butter or margarine   4 ounces Blue Cheese, room
         temparature

Whip butter until light and creamy. Whip in Blue Cheese until completely blended.

Mustard Sauce

2 tablespoons soy sauce   ¼ teaspoon dry mustard
½ cup brown sugar   ¼ teaspoon ground ginger
¼ cup vinegar   ¼ teaspoon salt
½ cup apricot nectar   Few drops Tabasco sauce
1 tablespoon catsup

Combine all ingredients in saucepan and bring to a boil to dissolve sugar. Serve hot or cold.

Horseradish Sauce

½ cup dairy sour cream   ¼ teaspoon salt
1 tablespoon horseradish   Dash paprika

Blend sour cream, horseradish and salt. Use paprika as garnish.

Chili

2 pounds ground chuck
1 bell pepper
2 medium onions
2 or 3 cloves of garlic,
   chopped
1 pound dried kidney beans, cooked
1 can of tomatoes
1 can tomato soup
3 tablespoons chili powder

Brown ground chuck and season with salt, pepper, and Worcestershire sauce to taste. Brown the bell pepper, onions, and garlic in oil and add to ground chuck.

Add the above mixture to the kidney beans, then add tomatoes, tomato soup, and chili powder. Add water if needed. Let simmer one hour.

Mrs. Howard F. Watson
Tuscumbia

Chili Con Carne With Tomatoes

1 pound ground beef
2 medium onions, chopped
1 medium bell pepper,
   chopped
1 can stewed tomatoes
1 can tomato paste
3 teaspoons chili iowder
1½ teaspoon salt
⅛ teaspoon cayenne pepper
   (double if you like
   it hot)
⅛ teaspoon paprika
1 can kidney beans
2 cups water

Cook and stir ground beef, onion and bell pepper in a large skillet until meat is browned and onion is tender. Drain off fat. In a stew pot add remaining ingredients along with meat mixture, omitting beans.

Heat to boiling. Reduce heat; cover and simmer two hours, stirring occasionally. (Or cook uncovered about 45 minutes.) Stir in beans; heat. Makes five or six servings.

Mrs. Danny W. DeLano
Russellville

Ed's Red

5 or 6 pounds good hamburger
1 large can mixed vegetable
   juices
3 or 4 cans chili-style red
   beans
2 or 3 kinds of chili powder
Seasoning salt
Garlic powder (not salt)
Crushed chili peppers
Black pepper

Put meat (without browning) and vegetable juices into a large pot and simmer (do not boil) for several hours. Pour off the grease and add beans. This is the "base," from here the recipe depends upon the preferences of the chef.

Add mixture of chili powders, seasoning salt and garlic powder, crushed chili peppers and black pepper to taste.

This mixture is "green." Put into freezer containers and store in deep freeze for at least one month.

Ed Newman
Florence

Chili

3 pounds ground beef
3 medium to large onions, diced
1 green pepper, diced
2 12-ounce cans tomato sauce or 2 quarts home-canned tomatoes, or 4 1-pound cans tomatoes

6-8 teaspoons chili powder (according to taste)
2 cloves garlic, minced
3 tablespoons sugar
3 teaspoons salt
3-4 1-pound cans of chili beans

Cook onions and green pepper in melted butter. Add meat, brown. Add other ingredients and simmer slowly 3 to 4 hours.

Billy Townsend
Florence

Betty's Chili

1 pound ground beef
1 pound lean beef small cubes
3 garlic cloves
1½ tablespoons paprika
3 tablespoons chili powder
1 tablespoon salt

6 cups water
2 cans pinto beans or kidney beans, drained
3 tablespoons cornmeal
3 tablespoons flour

Boil lean in 3 cups water until tender. Cut into small pieces. Brown ground beef. Add all other seasonings. Cook covered for 4 hours slowly. Stir ocassionally. Add 3 more cups water; cook 1 more hour. Add beans. Thicken with cornmeal and flour.

Mrs. Robert Burdine
Florence

Quick Homemade Chili

1 pound lean ground beef
½ cup chopped onion
½ cup clove garlic, minced
½ medium green pepper, chopped
1 can (15 ounces) kidney beans, undrained

2 cans (8 ounces each) tomato sauce
1 teaspoon salt
1 to 2 teaspoons chili powder

Lightly brown beef in skillet, add onion and garlic and cook until tender. Add remaining ingredients. Simmer, stirring occasionally for 45 minutes.

Mrs. Troy Trousdale
Sheffield

Chili Con Carne

2 cups cooked pinto beans
1 cup beef, coarsely chopped
1 medium onion
1½ cups water

1 pint canned tomatoes
1 teaspoon chili powder
1 teaspoon salt

Drain beans. Add meat, chopped onion, tomatoes, chili powder and salt. Cook slowly for one hour until meat is done (ground beef can be used). Add water if needed during cooking to keep it a thick, rich soup consistency.

Evelyn Pless
Cherokee

Oriental Beef

2 onions, sliced lengthwise
2 cups sliced celery, cut in
  1-inch pieces
3 tablespoons margarine
½ cup raw rice
1 pound hamburger
1 can cream of chicken soup
1 can cream of mushroom soup
1½ cups water
¼ cup soy sauce
¼ teaspoon pepper
1 can bean sprouts
Chinese noodles

Brown onions and celery in margarine; set aside. In same pan, brown rice and hamburger; set aside. Combine in large greased casserole the soups, water, soy sauce and pepper. Add onion and meat mixture. Stir in bean sprouts lightly. Bake, covered, at 350 degrees for 30 minutes. Uncover and bake 30 minutes longer. Serve with warm noodles. Yield: 6 servings.

Mrs. Joan Pugh
Florence

No-Peep Stew

2 pounds of stew meat
6 carrots
6 potatoes
4 onions
1 cup of chopped celery
1 quart of tomatoes
1½ teaspoons of salt
¼ teaspoon of pepper
1 tablespoon of sugar
3 tablespoons of tapioca
1 slice of bread (broken)

Mix together well and put in covered pan. Bake at 250 degrees for five hours. You never have to look at it.

Enchilada Pepper Pot

2 pounds ground beef
1 medium onion, chopped
2 teaspoons salt
2 cans (16 ounces each) kidney
  beans
2 ounces Cheddar cheese,
  shredded
1 clove garlic, minced
1 can (16 ounces each)
  tomatoes
1 can (15 ounces each)
  tomato sauce
1 can (4 ounces) green chilies
1 package (10 ounces) corn tortillas

Brown ground beef and onion in Dutch oven or large pot on grill. Pour off drippings; season meat with salt. Drain beans; reserve liquid. Heat beans in ½ cup reserved liquid and mash with a slotted spoon or fork. Stir cheese and garlic into beans to combine thoroughly. Add remaining bean liquid, tomatoes, tomato sauce and green chilies to meat; cover tightly and cook 30 minutes. Dip tortillas, two or three at a time, into hot meat mixture to soften. Remove tortillas, one at a time, to waxed paper. Place approximately 3 tablespoons bean mixture down enter of each and fold two edges of tortilla up to overlap on top, enclosing bean mixture. Cut square of heavy duty aluminum foil 2 inches longer than diameter of pan, pierce several times with fork and place over meat mixture. Place filled tortillas on foil, cover tightly and cook at low temperature 15 to 20 minutes. To serve, remove tortillas and foil and serve tortillas with ground beef mixture. Serves 6 to 8.

Pan Barbecued Steak

2 pounds round steak,
  1½ inches thick
½ teaspoon salt
½ teaspoon black pepper
3 tablespoons shortening
⅓ cup minced celery
⅓ cup minced onion

½ clove garlic, grated
2 tablespoons brown sugar
2 teaspoons prepared
  mustard
2 tablespoons lemon juice
Dash Tabasco sauce
1 can tomato soup

Sprinkle steak with salt and pepper, pound thoroughly. Melt shortening in a heavy saucepan or skillet. Brown onion, celery, and garlic in hot fat; add remaining ingredients and cover. Cook in a moderate (350) degree oven for 1½ hours or until tender. Double all the sauce ingredients for additional barbecue sauce to serve over fluffy rice or mashed potatoes.

Mrs. Harlon McMurtrey
Killen

Sweet Sour Beef Balls With Pineapple And Peppers

Meatballs:
1 pound ground beef
1 egg
1 tablespoon cornstarch
1 teaspoon salt
2 tablespoons onion,
  chopped
Few grains of black pepper
Sauce:
1 tablespoon oil
1 cup pineapple juice
3 tablespoons cornstarch

1 tablespoon soy sauce
3 tablespoons vinegar
6 tablespoons water
½ cup sugar
Condiments:
3 large bell peppers, each
  cut into 12 to 15
  lengthwise strips
4 slices fresh or canned
  pineapple
Handful of cherry tomatoes
  (for color)

Mix meatball ingredients and form into 18 or more balls. Brown them in a small amount of oil, drain. Now for the sauce. Cook oil and pineapple juice over low heat for a few minutes. Add rest of sauce ingredients. Cook until juice thickens, stirring constantly. Add meatballs and condiments. Heat thoroughly. Serve over hot rice.

Las Cruces, New Mexico

Ground Beef Casserole

1 pound ground beef
1 medium onion
½ cup brown sugar
1 cup catsup

1 tablespoon Worcestershire
  sauce
1 large can pork and beans
  (31 ounce)

Brown ground beef with onion. Mix all ingredients well. Pour in casserole and bake 30 to 45 minutes on 350 degrees. (You may put bacon on top if desired.)

Mrs. James H. Cross

Lynda's 7-Layer Casserole

1 cup canned whole kernel corn, drained

1 cup uncooked rice

Sprinkle with salt and pepper. Pour one small can tomato sauce and ½ cup water over ingredients.

½ cup finely chopped onion

¾ pound ground beef

½ cup finely chopped green pepper

Sprinkle with salt and pepper. Pour second can of tomato sauce and ¼ cup of water over ingredients. Cover meat with 4 strips bacon cut in half.

Cover and bake at 350 degrees for an hour. Uncover and bake 30 more minutes, until bacon is crisp. Yields 4-6 servings.

Las Cruces, New Mexico

Mock Steak In Mushroom Gravy

1½ pounds ground beef

1 cup of prepared herbed stuffing

1 can mushroom soup

1 can of water

Prepare the stuffing according to instructions on the package. Add the meat and mix well. Form into patties and brown in a small amount of oil. Drain. Add mushroom soup and water; stir until smooth. Cover and simmer until gravy becomes thick and brown, occasionally spooning gravy over the patties (Approximately 45 minutes to an hour.)

Mrs. Glenda Weir
Florence

Quick Lasagne

½ cup chopped onion

1 clove garlic, minced

2 tablespoons salad oil

1 pound ground beef

1 8-ounce can tomato sauce

1 6-ounce can tomato paste

1 cup water

1 teaspoon salt

½ teaspoon crushed oregano

¼ teaspoon black pepper

8 ounces lasagne noodles, cooked and drained

2 cups cottage cheese

½ cup shredded Parmesan cheese

8 ounces sliced Mozzarella cheese

Saute' onion and garlic in hot oil. Add meat; brown. Add tomato sauce, tomato paste, water and seasonings; cover and simmer 20-30 minutes. Place half of noodles in bottom of 13 x 9-inch baking dish. Spread half the cottage cheese and Parmesan cheese over noodles. Top with half the Mozzarella cheese slices and half of the meat sauce. Repeat layers. Bake at 350 degrees for 45 minutes. Serves 6 to 8. TO MAKE AHEAD: Assemble casserole. Refrigerate. Allow 15 minutes longer for baking.

Billy Townsend
Florence

Lasagna

2 pounds lean ground beef
Vegetable oil
2 medium onions, chopped
2 garlic cloves, crushed
1 jar (14 ounce) spaghetti sauce
1 can (1 pound) stewed tomatoes

1 can (3 ounce) mushrooms
½ pound lasagna noodles
1 package (8 ounce)
  mozzarella cheese,
  sliced thin
1 carton sour cream

Cook ground beef in a little vegtable oil in a large, deep frying pan until brown, stirring often with a fork. Drain off any excess fat. Add onions, garlic and spaghetti sauce, tomatoes and undrained mushrooms. Mix well. Simmer 20 minutes or until onions are soft. Cook lasagna according to package directions. Drain and rinse with cold water. Put ½ lasagna in a casserole. Cover with ½ the tomato-meat sauce. Top with slices of mozzarella cheese. Spread ½ sour cream over the cheese. Repeat, ending with slices of mozzarella cheese. Cover casserole. Bake at 350 degrees for 40 minutes. Remove cover; continue baking until mozzarella melts and browns slightly. This can be made 1 to 2 days ahead of serving. Serves 8.

Mrs. James Patton
Sheffield

Lasagne II

¾ package lasagne noodles,
  cooked
3 pounds ground beef or 2 pounds
  ground beef and 1
  pound sausage
3 large onions, chopped
1 large green pepper, chopped
2 stalks celery, chopped
  (if desired)
1 large can tomato paste or
  1 small can tomato paste
  and 2 small cans tomato
  sauce
1 (1 pound) can tomatoes

2 bay leaves
Seasonings to taste:
  salt, pepper, galric
  powder, Tabasco, Worcestershire
  sauce, rosemary, sweet
  basil, oregano
1¼ pounds grated cheese
1 pound cottage cheese
¾ pounds Mozzarella cheese,
  grated
Parmesan cheese
Baking pan 10 inches wide,
  2½ inches deep, and
  15½ inches long

Brown meat, onions, green pepper, and celery in Dutch oven. Drain off fat. Add tomato paste and tomatoes. Add enough water until it is the desired consistency. Add all seasonings to taste. Simmer for 3 hours. Alternate layers of sauce, noodles, and cheese in baking pan. Bake for 30 minutes in 350 degree oven. Let stand for 5 to 10 minutes before serving.

Mrs. Edward Mullen
Florence

Five Hour Stew

1 stalk celery, chopped
2 pounds stew meat (do not
  brown meat)
2 potatoes, diced
2 onions, diced
1 cup carrots, sliced

1 small can peas
1 can tomato soup
½ can water
Corn and/or butterbeans may
  be added if you prefer
Salt and pepper to taste

Combine ingredients in casserole dish. Cover and cook at 275 degrees for 5 hours.

Mrs. Dorothy H. Smith
Florence

Lay-A-Bed Stew

2 pounds stew meat (boneless
  stew beef)
1 small can English peas
1 cup diced carrots
1 large potato, diced

2 onions
1 can tomato soup
½ can of water, soup can
2 teaspoons salt
1 teaspoon pepper

Combine ingredients. Put in 2 quart casserole. Bake for 5 hours at 275 degrees, covered.

Mrs. F.E. Hooks
Florence

Linda's Meat Sauce

2 pounds lean stew meat
4 tablespoons margarine
2 stalks celery, diced
1 small onion, diced

2 jalapenos, diced
1 teaspoon garlic salt
Salt and pepper

In skillet, melt margarine and saute vegetables until soft. Add meat, seasonings; cook until meat is browned and well done. At this point, meat may be varied by adding 1 package of gravy mix and a cup of water, stirring until thickened or 1 cup of spaghetti sauce. Heat thoroughly. Serve over rice.

Barbecue Marinade

1 cup catsup
½ cup naturally brewed soy
  sauce
½ cup water

¼ cup vinegar
2 tablespoons brown sugar
1 clove garlic, crushed
1 bay leaf

Combine catsup, soy sauce, water, vinegar, brown sugar, garlic and bay leaf. Cook slowly, stirring occasionally, 5 to 10 minutes. Cool.

Helen Smith
Calhoun, Kentucky

Joyce's Freezer Meat Sauce

3 pounds ground beef
3 cloves garlic, minced
2 chopped medium green peppers
2 large sliced onions
1 cup boiling water
3 8-ounce cans tomato sauce
2 6-ounce cans tomato paste
1 tablespoon salt
½ teaspoon pepper
1 teaspoon paprika
1 teaspoon garlic salt
1 teaspoon celery salt
½ teaspoon parsley flakes
2 teaspoons oregano
2 teaspoons sugar

Brown ground beef in large kettle until brown, add water and remaining ingredients. Simmer uncovered for two hours, until thick. Cool quickly, freeze in one pint containers, makes 6 pints.

Reheat frozen sauce in double boiler.

Barbecue Sauce for Meats

½ pound butter
1 cup vinegar
2 cups tomato catsup
4 tablespoons Worcestershire sauce
1 tablespoon Tabasco sauce
1 tablespoon salt
3 tablespoons mustard
Dash red pepper
Juice of 1 lemon

Melt butter, add vinegar, then other ingredients. Bring to a boil and let simmer a few minutes. Makes 3½ to 4 cups. (Great with chicken or barbecued pork.)

Mrs. Robert E. Brown
Madisonville, Kentucky

Spaghetti Sauce with Cheese

2 pounds ground chuck
1 large onion, chopped
1 medium clove garlic, minced
1 medium green pepper, chopped
1 can (1 pound, 12 ounces) whole tomatoes, chopped and undrained
1 can (6 ounce) tomato paste
2 tablespoons Worcestershire sauce
1 can (3 ounce) sliced mushrooms, undrained
2 teaspoons chili powder
1 package (8 ounce) pasteurized process cheese spread
Cooked spaghetti

Crumble meat into skillet, add onion, garlic and green pepper. Cook over moderate heat. Drain off grease. Add tomatoes, tomato paste, Worcestershire, mushrooms, and chili powder. Mix well. Bring to boil, reduce heat and cover. Simmer about 30 minutes. Add cheese and cook 10 minutes, stirring occasionally. Serve over spaghetti.

Mrs. Earle Trent
Florence

Great Classic Recipe

It took the culinary expertise of two great countries, Austria and France, to produce a recipe—Cordon Bleu—so perfect that it received the famed blue ribbon award over 200 years ago.

Austria, so well known for its many specialties using ham and swiss cheese slices, crossed the Alps into France and sandwiched the ham and swiss between a truly French favorite, thin slices of veal. This combination, dipped into beaten egg and sautéd in butter, became the famous Cordon Bleu as we know it today. Its reputation has spread throughout Europe and the United States.

Even though Cordon Bleu is a classic recipe, it is one you need never be afraid of because of its ease in preparation. Simply cross the Alps at home and blend an authentic Alpine taste with ham and veal by using Austrian Swiss cheese slices, an imported influence easily obtainable in most supermarkets.

So, if you're looking for a special dish to serve on that special Saturday night, remember the perfect Austrian and French union, a Cordon Bleu so named by its own fame—its own blue ribbon.

Cordon Bleu

12 veal cutlets (3 to 4 ounces
  each)
Salt and pepper, to taste
3 slices from 1 package (6-ounces)
  Austrian Swiss Cheese,
  cut in half
2 tablespoons water

3 slices Austrian Swiss cheese,
  finely diced
3 slices boiled ham, cut in half
2 eggs, beaten with water
2 tablespoons butter
2 tablespoons vegetable oil

Pound veal cutlets very thin. Sprinkle with salt and pepper. Put together two cutlets like a sandwich with a half-slice of cheese and a half-slice of ham as the filling. Secure with toothpicks. Dip veal into beaten egg, then into diced cheese. Let stand ten minutes. Melt butter and oil in frying pan and sauté veal, slowly, until brown (about 20 minutes). Serve immediately with asparagus spears. Serves 6.

Roast Rack Of Lamb

To roast lamb rack, put in roasting pan and season with salt, pepper and Rosemary. Roast in preheated 375 degree oven 45 minutes, or until meat thermometer registers 145 degrees to 150 degrees for rare. Roast 10 to 15 minutes longer for well done.

Beef Brisket

4-6 pound boned beef brisket
Pinch each of heavy celery
   salt, onion salt
   and garlic salt

Salt and pepper to taste
1 small bottle Worces-
   tershire sauce
1 bottle liquid smoke

Combine ingredients and pour over beef, wrap in foil and soak in mixture overnight in refrigerator. Cook at 250 degrees for 6 hours. Drain, saving juice for later use, and return meat to oven. Add barbecue sauce, ½ bottle at a time.

Barbecue Sauce For Basting

1 pint cooking oil
1 pint vinegar
½ pound margarine
6 lemons

½ small box paprika
Red pepper to taste
Black pepper to taste

Melt margarine in saucepan, and add remaining ingredients—stirring constantly. Heat sauce almost to boiling point, stirring frequently. Let stand 15 minutes before use. Use for basting poultry, pork or beef. Sauce may be stored in tightly closed jar in refrigerator one week or in freezer indefinitely.

Anthony Haid
Muscle Shoals

Corned Beef

Corned beef brisket, unseasoned   Pepper

Place brisket in large pot, covered with water. Cook slowly over low heat three to four hours. Remove from heat and cool in same water. When completely cool, remove brisket from water, sprinkle with pepper and wrap tightly in plastic wrap or aluminum foil. Slice very thin and serve on rye or pumpernickle bread with a little mustard.

Bob Morrow
Florence

Mexican Casserole

1 pound ground beef
1 small can tomato paste
1 can white cream style corn
½ pound sharp cheddar cheese,
   grated

1 6 ounce package egg
   noodles
2 large hot onions, chopped
1 can water
2 tablespoons chili powder

Combine tomato paste, water, corn, chili powder and half the grated cheese in a large skillet. Brown meat and onions together in another skillet. Salt and pepper to taste. Pour off grease from meat and add tomato mixture to meat. Simmer. Boil noodles in salted water. Drain and add to tomato mixture. Cool 5 minutes. Top with remaining grated cheese. Bake in a moderate oven until bubbly and hot.

Mrs. Howard Kirkpatrick
Florence

Beef Patty Melt

2 pounds ground beef	12 slices (¾ to 1 ounce each)
12 slices rye bread	Swiss or Colby cheese
Butter or margarine	Salt and pepper
¾ cup Thousand Island dressing	

Spread bread with butter or margarine and place, spread side down, on hot baking sheet on grill or on grill top. Toast until golden brown on one side. Wrap to keep warm. Divide ground beef into 6 equal portions and shape into oval patties (the size of bread slices) about ½ inch thick. Place on grill and broil at moderate temperature 15 to 17 minutes, until almost desired doneness, turning occasionally. Season with salt and pepper. To assemble sandwiches, place 1 cheese slice on untoasted side of each slice of bread, spread each cheese slice with 1 tablespoon dressing, place patties on half the spread slices of bread and top with remaining slices, prepared side down. Wrap each sandwich in 12x17-inch piece of heavy duty aluminum foil, folding edges to seal. Heat packets on grill, 5 minutes on each side. Serves 6.

Patricia A. Chesnut
Greeneville, Tennessee

Johnny Mizetti

1 pound chuck or ½ beef and	1 can tomato soup
½ pork	1 small can mushrooms
2 medium onions	½ pound sharp cheese, grated
2 green peppers	1 package thin noodles
½ bunch celery	2 tablespoons soy sauce

Brown onion in fat, add meat and brown. Add chopped pepper, onion and celery. Then tomato soup, mushrooms and diced cheese. Let simmer. Cook noodles in salt water, and combine with other ingredients and salt and pepper to taste. Add the soy sauce. Bake in a greased casserole and bake 45 minutes at 350 degrees.

This recipe for Johnny Mizetti was given to me by a friend in Nashville, Tennessee, Mary Deckard. Her aunt had it in the Nashville Banner about 20 years ago. It is great served with either a tossed salad or fresh fruit salad and garlic French bread.

Mrs. James C. Mitchell
Florence

Cheddarburger Skillet

1 pound ground beef	¼ cup water
1 medium onion, chopped	2 cans (16 ounces each) whole
1 can cream of mushroom soup	potatoes, drained and
1 can cheddar cheese soup	sliced

In skillet, brown beef and cook onion until tender (use shorteing if necessary). Stir to separate meat; pour off fat. Stir in soups and water; add potatoes. Heat; stir occasionally. Garnish with tomato wedges and parsley if desired. Makes 6 (1 cup) servings.

Ouida Thompson
Sheffield

Reuben Cocktail Treat

24 slices cocktail rye
  bread
1½ packages (3 ounces
  each) thinly sliced
  corned beef

8 ounce can sauerkraut,
  drained and snipped
1½ cups mozzarella cheese
Thousand Island dressing

Arrange rye slices on baking sheet. Spread each slice with about one teaspoon Thousand Island dressing. Arrange folded beef slices on top. Spread one rounded teaspoon sauerkraut over beef. Top with cheese. Bake in preheated 400 degree oven 6-8 minutes or until cheese melts and browns lightly. Makes 24 treats.

Mrs. E.B. Anderson, Sr.
Florence

Take-Along Beef Pasties

3½ cups chopped cooked beef
1 beef bouillon cube
¼ cup boiling water
1 cup chopped cooked potatoes
1 cup chopped cooked carrots
1 large onion, chopped
¼ cup sweet pickle relish

¼ cup catsup
½ teaspoon salt
¼ teaspoon ground savory
⅛ teaspoon pepper
Pastry for two 9-inch
  double crust pies

Crush bouillon cube, stir in boiling water and reserve. Combine beef, potatoes, carrots, onion, pickle relish and catsup. Sprinkle salt, savory and pepper over meat mixture; add bouillon and mix to combine. Divide pastry in half and roll each portion into an 11x16½-inch rectangle. Cut each into six 5½-inch squares. Place ⅓ cup of meat mixture in center of each pastry square, brush edges with water, fold into a triangle, and press edges together with a fork to seal and pierce tops with tines of a fork. Place pasties on baking sheets and bake in a hot oven (425 degrees) 30 minutes or until pastry is lightly browned. Remove from pan immediately and place on wire rack. Chill before packing. Serves 6 with 2 pasties each. May also be served hot.

Sloppy Joe Grill

½ pound ground beef
½ cup barbeque sauce
¼ cup water
2 tablespoons chopped green pepper

2 tablespoons chopped onion
16 white bread slices
Single cheese slices
Soft margarine

Brown meat; drain. Add barbeque sauce, water, green pepper and onion. Simmer 15 minutes. For each sandwich, spread slice of bread with 2 tablespoons meat mixture. Top with process cheese food and second slice of bread. Spread bread with margarine. Place sandwiches on cookie sheet; broil on each side until golden brown. Makes 8 sandwiches.

South-Of-The-Border Submarines

4 pounds ground beef
2 small onions, chopped
2 packages (1½ to 1¾ ounces
   each) taco seasoning
   mix
2 teaspoons salt

1 can (15 ounces) tomato sauce
8 ounces (2 cups) shredded
   sharp Cheddar cheese
1 cup sliced stuffed green olives
2 loaves unsliced Vienna bread

Lightly brown ground beef and onion in large frying pan or Dutch oven. Pour off drippings. Sprinkle taco seasoning and salt over meat. Stir in tomato sauce, 1 cup shredded cheese and olives and cook 5 to 10 minutes, stirring occasionally. Slice loaves of bread in half lengthwise. Remove bread to form "boats," hollowing inside of loaves until sides and bottom are about ¾ inch thick. Make 2 cups crumbs from removed bread and stir into meat mixture. Lightly toast loaves on grill, cut side down. Spoon meat mixture into bread "boats," rounding top. Sprinkle remaining cup of cheese over meat. Wrap each "boat" loosely in heavy duty aluminum foil. Place on grill and heat at low to moderate temperature 20 to 25 minutes. To serve, remove submarines from foil and cut each "boat" into slices approximately 1¼ inches thick. Serves 16 to 20.

Hamburger Stuffed Bread

1 (1 pound) round loaf crusty
   white bread
1 pound ground beef
2 tablespoons oil
1 green pepper, diced
½ cup celery, diced
1 teaspoon salt

¼ teaspoon pepper
1 tablespoon Worcestershire
   sauce
1 (10¾ ounce) can cheddar
   cheese soup
2 slices cheddar cheese

Cut top off bread and reserve; hollow out remainder of loaf to form a crust shell. Tear enough bread into small pieces to make 2 cups; set aside. Brown beef in oil; mix in remaining ingredients except bread pieces and cheese slices. Simmer for 4 to 5 minutes. Stir in bread pieces and mix well. Fill crust shell with meat mixture. Cut cheese slices in half diagonally and place on top. Bake on ungreased baking sheet at 350 degrees for 5 to 8 minutes or until cheese melts. Replace top on bread; cut in wedges to serve. Yield: 6 to 8 servings.

Mrs. Claire S. Pitts
Sheffield

Sloppy Joes

2 pounds ground beef
1 cup chopped celery
1 cup green pepper
1 cup chopped onion
2 cups barbecue sauce

2 cups water
1 cup 3-minute oats
2 tablespoons flour
1 teaspoon salt

Combine beef, green pepper, celery and onion in skillet and cook until meat is browned. Add remaining ingredients and simmer for 35 minutes. Serve hot on buns.

Lela Hall
Leighton

132

Big Burgers

2 cups self-rising flour
2 cups mashed potato flakes

¾ cup butter or margarine,
  softened
¾ cup milk

Filling

1 pound ground beef
1 tablespoon catsup
1 tablespoon prepared mustard,
  if desired
11 ounce can condensed cheddar
  cheese soup

¼ cup chopped onion or 1
tablespoon instant
  minced onion
½ teaspoon salt
¼ teaspoon pepper

Topping

2 tablespoons milk
½ cup mashed potato flakes

2 tablespoons butter or margarine,
  melted

Meat and potatoes take a new shape. Preheat oven to 425 degrees. (To measure flour, lightly spoon into measuring cup; level off.) In large bowl, combine flour and flakes. Cut butter in thoroughly with a fork; stir in milk. Press half the dough into a 10-inch circle on ungreased cookie sheet. Brown ground beef; drain. Stir in next six ingredients. Spread to within ¼-inch of dough edge. On waxed paper, press or roll out remaining dough into an 11-inch circle. Place over filling and seal edge; brush with milk. Sprinkle with mixture of melted butter and potato flakes. Bake 20 to 25 minutes, until golden brown. (Refrigerate any leftovers.) 4 to 6 servings.

Beef And Cheese Dogs

2 pounds ground beef
1 cup (4 ounces) shredded
Monterey Jack cheese
1½ teaspoons salt
⅛ teaspoon pepper

1 small onion, chopped
½ cup Russian dressing
¼ cup horseradish mustard
6 hot dog buns (toasted, if
  desired)

Lightly combine ground beef, cheese, salt and pepper; divide into 6 equal portions and mold into rolls the shape of frankfurters. Place on grill and broil at moderate temperature 20 to 30 minutes, to desired doneness, turning occasionally. Combine onion, Russian dressing and horseradish mustard in small saucepan and cook on grill 10 minutes, stirring occasionally. Serve beef and cheese rolls on hot dog buns. Serve with sauce. Serves 6.

Ron Chesnut
Greenville, Tennessee

Zesty Submarine

1 loaf (1 pound) French bread
Soft butter or margarine
1 tablespoon wine vinegar
1 tablespoon olive oil
¼ teaspoon garlic salt
4 or 5 crisp lettuce leaves
½ pound sliced salami

2 tomatoes, sliced
Salt and pepper
4 ounces sliced Swiss cheese
½ pound sliced boiled ham
½ cucumber, thinly sliced
1 large onion, sliced

Cut bread horizontally in half. Spread bottom half with butter. Stir together vinegar, oil and garlic salt; dip lettuce leaves into mixture. Layer lettuce, salami and tomatoes on buttered bread; season with salt and pepper.. Layer remaining ingredients on tomatoes. Place top half of bread on filling; secure loaf with picks. Makes 6 servings.

Italian Submarine: Omit vinegar, oil ane garlic salt; spread top half of bread with 3 tablespoons prepared mustard.

Sandra Goforth
Waterloo

Glazed Gourmet Beefburgers

2½ pounds ground beef
1½ teaspoons salt
1 teaspoon dry mustard
¼ teaspoon pepper
½ cup chili sauce

¼ cup finely chopped green pepper
1 tablespoon capers, drained
¼ tablespoon grape jelly

Sprinkle salt, mustard and pepper over ground beef. Add green pepper and capers and lightly combine. Shape into 6 patties ½ inch thick. Place on grill and broil at moderate temperature 6 minutes on each side. Combine chili sauce and jelly in small saucepan and cook until jelly is melted, 3 to 5 minutes. Brush sauce on patties and continue cooking to desired doneness, turning and brushing with sauce occasionally. Serves 6.

Stuffed Superburgers

2 pounds ground beef
1 package (3 ounces) cream cheese
¼ cup dairy sour cream
½ teaspoon dill weed
2 cups toasted bread cubes
¼ cup chopped mushrooms

¼ cup chopped pitted ripe olives
1 tablespoon instant minced onion
⅓ cup water
2 teaspoons salt
¼ teaspoon pepper

Cream together cream cheese, sour cream and dill weed. Stir in toasted bread cubes, mushrooms and olives. Stir instant minced onion into water and let stand 5 minutes. Sprinkle salt and pepper over ground beef, add onion and water and lightly combine. Shape into 12 thin patties 4 to 5 inches in diameter. Place an equal amount of cheese stuffing in center of each of 6 patties: top with remaining patties, pressing edges together securely to seal. Place burgers on grill 3 to 4 inches from heat and broil at moderate temperature 8 to 12 minutes on each side, or until done. Serves 6.

Quick Pizza

2½ pounds lean hamburger
meat
1 pound ground pork (Boston
Butt)
½ teaspoon ground oregano
¼ teaspoon garlic powder
8 ounces tomato paste

2 cups tomatoes (Pureed in
blender)
6 large buns
12 tablespoons catsup
1 pound Cheddar Cheese (grated
fine)

Cook meat over high heat, stirring constantly until done. Drain off excess fat. Return to heat, add tomato paste, tomatoes, oregano, garlic powder, and salt to taste. Simmer 20 minutes. Open buns, roll flat with dough roller. Spread meat mixture on open buns. (Approximately ½ cup per bun): Add 1 tablespoon catsup and sprinkle with cheese. Bake in 375 degree oven 15 minutes before serving. These may be frozen on tray, then wrapped individually for future use.

Mrs. E.F. Stansell
Florence

Crazy Crust Pizza
Batter

1 cup self-rising flour
1 teaspoon Italian seasoning
or leaf oregano

⅛ teaspoon pepper
2 eggs
⅔ cup milk

Topping

¼ cup onion
1½ pounds ground beef, or
sausage or 1 cup thinly
sliced Pepperoni sausage
1 can (4 ounces) mushrooms
1 cup (4 ounces) Mozzarella
cheese, shredded

1 can (8 ounces) tomato sauce
or pizza sauce or add
1 to 2 teaspoons leaf
oregano and ¼ teaspoon
pepper to tomato
sauce

Brown ground beef or sausage (there is no need to brown pepperoni) and drain well. Set aside. Lightly grease and dust with flour or cornmeal a 14 or 12-inch pizza pan or a 15 by 10-inch jelly roll pan. Prepare batter by spooning flour into a cup and leveling off to measure. Combine flour, seasoning, pepper, eggs and milk in a bowl, mixing until smooth. Pour batter into prepared pan, tilting so batter completely covers the bottom. Arrange the topping with meat, onion and mushrooms over batter. Bake on a low rack for 25 to 30 minutes until pizza is golden brown. Remove from oven; drizzle with tomato sauce and sprinkle with cheese. Return to oven for 10 to 15 minutes.

Gladys Hickman
Florence

Homemade Pizza

Spread 1 8-ounce can of oven-ready biscuits over a greased pizza pan or baking sheet. Mix 1 8-ounce can of tomato sauce with these spices: ¼ teaspoon garlic powder, ½ teaspoon oregano, ½ teaspoon freeze-dried chives. Then spread 1 cup or 4-ounce package each of shredded Mozzarella and cheddar cheese. Cook for 8 to 10 minutes at 450 degrees. Makes 1 pizza.

Miss Vicki Sheridan
Sheffield

Herbed Leg Of Lamb

1 leg of lamb, about 6 to 7 pounds
Salt and pepper
1 clove garlic, cut into slivers
1 teaspoon crumbled rosemary
¼ cup olive oil
¼ cup red wine vinegar

The day before: Ask butcher to leave the shank bone on leg, so whoever does the carving can use bone as a handle to hold roast in proper position to slice off long thin, lengthwise pieces. Sprinkle lamb with salt and pepper. Cut small slashes in meat and stuff with slivers of garlic. Mix rosemary, oil, and vinegar in bowl, brush over lamb, then let roast stand in refrigerator overnight. On serving day: Bring lamb to room temperature. Place on rack in shallow roasting pan, and roast 325 degrees for 2 to 2½ hours or until well-done. Serves 6 to 8.

Mrs. John E. Higginbotham
Florence

Lamb Riblets With Orange Sauce

1 medium tomato, skinned and cubed
½ cup dark corn syrup
Grated rind of 2 medium or large oranges (3 to 4 tablespoons)
¼ cup orange juice
¼ cup cider vinegar
1 medium onion (peeled, sliced thin and separated into rings)
2 teaspoons prepared mustard
1 teaspoon Worcestershire sauce
1 teaspoon celery seed
½ teaspoon salt
3 pounds (about) lamb riblets (lamb breast)
1 tablespoon cornstarch
2 tablespoons cold water

In a small saucepan stir together the tomato, corn syrup, orange rind, orange juice, vinegar, onion, mustard, Worcestershire, celery seed and salt. Over medium heat bring to a boil; reduce heat and simmer 10 minutes.

Meanwhile cut riblets into 1-rib pieces; if ribs are long, cut in half crosswise with a cleaver. Place riblets in a 4 or 5-quart Dutch oven or similar heavy casserole. Pour orange mixture over them. Cover tightly and bake in a preheated 350-degree oven until riblets are tender—1 to 1¼ hours.

Transfer riblets to a broiler rack set over broiler pan or to rack over shallow roasting pan. Broil 6 inches from heat source, turning and basting several times with liquid in Dutch oven, until browned—5 to 6 minutes.

Skim as much fat as you can from liquid in Dutch oven—there should be about 2 cups including a small amount of fat. Mix cornstarch and water until smooth and add to liquid. Bring to a boil, stirring constantly, and boil 1 minute. Serve ribs and sauce with hot cooked rice. Makes 4 servings.

Martha Reed

Leg Of Lamb (Greek Style)

2 cloves garlic, crushed
¼ cup lemon juice
¼ teaspoon coarse ground
  black pepper
¼ teaspoon ground or crushed
  anise seed

½ pint (1 cup) plain yogurt
1 leg of lamb (6-7 pounds)
  boned, trimmed and
  butterflied

Combine all marinade ingredients in large, shallow, glass baking pan. Dip lamb in marinade, coating both sides. Allow to marinate, covered, in refrigerator several hours or overnight. Preheat oven to 500 degrees. Place lamb in shallow baking pan. Roast for 30 minutes. Baste with marinade. Turn and roast 15 minutes longer. Outer thin parts of lamb will be well done. Thick portions will be slightly pink. Slice thinly on the diagonal. Makes 8 servings.

Roast Lamb With Peaches And Chutney Glaze

1 can (1 pound) sliced cling
  peaches

⅓ cup chutney
Frenched lamb rack

Drain peaches, reserving half the syrup. Mix syrup with the chutney. Put lamb in roasting pan and baste with chutney mixture. Roast in preheated 375 degree oven, basting frequently with glaze, 45 minutes, or until meat thermometer registers 145 degrees to 150 degrees for rare. Roast 10 to 15 minutes longer for well done. When roasted to desired doneness, arrange peaches around meat, baste with glaze and put back in oven a few minutes to heat. Makes 4 servings.

Zucchini With Lamb Stuffing

Pick out zucchini 6 to 8 inches long for this main dish; plan on two halves for each serving.

4 zucchini (6 to 8 inches long)
1 pound ground lamb
2 tablespoons fine dry bread
  crumbs
1 tablespoon catsup
½ teaspoon meat seasoning sauce
  or Worcestershire

¼ teaspoon garlic salt
⅛ teaspoon pepper
½ teaspoon salt
1 egg
3 tablespoons freshly grated
  Parmesan cheese

Cut off ends of zucchini and scrub well. Drop into boiling water and cook until slightly tender, about 5 minutes. Remove from heat and plunge into cold water; drain.

When cool enough to handle, cut lengthwise and scoop out pulp with a spoon, leaving shell at least ¼-inch thick. Mash or finely chop zucchini pulp and add lamb, crumbs, catsup, meat seasoning sauce, garlic salt, pepper, salt, and the egg. Mix lightly; heap meat mixture in zucchini shells, arranged in a shallow baking dish. Sprinkle with Parmesan.

Bake, uncovered, in a 350 degree oven for about 30 minutes. Serve hot. Serves 4.

Orange Venison Roast

Venison roast
1 slice bacon, cut in small
  pieces
2 cloves garlic, mashed

1 bay leaf
2 cloves
1 cup orange juice
Salt and pepper

Cut small slits in meat and insert bacon pieces, garlic, salt and pepper. Place in roast pan after searing. Top with by leaf and cloves. Roast until tender at 350 degrees, basting often with orange juice.

Mrs. John H. Carter
Waterloo

Venison Roast

2 cups buttermilk
2 cloves garlic, pressed
1 4-5 pound roast (loin or
  round)
1 stick butter
4 cloves garlic
¼ cup plain flour

1 can cream of mushroom
  soup
1 envelope dried onion soup
2 cups water
1 cup cooking sherry
Salt and pepper to taste

Soak meat overnight in mixture of buttermilk and 2 cloves pressed garlic. When ready to cook, rub meat with remaining garlic, salt and pepper, then dredge with flour. Melt butter in bottom of Dutch oven and brown venison on both sides. Add onions. soups, water and sherry. Place venison in a 350 degree oven and bake 20 minutes for each pound of roast for medium well. A little longer is required for well done.

Mr. Rogert Hughes
Florence

Roast Venison

6 to 8 pound roast of venison
Flour, salt and pepper
6 strips of bacon

1 large onion
2 cans tomato soup

Wipe roast with a cloth soaked in vinegar. Dredge with flour mixed with salt and pepper. Lay ,strips; of bacon over top of roast, add onion rings and fasten on with toothpicks. Place in very hot oven (500 degrees) for 15 minutes, then reduce heat to moderate (350) and roast 20 minutes to the pound. About 40 minutes before the end of cooking time, pour soup over roast. Continue cooking, basting occasionally. 10 to 12 servings.

Lamb Chops With Minted Fruits

8 lamb rib or loin chops, 1 inch
   thick
4 slices process Swiss cheese

4 thin onion slices
Minted Fruits (Below)

Set oven control at broil and-or 550 degrees. Broil chops 3 inches from heat about 7 minutes or until brown. Cut cheese to fit chops; set aside. Turn chops; broil 5 to 7 minutes longer. Place onion and cheese slice on each chop; broil 2 minutes or until cheese begins to melt. Serve with Minted Fruits. Makes 4 serving.

Minted Fruits

1 can (16 ounces) pear halves,
   drained and quartered
1 can (13½ ounces) pineapple
   chunks, drained

⅓ cup mint-flavored apple jelly
1 tablespoon butter or margarine
1 tablespoon lemon juice

In small saucepan, cook and stir jelly, butter and lemon juice until jelly is melted. Stir in pears and pineapple, heat through. Serve hot in small individual dishes.

Sandra Goforth
Waterloo

Veal Piccata

4 pieces scallopini of veal
2 tablespoons flour
4 tablespoons margarine
1 clove garlic

¼ cup dry vermouth
1 tablespoon lemon juice
½ lemon, sliced

Pound veal with wooden mallet until very thin (⅛-inch). Dredge lightly in flour, shaking off excess. In skillet melt 3 tablespoons margarine. Crush clove and place in skillet until golden brown. Discard clove. Place veal in skillet and cook quickly, just until brown, about 1 to 2 minutes on each side. Remove onto serving dish. Add remaining margarine, wine and lemon juice. Simmer for 3 minutes, scraping bottom of pan to loosen drippings. Pour sauce over veal. Garnish with lemon slices and serve. Makes 4 servings.

Enchilada Casserole

1 pound ground beef
1 tall can green tomatoes
   and chilies
1 small can whole
   green chilies

¼ pound grated cheese
1 can cream of mushroom soup
1 can cream of chicken soup
1 medium onion
1 package tortillas

Brown onion and beef. Drain, add soups, tomatoes and chilies and chopped green chilies. Cover and simmer about 15 minutes. Alternating beef mixture, tortillas and cheese layer in a 2-quart casserole, bake at 350 degrees for 30 minutes.

Ellen McGee
Florence

Moussaka

Meat Sauce

2 tablespoons butter or margarine
1 cup finely chopped onion
1½ pounds ground chuck or lamb
1 clove garlic, crushed
½ teaspoon dried oregano leaves
1 teaspoon dried basil leaves
½ teaspoon cinnamon
1 teaspoon salt

Dash of pepper
2 cans (8 ounce) tomato sauce
2 eggplants (1 pound, 4 ounce
 size), washed and
 dried
Salt
½ cup butter or margarine,
 melted

Cream Sauce

2 tablespoons butter or margarine
2 tablespoons flour
½ teaspoon salt
Dash of pepper
2 cups milk

2 eggs
½ cup grated parmesan cheese
½ cup grated cheddar cheese
2 tablespoons dry bread crumbs

Meat sauce: In hot butter in 3½ quart Dutch oven, saute onion, chuck, garlic, stirring until brown (about 10 minutes). Add herbs, spices, tomato sauce; bring to boil while stirring. Reduce heat; simmer uncovered for ½ hour. Half unpared eggplant lengthwise; slice crosswise, ½ inch thick. Place in bottom of broiler pan; sprinkle lightly with salt; brush lightly with melted butter. Broil 4 inches from heat, 4 minutes per side or until golden.

Cream sauce: In medium saucepan, melt butter. Remove from heat; stir in flour, salt, and pepper. Add milk gradually. Bring to boil, stirring until mixture is thickened. Remove from heat. In small bowl, beat eggs with wire whisk. Beat in some hot cream sauce mixture; return mixture to saucepan. Mix well and set aside. Preheat oven to 350 degrees.

To assemble casserole: In bottom of a shallow 2 quart baking dish (12x7½x2 inches), layer half of eggplant, overlapping slightly; sprinkle with 2 tablespoons each grated parmesan and cheddar cheeses. Stir bread crumbs into meat sauce; spoon evenly over eggplant in casserole. Sprinkle with 2 tablespoons of each cheese. Layer rest of eggplant slices, overlapping as before. Pour cream sauce over all. Sprinkle top with remaining cheese. Bake 35 to 40 minutes. If desired, brown top a little more under broiler, about 1 minute. Cool slightly to serve. Cut in squares. Makes 12 servings.

Mrs. John E. Higginbotham
Florence

Ham Loaf With Orange Sauce

1½ pounds ham, ground
¼ pound milk pork sausage, optional
2 cups corn falkes, crushed
½ cup sweet milk
¼ teaspoon pepper

Combine all ingredients and form into loaf. Bake in preheated 300 degree oven for 45 minutes. Serve hot with Orange Sauce.

Orange Sauce

1 cup sugar
¼ teaspoon salt
2 tablespoons cornstarch
1 tablespoon flour
1¼ cups orange juice
¼ cup cup lemon juice
½ cup water
1 tablespoon butter
1 teaspoon each orange and lemon rind, grated

Mix sugar, salt, cornstarch and flour in sauce pan. Mix sugar, salt, cornstarch and flour in sauce pan. Stir in orange juice, lemon juice and water. Cook over low heat, stirring until it boils. Boil three minutes. Remove from heat; mix in butter and orang and lemon rind.

John's Ham Hash

4 medium potatoes, peeled
  and cooked
1 small onion
½ green pepper
Diced ham
¼ teaspoon salt
⅛ teaspoon pepper
Dash of thyme leaves
3 tablespoons butter or margarine

Force first 4 ingredients through coarse blade of food chopper or chop coarsely. Stir in seasonings. Heat butter in skillet, add mixture and cook, stirring frequently, until browned. Makes 4 to 6 servings.

Betty V. Ballinger
Madisonville, Kentucky

Eggplant Stuffed With Ham

1 large eggplant
Salted water
1 small onion, minced
1 green pepper, chopped fine
2 tomatoes, quartered
2 tablespoons butter
½ teaspoon salt
⅛ teaspoon black pepper
1 cup diced boiled ham
Bread crumbs

Wash and dry eggplant. Cut a slice from the top, scoop out inside to within half inch of skin. Cover shell and top with salted water and set aside. Chop eggplant pulp, combine with onion, pepper, tomatoes. Cover and cook in small amount of boiling salted water until tender. Drain, mash, add butter, salt, black pepper and ham. Drain shell, fill with mixture, and place in shallow baking dish. Sprinkle top with bread crumbs. Bake at 350 degrees for 25 minutes.

Mrs. J.P. Poe
Florence

Ham And Cheese Pie

1 (8-inch) pie crust, uncooked
5 medium eggs
Dash Tabasco sauce
Salt and pepper

1 cup cooked, diced ham
4 ounces Swiss or brick cheese,
grated

Put ham in pie crust. Sprinkle cheese over ham. Beat eggs with Tabasco, salt and pepper. Pour eggs into crust. Bake at 375 degrees for 20 to 25 minutes until eggs are set. Bacon can be used instead of ham.

Mrs. Edward Mullen
Florence

Ham And Eggs Pie

¼ cup butter or margarine
¼ cup flour
1 teaspoon salt
¼ teaspoon paprika
1 teaspoon mustard

1 tablespoon horseradish
2½ cups milk
1½ cups diced ham
1½ cups grated cheese
3 hard boiled eggs, sliced

Make a cream sauce of the first seven ingredients. Place ham and egg slices in the bottom of casserole. Pour over this the cream sauce. Top with grated cheese. For the crust, use butter flaked canned biscuits, split in half, enough to cover casserole. Bake at 425 degrees for about 30 minutes.

Mrs. Gene Hayes
Florence

Wine-Marinated Pork Roast

1 3-pound loin roast, boneless
1 garlic clove, halved
1½ teaspoons salt
1 teaspoon paprika
½ teaspoon pepper

1 cup dry white wine
½ cup chicken broth
1 (4-ounce) jar diced pimientos,
drained

Day before:
Rub pork with garlic, salt, paprika, and pepper. Place in shallow baking dish and pour wine over roast, cover and refrigerate. Turn occasionally. About 2¾ hours before serving place roast on rack roasting pan. Insert meat thermometer into center. Roast 2¼ hours or till thermometer reaches 170 degrees. Place roast on platter and remove strings.

For sauce:
Strain marinade and mix with 2 tablespoons of drippings from roast pan along with chicken broth and pimientos. Bring to a boil quickly, reduce heat to medium, cook 5 minutes, stirring occasionally. Makes 10 to 12 servings.

Phillip Beasley

Spicy Ham And Fruit

¼ cup butter or margarine
½ medium green pepper, chopped
Diced ham
1 can (8 ounces) pineapple rings
2 tablespoons brown sugar
1½ tablespoons cornstarch
1½ tablespoons cider vinegar
1½ teaspoons prepared mustard
⅛ teaspoon pepper
1⅓ cups packaged precooked rice
⅛ teaspoon ground cloves

Melt half the butter in skillet. Add green pepper and ham and saute 5 minues. Drain pineapple, reserving syrup. Cut rings in bite-size pieces. Mix syrup, ¾ cup water and next 5 ingredients. Stir into ham mixture and cook, stirring, until thickened. Add pineapple and heat. Prepare rice as directed on package, then add remaining butter and the cloves. Serve with the ham mixture. Makes 4 servings.

Smoked Ham Hock Chops

To cook skinned ham hocks, put in large kettle, cover with water and add 1 each sliced onion and carrot. Bring to boil, cover and simmer 2 hours, or until tender. For boiled dinner, add cut carrots and potatoes last ½ hour of cooking and cabbage last 10 to 15 minutes. Broth can be used to make bean or pea soup.

M.B. Anderson
Florence

Ham-Cheese-Potato Casserole

6 medium potatoes, peeled, cooked and diced
3 tablespoons butter or margarine
3 tablespoons flour
1½ cups milk
Diced ham
2 cups diced process Cheddar cheese
1 can (4 ounces) pimientos, drained
Salt and pepper

Force first 3 ingredients through medium blade of food chopper. Spread in buttered shallow 1½ quart baking dish. Cover with the potato. Melt butter in saucepan. Blend in flour. Add milk and cook, stirring, until thickened. Season to taste with salt and pepper and pour over ingredients in baking dish. Bake in preheated 350 degree oven about 40 minutes. Makes 6 servings.

Ham Steak

1½ pound ham steak, cut ¾-inch thick
1 cup cooking sherry
¼ cup brown sugar
1 can cranberry sauce

Mix sherry, sugar and cranberry sauce. Place ham in shallow baking dish. Cover with sauce and bake uncovered in 350 degree oven 1 to 1½ hours. Serves 4-6.

Mrs. John H. Carter
Waterloo

Ham Steak a la France

1 (2-2½ pounds) fully cooked
  center-cut ham steak,
  1½ inches thick
Whole cloves
1 cup dry sherry
4 tablespoons melted butter
  or margarine

2 cups (8 ounces) Gruyere
  or Swiss cheese
  triangles or slices,
  coarsely grated
6 slices white bread, toasted
  crusts removed
1 bunch watercress

Prepare ham steak the day before serving. Score side of steak ¼ inch deep at ½ inch intervals. Insert cloves evenly in two rows. Place ham steak in heavy-duty plastic bag. Add sherry; seal securely with twister. Place bag in pan (in case of leakage) and refrigerate overnight, turning once. Preheat broiler or barbecue grill. Brush ham steak with melted butter. Grill at medium heat 4 inches from heating element for 15 minutes on one side. Baste with marinade now and then. Trun; baste with butter and marinade and grill about 7 minutes, or until it's as brown as you like.

Turn steak again. Sprinkle with grated Gruyere. Allow cheese to melt and brown slightly for 2-3 minutes under broiler.

Meanwhile brush toast with remaining melted butter and arrange on serving board. Center ham steak on board. Garnish with watercress. Cut in thin slices across grain of meat, serving 2 toast triangles with each portion. Serves 4-6.

Casserole

1 pound pork sausage
2 medium potatoes
1 medium onion

3 medium carrots
1 can of cream of mushroom
  soup

Slice potatoes, onions, and carrots. Place in a baking dish one layer at a time starting with sausage. Then pour the mushroom soup over the layers. Bake in a 350 degree oven for 1 hour.

Addie C. Montgomery

Ham Glazes For Baked Ham
Orange Glaze:

1 cup firmly packed brown sugar
1 teaspoon dry mustard
¼ cup orange juice

¼ cup vinegar
1 tablespoon grated orange
  rind

Cola Glaze:

1 cup firmly packed brown sugar
1 teaspoon dry mustard

¼ cup bottled cola

Cranberry Glaze:

½ cup cranberry sauce, heated
½ cup brown sugar

1 teaspoon ary mustard
1 tablespoon vinegar

Ethel Rutherford
Cherokee

Layered Ham & Chicken Casserole

1 cup cooked ham, cubed
1 cup cooked chicken, cubed
½ cup celery, chopped
⅓ cup green pepper, chopped
¼ cup green onions, chopped
2 hard cooked eggs, chopped
2 tablespoons pimiento, chopped

⅓ cup green or ripe olives, sliced
1 can cream of chicken soup
1 can cream of mushroom soup
1 large package wide noodles,
   cooked
Potato chips or bread crumbs

Combine meats, vegetables, eggs, pimientos and olives. Mix the two cans of soup. Place a layer of noodles in a well buttered casserole dish, add a layer of the meat mixture and a layer of the soup. Alternate layers until all ingredients have been used, ending with soup. Top with crushed potato chips. Yields 8-10 servings.

Mrs. Joan Pugh
Florence

Mustard Sauce For Ham

⅓ cup vinegar
⅛ cup rum
2 tablespoons butter
2 egg yolks

¼ cup brown sugar
4 tablespoons prepared mustard
Water as needed

Combine ingredients and mix very well. Cook and stir over low heat until thickened. If desired, stir in a little water 1 teaspoon at a time until sauce consistency is to taste. Makes about 1 cup. Some people prefer their baked ham unadorned with glazes or crusts. In this case, serve your ham with Mustard Sauce on the side. Do not use both crust and sauce with the same ham.

Baked Ham With Savory Crust

1 ready-to-eat ham, 6 to 8 pounds
1 cup brown sugar
2 tablespoons prepared mustard
¼ teaspoon ground cloves

½ cup rum
⅔ to ½ cup packaged plain
   bread crumbs

Bake or heat ham as directed on wrapping, usually about 15 minutes per pound. Combine remaining ingredients and spread over scored fat surface of ham about 45 minutes before ham is done. Continue baking until done. Serves 12 to 14.

Sweet Sour Ham

2 slices ham
2 cups water
4 teaspoons soy sauce
½ teaspoon salt

3 tablespoons sugar
3 tablespoons vinegar
2 tablespoons cornstarch

Cut ham in serving pieces, place in skillet. Mix sugar, salt, soy sauce, cornstarch and water. Cook until thickened. Pour over ham and cook several minutes. Serves 6 to 8.

Baked Smoked Ham With Piquant Glaze

7 to 10-pound boneless smoked
"fully-cooked" ham

Piquant Glaze

Place ham on a rack in an open roasting pan. Insert roast meat thermometer so the bulb is centered in the thickest part. Do not add water. Do not cover. Roast in a slow 325 degree oven until thermometer registers 140 degrees. Allow approximately 15 to 18 minutes per pound. Spread ham with Piquant Glaze 10 minutes before end of cooking time.

Piquant Glaze

⅓ cup sugar

1 tablespoon cornstarch

¼ cup water

2 tablespoons vinegar

2 tablespoons sweet pickle relish

1 tablespoon prepared horseradish

Mix sugar and cornstarch in small saucepan. Add water and vinegar; cook until thickened, stirring constantly. Stir in relish and horseradish and cook 1 minute.

Hurry Up Ham

1 ham sliced, about 1 to 1½ pounds

1 can (1 pound) fruit cocktail

¼ cup firmly packed brown
sugar

¼ cup prepared yellow
mustard

1 tablespoon corn starch

Brown ham on both sides in large ungreased skillet. Remove from skillet and keep warm. Drain fruit, saving syrup. Add water to syrup to make 1 cup. Stir together brown sugar, mustard, and corn starch until smooth. Add to syrup, stirring to mix well. Pour into skillet and cook over medium heat, stirring constantly, until thickened. Stir in drained fruit; heat 5 minutes. Serve over ham. 4 to 6 servings.

Mrs. Robert E. Brown
Madisonville, Kentudky

Ham Loaf

1 tablespoon gelatin

¼ cup cold water

2 cups cooked ham, ground

½ cup celery, finely chopped

1 cup mayonnaise

½ pimiento, diced (optional)

½ green bell pepper, finely
chopped or shredded

¼ small onion, grated finely

4 hard boiled eggs, finely diced

1 tablespoon lemon juice

Soften gelatin in cold water, melt over hot water and add to other ingredients in mixing bowl. Add mayonnaise last and spoon into individual molds. Serve on crisp lettuce with teaspoon of mayonnaise on top and stuffed olive or two for garnish.

This salad is better if made one or two days ahead of time to serve. Holiday ham left-overs are ideal to use in this recipe.

Mrs. Thomas McCutcheon, Sr.
Russellville

Molasses Glazed Ham

Preheat oven to 325 degrees. Place boneless part of ham fat side up in shallow pan. If pre-cooked ham, bake 12 minutes per pound; if not 25 minutes per pound . Before end of baking time take ham from oven. Remove rind, score surface, stud with cloves. Combine 2 tablespoons molasses and 2 tablespoons prepared mustard. Brush over ham, continue baking until done.

Donna M. Hayes
Florence

Country Fried Ham And Red Eye Gravy

Soak slices of ham in enough cold water to cover for 1 hour. Drain, then fry ham in a greased skillet. Drain off excess fat, add a little water to the drippings and about a tablespoon of strong coffee for color. Bring to a boil and serve with ham.

Mrs. Joan Pugh
Florence

Spiced Ham Glazed With Guava Jelly

1 7 to 8-pound tenderized
ready-to-eat ham
Whole cloves
1 teaspoon powdered mustard

1 teaspoon warm water
1 cup guava jelly
2 tablespoons light corn syrup
1 tablespoon white vinegar

Place tenderized ham on rack in large baking pan. Bake, uncovered, in preheated 325 degree oven for 25 minutes per pound. Remove ham from oven; score diagonally in 1-inch diamonds. Stud each with a whole clove. Combine mustard and warm water; let stand for 10 minutes for flavor to develop. Melt jelly in 3-cup saucepan. Add syrup, vinegar and mustard. Mix well. Heat only until blended with jelly. Spoon or brush generously over ham. Return to oven. Bake 10 minutes in 350 degree oven. Spoon or brush jelly mixture over ham again. Bake 15 minutes or until beautifully brown. Let stand at room temperature 20-30 minutes before slicing. (Ready-to-eat ham: bake for 12-15 min. per pound). Yield: 12-15 servings.

Mrs. G.E. Smith
Leighton

Caramel Ham Loaf

½ pound ground beef
1 pound ground ham
5 slices bread, soaked in
¼ cup milk
3 beaten eggs

½ teaspoon salt
½ teaspoon dry mustard
½ cup brown sugar
Whole cloves

Mix meats, soaked bread, eggs, salt and mustard. In bottom of a buttered loaf tin, sprinkle the brown sugar and a few cloves. Pack meat on top and bake at 350 degrees for 1 hour. Place in individual custard cups for parties. Serves 6.

Mrs. Clayton Hardie
Florence

Ham And Asparagus Pie

3 tablespoons margarine
1 tablespoon cornstarch
¾ teaspoon salt
⅛ teaspoon pepper
1 cup milk
¼ cup mayonnaise
2 cups diced cooked ham

2 packages (10 ounces) unfrozen
   cut asparagus, cooked
   and drained
1 tablespoon lemon juice
1 baked 9 inch pastry shell
¼ cup grated Parmesan
   cheese

Melt margarine in saucepan over medium heat. Stir in next 3 ingredients. Remove from heat. Gradually stir in milk until smooth. Cook over medium heat, stirring constantly, until sauce comes to boil and boils 1 minutes. Stir small amount of hot mixture into mayonnaise, then stir into mixture in saucepan. Add ham, asparagus and lemon juice, cook until heated. Turn into pastry shell. Sprinkle with cheese. Broil about 2 minutes or until lightly browned. Makes 6 servings.

Mrs. Joan Pugh
Florence

Pork Chop Supreme

6 pork chops
1 cup rice
2 beef bouillon cubes
1 cup water (warm)

1 can cream mushroom soup
1 onion (medium sliced)
1 bell pepper (sliced)
1 tomato (sliced)

Salt and pepper pork chops and brown in a small amount of fat. Dissolve bouillon in the cup of warm water; put rice in mushroom soup and add all this in a greased casserole. Place pork chops on top of this mixture. Garnish each chop with the slices of onion, pepper and tomato. Pour ½ cup of bouillon on top of this. Cover with foil and bake 1 hour at 350 degrees. Makes six servings.

Mrs. Neca Allgood
Lexington

China House Special Pork

Pork, (preferably rib-eye), cut
   into small pieces

Water chestnuts
Bamboo shoots

Brown for about 30 seconds in wok, using vegetable or peanut oil. Remove from wok, and combine:

Ginger
Green onion
Garlic
Red pepper
1 teaspoon salt

4 teaspoons soy sauce
4 teaspoons cooking wine
2 teaspoons sugar
1 teaspoon sememi oil
2 teaspoons cornstarch

Mix with pork mixture, and fry for about one minute.

Sun-See Hsu
Florence

148

Pork Apple Pie

3 cups pork cut into 1-inch
   cubes
2 tart apples, peeled and
   thinly sliced
4 tablespoons brown sugar
½ teaspoon cinnamon
1 cup pork gravy

3 cups mashed sweet potatoes
3 tablespoons butter or
   margarine
¼ cup cream
1 teaspoon salt
⅛ teaspoon pepper

Arrange pork and apples in alternate layers in a greased 8-inch pan. Sprinkle each layer of apples with brown sugar and cinnamon. Pour pork gravy over apple-pork mixture. Combine mashed sweet potatoes and butter. Beat in cream until smooth; add salt and pepper. Spread sweet potato mixture over pork and apples. Bake at 350 degrees for 45 minutes. Yields 6 servings.

Mrs. Joan Pugh
Florence

Pork Chop Casserole

6 medium pork chops
2 cups noodles, cooked
1 can cream of chicken soup

1 cup grated cheese
1 cup sweet milk
Salt and pepper to taste

Brown pork chops on both sides in butter. Have noodles cooked. Place chops (after removing any bones) in an oblong baking dish that has been greased with butter. Spoon some of the noodles over the chops and cover with half the can of undiluted soup and half of cheese. Repeat for second layer starting with noodles. Pour milk over the top. Sprinkle with salt and pepper. Dot top with butter. Bake at 350 degrees for 1 hour.

Mrs. J.B. Elledge
Leighton

Cherry Sausage Bits

Meatballs

1 pound ground beef
1 pound bulk pork sausage
1 cup quick or old fashioned
   oats, uncooked

½ cup chopped pecans
1 egg
1 teaspoon salt

Sauce

1 21-ounce can cherry
   pie filling

½ cup dry sherry

For meatballs, combine all ingredients; mix well. Shape to form 1-inch balls. Bake in two 15½-inch jelly roll pans in preheated hot oven (400 degrees Farenheit) about 10 minutes. Drain.

For sauce, combine pie filling and sherry in large chafing dish; cook over medium heat until mixture comes to a boil. Add meatballs to cherry sauce; keep warm over very low heat to serve. Makes about 7½ dozen meatballs. Variation: Substitute orange juice or apple cider for dry sherry.

149

Pork Cutlets With Tomato

4 pork cutlets
Salt and pepper
Flour
2 tablespoons margarine

1 small onion, chopped
1 clove garlic, minced
1 beef or chicken bouillon cube
½ cup tomato juice

Season cutlets lightly with salt and pepper. Roll in flour and brown on both sides in the margarine in skillet. Remove meat and brown onion and garlic lightly in the drippings. Add remaining ingredients and ¾ cup water and bring to boil. Put pork back in skillet, cover and simmer about 30 minutes. Good with rice, noodles or mashed potatoes. Makes 4 servings.

Kathy Jordan

Sweet-And-Sour-Pork

1 egg yolk
Self-rising flour
Pork (preferably rib-eye), cut
   into small pieces
Soy sauce
Sugar
Vinegar
Tomato sauce

Pineapple
Ginger
Green onion
Garlic powder
Green pepper
Carrots
Cucumbers

Beat egg yolk and flour together to make a fairly thick batter. Dip browned cubes of meat into batter, and fry in vegetable oil in wok for about 30 seconds or until brown. Combine all other ingredients, to taste, to make the sweet-and-sour sauce. The meat chunks are dipped into the sauce as they are eaten.

Sun-See Hsu
Florence

Zesty Orange Pork Steaks

2 pounds smoked pork shoulder
   butt
1½ cups orange juice
1 teaspoon grated orange peel
⅓ cup firmly packed brown sugar

¼ cup spicy brown mustard
1 tablespoon vinegar
½ teaspoon ground ginger
Dash ground cloves

Cut pork shoulder in ¾-inch slices; place in shallow baking dish. Combine remaining ingredients; bring to boil; stir until well blended; pour over slices. Cover; marinate in refrigerator overnight.

Remove meat from marinade; pour liquid into small saucepan. Boil 5-10 minutes, until mixture is reduced and sauce is a good consistency for basting. Broil pork slices about four inches from source of heat 15-20 minutes, turning frequently and basting with sauce. To serve, pour any extra sauce over pork; garnish with orange slices and parsley. Makes four to six servings.

Sweet-Sour Spareribs

3 pounds spareribs
Salt and pepper to taste
1 onion, chopped
2 stalks celery, chopped
½ green pepper chopped
2 tablespoons salad oil
1 tablespoon cornstarch
1 can (8¼ ounces) pineapple
  tidbits, undrained
1 cup water
¼ cup vinegar
1 tablespoon soy sauce

Put spareribs, meaty side up, in a shallow pan. Season with salt and pepper. Bake at 400 degrees for 30 minutes. Combine onion, celery, green pepper, and salad oil; cook for 5 minutes over medium heat. Blend in cornstarch, add pineapple, water, vinegar, and soy sauce. Bring mixture to a boil. Pour over ribs. Bake at 350 degrees for 1 hour, basting occasionally. Yields four servings.

Ruth Gobbell
Florence

Sweet And Sour Pork

1½ pounds pork
2 tablespoons bacon grease
1 (No. 2 can) pineapple chunks
  and juice
½ cup water
⅛ cup vinegar
½ cup brown sugar
2 tablespoons cornstarch
½ teaspoon salt
1 tablespoon soy sauce
1 onion, sliced
1 green pepper, sliced
1 carrot, sliced (optional)
1 can water chestnuts,
  sliced (optional)
Egg and flour
Rice

Slice pork in 1-inch strips and dip in egg; cover with flour. Brown in bacon grease. In saucepan, combine drained pineapple and next 6 ingredients. Cook over medium heat until mixture thickens and is clear. Add to pork and cook 10 minutes (or longer if desired.) Add onion, pepper, pineapple chunks, carrot, and water chestnuts. Cook until thoroughly hot. (Vegetables should be crunchy, but I prefer to cook them longer.) Serve over rice. Serves 4. Sauce is better when made the day before and refrigerated for 24 hours.

Mrs. J.E. Tease
Florence

Calopie

1 pound pinto beans
2-3 pound pork roast
1 tablespoon garlic
2 tablespoons chili powder
1 tablespoon cumin seed
1 teaspoon oregano
1 small can green chilies
3 teaspoons salt

Mix together all ingredients and cover with water. Cook on very low heat for about 6 hours. A good main dish.

Nancy Dickerson
Killen

Barbecued Wieners

6 wieners
3 tablespoons butter
½ cup chopped onion
1 can tomato sauce (8 ounce)
4 teaspoons sugar

3 teaspoons vinegar
4 teaspoons Worcestershire sauce
1 teaspoon mustard
½ teaspoon black pepper
1 teaspoon paprika

Boil wieners 10 minutes. Split lengthwise and place in a greased baking dish. Brown onion in butter. Add rest of ingredients to onion and bring to a boil. Pour sauce over wieners and bake in 350 degree oven for 30 minutes. Can be served on buns or as a meat dish.

Mrs. Tony Glover
Killen

Barbecued Spareribs

4 pounds spareribs
2 onions
½ cup catsup
1 teaspoon salt

1 teaspoon Worcestershire sauce
1 tablespoon vinegar
1⅛ teaspoons chili powder
1 cup water

Cut ribs into serving size and brown in heavy pan on top of stove. Slice onions over the top and add other ingredients. Cover and cook in moderate oven 350 degrees, about 2 hours. Yields six servings.

Mrs. W.V. Gardner
Muscle Shoals

Barbecued Ham Slices

1 cup brown sugar
3 tablespoons catsup
1 tablespoon soy sauce
1 teaspoon dry mustard
1 cup crushed pineapple

2 tablespoons green pepper flakes
1½ tablespoons cornstarch
¾ to 1 inch thick ready to eat ham slices

Combine 1 cup water and brown sugar in sauce pan. Add catsup, soy sauce, mustard, pineapple and pepper flakes. Bring to boil, simmer for 10 minutes. Dissolve cornstarch in ¼ cup cold water, add to sauce. Cook, stirring, until sauce is clear and thick. Cook ham on stove for about 8 minutes, basting frequently with sauce. Serve with additional sauce.

Mrs. Marshall Pennington
Tuscumbia

Barbecue Lover's Barbecue Sauce

1 can onion soup
1 can (10¾ ounces) tomato soup
2 tablespoons cornstarch
2 large cloves garlic, minced

¼ cup vinegar
3 tablespoons brown sugar
1 tablespoon Worcestershire sauce
⅛ teaspoon hot pepper sauce

Combine all ingrdients in a bowl.

Mrs. Dorothy Clement
Russellville

152

Barbecued Pork Burgers

1 tablespoon cooking oil
¼ cup chopped onion
8 ounce can tomato sauce
¼ cup bottled steak sauce
2 tablespoons brown sugar
Dash of salt
2 cups thinly sliced roast pork
8 hamburger buns, split and
    toasted

Heat oil in skillet, sauté onion until tender. Stir in tomato sauce, steak sauce, sugar and salt. Bring to a boil. Add pork, cover and simmer for 10 minutes. Spoon over bun halves.

Christine Harrison
Killen

Frankburger Loaf

2 eggs, slightly beaten
¼ cup prepared yellow mustard
¼ cup catsup
1½ cups soft bread crumbs
1½ pounds ground beef
3 or 4 frankfurters, thinly
    sliced

Combine eggs, mustard, and catsup in large bowl. Add bread crumbs and beef; mix lightly. In shallow baking pan spread ½ the meat mixture forming a loaf about 1-inch thick. Sprinkle with ½ the frankfurters. Spread with remaining meat mixture and top with frankfurters. Bake at 350 degrees for 50 to 60 minutes. Six servings.

Frankly Mexican Casserole

1 package (5⅝ ounce) scalloped
    potatoes
½ pound frankfurters,
    sliced
1 can (1 pound kidney beans,
    drained and rinsed
1 tablespoon butter
¼ cup fine dry bread crumbs
½ teaspoon chili powder

Prepare potatoes as directed on package except use 2-quart casserole and increase boiling water to 2⅔ cups. Stir in frankfurters and beans. Bake at 400 degrees for 35 minutes. Melt butter in small pan; stir in bread crumbs and chili powder. Sprinkle over casserole and bake 10 to 15 minutes longer, until potatoes are tender. 5 to 6 servings.

Pork And Sauerkraut

4 or 5 pound pork loin roast
3 large cans shredded sauerkraut
1 large onion
Salt and pepper to taste

Place roast in small roaster and cook in moderate oven, 325 to 350 degrees, until meat is tender. Place sauerkraut on top, leaving juice from meat in pan. Chop onion fine and add to kraut. Cover and cook three to four hours. Check occasionally to see if meat has come loose from bone. If so, remove bone carefully so as not to miss any. Stir kraut and meat together thoroughly. Can be used immediately or placed in refrigerator for two or three days. This will actually add to the flavor. Serves 6-8.

Mrs. Ouida Thompson
Sheffield

Baked Pork Chops

6 loin pork chops cut 2 inches
   thick
6 tablespoons fat
2 onions sliced thin
1 green pepper, chopped
1 can pimientos, with juice

½ can (No. 2) tomatoes
½ teaspoon Worcestershire
   sauce
Salt and pepper to taste
1 cup rice, measured and cooked

Brown pork chops in fat. Place in roaster or Dutch oven. Mix all ingredients except rice. Spoon onto chops. Put rice on top of all. Cover. Cook in oven (300 degrees) for 2 hours, basting with juices occasionally.

Mrs. Donald E. Holt
Florence

Pork Chop Dinner

4 to 6 pork chops
Salt and pepper to taste
Salad oil
2½ cups water

1 envelope (8 ounces) onion
   soup mix
1 cup uncooked rice
1 green pepper, chopped

Season pork chops with salt and pepper. Brown on both sides in hot oil. Remove chops and add onion mix and water to pan drippings; bring to a boil. Place rice and green peppers in a shallow 2-quart casserole dish and top with pork chops. Pour soup mixture over chops and bake at 350 degrees for 1 hour.

Lela Hall
Leighton

Stuffed Pork Chops

¼ cup margarine or butter
½ cup water
3½ cups crouton stuffing, herb
   seasoning

8 to 10 pork chops, 1 inch thick,
   cut with pockets
Salt
Pepper

Heat oven to 350 degrees. Place margarine and water in a saucepan. Bring to a boil. Remove from heat. Add croutons all at once, tossing lightly until croutons are evenly and thoroughly moistened.

Fill pork chops with prepared stuffing. Fasten edges with wooden toothpicks. Place stuffed chops, flat side down, in a single layer, shallow baking pan; do not crowd. Sprinkle with salt and pepper. Cover pan tightly with aluminum foil. Bake in a moderate oven about 1 hour. Uncover and continue baking about 30 minutes, until browned and tender. Serve with cinnamon apple wedges or hot spiced applesauce.

Mrs. Jerry Turbyfill
Florence

Pork Chop One-Dish Meal

6 pork chops	3 medium onions, quartered
1 teaspoon salt	½ cup shortening
½ teaspoon pepper	½ cup water
1½ cups sliced carrots	1 teaspoon salt
6 small potatoes	½ teaspoon pepper

Brown chops in shortening, adding 1 teaspoon salt and ½ teaspoon pepper when chops are turned. Add vegetables, water, and remaining salt and pepper. Cover and continue to cook over low heat for 1 hour or until meat is fork tender. Yield: 6 servings.

Mrs. Neca Allgood
Lexington

Pork Chops and Rice

6 pork chops	3 tablespoons chopped onion
½ cup uncooked rice	2 teaspoons salt
3¾ cups strained tomatoes	¼ teaspoon pepper
3 tablespoons chopped green peppers	2 tablespoons shortening

Salt and pepper chops and roll in flour. Melt fat in skillet on high heat and brown chops on both sides. Mix in the uncooked rice, tomatoes, salt, pepper, onions and green peppers and pour over chops.

Place lid on skillet. When steam escapes freely from vent in cover, turn heat on low and simmer. Do not remove lid until cooking period is over. Cook 45 minutes.

Mrs Byron Barnett
Sheffield

Glazed Pork Chops

6 pork chops, salted	1 teaspoon mustard
1 cup brown sugar	Dash of ginger
2 tablespoons vinegar	

Heat oven to 350 degrees. Arrange chops in glass baking dish. Mix sugar, vinegar, mustard and ginger together. Spread over chops. Bake uncovered 1-1½ hours depending on thickness of chops.

Evelyn Taylor
Cherokee

Country-Style Pork Chops

4 medium carrots, peeled
2 small white turnips,
  peeled
2 ribs celery
4 leeks, white part only,
  or 8 green onions,
  white part only
4 small white onions,
  chopped

1 can (28 ounce) tomatoes
⅛ teaspoon marjoram
  leaves
1 bay leaf
¼ cup chopped parsley
¾ teaspoon salt
¼ teaspoon pepper
⅓ cup consommé
4 butterfly pork chops

Cut first 4 ingredients in 1½'' julienne strips. Put in kettle or Dutch oven with next 7 ingredients. Add consommé and bring to boil. Cover and simmer 5 minutes. Arrange chops on vegetables, cover and simmer 1 hour, or until all is done. Put vegetables in center of hot platter and surround with chops. Makes 4 servings.

Oven Barbecued Pork Chops

1 cup catsup
¼ cup vinegar
2 tablespoons brown sugar
1 tablespoon soy sauce
1 tablespoon horseradish mustard
2 tablespoons grated onion

1½ teaspoons salt
½ teaspoon Accent
½ teaspoon pepper
1 tablespoon salad oil
½ cup water
6 pork chops

Combine first 9 ingredients in a saucepan. Simmer over low heat for 10 minutes.

Meanwhile, brown pork chops in salad oil on both sides. Place in baking dish and cover with sauce. Add water, cover with foil and bake one hour and 20 minutes at 350 degrees. Uncover and continue baking 10 minutes more.

Mrs. Robert M. Metcalfe
Madisonville, Kentucky

Johnnie Mazetti

2 pounds ground pork
2 medium-size diced onions
1 medium can tomatoes
1 medium can tomato juice
Salt and Pepper to taste
1 pound Velveeta cheese

1 pound wide noodles, cooked
  until tender in salt
  water
2 small cans sliced mushrooms

Sear ground pork and onion in 1 tablespoon fat. Add tomatoes and tomato juice. Salt and pepper to taste. Cook slowly for two hours, then add noodles, sliced mushrooms and cheese. Cook slowly one hour, stirring often. Tastes even better after standing awhile. Serves 12-15 people.

Mrs. Bailey Anderson
Florence

Party Pork Barbecue

1 pound pork shoulder steak,
  cut into 1-inch cubes
¼ cups flour
⅛ teaspoon pepper
1½ teaspoons salt
2 tablespoons shortening or
  oil
1 medium green pepper, cut
  into 1-inch strips

1 small onion, sliced
1½ cups pineapple tidbits,
  undrained
¼ cup catsup
1 tablespoon Worcestershire
  sauce
1 tablespoon salad mustard
½ cup chopped celery

Coat pork with flour mixture, salt and pepper. Brown in oil in a large frying pan. Add celery, green pepper, onion, pineapple, catsup, mustard and Worcestershire sauce. Cover and simmer for 30 minutes. Serve over rice. This can be made ahead and frozen. Serves five to six.

Mrs. Gertrude Snider
Sheffield

Breaded Pork Cutlets

4 pork cutlets
Seasoned flour
2 eggs, slightly beaten
Fine dry bread crumbs
Butter

Vegetable oil
Lemon slices
Rolled anchovies, if desired
Chopped parsley

Dip each cutlet in flour, then in egg and finally in crumbs. Saute in ½ inch combined butter and oil in large skillet until well browned on both sides and cooked through. Arrange on hot platter and top each with a slice of lemon. If desired, put an anchovy in center of each lemon slice. Sprinkle with parsley. Makes 4 servings.

John Ballinger
Madisonville, Kentucky

Grits Scrapple

9 cups water (salted)
1 pound pork sausage

1 medium onion, chopped
2 cups grits

Break sausage into small pieces. Add sausage and onion to boiling water. Lower heat to low and cook for 30 minutes. Add grits and cook until thick. Pour into a shallow pan and refrigerate.

Slice mixture 1-inch thick after it has become hard. Roll in flour and fry until golden brown.

Mrs. Gertude Snider
Sheffield

Blue Ribbon Casserole

1 pound wieners (cut into 1" slices)
2 packages (10 ounces each) frozen French fries
1 can (11 ounce) cheese soup
¼ cup chopped onions
¼ cup milk
¼ cup chopped pimiento
¼ cup chopped bell pepper

Bake French fries according to directions. Combine wieners, soup, milk, onion, pimiento and green pepper. Arrange half of the baked French fries in bottom of a 1½ quart casserole dish. Pour half of the wiener mixture over the French fries. Repeat layers. Bake in a 400 degree oven for 15 to 20 minutes. Serves 4 to 6.

Ruth Huckaba
Rogersville

Creole Franks

1 pound all-beef wieners, cut in thin slices
4 tablespoons margarine
1 large onion, chopped
1 can tomatoes, drained slightly
½ green pepper, chopped
1 can tomato soup, undiluted
1 teaspoon chili powder
1 teaspoon salt
2 teaspoons sugar
Dash black pepper

Brown wieners, onion and pepper in skillet with margarine on medium high. Add tomatoes, soup and seasonings. Cover and bring to steaming on high heat. Turn to low for 15 minutes and serve over steamed rice.

James Coburn
Florence

Corn-Covered Wieners

⅔ cup self-rising cornmeal
1 cup self-rising flour
¼ teaspoon salt
2 tablespoons sugar
2 tablespoons shortening
1 egg, slightly beaten
¾ cup milk
1 pound wieners

Combine cornmeal, flour, salt and sugar. Cut in shortening until mixture resembles fine crumbs. Combine egg and milk; add to crumb mixture, stir until mixed. Insert wooden skewers into wieners. Spread wieners with mixture. Fry in deep fat. Serve with chili sauce or catsup. Yield: 12 to 14 servings.

Mrs. Preston White
Rogersville

Corn Dogs

⅔ cup enriched corn meal
1 cup plain flour
1½ teaspoons baking powder
1 teaspoon salt
2 tablespoons sugar

2 tablespoons fat
1 egg, slightly beaten
¾ cup sweet milk
1 pound wieners
Deep fat

Mix first eight ingredients. Insert wooden skewers into wieners; dip into mix. Fry until brown in deep fat. Serve with tomato catsup or chili sauce.

Mrs. Preston White
Rogersville

Corn Dogs

Hot dogs
½ cup cornmeal
1 tablespoon sugar (optional)
1 teaspoon salt

⅓ cup milk
1 egg
4 drops tabasco sauce
2 tablespoons dry mustard

Parboil wieners and prepare whole or cut the whole wiener into ½-inch pieces.

Mix together cornmeal, sugar, salt, milk, egg, tabasco sauce, and mustard for batter. Dip wieners into batter and fry in hot deep fat until golden brown. Drain.

Donna M. Hayes
Florence

Open Pork And Bean Sandwiches

1 pound can pork and beans
6 slices buttered bread

6 slices mild cheddar cheese
12 slices bacon

Pre-heat broiler. Arrange pork and beans equally on bread slices. Top with cheese. Arrange 2 slices of bacon on each cheese slice. Broil until bacon is crisp.

Christine Harrison
Killen

Roast Pork And Vegetables

Frenched pork loin
Salt and pepper
6 medium yams, cooked
  and peeled

2 pounds small white onions,
  peeled and cooked
¾ cup cider or apple juice
Spiced pears (optional)

Rub pork loin with salt and pepper and put on rack in shallow baking pan. Roast in preheated 325 degree oven 35 minutes to the pound, or until meat thermometer registers 170 degrees. Arrange yams and onions on rack beside pork and bake, basting frequently with the cider, 15 minutes. Put on platter and, if desired, garnish with spiced pears. Makes 6 servings.

Mrs. Ron Chesnut
Greeneville, Tennessee

Barbecue Lover's Meatballs

1 pound ground beef
½ pound bulk sausage

½ cup soft bread crumbs
1 egg, slightly beaten

Mix thoroughly beef, sausage, crumbs and egg. Shape into 24 meatballs; brown and pour off fat. Add Barbecue Lover's Barbecue Sauce mixture. Cover; cook over low heat for 20 ninutes or until done. Stir often. Serve with rice. Makes 6 servings.

Mrs. Dorothy Clement
Russellville

Ham & Cheese Sandwiches

4 slices cooked ham, ¼-inch
thick and same size
as bread
4 slices firm-type bread,
lightly toasted
Prepared mustard

4 slices Swiss cheese, ⅛-inch
thick and same size
as bread
Parsley
Tomato slices and wedges

Put ham slice on each slice of bread. Spread a thin coat of mustard on ham and top with a slice of cheese. Put on a baking sheet and bake in a very hot oven (450 degrees) for 10 minutes, or until cheese is melted and sandwiches are heated. Top half the slices with remaining slices to make 2 doubledecker open-faced sandwiches. Garnish with parsley and tomato slices and serve with tomato wedges.

Donna M. Hayes
Florence

Sausage Sweet Potato Casserole

8 medium sweet potatoes
2 tablespoons butter
1 teaspoon salt

2 eggs, well beaten
1 tablespoon heavy cream
1 pound small pork sausages

Boil sweet potatoes until tender, drain and peel. Mash and beat well adding all ingredients and enough cream to make mixture light and fluffy. Pour into casserole and press sausages into surface. Bake at 400 degrees about 15 minutes or until sausages are brown. Reduce heat to 350 degrees and cook 10 minutes more. Serves 6.

Jean Allen
Florence

Company Pork Chops

6 pork chops, ½ inch thick
¾ cup onion, chopped

¾ cup chili sauce

Brown pork chops in skillet. Drain, Mix onion and chili sauce. Place pork chops in oiled baking dish. Spread onion and chili sauce over them. Cover and bake at 350 degrees for 1 hour, or until chops are tender.

Mrs. James A. Gafford
Florence

Umbrella Party Sandwich Loaf

1 pound round loaf unsliced
   white bread

6 tablespoons butter, softened

Egg Filling

4 hard-cooked eggs, coarsely
   chopped
¼ cup crumbled Blue cheese
¼ cup chopped pimiento

2 tablespoons dairy sour cream
2 tablespoons chopped parsley
½ teaspoon salt
⅛ teaspoon cayenne

Ham Filling

1 cup finely chopped ham
¾ cup (3 ounce) shredded Cheddar
   cheese
½ cup dairy sour cream

¼ cup chopped pimiento-stuffed
   olives
1 teaspoon dry mustard
¼ teaspoon paprika

Frosting

2 packages (8 ounce) cream
   cheese
¼ cup milk
1 teaspoon white vinegar
½ teaspoon salt

Ham strips
Short pimiento strips
1 hard-cooked egg, sliced
Parsley
Celery stalk

To prepare Egg Filling: In a small bowl, blend together eggs, blue cheese, pimiento, 2 tablespoons sour cream, parsley, salt and cayenne. Chill. (Makes 1½ cups). To prepare Ham Filling: In a small bowl blend together ham, ¾ cup Cheddar cheese, ½ cup sour cream, celery, olives, mustard and paprika. Chill. (Makes 2 cups). To prepare Sandwich Loaf: Remove crusts from bread; slice crosswise into three slices. Butter cut surface of slices. Spread Ham Filling on bottom slice of bread. Cover with second slice of bread. Top with Egg Filling. Top with last slice of bread. Cover with damp towel or protective wrap and chill thoroughly. Cut loaf in half to form top of umbrella and frost about 1 hour before serving. To prepare Frosting: In a small mixing bowl beat cream cheese, milk, vinegar and salt until fluffy. Spread on sides and top of loaf. Decorate top of one loaf half to resemble an umbrella (can be used for ceterpiece). Form 7 spokes with ham strips, place short pimiento strips in between spokes. Create scalloped effect on the edge using halved egg slices with parsley garnish. Cut a short piece from the celery stalk for the tip of the umbrella; insert a toothpick into rest of stalk and fasten to loaf for handle. Allow to stand at room temperature shortly before serving. Serve undecorated half first, cutting into wedges. Makes 14-16 servings.

Mrs. John Ballinger
Madisonville, Kentucky

Bill's Goulash

1½ pounds ground chuck
½ cup chopped onions
1 No. 303 can whole tomatoes
1 small can tomato sauce

1 package (seven ounce)
 spaghetti
1 clove garlic, chopped
½ cup grated cheddar cheese
Salt and pepper to taste

Brown meat with onions and garlic in butter over low heat. Cook spaghetti according to package directions, drain.

In casserole dish, place a layer of spaghetti, then a layer of the meat mixture and a layer of tomatoes. Repeat the process adding salt and pepper as you go. Pour tomato sauce over all and let soak in. Bake in 350 degree oven for about 30 minutes. Just before serving, top with grated cheese and return to oven until cheese melts.

Bill Cornelius
Florence

Brazilian Pilaf With Ginger Glazed Pork

3½ teaspoons salt
2½ teaspoons ground ginger
5-pound pork loin roast
1 cup orange juice
½ cup packed brown sugar
½ teaspoon ground cloves
1 cup chopped onion
2 tablespoons vegetable oil
1 cup rice

2½ cups water
1 large tomato, peeled,
 shredded, diced
1 banana, coarsely chopped
½ cup chopped cashews or
 peanuts
2 tablespoons shredded
 coconut, (optional)

Mix 2 teaspoons salt and 1½ teaspoons ginger. Rub meat with ginger mixture and let stand at room temperature 1 hour. Roast on rack in 325 degree oven for 2 to 2½ hours, or until meat thermometer registers 170 degrees. Meanwhile, in small saucepan, combine orange juice, brown sugar, 1 teaspoon ginger and cloves. Simmer over medium heat, stirring constantly about 10 minutes. Glaze roast with sauce mixture several times during last hour of roasting. Meanwhile prepare rice. Saute onion in oil in 3-quart saucepan until tender. Add rice, water and 1½ teaspoons salt. Bring to a boil; reduce heat. Cover tightly and simmer 20 minutes. Remove from heat. Let stand, covered, until all liquid is absorbed, about 5 minutes. Stir in tomato, banana and nuts. Serve rice sprinkled with coconut, if desired, with Ginger Glazed Pork. Makes six servings.

Seafood

Long before 56 B.C., when the Romans named it The Leaper, salmon was a highly prized food source for peoples of the world fortunate enough to live near the waters where it was plentiful. Today, thanks to modern canning methods, this delicious food can be enjoyed in many different dishes by people all over the world, no matter how far inland they live.

Few foods are as rich in nutrients as salmon. Not only is it an exceptionally good source of complete protein, containing all the essential amino acids, but it also contains Vitamins A and D as well as niacin and riboflavin from the B-complex group. Appreciable amounts of calcium and iron, as well as zinc, magnesium and phosphorus are also contained in canned salmon. Because the fat content in canned salmon is the polyunsaturated type, it is recommended for those on low cholesterol diets. There is no waste to canned salmon because the liquid, skin and tiny bones are not only edible, but contribute flavor and texture as well as nutrients.

All five varieties of salmon which are canned are equally nutritious, so your choice of salmon depends on its use. When color is important, as in salads and appetizers, choose Red or Sockeye salmon. When combining salmon with other ingredients in casseroles, soups and sandwich fillings, the less expensive Pink or Chum salmon is ideal.

Canned salmon is available in 15½ ounces, 7¾ ounces and 3¾ ounce cans. It is delicious used just as it comes from the can, or in countless varieties of main dishes, salads, soups, sandwiches and appetizers.

The versatility of this succulent seafood is evident as canned salmon takes a tour of the world in a variety of exciting main dish salads.

Northwest Salmon Platter

1 can (15½ ounces) salmon
or 2 cans (7¾ ounces)
salmon
1½ pounds potatoes
3 green onions, sliced
2 tablespoons minced
parsley
Lemony French Dressing

1 can (15 ounces) whole
green beans
Sliced cucumber
Crisp lettuce
Pimiento strips
2 tomatoes, sliced
Radish roses

Refrigerate salmon. Cook potatoes in boiling salted water until tender. Cool slightly. Peel and slice crosswide into ¼-inch rounds. Gently toss potatoes with sliced green onions, minced parsley and ⅓ cup dressing. Heat beans. Drain. Drizzle with 3 tablespoons dressing. Marinate potatoes and beans several hours. Drain salmon and break into chunks with a fork. Arrange salmon chunks over sliced cucumber on lettuce-lined platter. Arrange potatoes, green beans trimmed with pimiento stripes, sliced tomatoes and radish roses around salmon. Serve remaining dressing on the side. Makes six servings.

Curried Salmon Salad

1 can (7¾ ounces) salmon
3 cups steamed rice
⅓ cup chopped green onion
2 tablespoons salad oil
2 teaspoons curry powder
3 tablespoons lemon juice
3 tablespoons vinegar

3 tablespoons olive oil
1 teaspoon garlic salt
Lettuce
Cantaloupe and honeydew
  melon wedges
Green grape clusters
Parsley, for garnish

Drain salmon, reserving liquid. Flake salmon and combine with rice and reserved salmon liquid. Saute green onion in 2 tablespoons salad oil with curry powder added. Blend in lemon juice, vinegar, olive oil and garlic salt. Pour dressing over salmon-rice mixture and blend thoroughly. Refrigerate several hours to blend flavors. Spoon salad into center of lettuce-lined bowl or platter. Arrange fruit around salad. Garnish with parsley. Serve with a selection of condiments such as chopped cucumber, sieved hard-cooked egg, chopped peanuts and crisp bacon bits. Makes 4 to 6 servings.

Steamed Rice: Place 2¼ cups water and 3 chicken bouillon cubes in saucepan. Bring to boil. Slowly add 1 cup rice. Cover and cook over low heat 20 minutes. Cool slightly.

Salmon Loaf

1 pound can pink salmon,
  drained and falked
1 can cream of celery soup
½ cup chopped onion
1 tablespoon lemon juice

½ cup mayonnaise
1 egg, beaten
1 cup dry bread crumbs
¼ cup chopped green peppers
1 teaspoon salt

Combine and pour into greased loaf pan. Bake at 350 degrees for one hour.

Mrs. Walter Shaff
Florence

Oriental Salmon

1 can (7¾ ounces)salmon
2 cups shredded cabbage
2 cups fresh bean sprouts
  or 1 can (16 ounces)
  beans sproutes,
  drained
½ cup sliced water chestnuts

3 tablespoons cider vinegar
2 tablespoons soy sauce
1 tablespoons lemon juice
2 teaspoons sugar
¼ teaspoon ground ginger
2 tablespoons salad oil
1 tablespoon sesame seeds

Drain and flake salmon, reserving 1 tablespoon liquid. Toss salmon with cabbage, bean sprouts and water chestnuts. Combine reserved salmon liquid, cider vinegar, soy sauce, lemon juice, sugar and ginger. Add oil slowly, beating constantly. Add dressing to salad and toss, coating ingredients well. Sprinkle sesame seeds on top. Serve immediately. Makes four servings.

Salmon Roll

1 (1 pound) can salmon (2 cups)
1 (8 ounce) package cream
  cheese, softened
1 tablespoon lemon juice
2 teaspoons grated onion
1 teaspoon prepared
  horseradish
¼ teaspoon liquid smoke
½ cup chopped pecans
¼ teaspoon salt
3 tablespoons snipped fresh
  parsley

Drain and flake salmon, removing skin and bones. Combine salmon, cream cheese, lemon juice, onion, horseradish, salt and liquid smoke. Mix thoroughly. Chill several hours. Combine pecans and parsley. Shape salmon mixture into 1 large mound or small rolls. Roll in nut mixture. Chill, serve with crackers.

Mrs. Donald E. Holt
Florence

Lomi Salmon

1 pound salted salmon
5 large peeled tomatoes
1 medium onion, finely
  chopped
1 stalk green onion, finely
  chopped

Soak salmon in water for about three hours. Remove skin and bones and shred finely. Mash tomatoes to a pulp. Mix all ingredients and chill. Add several ice cubes ½-hour before serving.

Isao Hashimoto

Congealed Salmon Salad

¾ teaspoon salt
¾ teaspoon dry mustard
½ teaspoon Worcestershire
  sauce
1 teaspoon grated onion
2 tablespoons lemon juice
½ cup mayonnaise
½ cup cooked peas
½ cup sliced celery
2 teaspoons chopped parsley
1 cup flaked salmon
1 tablespoon plain gelatin
¼ cup cold water
1 cup boiling water

Mix salt, mustard, Worcestershire sauce, grated onion, and lemon juice with mayonnaise. Place peas, celery, parsley and salmon in bowl. Add mayonnaise mixture; toss lightly and chill. Soften gelatin in cold water. Add boiling water and stir until gelatin is dissolved. Chill. When slightly thickened, fold into seasoned, chilled salmon and vegetable mixture. Pour into a mold and chill until firm. Serve on salad greens with or without dressing. Serves 6.

Mrs. Tracy Gargis
Sheffield

Salmon Salad Platter

1 pound can salmon, drained
Romaine or crisp lettuce
¾ cup mayonnaise
1 tablespoon lemon juice
½ teaspoon dry mustard
1 cucumber, peeled

1 large tomato, peeled and
   cut into wedges
2 hard-cooked eggs, quartered
1 tablespoon chopped parsley
Salt and freshly ground pepper

Separate salmon into chunks and arrange in center of a platter lined with romaine leaves. Combine mayonnaise, lemon juice and mustard and spread over salmon. Slice cucumber thinly. Arrange cucumber slices, tomato wedges and egg quarters around salmon. Sprinkle with parsley and salt and pepper. Serves 4.

King Mackerel

2 king mackerel (4-5 pounds)
Butter
Grated onion

Parsley
Salt and pepper
Sauce

Prepare fire for indirect cooking. Place fish on heavy duty aluminum foil on grill. Season with above ingredients. Cook with lid closed and vents regulated for medium heat. Turn fish every fifteen minutes, being careful not to tear meat.

Anthony Haid

Baked Curried Fillets

1 pound fresh or frozen fish fillets
   (sole, haddock, cord,
   perch or bass)
Seasoning salt
Lemon juice or dry white wine
10 ounce can golden mushroom
   soup

3 thinly sliced green onions or 2
   tablespoons chopped onion
½ to 1 teaspoon curry powder
Freshly ground black pepper
Few celery seeds

If fish is frozen, defrost just enough to separate the fillets. Arrange in one layer in a shallow pan lined with foil. Sprinkle with seasoning salt and lemon juice. Bake at 450 degrees for 5 minutes if fresh and 7 minutes if fish is still icy. Carefully drain the juice into a small saucepan and boil until reduced by one third. Add remaining ingredients and heat thoroughly. Taste. Pour over the fillets and return to the oven. Bake 5 minutes longer and serve with fluffy rice and spinach. Serves 4. Calories per serving: 147.

Mrs. Donna M. Hayes
Florence

French Fried Fish

Fish
½ cup wheat germ or ¾ cup
   sifted whole wheat
   bread crumbs

1 tablespoon powdered milk
1 teaspoon salt
Vegetable oil

Cut fish in serving size pieces approximately 1 inch thick; bone and remove skin. Dip in batter or shake in bag containing wheat germ (or whole wheat bread crumbs), powdered milk, and salt. Let dry 10 minutes or longer. Heat vegetable oil to 360 degrees and fry fish until brown. Drain on paper towels.

Mrs. Nancy Gonce
Florence

Barbecued Cod Italian Style

1½ pounds cod fillets
¼ cup olive oil
1 clove garlic, finely chopped
¼ cup onion, finely chopped
1 bay leaf
2 or 3 sprigs fresh thyme or
   ⅛ teaspoon ground thyme

½ teaspoon salt
Fresh ground pepper to taste
1 can (8 ounces) tomato sauce
¼ cup water
2 or 3 sprigs parsley, chopped

Place cod fillets in flat pan. Heat olive oil and sauté garlic and onion over medium heat for 5 minutes. Add remaining ingredients and simmer for 5 minutes. Pour about two-thirds of the hot sauce over the fish in the pan. Refrigerate for 30 minutes to 2 hours. When ready to cook, place fillets in fish grill or on grill and cook about 4 inches from heat for about 5 minutes, basting with sauce (do not turn). Serve with any leftover sauce. Makes 4 servings.

Jere Medaris
Vicenza, Italy

Seviche

½ pound snapper or turbot,
   diced
Lemon and/or lime juice
1 medium onion, chopped
1 medium tomato, chopped

½ green pepper, chopped
½ cup vinegar
⅛ cup cooking oil
Oregano to taste
Catsup to taste

Place fish in shallow dish and cover with lemon juice. Let stand for 1 hour. Combine onion, tomato, and green pepper. Mix vinegar, oil, and oregano in saucepan and simmer for about 5 minutes. Cool. Drain lemon juice from fish and place fish in serving bowl. Add onion mixture and vinegar mixture. Stir in catsup. Chill well and serve with crackers.

Mrs. Stewart O'Bannon
Florence

Fish Plaki

1 medium onion, sliced
1 clove garlic, minced
2 medium tomatoes, sliced
1 cup chopped parsley
½ cup (1 stick) margarine

2 pounds frozen fish fillets, defrosted
½ teaspoon salt
½ teaspoon oregano
¼ teaspoon pepper
½ cup bread crumbs

In a large skillet sauté onion, garlic, tomatoes and parsley in one-quarter cup margarine. Set aside. Arrange fillets in 13½x8¾x1¾ inch baking dish and sprinkle with salt, oregano and pepper. Arrange sauteed mixture over fillets; sprinkle bread crumbs evenly over all. Dot with remaining margarine. Bake covered at 350 degrees for 35-40 minutes, or until fillets are fork-tender. Makes 6-8 servings.

Trout Marguery

4 fillets of trout
3 tablespoons olive oil
2 egg yokes, beaten
1 cup butter, melted
1 tablespoon lemon juice
1 cup shrimp, cooked and chopped

½ cup crabmeat
½ cup mushrooms sliced
1 tablespoon flour
¼ cup dry white wine
Paprika
Salt and pepper

Salt and pepper fillets. Place in a baking pan and add olive oil. Bake at 375 degrees. As fish bakes, prepare sauce. Place egg yolks in top of double boiler over hot water and add melted butter stirring constantly until mixture thickens. Blend in flour. Add lemon juice, shrimp, crabmeat, mushrooms, wine, salt and pepper to taste. Stir and cook for 15 minutes to heat thoroughly. Place baked fish on platter and cover with sauce. Serves 4.

Mrs. J. Douglas Evans
Florence

Tartar Sauce

1 cup mayonnaise
2 tablespoons chopped dill pickle
2 teaspoons chopped pimiento

1 teaspoon grated onion
1 tablespoon snipped parsley

Mix mayonnaise, pickle, parsley, pimiento and onion. Refrigerate. Makes one cup to serve with fish and seafood.

Mrs. Jerry L. Turbyfill
Florence

Oriental Tartar Sauce

Chop small white onion
Chop 2 small dill pickles

Chop 6 sprigs parsley

Mix all together with 3 tablespoons of mayonnaise. Good for fish dishes.

Hannah J. Phillips
Bear Creek

Scalloped Oysters I

1 pint oysters
2 cups cracker crumbs
½ teaspoon salt
Dash of pepper

½ cup melted butter
¼ teaspoon Worcestershire
  sauce
1 cup milk

Drain oysters, set aside. Combine cracker crumbs, salt, pepper and butter. Sprinkle ⅓ in a buttered 1 quart casserole dish and cover with a layer of oysters. Repeat layers, reserving a little of the crumb mixture for topping. Add Worcestershire sauce to milk. Pour over casserole. Sprinkle remaining crumbs over top. Bake at 350 degrees for 30 minutes or until brown. Makes 6 servings.

Mrs. Earle Trent
Florence

Scalloped Oysters II

1 pint fresh oysters
2 cups cracker crumbs, medium
  coarse
½ cup melted butter or margarine
½ teaspoon salt

Dash pepper
¾ cup cream
¼ cup oyster liquor
¼ teaspoon Worcestershire
  sauce

Drain oysters, saving liquor. Combine crumbs, butter, salt, and pepper. Spread ⅓ of the buttered crumbs in a greased 8x1¼ inch round pan or casserole dish. Cover with half the oysters. Using another third of the crumbs, spread a second layer, cover with remaining oysters. Combine cream, oyster liquor, and Worcestershire sauce. Pour over oysters. Top with last of crumbs. Bake in moderate oven (350 degrees) for 40 minutes. Makes 4 servings.

Mrs. Donald E. Holt
Florence

Crab Louis

2 cans (7½ ounces each) crabmeat
Louis dressing
4 tomatoes, quartered
4 hard-boiled eggs, quartered

Ripe or green olives
4 cups bite-size pieces, salad
  greens, chilled

Drain crabmeat and remove cartilage; chill. Prepare Louis dressing. Arrange crabmeat, tomatoes, eggs and olives on greens. Pour Louis dressing over salad. Makes 4 servings.

Sandra GoForth
Waterloo

Louis Dressing

¾ cup chili sauce
½ cup mayonnaise or salad
  dressing
1 teaspoon instant minced onion

½ teaspoon sugar
¼ teaspoon Worcestershire
  sauce
Salt

Mix all ingredients together. Adding salt to taste. Cover and chill 30 minutes. Makes 1¼ cups.

Sandra GoForth
Waterloo

Stuffed Lobster A La Bechamel

2 pounds lobster
1½ cups milk
Bit of bay leaf
3 tablespoons butter
3 tablespoons flour
½ teaspoon salt

Few grains Cayenne
Slight grating of nutmeg
1 teaspoon chopped parsley
1 teaspoon lemon juice
2 egg yolks
½ cup buttered crumbs

Remove lobster meat from sh ell and cut and dice. Scald milk with bay leaf, remove bay leaf and make a white sauce of butter, flour, and milk; add salt, cayenne, nutmeg, parsley, egg yolks slightly beaten, and lemon juice. Add lobster dice, refill shells, cover with buttered crumbs and bake until crumbs are brown. One-half chicken stock and one-half cream may be used for sauce if a richer dish is desired.

Stuffed Lobster Tails

6 lobster tails, about 8 ounces
  each
1 pound crab meat
1 egg
½ cup mayonnaise
2 tablespoons finely chopped
  green pepper

2 tablespoons finely chopped
  pimento
½ teaspoon dry mustard
1 tablespoons instant
  minced onion

Put lobster tails in a saucepan. Cover with water. Bring to a boil. Remove from heat and drain. Remove thin shell on under side of tails. Split meat lengthwise and spread open slightly. (The easiest way is to place the blade of a large knife flat across the lobster tail and press down on the blade until the shell cracks.) Remove any small pieces of shell from crab meat. Beat egg and stir in mayonnaise. Add remaining ingredients and mix well. Stir in crab meat. Fill lobster tails. Wrap each lobster tail in a double thickness of heavy duty foil. Seal top edges, leaving some space above the stuffing. Grill 5 to 6 inches from coals 25 to 30 minutes. Makes 6 servings.

To Bake: Do not wrap in foil. Place lobster tails in shallow baking pan and bake in 350 degree oven 30 minutes or until lightly browned.

Ron Chesnut
Greeneville, Tennessee

Frogs

Only the hind-quarters of frogs are cooked; wash and wipe them, flour them and fry a light brown in butter; or put them in a stew pan with butter, a sprinkling of flour and pepper and salt; shake them about over the fire for a moment; then add a very little water, simmer until tender and almost dry, then add a coffee cup of cream, butter the size of an egg, a little flour and chopped parsley, give a boil up and serve.

Baked Or Barbecued Shrimp

3 to 5 pounds medium or large
  unpeeled shrimp
6 to 8 sticks melted
  margarine

Cayenne pepper
10 to 12 cloves of garlic

In large baking pan, place washed unpeeled shrimp (with heads if possible). Pour melted margarine (do not use butter) over shrimp. Chop cloves of garlic fine and stir into mixture (Amount of garlic can be adjusted according to taste). Cover and let sit 1 to 2 hours. This helps the flavors to blend well. Sprinkle cayenne pepper freely over shrimp. Bake at 350 degrees for 1 hour or until done. Stir shrimp once while baking. Serve with a salad, rice and bread. Serve in large bowls with sauce poured over shrimp. The butter sauce makes an ideal dip for French bread.

Mrs. James Patton
Sheffield

Shrimp Egg Foo Yong

Shrimp, peeled
Egg, beaten

Onion

Brown shrimp in wok using vegetable oil. Remove from wok, and fry onion. Combine onion and shrimp, and add egg and fry.

To make Foo Yong Sauce:

Combine:
Salt
Black pepper
Soy sauce
Green onion

Garlic powder
Ginger
Water
Sugar

Serve sauce and pork in individual dishes

Sun-See Hsu
Florence

Shrimp Relish

1½ pounds large fresh shrimp,
  cooked and deveined
1 cup minced onions
1 cup snipped parsley
⅔ cup salad oil

⅓ cup vinegar
1 clove garlic, minced
1½ teaspoons salt
Speck of pepper

Few hours ahead:
In a large bowl, combine shrimp, onion and parsley. In a small bowl, mix salad oil, vinegar, garlic, salt and pepper. Beat well. Pour over shrimp. Refrigerate shrimp one hour or until served. At serving time, heap shrimp in serving dishes with a few on rim. Guests can spear with picks. Makes about 25 to 30.

Linda McDougal
Killen

Shrimp With Garlic Butter

10 to 16 ounces frozen, shelled
  and deveined shrimp
2 chicken boullion cubes
½ cup (or 1 stick) margarine
1 2-ounce can sliced mushrooms,
  drained
½ teaspoon garlic powder

1 tablespoon lemon juice
⅛ teaspoon pepper
1 tablespoon dry sherry or 2
  teaspoons sherry flavoring
1 tablespoon parsley flakes
1 tablespoon dry onion flakes

Dissolve boullion in metled margarine. Add shrimp and mushrooms. Sauté 4 to 5 minutes or until shrimp is pink (covered black skillet is best). Stir in remaining ingredients and heat thoroughly (approximately 1 minute). Serve over plain toast.

Clifford Delony
Tuscumbia

Shrimp Ring

1 can tomato soup
3 small packages cream cheese
1 envelope unflavored gelatin
1 cup mayonnaise
½ cup chopped celery

1 small onion, chopped
¼ cup green pepper, chopped
¼ cup cold water
Salt and pepper
1 cup finely cut shrimp

Dissolve gelatin in ¼ cup water. Heat soup to a boiling point. Dissolve cream cheese. Add gelatin. Cool. Add remaining ingredients. When thickened, add shrimp. Butter the mold, add mixture and refrigerate.

Mr. E.G. Dorris
Florence

Carolina Shrimp Pilau

3 ounces salt pork or
  bacon, diced
½ cup chopped onion
1 clove garlic, minced
1 cup rice
1 can (28 ounces) tomatoes
½ teaspoon salt

¼ teaspoon mace (optional)
⅛ teaspoon cayenne pepper
1 pound medium-size
  uncooked shrimp, peeled
  and deveined
1 cup chopped green pepper

In 10-inch skillet, fry salt pork until brown and crisp; remove and reserve. Saute onion and garlic in drippings until tender, about 5 minutes. Chop and drain tomatoes. Add enough water to tomato liquid to measure 2½ cups. Add rice to skillet; cook and stir over low heat 3 minutes. Add tomato liquid, tomatoes, reserved salt pork and seasonings to rice mixture. Bring to boil; reduce heat. Cover tightly and simmer 20 minutes. Remove from heat and stir in shrimp and green pepper. Let stand covered until all liquid is absorbed, about 5 minutes. Makes six servings.

Zippy Shrimp And Rice

1 cup chopped onions
2 cloves garlic, crushed
1 tablespoon butter or margarine
1 can (16 ounces) tomatoes
1 can (8 ounces) tomato sauce
½ cup water
1 tablespoon salt
¼ teaspoon pepper

1 teaspoon each sweet basil, oregano
 leaves, and prepared
 horseradish
1 pound cleaned and deveined
 shrimp
3 cups hot cooked rice
Grated Parmesan cheese,
 optional

Sauté onions and garlic in butter until tender. Add tomatoes, tomato sauce, water, seasonings, and horseradish. Simmer for 20 minutes or until slightly thickened. Stir in shrimp and cook 10 minutes longer. Serve over beds of fluffy rice. Sprinkle with Parmesan cheese, if desired. Makes 6 servings.

Sara's Shrimp Creole

Chop 2 onions, 2 stalks celery, 1 large bell pepper. Brown in 5 tablespoons bacon fat.

Add:
1 1-pound, 12 ounce can
 tomatoes
1 can large tomato paste
1 cup water
3 tablespoons flour

1 tablespoon sugar
1½ tablespoons vinegar
3 teaspoons salt
½ teaspoon garlic salt

Simmer all ingredients together for 1 to 1½ hours. Add 3 pounds of cooked shrimp. Serve over rice.

Shrimp Creole

1½ cups flour
¼ cup cooking oil
3 onions
2 cloves garlic
½ bell pepper
¾ can thick tomato paste

2 cups water
2 stalks celery
1 sprig parsley
1 bay leaf
Salt and red pepper
2 pounds raw shrimp

Make roux by browning flour in cooking oil. Chop 1 onion, garlic, bell pepper; add to roux. Add tomato paste and water; let simmer. Chop two onion tops, celery, parsley, and add to mixture. Add bay leaf for a few minutes, then remove. Season with salt and red pepper. Let simmer for 2 hours. Add shrimp. Cook until shrimp are tender.

Evelyn Pless
Cherokee

Shrimp-Okra Gumbo

1 large onion, finely chopped
1 pound sliced okra
2 tablespoons oil
1 pint peeled headless
  shrimp
2 tablespoons tomato sauce

1 clove garlic, finely chopped
Worcestershire sauce to taste
Salt and pepper to taste
Tabasco sauce to taste
2 cups hot water

Saute onion and okra in oil, stirring often, until okra is dry and slightly brown. Add shrimp; stir until pink. Add tomato sauce, garlic, Worcestershire sauce, salt, pepper, Tabasco sauce and water; simmer for 45 minutes to 1 hour. Yield: 4 servings.

Mrs. Joe L. Puckett Sr.
Muscle Shoals

Mardi Gras Gumbo

1 medium onion, chopped
1 clove garlic, minced
4 tablespoons butter
2 envelopes instant vegetable
  broth or 2 vegetable
  bouillon cubes
1 can (about 1 pound) tomatoes
1 can (about 1 pound) okra
1 can (about 7 ounces) minced
  clams

1 can (12 ounces) mixed
  vegetable juice
1 teaspoon salt
1 teaspoon sugar
¼ teaspoon bottled red pepper
  seasoning
1 tablespoon cornstarch
½ cup cold water
2 cans (about 5 ounces each)
  deveined shrimp (rinsed)
Rice

Saute onion and garlic in butter just until soft. Stir in vegetable broth, tomatoes, okra, clam, vegetable juice, and seasoning. Heat to boiling and simmer 10 minutes.

Stir cornstarch into water until smooth in cup. Stir into soup mixture. Cook, stirring constantly until soup thickens slightly and boils 3 minutes. Stir in shrimp. Cook 2 to 3 minutes. Pour over rice. Serves 6.

Kaye Ford
Sheffield

Crabburgers

1 cup crab meat (fresh or canned)
½ cup diced celery
2 tablespoons chopped onion

½ cup shredded cheddar cheese
½ cup mayonnaise

Mix all ingredients. Spread on toasted English muffins and broil a few seconds. Serve hot.

Mrs. John E. Higginbotham
Florence

Fish Gumbo

1 pound boneless fish cut in
   small pieces (turbot)
2 cups brown rice
1 chopped seeded banana
   pepper (optional)
¼ teaspoon oregano
½ teaspoon chili powder, dash
   of tabasco
2 cans beef gravy
1 button garlic, chopped fine
1 bay leaf

¼ cup butter or margarine
½ cup chopped onion
1 medium bell pepper
½ cup chopped celery
1 can (1 pound 12 ounce)
   tomatoes
1 can (15½ ounce) okra
1 cup water
¼ teaspoon dried thyme
   leaves
1 teaspoon salt and pepper
   or to taste

Mix all ingredients and let simmer. This is great for a slow cooker. Serve over additional brown rice if desired.

Ruby Anderson
Florence

Seven Sea Casserole

1 can mushroom soup
½ cup milk
1 package frozen peas (cooked)

1⅓ cup cooked rice
1 can tuna or shrimp

Combine soup and milk and heat to boiling. Place cooked rice in a two quart buttered casserole dish. Add tuna or shrimp and stir. Spread peas on top and pour soup over all and top with slices of American cheese. Bake at 350 degrees for about 20 minutes.

Evelyn Pless
Cherokee

Fish Creole With Rice

1 cup each chopped onions
   and celery
½ cup chopped green pepper
1 clove garlic, crushed
1½ tablespoons butter or
   margarine
2 tablespoons chopped parsley
1 teaspoon salt

⅛ teaspoon red pepper
1 bay leaf
1 can (14½ ounce) tomatoes
¾ cup water
1 pound fillets of flounder,
   cubed
1 tablespoon cornstarch
3 cups hot cooked rice

Sauté onions, celery, green pepper and garlic in butter until tender. Add parsley, seasonings, tomatoes, and ½ cup water. Cover and simmer 15 minutes. Add fish cubes and cook 15 minutes longer. Blend cornstarch and ¼ cup water. Stir into creole sauce and cook 2 minutes longer. Remove bay leaf. Serve over bed of fluffy rice. Makes 6 servings.

Peggy Scott
Eunice, Louisiana

Quick Tuna Casserole

1 large can tuna
1 regular size package potato chips

1 can mushroom soup
4 large slices cheese

Cover the bottom of a baking dish with crushed potato chips; spread tuna evenly over top. Lay cheese slices on top of tuna; cover with ½ can of mushroom soup. Repeat layers. If mixture seems dry add ½ can water. Cook in a 325-degree preheated oven for 25 minutes. Serves six.

Addie C. Montgomery
Tuscumbia

Tuna Casserole

1 can (7 ounces) white meat tuna
2 hard boiled eggs
1 cup English peas, drained

1 can mushroom soup
⅓ cup milk
Potato chips

Mix all ingredients together, except potato chips. Bake in a 350 degree oven for 25 minutes. During the last 10 minutes of baking, crumble potato chips over the casserole.

Mrs. Jack Thomason
Muscle Shoals

Chicken & Tuna Casserole

1 cup macaroni (raw)
½ cup chopped onion
¼ cup green pepper, chopped
3 tablespoons flour (Rye flour or corn starch)

2 tablespoons butter
1¼ cups milk
1 can tuna
1 can (10 ounces) cream of chicken soup

Cook macaroni until tender, drain. Simmer onion and pepper in butter. Add flour and milk. Cook until thick. Add chicken soup and cook until smooth. Then add macaroni and tuna. Bake for 30 minutes in a moderate oven.

Donna M. Hayes
Florence

Hot Tuna 'N Rice

For six servings prepare 1½ cups uncooked rice, following the directions on the package. While rice is cooking prepare creamed tuna as follows:

1 can (7 ounce) tuna
4 tablespoons maragarine
4 tablespoons self-rising flour

2 cups milk
⅛ teaspoon each of salt, pepper and paprika

Melt butter in double boiler, add flour and stir until blended and smooth. Add milk slowly, stirring constantly until mixture boils and thickens. Add seasonings and cook 5 minutes more. Add tuna and heat thoroughly. Serve over rice in individual plates. Can make ring of rice on serving platter and fill with creamed tuna. Garnish with stuffed olives or pickles.

Evelyn Pless
Cherokee

Salmon Chowder

1 pound can salmon
1 cup diced raw potatoes
1 cup canned tomatoes
1 small onion, cut fine
2 cups hot water

¼ cup butter
¼ cup flour
3 cups milk
2 teaspoons salt
¼ teaspoon pepper

Remove bones from salmon. Place it with its liquid in a saucepan with the potatoes, tomatoes, onion and water. Simmer for 20 minutes or until the potatoes are tender. Make a white sauce of the butter, flour and milk. Add to salmon mixture, season and serve immediately. Ten generous servings. Time: 30 to 35 minutes.

Mrs. Hattie K. Bailey
Rogersville

Fish Chowder

1 pound fillet of haddock
1½ cups diced raw potatoes
1 cup chopped celery
½ cup chopped onion
1 bay leaf
4 cups water
1½ cups instant nonfat dry
   milk solids

2 tablespoons margarine
3 tablespoons flour
2 teaspoons salt
Generous dash white pepper
Chopped parsley

In a large saucepan combine haddock, potatoes, celery, onion, bay leaf and water. Simmer 15 minutes, or until potatoes are fork-tender. Flake fish with fork into bite-size pieces. Remove bay leaf. Strain mixture, reserving liquid. Stir nonfat dry milk solids into liquid.

Melt margarine in a large saucepan. Blend in flour, salt and pepper. Gradually blend in reserved liquid mixture. Cook over medium heat, stirring constantly, until mixture comes to a boil. Add strained fish mixture, heat through. Serve hot garnished with parsley. Makes 7 servings.

Mildred Anderson
Florence

Clam And Cheese Chowder

1 package (5½ ounce) potatoes
   au gratin
2 cups water
1½ cups clam juice or chicken
   broth

1 cup milk
1 can (8 ounce) minced clams
2 tablespoons butter or margarine
1 teaspoon parsley flakes

Combine potatoes and seasoning mix from package with water and clam juice in large saucepan. Cover and simmer 15 to 20 minutes. Stir in milk, undrained clams, and butter. Heat gently 5 minutes longer. Sprinkle with parsley flakes. 5 to 6 servings.

Tuna Romanoff
(Chicken or Turkey can be substituted)

4 tablespoons butter
3½ cups rice cereal crushed
  to 2½ cups
¼ cup chopped onion
1 can mushroom soup
1 8-ounce package cream cheese
½ cup milk (evaporated)

½ cup sliced olives
3 ounces cooked and drained
  noodles
2 cans drained tuna
½ cup mozzarella cheese
  (shredded)

Preheat oven to 350 degrees. Melt butter in large skillet. Remove 3 tablespoons and mix with rice cereal crumbs. Set aside. Saute onion in remaining butter 5 minutes. Add soup, cream cheese, and milk. Heat and stir over low heat until smooth. Remove from heat. Stir in olives, noodles, tuna, and 1 cup rice cereal crumbs. Turn into 1½ quart baking dish. Sprinkle with cheese, then remaining crumbs. Bake 25 minutes. Garnish with paprika and parsley flakes. Serves 6.

Mrs. Brenda Heupel
Florence

Tuna Chop Suey

¼ cup (½ stick) margarine
1 cup sliced celery
1 medium onion, sliced
1 medium green pepper, cut
  in strips
1 clove garlic, minced
1 can (8 ounce) bamboo
  shoots, drained
1 can (8 ounce) water
  chestnuts, drained and
  sliced

1½ cups water
1 tablespoon soy sauce
½ teaspoon salt
2 tablespoons cornstarch
2 cans (7 ounces each) water-packed
  tuna, drained and
  flaked
Cooked rice

In a large skillet, melt margarine over medium heat. Lightly saute celery, green pepper, onion, garlic, bamboo shoots and water chestnuts. Mix one and one-quarter cups water, soy sauce and salt into skillet. Combine cornstarch with remaining water; slowly add to skillet, stirring constantly. Simmer until thickened. Fold in tuna and heat through. Serve over rice. Makes 6 servings.

Tuna Tantalizer

¾ cup quick or old
  fashioned oats, uncooked
1 6½ ounce can tuna,
  drained, flaked
½ cup chopped pimiento
½ cup pitted ripe olive
  halves

⅓ cup sweet pickle relish
1 8-ounce carton plain yogurt
2 tablespoons milk
½ teaspoon salt
½ teaspoon onion salt
¼ teaspoon pepper

Toast oats in shallow baking pan in preheated moderate oven (350 degrees Farenheit) about 15 minutes or until golden borwn. Cool. Combine all ingredients, mix well. Chill. Serve with assorted raw vegetables. Makes about 3 cups dip.

Seafood Casserole I

1 cup shrimp
1 cup crabmeat
4 tablespoons chopped onion
1 cup chopped celery
½ cup mayonnaise
½ teaspoon Worcestershire sauce
½ teaspoon salt
Pinch of black pepper
½ teaspoon dry mustard
Buttered bread crumbs
½ can mushroom soup

Mix all together except bread crumbs. Put in greased casserole dish. Put crumbs on top. Bake in 350 degree oven until lightly browned.

Mrs. Dorothy H. Smith
Florence

Seafood Casserole II

⅔ cups cooked shrimp
1 cup crab meat
⅓ cup onions, grated
3 tablespoons bell pepper, chopped
2 cups cooked rice
1 teaspoon salt
⅛ teaspoon pepper
1 teaspoon Worcestershire sauce
1 cup mayonnaise
1 cup English peas (optional)
1 cup buttered bread crumbs

Combine all ingredients (except bread crumbs). Put in greased casserole dish and sprinkle crumbs over top. Bake at 350 degrees for 30 to 40 minutes. Garnish with parsley. Serves six to eight.

M.B. Anderson
Florence

Crab Casserole

1 pound crab meat
1 onion, chopped
½ bell pepper, chopped
1 stick butter or oleo
3 stalks celery, chopped
1 teaspoon salt
¼ teaspoon pepper
1 can mushroom soup
2 eggs
Rice Krispies
1 cup corn flakes
½ teaspoon Worcestershire sauce
1 tablespoon mayonnaise

Melt butter in sauce pan. Sauté onion and bell pepper in melted butter. Add mushroom soup, corn flakes, egg, crab and other ingredients. Place in baking dish and top with crushed Rice Krispies. Bake 20 minutes at 400 degrees.

Evelyn Pless
Cherokee

Crepes St. Jacques

Crepes

½ cup all-purpose flour

1 egg, beaten

¼ cup water

½ teaspoon salad oil

Blend flour, egg, salt and water to pancake consistency. Heat salad oil in 6-inch frying pan. Pour batter to make very thin pancakes. Cook until done; keep hot while preparing filling.

Filling

1 tablespoon butter

2 tablespoons diced onion

1 clove crushed garlic

½ cup crabmeat

½ cup scallops

Salt and pepper to taste

1 teaspoon all-purpose flour

½ cup Chablis wine

½ cup heavy cream

Dash Worcestershire sauce

Freshly squeezed juice of

½ lemon

Hollandaise sauce

Melt butter in flat saucepan; simmer onion and garlic lightly. Add crabmeat and scallops, season to taste with salt and pepper, and sauté for 10 minutes. Add flour and mix well. Stir in wine, cream, Worcestershire sauce, and lemon juice. Distribute mixture evenly onto crepes and roll them up. Put in 500 degree oven for a few minutes. Cover with Hollandaise Sauce and serve hot. Yield: 4 servings.

Mrs. J. Douglas Evans
Florence

Spaghetti With Ripe Olive Clam Sauce

A variation on a favorite theme.

¾ cup canned pitted ripe
   olives

1 can (6½ to 8 ounces) minced
   or chopped clams

Milk

2 tablespoons butter

2 tablespoons flour

½ teaspoon salt

½ teaspoon Worcestershire
   sauce

2 teaspoons lemon juice

2 drops tabasco sauce

1 tablespoon minced parsley

Drain olives and slice. Drain clams; to clam liquid add enough milk to make 1¼ cups. In a 1-quart saucepan over low heat melt butter; stir in flour, salt and onion powder; remove from heat; gradually stir in milk mixture, keeping smooth. Cook over moderately low heat, stirring constantly, until thickened and boiling. Stir in Worcestershire, lemon juice, tabasco, clams, olives and parsley; reheat. Makes about 1¾ cups sauce, enough for ½ pound spaghetti, cooked—4 servings.

Salmon Patties

1 can (16 ounces) pink
  salmon
1 egg
⅛ cup chopped onion

½ cup flour
1½ teaspoons baking powder
1½ cups vegetable oil

Drain salmon, reserving ½ of liquid. Mix together salmon, egg, reserved liquid, and onion until sticky; stir in flour and baking powder. Form into small patties and fry until golden brown in hot oil.

Eddie Killen
Florence

Salmon Loaf

2 cups (1 can) canned
  salmon
½ teaspoon pepper
1 teaspoon salt
2 tablespoons lemon juice

½ cup hot milk
2 cups bread or cracker
  crumbs
3 egg yolks
3 egg whites

Remove skin, bone and drain salmon; flake. Pour hot milk over crumbs and add to flaked salmon, salt, pepper and lemon juice. Add beaten egg yolks and fold in stiffly beaten egg whites last. Pour into a well greased loaf pan. Bake 1 hour at 350 degrees.

Ethel Rutherford
Cherokee

Seaside Chowder

3 slices bacon
1 cup chopped onion
2 cups water
1 can (8 ounces) cut green
  beans
2 ounces (about 1 cup) sea-
  shell macaroni

½ pound (2 cups) shredded
  American cheese
1 to 1¼ cups milk
1 can (6½ ounces) chunk style
  tuna, drained and flaked
Generous dash pepper

In saucepan, cook bacon until crisp; remove and crumble. Pour off all but 2 tablespoons drippings; add onion and cook until crisp-tender. Stir in water and liquid from green beans. Bring to a boil; add macaroni and cook, uncovered, 6 minutes. Add bacon and remaining ingredients. Simmer 5-10 minutes more or until macaroni is tender; stir occasionally. Makes 4 servings. (Yield: about 5½ cups).

Lesa Armstrong
Florence

Vegetables

Wentachee Squash-Stuffed Apples

8 large Golden Delicious apples
1 cup apple cider
½ cup brown sugar
2 packages (12 ounces each)
  frozen squash

2 tablespoons butter or margarine
1 tablespoon brown sugar
½ teaspoon salt
½ teaspoon nutmeg

Core apples, being careful not to cut through blossom end. Cut ½-inch slice off top of each apple. Scoop out pulp leaving ¾-inch shells. Reserve pulp. Place apples in shallow baking dish. Combine cider and ½ cup brown sugar. Heat until sugar dissolves. Pour over apples. Bake at 325 degrees for 40 to 45 minutes, or until apples are tender, basting occasionally with syrup.

Meanwhile, chop reserved apple pulp. Place in saucepan with squash and butter or margarine. Cook until apple is tender and squash is thawed. Add 1 tablespoon brown sugar, salt and nutmeg. Beat with electric mixer until smooth. Pipe or spoon squash mixture into apple centers, mounding high. Sprinkle with additional nutmeg. Return to oven and bake 15 minutes longer, basting with syrup from pan. Makes eight servings.

Cheesy Cauliflower Italiano

3 tablespoons flour
¼ teaspoon salt
½ teaspoon garlic powder
½ teaspoon coarsely ground pepper
1 pound fresh cauliflower, cored,
  cleaned and cut vertically
  into thin slices, about
  4 cups
1 small onion, sliced in very thin
  slices

3 tablespoons butter or margarine,
  cut into small pieces
1 cup ripe olives, sliced
2 cups grated Mozzarella cheese
½ cup grated Parmesan cheese
2 tablespoons parsley, chopped
Paprika
¼ cup dry white wine
¾ cup milk

Preheat oven to 350 degrees. Combine flour, salt, garlic powder and coarsely ground pepper. In a greased 8-inch square casserole, layer ½ of each of the following ingredients in order: cauliflower, onion, flour mixture, butter pieces, olives, Mozzarella cheese and Parmesan cheese. Repeat layering with second ½ of ingredients, adding chopped parsley between olive slices and Mozzarella cheese. Sprinkle with paprika. Combine wine and milk; pour over. Bake uncovered in preheated oven 40 to 45 minutes or until golden and bubbly. Makes four to five servings.

Variation: For stronger cheese flavor, grated Romano cheese may be substituted for all or part of Parmesan cheese.

Squash Souffle

1½ pounds squash
9 crackers
¼ cup butter
2 eggs

1 large onion
1 cup grated cheese
½ cup milk
Salt and pepper to taste

Cook squash and onion together until tender, drain off water and mash until fine. Add salt, pepper, cheese, butter, egg yolks, and crackers that have been crumbled fine. Beat egg whites until very stiff and fold into mixture. Cook in a greased casserole at 350 degrees for 30 to 45 minutes. Serve hot.

Mrs. C.H. Holder
Florence

Mother's Squash Casserole

6 medium yellow squash, sliced
1 small onion, minced
1 teaspoon salt
1 egg well beaten
½ cup milk

1 can cream of mushroom soup
2 tablespoons butter or margarine
1 cup grated cheese
1 cup cracker crumbs

Cook squash in small amount of water in covered container until tender. Drain. Mix all ingredients, reserving a small amount of cheese and cracker crumbs for top. Place in greased baking dish. Sprinkle with reserved cracker crumbs and cheese. Bake in 350 degree oven about 30 minutes or until slightly brown on top.

Oma Gooch
Florence

Southern Summer Squash

6 or 8 small squash
2 medium onions, chopped
1 stick butter or margarine
3 large eggs

1 can cream of mushroom soup
½ teaspoon salt
1 cup of herb stuffing mix

Boil squash and onions until tender; drain and mash. Stir in remaining ingredients except herb stuffing. Spread ½ or ⅓ of stuffing mix on bottom of 1½ quart baking dish; then spread squash mix over stuffing mix and then top with the remainder of stuffing mix. Bake at 350 degrees for 25 to 30 minutes. Yield: 8 servings.

Mrs. Orville O. Sharp
Florence

Squash Casserole

1 pound yellow squash
1 pound zucchini squash
½ cup onion
1 cup evaporated milk
½ stick butter

1 cup grated sharp cheddar
 cheese
Bread crumbs
Salt

Boil squash witn onion until tender. Drain well and chop. Add milk, butter, cheese and salt. Pour into casserole and top with bread crumbs. Bake at 350 degrees for 30 minutes. Serves 6.

Betty Ballinger
Madisonville, Kentucky

Squash Casserole

1½ pounds fresh or frozen squash
  or 2 16-ounce cans
Salt and pepper
1 jar (2 ounces) pimentos, chopped
1 medium onion, chopped finely
1 cup sour cream
1 can cream of chicken soup
4 small carrots, grated
1 package cornbread or herb
  stuffing
½ cup margarine, melted

Cook squash in small amount of water until tender. Drain and mash, season to taste. Stir in remaining ingredients, reserving half the stuffing, which has been mixed with melted margarine. Line a casserole with reserved stuffing. Set aside enough stuffing to sprinkle on top. Fill casserole with squash mixture and top with remainder of stuffing. Bake at 350 degrees for 30 minutes. May be prepared the day before and baked when needed. This can also be frozen. Serves eight.

Emma Jeffreys
Leighton

Squash Pie

1 cup cooked squash
1 cup cream
¾ cup sugar, white or brown
3 eggs
3 tablespoons vanilla
½ teaspoon ginger
½ teaspoon nutmeg
½ teaspoon salt
¼ teaspoon mace
White of 1 egg
Bread crumbs

To one cupful of cooked squash which has been put through a sieve or one cupful of canned squash, add the cream and sugar. Beat the three eggs slightly and add to the squash and cream mixture with the vanilla, ginger, nutmeg, salt and mace. Line a pie plate with pastry. Brush the pastry with the white of an egg and sprinkle lightly with bread crumbs. Pour in the squash mixture and bake as caramel custard pie. This pie is delicious spread with honey and topped with whipped cream.

Mrs. Joan Pugh
Florence

Stuffed Green Peppers

4 medium green peppers
½ pound ground beef
1 cup cooked rice
1¼ teaspoon salt
1 slightly beaten egg
2 tablespoons minced onion
½ cup condensed tomato soup
½ cup grated cheese

Remove stems and seed from green peppers. Blanch them in hot water for 10 minutes or until tender. Place upright in a 1½ quart casserole dish.

Combine ground beef, cooked rice, salt, egg, minced onion and tomato soup. Mix well. Fill peppers with mixture and bake 30 minutes in a 350 degree oven. Pour remainder of soup over peppers and sprinkle with cheese. Bake 15 minutes longer.

Evelyn Pless
Cherokee

Copper Carrot Pennies

1 pound carrots
1 green pepper, sliced in rings
1 onion (sliced in rings)
1 can tomato soup

½ cup salad oil
1 teaspoon Worcestershire sauce
1 cup vinegar
Salt and pepper to taste

Marinate tomato soup, salad oil, Worcestershire sauce, vinegar, and salt and pepper; set aside. Scrap, slice and boil carrots in salted water until tender. Drain and cool. In bowl, alternate layers of carrots, pepper rings and onion rings. Pour marinade over vegetables. Refrigerate 12 to 24 hours before serving. Serve cold.

Mrs. Donald E. Holt
Florence

Glazed Carrots

1 small can or 10 medium carrots
½ cup brown sugar
¼ cup water from carrots

1 tablespoon butter
¼ teaspoon salt

Put carrots in pan after water has been drained, reserving ¼ cup. Meanwhile, combine remaining ingredients in saucepan and boil five minutes. Pour hot syrup over carrots. Bake in a moderate oven 15 minutes.

Ruth Gobbell
Florence

Flatwoods Black-Eyed Peas

2 cups black-eye peas (swell at least two hours)
2 small hamhocks (hog knuckles)

¼ cup finely chopped onions
¼ teaspoon salt
¼ teaspoon ground red pepper

Place hamhocks in 2½ cups of water in a medium boiler. Cook on medium for 1 to 1½ hours. Add peas and cook for 30 minutes. Add onions, salt and pepper. Simmer for 10 more minutes. Serves two to four.

Debbie J. Carter
Leighton

Hopping John

1 cup dried black-eyed peas
¼ pound salt pork, diced
1 medium green pepper, chopped
1 medium onion, chopped

1 cup uncooked regular rice
1 tablespoon butter
Pinch of cayenne pepper
Salt and pepper to taste

Pick over peas, wash thoroughly. Place in a heavy saucepan; cover with water. Soak overnight; drain. Add salt pork, green pepper, onions. Cover with water and simmer two hours or until peas are tender. Cook rice according to package directions. When peas are done and water has cooked very low, add remaining ingredients. Cover and cook over low heat until all liquid is absorbed. Serve hot. Yield 4 to 6 servings.

Ruth Gobbell
Florence

Green Bean Casserole

2 packages frozen cut green
  beans or 2 1-pound
  cans, drained
1 teaspoon salt
¾ cup milk

1 can (10½ ounce) condensed
  cream of mushroom
  soup
⅛ teaspoon ground black pepper
2 tablespoons diced pimiento
1 can (3-ounce) french fried
  onions

Cook frozen beans in salted water; drain. If using canned beans, omit salt. Combine milk, soup, pepper; pour over beans. Add ½ can onions. Pour into 1½ quart casserole. Bake at 350 degrees for 20 minutes. Garnish with ½ can onions and pimiento. Bake 5 minutes. Serves 6.

Donna M. Hayes
Florence

Green Beans Horseradish

2 (No. 2) cans green beans
1 onion, sliced
3 slices bacon, cut up
1 cup mayonnaise
2 hard boiled eggs, chopped
1 heaping tablespoon horseradish

1 teaspoon Worcestershire sauce
Salt, pepper, garlic salt, celery
  salt, onion salt to
  taste
1½ teaspoons parsley flakes
Juice of 1 lemon

Cook beans with onion and bacon for at least 1 hour. Combine remaining ingredients and set aside at room temperature. When beans are ready to serve, drain and put in serving dish. Pour mayonnaise mixture over them. Serves 8.

Mrs. Harold V. Hughston
Tuscumbia

Frozen Green Bean Festive

2 10-ounce packages frozen
  French-style green beans
1 can cream of mushroom soup
¼ teaspoon celery salt

¼ teaspoon soy sauce
1 3½ ounce can French fried
  onions

Cook beans in one cup boilng water for three minutes or until beans lose raw taste. Drain. Reserve one-half cup liquid. Combine all other ingredients in 1½ quart casserole with one-half the onion. Arrange rest of onion on top. Bake in moderate oven (350 degrees) for 20-30 minutes. Makes 6 servings.

Evelyn Pless
Cherokee

Canned Beans With Vinegar

2 gallons green beans, broken
  up
1 gallon water

1 cup vinegar
1 cup sugar
¾ cup salt (hot iodized)

Break and wash beans. Place them in a large enamel dishpan. Pour 1 gallon of water over beans. Add vinegar, sugar and salt. Bring to a rolling boil and boil 30 minutes. Can beans using regular method.

Elsie Pierce
Sheffield

French Bean Casserole

2 cans French style beans (heated
   and drained)
3 tablespoons butter
1 teaspoon salt
1 (8 ounce) carton sour cream

2 tablespoons flour
2 tablespoons grated onions
½ cup grated cheddar cheese
1 small package corn flakes,
   crushed

Melt butter; stir in flour, salt, and onions. Remove from heat; add cheese gradually. Add sour cream and fold in beans. Put in greased 1½ quart casserole. Top with corn flakes. Bake at 350 degrees for 20 minutes.

Paula Doggett
Florence

Brussels Sprouts In Onion Butter

1 small onion, chopped
2 tablespoons butter or margarine
1 package (10 ounce) Brussels
   sprouts

1 cup chicken stock (canned
   or made from 1 bouillon
   cube and 1 cup water)
Salt and pepper to taste

Saute the onion in butter very slowly until soft and golden brown. Cook the sprouts in chicken stock, steaming them just until tender. Drain; toss with onion butter; season with salt and pepper.

Mrs. John D. Clement, Jr.
Muscle Shoals

Sweet And Sour Red Cabbage

½ cup water
3 tablespoons sugar
3 tablespoons vinegar
1 onion stuck with 6 to 9 cloves
1 tablespoon flour

1 medium head red cabbage,
   shredded fine
Boiling water, salted
¼ cup pork or bacon drippings
1 large apple, peeled and chopped

Cover cabbage with boiling salted water and simmer 10 minutes. Drain thoroughly. Put in large casserole. Stir into the cabbage the drippings, apple, water, sugar and vinegar. Push the onion well down in the middle. Cover and bake 1½ hours in slow oven at 325 degrees. Just before serving sprinkle the flour over mixture and stir it in. Remove the onion. Serves 6 to 8.

Mrs. John E. Higginbotham
Florence

Garlic Grits

4½ cups water
1 teaspoon salt
1 cup grits
1 stick oleo

1 roll garlic cheese
2 beaten eggs
½ cup sweet milk
Crushed corn flakes

Cook grits in water and salt as directed on box. Add oleo and melted garlic cheese. Add eggs and milk; mix. Place in greased casserole. Cover with butter and crushed corn flakes. Bake about 20 minutes at 350 degrees.

Mrs. George Barnett
Florence

Poor-Man Potatoes

4 large Irish potatoes, peeled
1 medium onion
3 strips bacon
½ teaspoon salt (optional)
¼ teaspoon black pepper
1 cup water

Slice potatoes and onion (either lengthwise or crosswise). Fry bacon and drain off fat. Place potatoes and onions in a skillet. Pour in 1 cup water. Bring to a boil on high and cut down to medium. When half done, place fried bacon on top, sprinkle with salt, pepper and ¼ of bacon drippings. Cook on low. Serves four to six.

Debbie Joy Carter
Leighton

Sweet Potato Casserole

3 cups cooked mashed sweet
   potatoes
1 cup sugar
2 eggs
Topping:
1 cup light brown sugar
1 cup chopped pecans
1 teaspoon vanilla
½ cup butter
⅓ cup milk

⅓ cup flour
⅓ cup butter

Add other ingredients to mashed potatoes and mix well. Put in greased casserole. Mix topping and crumble on top. Bake in 350 degree oven for 25-30 minutes.

Billy Townsend
Florence

Yummy Yams

4 pounds sweet potatoes, cooked
   and mashed
½ cup maragarine
⅓ cup orange juice
⅓ cup firmly packed brown
   sugar
¾ teaspoon salt
½ teaspoon apple pie spice
½ to ¾ cup pecan halves

Combine all ingredients except pecans in a large mixing bowl, mixing well. Pour into a greased 2½ quart casserole dish. Arrange nuts around edge of dish. Bake at 350 degrees for 45 minutes.

Lela Hall
Leighton

Sweet Potatoes And Apples

Wash and peel six medium-sized sweet potatoes. Cut crosswise and steam until nearly tender, using ½ cup water and 1 teaspoon salt. Do not overcook!

Pare and core three medium, tart apples and cut finely crosswise.

Grease a casserole dish and place alternate layers of potatoes and apples. Place ½ cup sugar, a dash of cinnamon and dots of butter between each alternate layer.

Pour over casserole any potato water left or use additional water to make ½ to ¾ cups.

Bake at 350 degrees covered for 30 minutes; uncover and bake 15 minutes more.

This dish is delicious served with pork roast or baked pork chops.

Mrs. Mava Streetman
Muscle Shoals

Ann's Sweet Potato Casserole

5 sweet potatoes
1 cup butter
1½ cups sugar
1 cup milk

Juice and grated rind of 1 orange
4 eggs
1 cup nuts, chopped and mixed
  with melted butter

Stew potatoes in jackets. Skin and mash. Add butter, sugar, milk, orange juice and rind, and eggs. Put in buttered casserole. Sprinkle buttered nuts on top. Bake at 350 degrees for 30 minutes.

Mrs. J.E. Tease
Florence

Sweet Potato Casserole

3 cups mashed sweet potatoes
1 cup sugar
⅓ cup milk

2 teaspoons vanilla
½ cup butter

Topping:

1 cup light brown sugar
½ cup flour

1 cup chopped nuts
½ cup butter

Add other ingredients to mashed potatoes and mix well. Put into a greased casserole. Mix topping and crumble on top of casserole. Bake in a 350 degree oven for 25 to 35 minutes.

Mrs. Pat Peck
Florence

Broccoli Casserole

3 cups cooked minute rice
1 stick butter or oleo
Salt
2 packages broccoli, cooked
  according to package
  directions and drained well

1 (8 ounce) jar cheese spread
1 can cream of chicken soup
1 small can water chestnuts

Mix rice and broccoli; add cheese spread, soup, and water chestnuts. Pour melted butter or oleo over top of casserole. Bake in 350 degree oven until bubbly. Can be frozen before baking.

Mrs. Joe Patterson, Jr.
Florence

Broccoli And Rice Casserole

2 cups instant rice, cooked
1 can cream of mushroom soup
1 (8 ounce) jar cheese spread
1 small or medium onion, grated

½ cup celery, chopped
4 tablespoons butter
2 packages chopped broccoli,
  cooked and drained

Saute onions, celery and butter. Combine all ingredients and bake in buttered casserole for 45 minutes in 350 degree oven. Serves 12.

Mrs. Claire S. Pitts
Sheffield

Creamy Scalloped Potatoes

2 pounds potatoes (about 6 medium) 2½ cups milk
3 tablespoons butter or margarine ¼ cup finely chopped onion
3 tablespoons flour 1 tablespoon butter or margarine
Salt and pepper

Heat oven to 350 degrees. Wash potatoes, pare thinly and remove eyes. Cut potatoes into thin slices to measure about four cups. Melt 3 tablespoons butter in saucepan over low heat. Blend in flour and seasonings. Cook over low heat, stirring until mixture is smooth and bubbly. Remove from heat. Stir in milk. Heat to boiling, stirring constantly. Boil and stir one minute.

In a greased 2-quart casserole, arrange potatoes in two layers, topping each with half the onion and one-third of the white sauce. Top with remaining potatoes and sauce. Dot with 1 tablespoon butter. Cover. Bake 30 minutes. Uncover and bake 60 to 70 minutes longer or until potatoes are tender. Let stand 5 to 10 minutes before serving.

Anita Pilkilton
Tuscumbia

Cheesy Scalloped Potatoes

1 can cheddar cheese soup 8 cups thinly sliced potatoes
1 can cream of mushroom soup 1 cup thinly sliced onions
½ cup milk 2 tablespoons butter
¼ teaspoon pepper

Combine soups, milk and pepper. In 2-quart baking dish (13 x 9 x 2) arrange alternate layers of potatoes, onions and soup mixture. Dot top with butter. Bake at 375 degrees for 1 hour. Uncover and bake 15 minutes more until done. Makes 8 servings.

James Coburn

Special Stuffed Potatoes

6 to 8 baking potatoes 1½ to 2 teaspoons salt
½ cup diced green pepper ⅛ teaspoon pepper
¼ cup butter or margarine ¼ cup shredded Cheddar
½ to ⅔ cup hot milk cheese

Scrub potatoes, prick each with a fork and wrap individually in aluminum foil and bake in hot oven (400 degrees F.) until done, approximately 1 hour. Cut slice from top of each potato immediately and scoop out centers, being careful not to break skins. Cook green pepper in butter or margarine for 2 to 3 minutes; remove green pepper and reserve. Mash potatoes; add the butter or margarine, hot milk, salt and pepper and beat until light. Fold in reserved green pepper and fill potato shells with mixture; return to foil wrappings, folding foil to make containers. Sprinkle shredded cheese on top. Return to oven and bake 15 minutes. Serves 6 to 8.

Rice Broccoli Casserole

1 cup raw rice
1 package frozen chopped broccoli
Margarine
¾ cup onion, chopped
¾ cup celery, chopped

1 can cream of chicken soup
1 can cream of mushroom soup
1 medium jar (8 ounces) cheese
 spread

Cook rice and broccoli as usual without salt. Saute onion and celery in margarine. Mix cream of chicken soup, cream of mushroom soup, and cheese spread. Add cooked rice and broccoli to other ingredients. Bake in greased casserole in 350 degree oven for 30 minutes.

Mrs. Ken Hewlett
Muscle Shoals

Broccoli Casserole Dixon

2 packages (10 ounces each)
 frozen broccoli
½ teaspoon monosodium glutamate
1 can condensed cream of chicken
 soup
Juice of one lemon

½ cup mayonnaise
6 slices processed American
 cheese
½ cup bread crumbs
2 tablespoons butter
1 teaspoon seasoned salt

Cook broccoli as package directs, but only for 5 minutes. Cut into 1-inch lengths. Put into a greased 2-quart casserole sprinkled with pepper and glutamate. Mix soup and mayonnaise and lemon juice. Spread this over broccoli. Top with cheese and bread crumbs that have been mixed with butter. Sprinkle seasoned salt over this. Bake at 350 degrees for 30 minutes. Serves 6 to 8 people.

Mrs. Edward J. Diskey
Key Largo, Florida

Broccoli Casserole

2 packages frozen, chopped
 broccoli (prepared according
 to package directions)
2 eggs
1 cup sharp, grated cheese

1 can cream of celery soup
1 cup mayonnaise
1 small onion, grated
Salt and pepper to taste

Mix all ingredients. Crumble bread crumbs or Ritz crackers over the top and pour one-half stick melted butter over all. Bake at 350 degrees for 20 minutes.

Mrs. Bailey Anderson
Florence

Eggplant Casserole
(Ratatouille Tyree Provencale)

2 or 3 medium eggplants
2 garlic buds, chopped
2 onions, chopped
2 bell peppers, slice some and
   chop rest
Medium jar of pimentos
½ cup chopped celery
½ pound fresh mushrooms
   or large jar stems
   and caps (use liquid,
   also)
2 or 3 ripe tomatoes

1 or 2 cans "Rotel" tomatoes
   and chilis
1 can stewed tomatoes
1 or 2 cans tomato sauce
2 fresh zucchini
2 teaspoons basil
1 teaspoon oregano or marjoram
2 teaspoons monosodium glutamate
3 teaspoons dehydrated parsley
Parmesan cheese (dry, in can)
1 package sliced bread crumbs
Olive oil

Slice eggplant into ¾ inch sections. Salt slices and let drain in colander and dry on paper towel. Remove stems from fresh mushrooms and chop. Chop tomatoes into large pieces and slice zucchini in ½ inch slices. Saute celery, bell pepper, garlic, and onion in olive oil until tender in electric skillet. Remove and reserve. Saute mushrooms, remove. Saute eggplant; keep adding olive oil until lightly browned. Saute zucchini. Mix tomatoes, sauce, spices, pimentos, and oil in 2 quart casserole dish. In casserole dish, place a layer of eggplant (and zucchini); a layer of ½ of celery, pepper, onion, garlic; a layer of tomato mix; and a layer of cheese slices broken in 2 inch pieces. Sprinkle with parsley and Parmesan. Repeat layers. Pour remaining tomato mix (add milk or water if liquid is needed) on layers. Top with bread crumbs, Parmesan, and parsley. Cook in oven at 325 degrees for 45 minutes or until top is brown and bubbly.

Karl Tyree
Florence

Scalloped Eggplant

1 medium eggplant, peeled
   and cut into 1-inch
   cubes
2 slices bread, cubed
½ cup grated cheese

¾ cup milk
1 dash pepper or to taste
1 egg, beaten
2 tablespoons chopped onion

Boil eggplant in salted water until it changes color. In a mixing bowl, mix together bread, milk, pepper and egg.

Drain eggplant and add to other ingredients. Place mixture in a buttered casserole dish and add ½ cup grated cheese or if preferred buttered bread crumbs. Bake 20 minutes in a 350 degree oven. Sprinkle 2 tablespoons onion over the top if desired.

Mrs. Gertrude Snider
Sheffield

Bubbly Vegetable Casserole

1 cup slivered almonds
¼ pound bacon, but into
  1-inch lengths
1 pound zucchini squash,
  sliced
1 pound eggplant, diced
1 large onion, cut
  into wedges
1 tablespoon flour

2 cups diced fresh tomatoes
  or 1 can (1 pound)
  tomatoes, undrained
1 teaspoon minced garlic
1½ teaspoons salt
¼ teaspoon pepper
1 teaspoon basil
1 package (6 ounces) sliced
  Swiss cheese

Saute almonds with bacon in 10-to-12-inch skillet. When almonds are lightly roasted and bacon crisp, remove from skillet with slotted spoon. Add zucchini, eggplant and onion to skillet; cover and cook over medium-low heat for 15 minutes, shaking pan or stirring often to prevent sticking. Mix in flour, then add tomatoes, breaking them up with spoon into chunks. Stir in garlic, salt, pepper and basil. Layer vegetable mixture, almonds, bacon and cheese slices in 2-quart baking dish, ending with bacon and almonds in ring on top. To serve right away, bake uncovered in pre-heated 400 degree oven for 15 to 20 minutes or until bubbly throughout. To serve later, cover and refrigerate. To heat, uncover and bake in preheated 400 degree oven for 30 to 35 minutes until bubbly throughout.

Norma Clare's Hominy Casserole

1 small onion
½ green pepper
½ stick butter
3 tablespoons flour
1 teaspoon salt
½ teaspoon dry mustard
Dash of Tabasco
1½ cups milk

¾ cup ground New York
  sharp cheddar
1 large can mushrooms
1 cup black olives
1 large can hominy
  (drained)
¾ cup bread crumbs

Saute onions and pepper in butter. When tender, add next four ingredients. Gradually add milk and cook until a sauce consistency. Add cheese, mushrooms and olives. Rinse hominy and mix with sauce. Put into casserole. Top with bread crumbs and bake at 375 degrees for 30 minutes. Serves 6 to 8. Can be frozen, too.

Asparagus Casserole

2 tablespoons butter
2 tablespoons flour
1 teaspoon salt
1 can condensed milk

4 hard-boiled eggs
1 can asparagus, drained
1 can slivered almonds
Soda crackers, broken up

Melt butter and add flour and salt. Slowly add condensed milk. Cook over low heat until thick. (Can be thickened with asparagus juice.) Layer in order crackers, sliced eggs, asparagus and cream sauce in a casserole dish. Repeat layers ending with sauce. Let stand a short time. If needed to heat, put in a warm oven for a few minutes.

Mrs. Roy Allen
Owensboro, Kentucky

Canned Green Tomatoes For Frying

Wash tomatoes and slice. Fill pint jars full of the slices. Cover with cold water. Add ½ teaspoon salt, seal and boil in hot water bath for 10 minutes.

When ready to use, drain all liquid and fry as you would fresh green tomatoes.

Mrs. J.H. Mitchell
Florence

Tomato Florentine

6 medium tomatoes
Salt
1 tablespoon all-purpose flour
½ teaspoon salt
½ cup milk
1 slightly beaten egg yolk
3 tablespoons butter, melted
1 10-ounce package frozen
   chopped spinach, cooked
   and well drained

Cut a slice, ¼ inch thick, off top of each tomato. Scoop out pulp, leaving shell ¼ inch thick. Sprinkle inside of each with salt. Combine flour and ½ teaspoon salt. Blend in milk. Stir in egg yolk and 1 tablespoon of melted butter; add to spinach. Cook and stir over medium heat just until mixture simmers. Fill tomatoes with spinach. Place in shallow baking dish. Top each with 1 teaspoon of butter. Bake at 375 degrees for 20 minutes. Serve hot. Yield: 6 servings.

Mrs. J. Douglas Evans
Florence

Gumbo

2 sticks margarine
2 cups flour
6 quarts hot water
1 quart or large can tomatoes
2 stems celery, chopped
3 medium onions
1 bell pepper, chopped
2 large cloves garlic, minced
3 carrots sliced thin
2 cans small green butterbeans (or
   equivalent frozen
   butterbeans)
2 pounds tender okra, chopped
1½ pounds Polish smoked sausage,
   sliced
2 cups cooked chopped turkey
2 cups cooked chopped chicken
2 cups crab meat
4 cups small shrimp
1 teaspoon Tabasco sauce
2 packages of frozen corn

Melt margarine in large heavy pot. When hot add flour gradually, stirring constantly, until oil is completely absorbed. Continue stirring until roux is a dark golden brown (about 15 minutes). Add 6 quarts hot water. Place on high fire, stirring occasionally, until roux is completely dissolved and water begins to boil. Reduce fire and add next 8 ingredients plus corn. Allow to simmer for three hours. After sausage has been cooked add to mixture. Add the remaining items and cook slowly for 20 minutes. 1 pint of oysters and 1 can of lobster may be added. After which simmer 10 to 15 minutes. Serve over hot rice. Garlic bread of French bread goes well with this.

Mrs. C.H. Holder
Florence

Stuffed Cabbage Rolls

1 large cabbage head
1 pound ground beef
1 cup rice (raw)
1 egg
1 can tomatoes
1 onion

1 teaspoon salt
1 tablespoon vinegar
½ medium-size onion (diced)
½ cup water
¼ teaspoon black pepper

Cut core out of cabbage; boil about 5 minutes. Take leaves apart and set aside to cool. Combine ground beef, uncooked rice, egg, salt, diced onion, water and black pepper and mix well; then roll small portions in cabbage leaves. Saute 1 onion in large pot in oil. Put layer of cabbage leaves on top of onions. Place cabbage rolls on top, layer by layer. Add tomatoes, vinegar and water to cover rolls. Season to taste. Cook slowly about 2½ hours.

Joyce Spicer Carrol
Florence

Steamed Cabbage With Sour Cream Dressing

1 small head cabbage
1 egg
1 cup sour cream
1 tablespoon fat
2 tablespoons vinegar
1 tablespoon lemon juice
1 teaspoon sugar

1 teaspoon salt
⅛ teaspoon pepper
⅛ teaspoon paprika
⅛ teaspoon mustard
Celery seeds
1 jar pimiento

Wash and shred the cabbage. Steam it until tender, about 25 minutes. Meanwhile place the sour cream in the top of a double boiler. Add the beaten egg, fat, vinegar, lemon juice, sugar, salt, finely chopped pimiento, pepper, paprika, mustard and a few celery seeds. Stir constantly until thick. Then pour immediately over the steamed cabbage which has been seasoned with salt, pepper and butter. Serves six.

Mrs. Joan Pugh
Florence

Onion Kuchen

2 medium onions, peeled, sliced
  and separated
3 tablespoons butter
1 package refrigerator biscuits
  (use 8)

1½ eggs
1 cup sour cream
½ teaspoon salt
1 teaspoon poppy seed

Saute onions in butter until soft. Place biscuits in round 8 or 9-inch ungreased pan covering bottom completely to form crust. Spoon onion mixture on top. Beat eggs in small bowl, blend in sour cream and salt. Spoon over mixture. Sprinkle on poppy seeds. Bake at 375 degrees for 30 minutes or until top sets. Serve warm. Serves 8.

Mrs. John Formby, Jr.
Florence

Mommie's Casserole Spaghetti

⅓ pound salted pork, (streak
of lean and streak
of fat)
1 cup onions, chopped

1 (1 pound) can tomatoes
⅓ of a 4-ounce package spaghetti
Thin sticks of Wisconsin cheese

Cut salted pork in very slender pieces and fry until almost brown; pour off excess fat and chopped onions. Continue to brown until onions are clear and almost brown. Add tomatoes; cover and simmer for about 30 minutes. Have ready spaghetti cooked without salt; drain thoroughly. In a 2½ quart baking dish pour ½ of cooked spaghetti and cover with ½ of tomato sauce; cover with thin sticks of Wisconsin cheese. Repeat layers, topping with remaining cheese slices. Cook in low to moderate oven for about 30 minutes.

Mrs. Leonard Burt
Sheffield

Olive-Cheese Spaghetti

1 (7 ounce) package thin spaghetti
1 pound ground chuck
1 (6 ounce) can tomato paste
1 (8 ounce) jar stuffed green
olives

¼ pound grated cheddar cheese
1 medium onion, chopped
1 cup water

Saute onions in small amount of cooking oil and add ground chuck. Cook until brown and drain excess fat. Add water juice from olives and olive halves. Simmer for a few minutes and add tomato paste. Stir well and mix in grated cheese until melted. Add cooked, drained spaghetti to sauce and mix well. Serves 6.

Mrs. Stewart O'Bannon

Macaroni Loaf

1¾ cup elbow macaroni
1 13-ounce can evaporated milk
¼ cup diced pimiento
½ pound grated cheddar cheese

1 teaspoon salt
¼ teaspoon pepper
2 eggs

Cook macaroni in salted water. Heat canned milk, pimientoes, cheese, salt and pepper in double boiler over hot water, stirring until smooth. Add drained macaroni. Stir in beaten eggs. Pour into buttered mold or an 8-inch loaf pan. Set pan in another pan of hot water. Bake about 350 degrees for 30 minutes or until set. Serve with seasoned lima beans, peas or broccoli spears with pimiento designs or strips on top.

Mrs. John Ballinger
Madisonville, Kentucky

Rice Roast

2 cups cooked rice
2 cups ground whole wheat
bread toast
¾ cup pecans or peanuts, broken
3 tablespoons minced onion
2 eggs, beaten

2 tablespoons each of chopped
pimento and sweet
green pepper
2 cups canned or fresh cooked
tomatoes
1 teaspoon salt
⅛ teaspoon paprika
¾ cup grated cheese

Mix well, form into a loaf and bake 1 hour in moderate oven. Sprinkle ¾ cup grated cheese over loaf a few minutes before removing from oven and serve hot.

Mrs. Tracy Gargis
Sheffield

Rice-Ham Medley

⅔ cup long grain rice (2
cups after cooking)
½ cup diced celery
1 4½ ounce can deviled ham
1 beaten egg

½ cup (2 ounce) shredded
natural cheddar cheese
2 slices bacon, crisp cooked,
drained and crumbled

In bowl, combine cooked long-grain rice, diced celery, deviled ham, and beaten egg; turn into medium skillet. Cook and stir over medium heat until mixture is heated through, about 10 minutes. Top rice mixture with shredded cheese and crumbled bacon. Cover and cook over low heat until cheese is melted, about 5 minutes. Yield: 4 servings.

Mrs. Gene Mance
Muscle Shoals

Suppli al Telefono
(Rice Croquettes)

3 tablespoons butter
⅓ cup flour
1 cup milk
2 cups uncooked natural
rice

1 cup grated sharp
cheese or mozarella
1 tablespoon chopped parsley
1 teaspoon paprika
Salt to taste

Boil rice. Advise boiling 2¾ cup water, add rice, bring to boil, then reduce heat and simmer for 30 minutes covered.

While rice simmers melt butter, add and blend over low heat for 4 minutes the flour. Stir in slowly the milk. Cook and stir this sauce with wooden spoon until thick and smooth. Place in oven 350 degrees for 20 minutes. Meanwhile combine the rice, cheese, parsley, paprika, salt and when ready, the sauce. Cool and shape into balls. Roll in dried bread crumbs and deep fat fry. Drain and serve at once. You may save rolled balls in refrigerator 1-2 days before frying. Makes about 40 croquettes. A favorite in southern Italy.

Elizabeth A. Medaris
Villaggio della Pace
Vicenza, Italy

Green Peas And Beef

Adapted From A Chinese Cookbook

1 teaspoon cornstarch
1 egg white
½ pound ground beef
  round
1 tablespoon dry sherry
1 tablespoon soy sauce

½ teaspoon sugar
2 tablespoons peanut oil
1 cup frozen extra-fancy
  petite peas (from a
  10-ounce package), thawed

In a small mixing bowl stir together (do not beat) the cornstarch and egg white until smooth; add beef and mix together well with your fingers. In a cup stir together the sherry, soy sauce and sugar. In a 10-ounce skillet heat the oil; add beef; over moderate heat crumble with a fork until meat loses its red color. Stir in sherry mixture; stir in peas; cover and simmer a few minutes to heat peas. Makes 2 large servings.

Middle Eastern Pilaf

½ cup chopped onion
3 tablespoons butter or
  margarine
1 tablespoon olive oil
1 cup rice
½ cup slivered almonds
2½ cups chicken broth
1½ teaspoons salt

¼ teaspoon pepper
⅓ cup golden raisins
2 tablespoons fresh chopped
  parsley
1½ teaspoons fresh chopped
  mint leaves or ½
  teaspoons dried mint
  leaves

Saute onion in butter and oil in medium saucepan until tender, about 5 minutes. Add rice and almonds. Cook over low heat stirring constantly, until rice is golden. Add chicken broth, salt and pepper. Heat to boiling; reduce heat. Cover tightly and simmer 20 minutes. Remove from heat and stir in remaining ingredients. Let stand, covered, until all liquid is absorbed, about 5 minutes. Makes six servings.

Quickie Curry

1 tablespoon curry powder
2 tablespoons butter
1 cup chopped onions
2 tablespoons flour
¼ teaspoon garlic powder
1 can (14 ounces) chicken broth
1 fresh pear

3 cups cooked chicken or turkey,
  cut into julienne strips
  or diced
Salt and pepper to taste
2 cans (3½ ounces each) fried
  noodles or 3 to 4 cups
  steamed rice

Fry curry powder in butter over low heat two to three minutes. Add onion and flour; cook and stir until onion is limp. Add garlic and broth. Cook and stir until thickened. Core and dice pear. Add pear and chicken to curry mixture; heat through. Season to taste. Serve over noodles or rice. Makes about three cups curry, three to four servings.

Desserts

Prize Chocolate Cake

4 ounces chocolate squares
1 cup milk
1 cup cake flour, sifted
¼ teaspoon salt

2 teaspoons baking powder
4 eggs, separated
1⅔ cups sugar
1 teaspoon vanilla

Grate chocolate in a saucepan and add milk. Cook over low heat, stirring constantly, until thickened. Cool, sift flour, salt and baking powder together. Beat egg yolks and add sugar and vanilla and beat until fluffy. Add sifted dry ingredients and chocolate mixture alternately in small amounts, beating well after each addition. Fold in stiffly beaten egg whites. Pour into greased pan and bake in a moderate oven (350 degrees) for 30 minutes. Makes 1 9-by-9-inch cake.

Lela Hall
Leighton

Peppermint Frosting

¼ cup crushed peppermint
  stick candy
½ cup milk

1 pound confectioners'
  sugar (sifted)

Heat candy and milk over hot water in a double boiler until candy is melted. Add enough confectioners' sugar to make frosting thick enough to spread on cake.

Lela Hall
Leighton

Scratch Chocolate Cake

2 cups self-rising flour   2 cups sugar

Put in bowl and set aside. In a saucepan bring to a boil 1 stick oleo, ½ cup shortening, 4 tablespoons cocoa and 1 cup water. Add mixture to flour and sugar and then add 2 beaten eggs, ½ cup buttermilk, 1 teaspoon soda, and 1 teaspoon vanilla. Bake at 400 degrees till done.

Icing

In the same saucepan add 1 stick oleo, 4 tablespoons cocoa, 6 tablespoons milk and bring to a boil and pour over 1 box powdered sugar, 1 teaspoon vanilla. Add hot icing to hot cake.

Mrs. Jane Sherrell
Muscle Shoals

Tunnel of Fudge Cake

1½ cups soft butter
6 eggs
1½ cups sugar
2 cups flour (regular or
    instant blending)

1 package Double Dutch fudge
    butter cream frosting mix
2 cups chopped walnuts

Cream butter in large mixing bowl at high speed of mixer. Add eggs, one at a time, beating well after each. Gradually add sugar. Continue creaming at high speed until light and fluffy. By hand, stir in flour, frosting mix, and walnuts; blend. Pour batter into greased bundt pan. Bake at 350 degrees for 60 to 65 minutes. Cool two hours. Remove from pan. Cool completely before serving.

Evelyn Pless
Cherokee

Texas Fudge Cake

1 stick oleo
½ cup shortening
1 cup water
2 cups flour
2 cups sugar

4 tablespoons cocoa
½ cup buttermilk
2 eggs
1 teaspoon vanilla
1 teaspoon soda

Mix oleo, shortening, water and bring to a boil. Pour in dry ingredients and add buttermilk, eggs and vanilla. Mix well and pour in greased pan and bake 25 minutes at 400 degrees (13 x 9 pan).
Mix and bring to a boil:

1 stick oleo
4 tablespoons cocoa

7 tablespoons milk

To this add a box of confectioners' sugar, 1 teaspoon vanilla and 1 cup chopped pecans. Pour on cake while still warm.

Nancy Wallace
Sheffield

Ohio State Devils Food Cake

3 cups dark brown sugar
¾ cup butter
3 eggs
¾ cup sour milk
1 teaspoon vanilla flavoring

¾ cup cocoa
¾ cup boiling water
1½ teaspoons soda
3 cups cake flour, sifted

Combine cocoa, boiling water and soda; let cool while creaming shortening. Add sugar gradually, creaming thoroughly. Add cocoa mixture after each egg. Add unbeaten eggs. Add milk and flour alternately, beginning with flour and ending with flour. This makes a large cake. Can be made in three layers. Bake 40 minutes at 350 degrees.

Jean Allen
Florence

Devil's Food Cake

½ cup cocoa
½ cup boiling water
2½ cups cake flour, sifted
1 teaspoon baking powder
½ teaspoon salt
½ cup vegetable shortening

1½ cups sugar
2 eggs
1 cup buttermilk
1 teaspoon soda
2 teaspoons vanilla

Mix cocoa with boiling water and cool. Sift flour, salt and baking powder together. Cream shortening, sugar and eggs until light and fluffy. Add cocoa mixture. Mix buttermilk with soda and add alternately with flour mixture. Let stand for 10 minutes. Pour into 2 9-inch layer pans and bake for 25 minutes at 350 degrees or until cake leaves sides of pan. Frost with Seven Minute Frosting.

Seven Minute Frosting

2 egg whites
1½ cups sugar

5 tablespoons cold water
1½ tablespoons light corn syrup

Put egg whites, sugar, water and corn syrup in top of double boiler. Beat with rotary beater until thoroughly mixed; place over rapidly boiling water, beat constantly with rotary egg beater and cook seven minutes or until frosting stands in peaks. Remove from heat; add vanilla and beat until thick enough to spread.

Mrs. Eddie Ross
Florence

Marshmallow Fudge Cake

½ cup margarine
1 cup sugar
4 eggs
1 teaspoon vanilla
1 cup self-rising flour

1 (16 ounce) can chocolate syrup
1 cup chopped nuts
1 (7 ounce) jar marshmallow
cream

Combine margarine and sugar and beat until creamy. Add eggs one at a time, beating after each. Add vanilla. Add flour and chocolate syrup. Mix well and stir in nuts. Bake in a 350 degree oven for 30 minutes in 13 x 9 x 2 inch baking pan. Spread marshmallow cream on cake while hot. Pour fudge topping over all.

Fudge Topping

2 cups sugar
½ cup cocoa
½ cup margarine

½ cup milk
1 tablespoon corn syrup

Combine ingredient. Stir and bring to a boil. Boil one minute. Remove from heat and beat 1 minute. Pour over cake.

Mrs. E.P. Garrett
Tuscumbia

Phillip's Chocolate Cake

1 cup shortening
2 cups sugar
4 eggs, separated
1 package of German sweet chocolate
½ cup boiling water

2½ cups cake flour
½ teaspoon salt
1 teaspoon soda
1 cup buttermilk
1 teaspoon vanilla extract

Cream shortening; add sugar and egg yolks one at a time. Melt chocolate in boiling water, then let cool before adding to other ingredients. Add cooled chocolate to shortening, egg yolks and sugar. Mix thoroughly. Combine dry ingredients and then alternate with buttermilk when mixing with cream mixture. Beat egg whites stiff and then fold into creamed mixture. Add vanilla. Bake in three 8-inch or 9-inch layer pans at 350 degrees for about 40 minutes.

Frosting

1 6 ounce package semisweet
  chocolate bits
1 6 ounce package of butterscotch
  pieces

½ cup strong hot coffee
3 cups sifted powdered sugar

Melt chocolate and butterscotch pieces over double boiler. Remove from heat and add coffee and sugar. Beat until smooth.

Phillip Beasley

Rocky Road Chocolate Cake

⅔ cup soft shortening
1½ cups sugar
3 eggs
2 squares unsweetened chocolate,
  melted

2¼ cups sifted flour
1 teaspoon salt
1 teaspoon soda
1 cup buttermilk

Grease and flour a 13 x 9 inch pan. Cream shortening and sugar; add eggs, one at a time and beat well. Blend in melted chocolate. Add flour and salt alternately with buttermilk and soda. Pour into pan and cook at 350 degrees for 40 to 45 minutes. Loosen edges.

Icing for Rocky Road Chocolate Cake

3 squares unsweetened chocolate
3 tablespoons butter
1 package powdered sugar
⅛ teaspoon salt

7 tablespoons milk
1 teaspoon vanilla
½ cup chopped pecans
1 cup cut marshmallows

In double boiler, melt butter and chocolate. Sift powdered sugar and salt in a bowl. Add milk and vanilla. Add chocolate and butter. Sprinkle nuts and marshmallows on top of cake. Pour icing over all.

Mrs. Earl Keeton
Cherokee

White Chocolate Cake

4 ounces white chocolate
½ cup boiling water
1 cup butter or margarine
2 cups sugar
4 egg yolks, unbeaten
1 teaspoon vanilla

2½ cups sifted cake flour
½ teaspoon salt
½ teaspoon baking soda
1 cup buttermilk
4 egg whites, stiffly beaten

Melt chocolate in boiling water. Cool. Cream butter and sugar until fluffy. Add egg yolks, one at a time, and beat well after each addition. Add melted chocolate and vanilla. Mix well. Sift together flour, salt and soda. Add alternately with buttermilk to chocolate mixture. Beat well. Beat until smooth. Fold in egg whites.

Pour into three deep 8 or 9-inch layer pans, lined with paper. Bake in a moderate oven, 350 degrees, for 30 to 40 minutes.

Icing

8 ounces white chocolate
Dash salt
4 tablespoons butter
1½ cups confectioners' sugar

4 tablespoons hot water
2 egg yolks
1 teaspoon vanilla

Melt chocolate, blend in sugar, salt and hot water. Add yolks; beat well. Add butter, two tablespoons at a time, beating well after each addition. Stir in vanilla. Makes about 1½ cups, or enough to cover cake and between layers, too.

Mrs. W.C. Sumner
Florence

Pauline's White Chocolate Cake

2 cups sugar
¼ teaspoon salt
4 whole eggs
2 teaspoons vanilla
1 cup coconut
2 sticks oleo

2 cups flour
¼ teaspoon baking powder
1 cup buttermilk
1 cup nuts
3 block white chocolate (1 pound makes 3 cakes)

Melt oleo and chocolate in double boiler. Mix sugar, flour, salt; add to butter-chocolate mixture. Add eggs one at a time beating after each addition. Add baking powder, buttermilk, and vanilla, mix well. Fold in coconut and nuts. Bake in 3 layers at 350 degrees.

Icing

2¼ sticks oleo
1 cup evaporated milk
1 cup nuts

2 cups sugar
2 teaspoons vanilla
1 cup coconut

Cook oleo, sugar and milk in double boiler to soft ball stage. Add nuts and coconut, beat and then spread on cooled cake.

Pauline Hillis
Florence

Coca Cola Cake I

2 cups sugar
2 cups plain flour
½ cup margarine (1 stick)
½ cup cooking oil
1 cup Coca Cola
3 tablespoons cocoa
½ cup buttermilk
1 teaspoon soda

1 teaspoon vanilla
2 eggs
½ cup margarine
3 tablespoons cocoa
6 tablespoons Coca Cola
1 box confectioners' sugar
1 teaspoon vanilla
1 cup chopped pecans

Mix sugar and flour in large bowl. In saucepan, mix and bring to boil, ½ cup margarine, cooking oil, 1 cup Coca Cola, and 3 tablespoons cocoa. Pour mixture over flour and sugar mixture and mix well. Add buttermilk, soda, 1 teaspoon vanilla and eggs. Mix well. Bake in a greased 9x13 inch pan at 350 degrees for 40 to 45 minutes. Bring ½ cup margarine, 3 tablespoons cocoa, and 6 tablespoons Coca Cola to a boil. Mix in confectioners' sugar, 1 teaspoon vanilla, and chopped pecans. While hot, spread on cooled cake.

Mrs. C.W. Cochran, III
Florence

Coca-Cola Cake II

2 cups sugar
2 cups plain flour
3 sticks oleo
6 tablespoons cocoa
1 cup Coca Cola
½ cup buttermilk
2 eggs, well beaten

1 teaspoon soda
1 teaspoon vanilla
½ cup small marshmallows
6 tablespoons Coca Cola
1 teaspoon vanilla
¾ to 1 box powdered sugar
1 cup pecans

Blend together sugar and flour. Mix 2 sticks oleo, 3 tablespoons cocoa, and 1 cup Coca Cola together and bring to boil. Add to flour and sugar mixture. Mix together buttermilk, eggs, soda, vanilla, and marshmallows. Add to first mixture and mix by hand (not electric mixer.) Pour mixture in greased oblong pan and bake at 350 degrees for 45 minutes. During last 5 minutes of baking time, mix 1 stick oleo, 3 tablespoons cocoa, and 6 tablespoons Coca Cola. Bring to boil, remove from heat and add vanilla, powdered sugar and pecans. Pour over cake.

Mrs. Joe Patterson, Jr.
Florence

Sheath Cake

Put in saucepan and melt:

1 stick margarine

½ cup shortening

Stir in:

4 tablespoons cocoa

1 cup water

Bring to a boil and let cool. Mix well in mixing bowl:

2 cups sugar
½ teaspoon salt

2 cups flour (use self-
    rising for best results)
1 teaspoon cinnamon

Add:

½ cup buttermilk
2 beaten eggs

1 teaspoon soda
1 teaspoon vanilla

Stir first mixture into dry ingredients and mix well.

Bake in 2 greased layer cake pans or one 8x13x2-inch pan in 350 degree oven for 45 minutes. Remove from oven and make following frosting to pour on cake while still warm. Mix together:

1 stick oleo
6 tablespoons milk or cream

4 tablespoons cocoa

Bring to boil. Remove from heat, add 2 cups confectioners' sugar and 1 cup nuts. Blend well and pour over cake. Cut in squares. Freezer storage time: 2 months. Note: I double the icing recipe for my cake in 2 large loaf pans.

Mrs. W.T. Arthur
Sheffield

Chocolate Sheath Cake

2 cups sugar
2 cups flour
1 teaspoon soda
1 teaspoon cinnamon
1 cup water
1 stick margarine

½ cup all-vegetable cooking oil
4 tablespoons cocoa
½ cup buttermilk
2 eggs, slightly beaten
1 teaspoon vanilla extract

Sift together the sugar, flour, soda and cinnamon. Set aside. In a saucepan place the water, margarine, oil and cocoa. Bring to a boil and pour over dry ingredients, mixing well. Set aside. Mix together the buttermilk, eggs and vanilla extract; add to chocolate batter. Pour batter into greased and floured 13x9x2 inch pan. Bake at 400 degrees for 20 minutes. Start chocolate icing about 5 minutes before cake is done and frost cake in pan.

Icing for Chocolate Sheath Cake

1 stick margarine
4 tablespoons cocoa
6 tablespoons milk

1 1 pound box powdered sugar
1 teaspoon vanilla extract
1 cup chopped pecans

Place margarine, cocoa and milk in a saucepan. Bring to a boil, being careful not to let it scorch. Then add powdered sugar, vanilla extract, and pecans. Spread over hot cake.

Mrs. H.M. Hunnicutt
Cloverdale

Salad Dressing Cake

1½ cups sugar	3 tablespoons cocoa
2 cups flour	2 teaspoons soda
Pinch of salt	1 teaspoon vanilla
1 cup salad dressing	1 cup warm water

Mix all ingredients together and beat for 2 minutes. Bake in 2 layer cake pans at 350 degrees for 3 minutes.

Icing

1½ cups sugar	⅓ stick margarine
⅔ cup milk	

Heat ingredients over low heat and then cool until thickens and pour over cake.

Mrs. Ira Johnson
Killen

Mayonnaise Cake

2 cups plain flour	4 tablespoons cocoa
1½ cups sugar	1 cup water
1½ teaspoons soda	2 teaspoons vanilla
1½ teaspoons baking powder	1 cup mayonnaise

Mix all ingredients together and bake in a greased loaf pan for 35 minutes at 350 degrees. Allow cake to cool before cutting.

Addie C. Montgomery
Tuscumbia

Chocolate Sheath Cake

1 stick oleo	1 cup water
4 tablespoons cocoa	2 eggs
½ cup shortening	1 teaspoon soda
2 cups sugar	1 teaspoon vanilla
2 cups unsifted flour (plain)	1 cup buttermilk

Put oleo, cocoa and shortening in 2 quart saucepan; bring to boil. Pour over sugar and flour, stir and add remaining ingredients; stir well. Bake in 12 x 15 inch flat pan for about 25 minutes on 400 degree heat.

Frosting For Chocolate Sheath Cake

4 tablespoons cocoa	1 1-pound box powdered sugar
1 stick oleo	1 cup pecans
½ cup milk	1 teaspoon vanilla

Bring cocoa, oleo and milk to a boil in saucepan, add remaining ingredients. Pour over hot cake.

Evelyn Pless
Cherokee

Red Velvet Cake

½ cup shortening
1 teaspoon vanilla
1 tablespoon vinegar
2 cups cake flour
1 cup buttermilk

1½ cups sugar
1 ounce red food coloring
2 whole eggs
1 tablespoon cocoa
1 tablespoon soda

Cream shortening and sugar together, add vanilla and coloring, mix. Add eggs, cream well. Sift measured cake flour with cocoa three times; add to the above mixture, alternate with buttermilk ending with buttermilk. Fold in soda mixed with vinegar. Bake in two 9-inch pans at 350 degrees for 30 minutes.

Vickie Rikard
Tuscumbia

Red Velvet Cake

1 cup cooking oil
1½ cups sugar
1 to 2 ounces cake coloring
2 cups plain flour
1 tablespoon cocoa

½ teaspoon salt
1 cup buttermilk
1 teaspoon vanilla
1 teaspoon soda
2 eggs

Cream oil, sugar and coloring, then add 2 eggs, one at a time. Add remaining ingredients and blend well. Beat at medium speed for three minutes. Bake at 350 degrees for 25 to 30 minutes.

Filling For Red Velvet Cake

¼ cup flour
1 cup sweet milk
1 cup cooking oil
1 cup sugar

¼ teaspoon salt
1 cup coconut
1 cup nuts

Cook milk and flour, stirring constantly. When thick set aside and cool. Cream oil, sugar, salt and coconut, then add to milk and flour mixture. Add nuts and spread on cool cake.

Mrs. Gracie Wisdom
Killen

Laurine's Red Earth Cake

½ cup shortening
1½ cups sugar

Cream and add 2 whole eggs and beat well after each addition.

Make a paste of:

3 tablespoons cocoa
1 teaspoon red food coloring

3 tablespoons hot coffee
1 teaspoon soda

Add to creamed mixture. Add 1 teaspoon vanilla and a pinch of salt. Add 2 cups minus 2 tablespoons flour, alternately with 1 cup sour milk or buttermilk, beating well after each addition. Bake in two 8 inch greased and floured pans for 30 minutes. Icing:

1 box powdered sugar
1 stick butter
1 teaspoon red food coloring

3 tablespoons coffee
3 tablespoons cocoa
1 teaspoon vanilla

Mix well and spread on cake.

Mrs. James A. Gafford
Florence

Chocolate Velvet Cake

2 cups cooking oil
2 cups sugar
2 eggs
2½ cups plain flour
1 teaspoon salt

1 teaspoon soda
1 teaspoon vanilla
1 tablespoon vinegar
1 cup buttermilk
½ cup plus 2 tablespoons cocoa

Mix cooking oil, sugar and eggs, mix well. Sift flour, add salt and soda, sift again. Add to cooking oil mixture. Mix butter, milk, cocoa and vinegar. Add all mixtures together and beat 3 minutes on high speed. Add vanilla and beat 1 more minute. Bake in oblong pan (or makes three layers) at 350 degrees for about 35 minutes.

Icing For Chocolate Velvet Cake

1 stick oleo
1 pound box powdered sugar,
   sifted

1 teaspoon vanilla
1 8 ounce package cream cheese
1 cup nuts, broken up

Mix all ingredients together, spread while cake is still hot.

Mrs. Racene Pace
Leighton

German Sweet Chocolate Pudding Cake

1 package (2 layer size)
   yellow cake mix
1 package (4-serving-size
   vanilla instant pudding
   and pie filling
4 eggs

1 package (4 ounce) German
   sweet chocolate, melted
1¼ cup buttermilk (or substitute
   ½ cup sour cream and
   ¾ cup water)
¼ cup oil

Combine all ingredients in large mixer bowl; blend. Beat four minutes at medium speed. Pour into three greased and floured 9-inch layer pans. Bake at 350 degrees for 30 minutes or until cake springs back when lightly pressed. Cool in pans 15 minutes. Remove and finish cooling on racks. Fill with coconut fillng.

Coconut Filling

Combine one cup evaporated milk, one cup sugar, three egg yolks, slightly beaten, ½ cup butter or margarine and one teaspoon vanilla in saucepan. Cook and stir over medium heat until thickened, about 12 minutes. Remove from heat. Add 1⅓ cups flake coconut and one cup chopped pecans. Cool, beating occasionally, until of spreading consistency. Makes 2½ cups.

Sandra Goforth
Waterloo

Whipped Cream Pound Cake

½ pound butter or
   margarine
3 cups sugar
1 teaspoon baking powder
6 eggs

3 cups flour
½ pint whipping cream
   (do not whip)
2 teaspoons vanilla

Cream together butter, sugar, and baking powder. Add eggs, one at a time, beating well after each egg. Add flour and whipping cream alternately to the above mixture, beginning with flour and ending with flour and beating well after each addition. Add vanilla. Beat well. Bake in tube pan for one hour and 20 minutes at 325 degrees. Do not preheat oven. Cool before removing from pan.

Mrs. G.K. Counts
Florence

Old-Fashioned Pound Cake

4 sticks margarine
3 cups sugar
4 cups cake flour

1 cup sweet milk
6 eggs
2 tablespoons lemon flavor

Cream sugar and margarine, add sweet milk and then add flour, one cup at a time. Add eggs one at a time. Beat until creamy and add the lemon flavor. Pour into well greased and floured tube pan and bake 1 hour and 15 minutes at 350 degrees or until done.

Mrs. Rosie B. Groce
Russellville

Christmas Pound Cake

1 pound butter or oleo
1 pound sugar
1 pound flour (4 cups all
   purpose or 4½ cups
   cake flour)
2 cups white raisins
1 pound pecans (chopped
   coarsely)

½ to 1 cup candied cherries
½ to 1 cup candied pineapple
1½ teaspoons baking powder
½ teaspoon salt
4 tablespoons lemon extract
   (2 ounce bottle)
6 eggs

Cream butter, sugar and extract. Sift flour once, and measure. Sift twice more, adding baking powder and salt to last sift. Add eggs, one at a time, to creamed mixture, alternating with flour, beating well after each addition. This makes a very stiff batter so will probably have to be beaten by hand. Then add nuts, raisins, and candied fruits which have been coated with a little of the flour. Bake in large round tube pan which has been lined with brown paper and greased. Bake at 300 degrees for 2 hours, or until done when tested.

Miss Mary Harris
Tuscumbia

Pound Cake

1 cup shortening
1 stick margarine
3 cups sugar
6 eggs
3 cups flour
½ teaspoon ground nutmeg

½ teaspoon baking powder
½ teaspoon salt
1 cup milk
1 teaspoon almond extract
1 teaspoon vanilla extract

Cream shortening, margarine and sugar. Add eggs one at a time, beating after each addition. Sift flour, nutmeg, baking powder and salt. Add to mixture alternately with milk, beating after each addition. Add almond and vanilla extract. Pour into greased and floured tube pan. Cook at 325 degrees for 1 hour 20 minutes.

Mrs. R.W. Weaver
Florence

Neapolitan Pound Cake

8 ounce package cream cheese,
   softened
4 eggs
1 package white cake mix
¾ cup milk or water

¾ cup strawberry flavored
   milk drink mix
1 teaspoon vanilla
1 cup chocolate flavored
   milk drink mix

Preheat oven to 350 degrees (325 degrees for colored fluted pan). Grease and flour 12 cup fluted tube pan. In large bowl; blend cream cheese and eggs until smooth. Blend in cake mix and milk. Beat 2 minutes at highest speed. Put 2 cups batter in pan. Add strawberry milk drink mix to 2 cups of batter; pour over vanilla batter. Add chocolate milk drink mix to remaining batter; pour over strawberry batter. Bake 55 to 65 minutes or until toothpick inserted in center comes out clean. Cool upright in pan 45 minutes. Loosen edges; remove from pan. Cool completely. If desired sprinkle with powdered sugar or serve with ice cream and chocolate sauce.

Mrs. Joan Pugh
Florence

Buttermilk Pound Cake

½ cup (1 stick) butter
½ cup shortening
2½ teaspoons vanilla extract
2 cups sugar
5 eggs

3 cups sifted plain flour
½ teaspoon salt
½ teaspoon soda
½ teaspoon baking powder
1 cup buttermilk

Heat oven to 325 degrees. Grease and dust with flour a ten-inch tube pan. Cream butter and shortening together; add vanilla gradually. Cream in sugar. Add eggs one at a time, beating well after each addition. Sift dry ingredients together and add to creamed mixture alternately with buttermilk.. Pour batter into prepared pan and bake. Bake for 1¼ hours.

Mrs. Larry W. Hester
Muscle Shoals

Coconut Pound Cake

2 sticks margarine	1 teaspoon vanilla
½ cup shortening	3 cups plain flour
3 cups sugar	1 cup sweet milk
6 eggs	1½ cups coconut

Cream margarine, shortening, and sugar together. Add eggs, one at a time; add vanilla. Add flour and milk alternately; mix in coconut. Cook 1½ hours at 275 degrees.

Glaze

1 cup sugar	1 teaspoon vanilla
½ stick margarine	1 cup coconut
½ cup evaporated milk	

Boil all ingredients except coconut for 2 minutes. Add coconut. Spread mixture over cake and let cool a little.

Mrs. John D. Clement, Jr.
Muscle Shoals

Coconut Pound Cake

1 cup shortening	1 teaspoon salt
2 cups sugar	1 teaspoon coconut extract
2 cups flour	1 can flaked coconut
1½ teaspoons baking powder	1 cup buttermilk
5 eggs	

Cream sugar and shortening; add eggs one at a time, beating well after each. Combine dry ingredients. Add buttermilk. Add extract and coconut. Bake in tube pan, grease and flour. Bake one hour at 350 degrees until well browned.

Icing

1 cup sugar	½ teaspoon coconut extract
1 cup water	

Mix all together and cook until it boils (1 minute). Pour over cake while icing is hot.

Alice Marshall
Tuscumbia

Vanilla Butternut Pound Cake

½ cup cooking oil	3 cups flour
2 sticks margarine	1 6-ounce can milk plus water to
3 cups sugar	make one cup liquid
¼ teaspoon salt	2 tablespoons vanilla and butternut
5 large eggs	flavoring

Cream oil, margarine, sugar, and salt for 5 minutes. Add eggs one at a time. Add flour and milk alternately ending with flour. Fold in flavoring by hand. Pour into greased tube pan. Place cake in cold oven. Bake for one hour and forty-five minutes in a 325 degree oven. Do not open oven door while baking. Remove cake from pan immediately.

Mrs. Glen Stewart
Tuscumbia

Pineapple Pound Cake

2½ cups sugar
2½ cups flour, all-purpose
4 eggs (large) room temperature
3 sticks margarine

1 teaspoon vanilla
¾ cups unsweetened pineapple
juice

Cream sugar and butter; add eggs one at a time and beat well. Add flour, vanilla and pineapple juice; beat four minutes. Bake at 325 degrees (use tube pan) for one hour and fifteen minutes. Use favorite glaze but instead of water or milk use pineapple juice and top with crushed pineapple.

Mrs. Ernest Moore
Florence

Pineapple Pound Cake

½ cup shortening
½ cup margarine
2¾ cups sugar
6 large eggs
3 cups sifted all-purpose flour

1 teaspoon baking powder
¼ cup milk
1 teaspoon vanilla
¾ cup pineapple and juice

Topping

¼ cup margarine (½ stick)
1½ cups powdered sugar

1 cup pineapple (drained)

METHOD: Cream shortening, margarine and sugar together. Add eggs one at a time beating well after each addition. Sift together baking powder and flour. Add to shortening, margarine and sugar mixture the ¼ cup milk and vanilla. Add pineapple. Add flour mixture gradually; beating well. Pour topping over cake while it is hot.

Mary Doris Cain
Florence

Orange Rum Pound Cake

2 packages pound cake
mix (17 ounces each)
2 tablespoons shredded
orange peel
2 teaspoons shredded
lemon peel

1 cup sugar
1 cup orange juice
2 tablespoons lemon juice
2 tablespoons rum

Prepare mixes according to package directions, adding orange and lemon peel. Turn into greased and floured 10-inch angel food pan or fluted bundt pan. Bake at 350 degrees for one to one and one-fourth hours till done. Cool in pan 10 minutes; remove to wire rack and cool 20 minutes more. Place on serving platter. Using a skewer, punch holes in top of cake at one-inch intervals. Combine sugar, juices and rum. Bring to boil. Spoon slowly over cake a small amount at a time, allowing cake to absorb sauce. Chill cake until serving time.

Las Cruces, New Mexico

Favorite Date Nut Pound Cake

1 pound butter
2 cups sugar
6 eggs
1 1-ounce bottle lemon extract

4 cups all-purpose flour,
  divided
1 pound dates, chopped
1 pound (4 cups) pecans and
  walnuts, chopped fine

Cream butter well; add sugar and beat until smooth and fluffy. Add eggs one at a time beating well after each. Add flavoring. Sprinkle one cup flour over nuts and dates. Add three cups to creamed mixture. Add dates and nuts, mix well and spoon into well greased 10-inch tube pan. Bake at 300 degrees for 2 hours. Remove from oven and turn upside down for a few minutes.

Mrs. J.P. Poe
Florence

Chocolate Pound Cake

2 sticks butter
2 cups sugar
4 eggs
½ teaspoon soda
1 cup buttermilk

2½ cups plain flour
  sifted 3 times
1 cup chocolate syrup
1 bar German chocolate
1 teaspoon vanilla

Cream butter and sugar; add eggs one at a time. Dissolve soda in buttermilk; add flour and milk alternating; add chocolate syrup, melted chocolate and vanilla. Bake 1¼-1½ hours at 325 degrees.

Rhonda Rickard
Florence

Pudding Cake

1 package yellow cake mix
1 package instant pudding mix
6 eggs

1 cup milk
½ cup oil

Mix together all ingredients with an electric mixer at a high speed for at least 2 minutes (or until mixed well). Grease tube pan; it may be necessary to put wax paper around bottom of the pan where it divides. Bake at 325 degrees for an hour. Test with a toothpick to see if it comes out clean. This may be used with different cake mixes and different kinds of instant puddings which you may think will combine to make a good flavor. A very moist cake which doesn't need a frosting unless wanted.

Las Cruces, New Mexico

Chess Cake

1 package yellow cake mix
2 eggs

1 stick of oleo

Mix well and pat in the bottom of a 13x9x2 inch pan.

2 eggs
1 package (8 ounces) cream
cheese

1 pound powdered sugar
½ teaspoon vanilla

Mix all ingredients together and pour over crust. Bake at 350 degrees for 40 minutes. Sprinkle the top with powdered sugar.

Mrs. W.A. Reid Jr.
Tuscumbia

Scratch Chess Cake

1 cup butter or oleo
1 pound light brown sugar
½ cup white sugar
4 eggs
2 cups sifted flour

1 teaspoon baking powder
1 teaspoon vanilla
Pinch of salt
1 cup chopped pecans

Heat butter and sugar on low heat, cool and add other ingredients in order. Pour into 2 8-inch pans that have been greased and floured. Bake for 40-50 minutes at 300 degrees. Cut in squares and roll in powdered sugar while still warm.

Mrs. Rufus L. Sherrod
Cumberland City, Tennessee

Gooey Butter Cake

Oil 9 x 13-inch pan. Mix pound cake mix, 1 stick melted butter and 2 eggs; spread in pan and set aside. Mix:

1 box confectioners' sugar
1 8-ounce package cream cheese

2 eggs
1 teaspoon vanilla

Spread into pan on top of pound cake mixture. Put in cold oven and bake at 350 degrees for 45 minutes.

Lillian Counce
Tuscumbia

Pecan Christmas Cake

2 cups butter (1 pound)
2 cups sugar
6 eggs
1 tablespoon lemon juice
1 teaspoon grated lemon rind
1 tablespoon vanilla

1½ cups golden raisins
4 cups chopped pecans
3 cups sifted flour
¼ teaspoon salt
1 teaspoon baking powder

Cream butter and sugar unti fluffy. Beat in eggs, one at a time. Add lemon juice, rind and vanilla. Mix raisins, nuts and ¼ cup flour. Sift remaining dry ingredients, alternately fold nuts and raisins and dry ingredients into creamed mixture. Spoon into greased, paper-lined 10" tube pan; bake in slow oven (300 degrees) about 1 hour and 50 minutes. Cool, then remove from pan.

Mrs. W.C. Sumner
Florence

Christmas Cake

8 ounces cream cheese
1 cup margarine
1½ cups sugar
1½ teaspoons vanilla
4 eggs
2¼ cups plain flour

1½ teaspoons baking
  powder
½ cup maraschino cherries,
  chopped
½ cup pecans, chopped

Blend cream cheese, margarine, sugar and vanilla. Add eggs, one at a time. Add 2 cups flour and mix well. Combine remaining flour with cherries and nuts. Fold into batter. Pour into a lightly greased bundt pan and bake at 325 degrees for 1 hour, 20 minutes. Cool 5 minutes. Remove from pan and top with glaze and additional cherries and nuts, if desired.

Glaze

1½ cups powdered sugar

2 tablespoons milk or 1
  tablespoon cherry juice

Combine and mix until smooth. Use over Christmas Cake.

Mrs. Walter Shaff
Florence

Christmas Angel Cake

1 cup sifted cake flour
2½ cups sugar
2 tablespoons sugar
12 egg whites

1½ teaspoons cream of
  tartar
½ teaspoon salt
1½ teaspoons vanilla extract
½ teaspoon almond extract

In bowl combine flour and 1 cup of sugar. In another bowl combine egg whites, cream of tartar and salt. Beat until foamy. Slowly add remaining sugar. Beat until stiff. Blend in vanilla and almond. Slowly blend flour mixture into egg whites mixture. Place batter in an ungreased 10-inch tube pan. Bake 375 degrees for 30 to 55 minutes. Invert on a wire rack to cool. Yields 1 10-inch cake. Can use topping of whipped cream and chopped cherries.

Lou Ware
Tuscumbia

Christmas Special Coconut Cake

1 cup butter or shortening
2 cups sugar
1½ cups plain flour
1½ cups self-rising flour

4 large eggs
1 cup milk
1 tablespoon vanilla or butternut
  flavoring

Cream shortening and sugar and beat until fluffy. Add 1 egg at a time and beat until lemon colored. Add flavoring. Add milk and flour alternately. Bake in 9-inch pans, greased and floured for 20-25 minutes at 300 degrees. Pierce with fork before removing from pans. This will make 2 three-layer cakes or one four-layer cake.

Moistening

2 cups sugar
1 cup sweet milk

1 coconut (grated)
1 can crushed pineapple (Small)

Heat milk and sugar to dissolve. Add coconut and pineapple. Cook 2 minutes. Spoon over layers.

Frosting

2 sticks of margarine
¼ cup sweet milk

1 cup sugar

Melt and cool, add 1 box coconut and 1 box powdered sugar. Spread on layer top and side. Sprinkle with coconut and place in refrigerator to set. This cake can be made and frozen and is good and fresh for a long time.

Mrs. Neca Allgood
Lexington

Christmas Jam Cake

1 cup butter
2 cups sugar
6 whole eggs
4 cups all purpose flour
2 teaspoons nutmeg
2 teaspoons cinnamon
2 teaspoons allspice
1 cup buttermilk

2 teaspoons vanilla
1½ cups blackberry jam
1 cup drained, crushed
  pineapple
1 cup chopped nut meats
1 cup seedless raisins
1 cup grated coconut
1 cup cherry preserves

In large bowl of electric mixer, mix butter and sugar until creamy. Add eggs and beat until well blended. Sift and measure and resift together flour, nutmeg, cinnamon and allspice. Add about half of the sifted flour mixture at a time to the batter alternately with the buttermilk and vanilla. Now add jam, pineapple, nut meats, raisins, coconut and preserves to batter. Bake in a 9-inch stem pan lined with brown paper and well greased just as in making a fruit cake. Bake at 300 degrees for 3 hours.

Mrs. R.W. Weaver
Florence

Old Fashioned Jam Cake

2 cups sugar
1½ cups butter or oleo
6 eggs
3 cups flour
1 cup buttermilk

2 cups of blackberry jam
2 teaspoons soda
1 teaspoon nutmeg
1 teaspoon allspice

Cream sugar and butter, sift flour, soda and spices. Add alternately flour mixture and eggs into creamed sugar and butter; last, add jam. Prehea oven 325 degrees and pour mixture into well-greased and paper lined pans. Cook about 30 minutes or until done.

Cooked Filling:

2 cups sugar
¾ cup butter

1½ cups sweet milk

Let filling come to boil. While cakes are still warm, pour a little filling at a time over each layer until it is used up. This makes the cake moist.

Mrs. Marjorie Y. Fisher
Sheffield

Kentucky Jam Cake

1 cup margarine, soft
2 cups sugar
5 eggs
1 cup seedless blackberry jam
3 cups sifted flour
1 teaspoon soda

½ teaspoon salt
½ teaspoon cloves
½ teaspoon allspice
1 cup buttermilk
1 cup chopped nuts
1 cup chopped dates

Cream margarine and sugar until light. Add eggs, one at a time, beating well after each addition. Add jam and beat well. Add sifted flour, soda, salt, cloves and allspice alternately with buttermilk, beating until smooth. Stir in nuts and dates. Pour into four 9" layer pans, lined on the bottom with paper. Bake in moderate oven (325 degrees) about 35 minutes. Cool and spread frosting between layers and on top of cake.

Caramel Frosting

In large saucepan. mix 2 cups packed light-brown sugar, 1 cup granulated sugar, 2 tablespoons corn syrup, 3 tablespoons butter, dash salt, ⅔ cup cream and 1 teaspoon vanilla. Bring to a boil, cover and cook three minutes. Uncover and cook to 236 degrees on a candy thermometer or until a small amount of mixture forms a soft ball when dropped in cold water. Cool five minutes; then beat until thick. If too stiff, add a little hot water.

Mrs. Stella Hammond
Lexington

Old Time Jam Cake

4 eggs
2 cups sugar
1 teaspoon cinnamon
½ teaspoon cloves
1½ cups jam
1 cup nuts

1 stick margarine
½ cup buttermilk
1 teaspoon soda
1 box seedless raisins
2½ cups flour

Mix all ingredients at one time and bake in layers until done at 350 degrees.

Filling For Old Time Jam Cake

1 grated coconut
2 oranges (chopped)
2 cups sugar

1 small can of crushed
   pineapple
2 tablespoons flour

Heat sugar, pineapple and oranges. Cool, add coconut and spread between layers.

Jam Cake

Neca Allgood
Lexington

2 cups flour
1 cup brown sugar
1 cup butter and lard mixed
1 cup buttermilk
1 cup raisins
1 cup blackberry jam

4 eggs
1 teaspoonful nutmeg
2 teaspoonfuls cinnamon
1 teaspoonful cloves
1 teaspoonful soda (level)

Cream butter and lard well, add sugar and beat thoroughly. Sift flour once and measure, add spices and sift again. Add flour and milk alternately. Add jam to the butter and sugar, before adding the flour. Dissolve the soda and a little of the milk and add last. Roll raisins in a little flour before putting them in the batter. Cook in loaf pan in moderate oven for one hour. Do not ice.

Mrs. Hattie K. Bailey
Rogersville

My Special Jam Cake

4 whole eggs, beaten well
1 cup buttermilk
2 cups sugar
1 cup butter
2 cups blackberry jam
2 level teaspoons soda

2 cups nuts
1 cup raisins
1 teaspoon cinnamon
1 teaspoon spice
1 teaspoon nutmeg
4 cups flour

Mix in order named and cook in 4 layer cake tins at 300 degrees. Put layers together with fruit filling listed below.

Filling

To 4 whole eggs, well beaten, add 3 cups sugar, ½ cup of milk, ½ cup butter and cook in double boiler until done and creamy thick. Add 3 cups of nuts, 1 cup of raisins, 1 cup of coconut, and cook 5 more minutes. Let cool until slightly warm and use.

Doris Simmons
Muscle Shoals

Orange Cream Cake

4 egg whites
¼ teaspoon cream of tartar
Sugar
6 egg yolks
1 cup all-purpose flour
¾ cup orange juice
1 teaspoon double-acting
  baking powder

½ teaspoon salt
2 cups heavy or whipping
  cream
3 tablespoons confectioners'
  sugar
2 tablespoons grated orange
  peel
Orange sections for garnish

Early in the day, preheat oven to 325 degrees. In small bowl with mixer at high speed, beat egg whites and cream of tartar until soft peaks form. Beating at high speed, gradually sprinkle in ½ cup sugar, 2 tablespoons at a time, beating until each addition of sugar is completely dissolved. (Whites should stand in stiff glossy peaks.) Do not scrape sides of bowl at any time; set aside. In large bowl with mixer at high speed, beat egg yolks until thick and lemon colored, continue beating, gradually sprinkling in ½ cup sugar; beat until mixture is pale yellow. Reduce speed to low, beat in flour, ¼ orange juice, baking powder and salt until well mixed, occasionally scraping bowl with rubber spatula. Fold egg-white mixture into yolk mixture until just blended. Line two 9-inch round cake pans with waxed paper (do not grease). Pour batter into cake pans; bake 40 minutes or until cake springs back when lightly touched with finger. Cool cakes in pans on wire racks 10 minutes; remove cakes from pans and cool completely on racks. With fork, prick holes in cake layers. In saucepan over medium heat, heat ⅓ cup water and ¼ cup sugar to boiling; boil 3 minutes. Stir in ½ cup orange juice; drizzle mixture evenly over cake layers and let stand 30 minutes. In small bowl with mixer at medium speed, beat cream and confectioner's sugar until soft peaks form. Fold in orange peel. Place one cake layer on platter; spread with ⅓ cup of whipped cream; top with second layer. Frost top and sides of cake with remaining whipped cream; garnish with orange sections. Refrigerate. Makes 10 servings. Keeps well for several days.

Mrs. Braxton W. Ashe
Sheffield

Ice Box Fruit Cake

1 can sweetened condesned
  milk
1 cup candied cherries
1 cup raisins

½ cup chopped pecans
1 small package dates
1 pound vanilla wafers

Empty condensed milk into large mixing bowl. Add crushed vanilla wafers. Mix in all other ingredients. Roll to about 2 inches in diameter, wrap in damp cloth and refrigerate. Slice to desired thickness.

Evelyn Pless
Cherokee

Fruit Cake Roll

1 pound marshmallows,
cut fine
1 can sweetened condensed
milk
1 box graham crackers,
crushed

1 box raisins ground with
2 cups nuts
1 pound mixed crystalized
fruit

Pour milk over marshmallows and let stand while preparing other ingredients. Roll graham cracker crumbs fine and save out ¾ cup crackers crums to use later to form the rolls. Mix all ingredients well and form into roll about 2 inches in diameter. Roll in graham cracker crumbs and wrap in waxed paper. Place in refrigerator overnight before slicing. Garnish slices with whipped cream and a small slice of cherry.

Mable Allison
Tuscumbia

Dark Fruitcake

2 sticks margarine
1½ cups sugar
5 large eggs
¼ cup pineapple juice
2 cups crushed graham
crackers
2 cups crushed chocolate
cookies

1 tablespoon baking powder
1 cup candied fruit
2 tablespoons flour
1 cup chopped nuts
1 cup coconut
1 cup drained pineapple
1 teaspoon each: rum, orange and
coconut extract

Cream margarine and sugar, add eggs, one at a time. Mix baking powder with crumbs and add to creamed mixture; alternate with pineapple juice. pieces are separated); mix well. Add extract and nuts. Bake in greased tube pan 1 hour and 15 minutes at 325 degrees. Cool in pan and glaze.

Glaze

1½ cups powdered sugar
2 tablespoons soft butter
Mix and pour over warm cake.

2 tablespoons pineapple juice or
lemon juice

Mrs. J.H. Mitchell
Florence

Autumn Fruit Cake

2 sticks oleo
2 cups sugar
5 eggs
1 pound box graham cracker
crumbs

1 can coconut
1 can pineapple (drained)
1 cup chopped nuts
1 teaspoon baking powder

Cream butter and sugar. Add eggs one at a time, beating well after each addition. Add other ingredients, except nuts. Mix thoroughly. Add nuts. Bake in a greased tube pan for one hour and ten minutes at 325 degrees.

Mrs. William R. Portwood
Russellville

White Christmas Fruit Cake

3 cups chopped mixed
  candied fruits
2⅔ cups (2 cans) falked
  coconut
1½ cups golden raisins
1½ cups chopped pecans
1½ cups chopped pecans
1½ teaspoons grated
  orange rind

3¾ cups sifted cake flour
1½ teaspoons baking powder
¾ teaspoon salt
1½ sticks margarine
1½ cups sugar
6 eggs
⅓ cup orange juice

Grease tube pan, line with waxed paper and grease. Combine fruit, coconut, raisins, nuts and orange rind in large bowl. Sift flour, baking powder and salt over fruit; mix well. Cream margarine with sugar unti fluffy. Beat eggs in one at a time; add juices. Pour over fruit mixture. Spoon in prepared pan and press down firmly. Bake at 275 degrees for three hours. Cool in pan.

Lela Hall
Leighton

White Fruit Cake

¾ pound oleo
2 cups sugar
5 cups plain flour
  (use about half to
  dredge fruits)
1 tablespoon vanilla extract
1 tablespoon lemon extract
1 teaspoon baking powder

½ teaspoon salt
Juice and grated rind
  of one lemon
1 pound candied cherries
1 pound candied citron
½ pound candied pineapple
1 pound white raisins
1 pound nuts

Cream oleo and sugar. Add eggs one at a time, alternating with sifted dry ingredients and vanilla and lemon. Beat well. Dredge chopped fruits, nuts with flour. With hands mix lightly and thoroughly. Bake in loaf or tube pan at 275 degrees up to 3 or 4 hours. Test with toothpick for doneness. This is a recipe that lends itself to freezing and will keep for months to use for slicing.

Mrs. Delbert F. Wombacher
Leighton

Favorite Fruit Cake

1 pound (4 cups) chopped pecans
1 pound chopped candied
  cherries
1 pound chopped dates

4 4-ounce cans coconut
2 14-ounce cans condensed
  milk

Place all ingredients in a very large bowl and mix well with hands. Spoon mixture into 2 loaf pans that have been lined with oiled brown paper. Bake at 350 degrees for 1½ hours. Cool.

Mrs. Brenda Heupel
Florence

Chocolate Fruit Cake

5 cups sifted cake flour
3 teaspoons baking powder
¼ teaspoon soda
½ teaspoon salt
3 teaspoons cinnamon
1 teaspoon allspice
1 teaspoon mace
½ teaspoon nutmeg
3 pounds raisins, finely cut
2 pound currants
½ pound dates, seeded and
    finely cut

1 pound citron, thinly sliced
3 teaspoons grated orange rind
1½ teaspoons grated lemon rind
1 pound butter
1 pound brown sugar
12 eggs, well beaten
4 squares unsweetened
    chocolate, melted
1 cup molasses
1 cup tart jelly
¾ cup orange juice
3 tablespoons lemon juice

Sift once, measure. Add baking powder, soda, salt and spices, and sift together three times. Sift cup of flour mixture over fruit and mix well. Combine orange and lemon rind with butter, creaming thoroughly. Add sugar gradually and cream together until light and fluffy. Add eggs and chocolate and blend; then molasses, jelly and fruit juices. Add flour gradually, beating well after each addition. Add fruit. Turn into pans which have been greased, lined with wax paper and greased again. If desired, sprinkle almonds, blanched and shredded over top before baking. If 8½ inch tube pans are used, bake 4-5 hours; in 8x4x3 inch loaf pans 3-4 hours; in 6x3x2 inch loaf pans 2½-3 hour. Makes about 12½ pounds.

Mrs. Joan Allen
Florence

Ice Box Fruit Cake

1 large can evaporated milk
2 cups flake coconut
1 bag marshmallows
1 box golden raisins
1 quart chopped pecans
1 box vanilla wafers
    (crumbled)

1 box Graham crackers
    (crumbled)
2 boxes candied cherries
    (chopped finely)
2 boxes candied pineapple
    (chopped finely)
1 teaspoon cinnamon
1 teaspoon vanilla

Mix all dry ingredients in a large pan. Heat milk over very low heat stirring constatnly to avoid scorching. Stir in marshmallows and continue to heat until marshmallows are melted. Pour over dry mixture. Mix thoroughly. Pack firmly in any shape pan desired which has been lined completely with wax paper. (Rub wax paper with butter before lining pan). Make now and store in refrigerator for Christmas.

Mrs. Bill Roberts
Lexington

Light Old Fashioned Fruit Cake

1 pound candied cherries
1 pound candied pineapples
1 pound mixed colored
  diced fruit
3 cups pecans
3¼ cups white raisins
3 tablespoons brandy flavoring
4 cups all-purpose flour

1½ teaspoon salt
½ teaspoon baking powder
1½ teaspoon cinnamon
1 teaspoon nutmeg
1 cup butter
2¼ cups sugar
6 unbeaten eggs

Sift flour, baking powder, salt, nutmeg and cinnamon together in bowl. Add pecans and all fruits together in larger mixing bowl. Then mix flour mixture to fruit mixture until all is well coated. Measure 2 cups of floured mixture and set aside. Cream butter, sugar and add eggs, one at a time, cream after each addition. Add brandy flavoring. Add this with fruit mixture in large bowl, mix well. Pour ⅓ of cake batter into tube pan. Sprinkle or arrange ½ of reserved floured fruit. Cover with another layer of batter. Another ½ cup of reserved floured fruit. Cover with another layer of batter. Do this until all is used. Do not shake the pan to smooth out batter. Bake slowly at 300 degrees for 3½ hours. While cake is still hot, brush with some sort of thick table syrup. Wrap in foil. Store in freezer. Remove from freezer approximately 1 week before serving.

Mrs. Racene Pace
Leighton

Black Beauty Fruitcake

1 cup seedless raisins
1 cup currants
¾ cup chopped pitted dates
¾ cup (4 ounces)
  chopped citron
¾ cup (4 ounces)
  chopped candied orange
  and/or lemon peel
1½ cups walnuts or pecans
1½ cups sifted all-purpose
  flour
½ teaspoon baking powder

½ teaspoon soda
¼ teaspoon salt
½ teaspoon each cinnamon, all-spice,
  and nutmeg
¼ teaspoon cloves
½ cu soft shortening
½ cup firmly packed brown
  sugar
2 eggs
¼ cup dark molasses
¼ cup grape juice or coffee

Combine fruits and nuts in large bowl. Coat with ½ cup of the sifted flour. Sift remaining 1 cup flour with baking powder, salt, soda, and spices. Cream shortening. Gradually add sugar, beating until fluffy.

Add eggs, one at a time, beating 1½ minutes after each addition. Combine molasses and grape juice or coffee. Add alternately with dry ingredients to creamed mixture. Fold into floured fruits and nuts. Spread evenly in prepared 9-inch square pan. Bake as directed for 40 to 45 minutes.

Evie Boyles
Russellville

English Rum Cake

½ pound candied pineapple
5 cups coarsely grated pecans
1 cup sugar
5 eggs

1 stick butter
1 cup rum
1 cup flour
2 teaspoons vanilla

Chop fruit extra fine. Pour rum over and let set overnight. Beat eggs until thick. Add sugar and then fold in the flour. Add fruit mixture and nuts. Pour into greased tube pan. Put cake in cold oven and set at 225 degrees. Bake 2½ to 3 hours. Let cake stand in pan 10 minutes before removing to cool on rack.

Mrs. Tracy Gargis
Sheffield

Rum Cake

Preheat oven to 325 degrees. Grease and flour 10-inch tube pan or large bundt pan. Either place chopped pecans in bottom of pan or later mix into cake batter.

In large mixing bowl, place these ingredients in order:

1 package white or yellow
  cake mix
1 large package instant.
  vanilla pudding mix
4 eggs

½ cup vegetable oil
¼ or ½ cup rum (according
  to taste)
½ cup cold water

Beat well; pour into pan. Bake one hour at 325 degrees. Take from oven. Pour glaze over cake, leaving cake in pan.

Glaze

Boil these ingredients for four minutes:

1 stick margarine
¾ cup sugar

¼ cup rum
¼ cup water

Pour over cake in pan. Cool one-half hour. Turn out onto plate.

Mrs. Jere Medaris
Vicenza, Italy

Quick Trick Fruitcake

1 package date bar cake mix
⅔ cup hot water
3 eggs
¼ cup flour
¾ teaspoon baking powder
2 tablespoons light molasses
1 teaspoon cinnamon

¼ teaspoon nutmeg
¼ teaspoon allspice
1 cup chopped walnuts
1 cup chopped candied
  fruits
1 cup raisins

Mix thoroughly. Bake in greased loaf or tube pan at 350 degrees.

Mrs. Frank Boswell
Red Bay

Carrot Cake

2 cups sugar
3 cups all-purpose flour
1 teaspoon soda
¼ teaspoon salt
2 teaspoons ground cinnamon
1½ cups buttery-flavored salad oil
1 teaspoon vanilla extract

3 eggs, beaten
1 cup crushed pineapple,
  well-drained
1¾ cups grated raw carrot
¼ cup peeled, grated apple
1 cup chopped pecans
Icing (recipe follows)

Combine sugar, flour, soda, salt, and cinnamon; set aside. Combine oil, vanilla, eggs, pineapple, carrots and apple; beat well. Stir in dry ingredients and pecans. Spoon batter into 3 greased 8-inch cake pans. Bake at 350 degrees for 25-30 minutes. Cool 10 minutes in pans; remove from pans, and cool completely. Spread icing between layers and on top and sides of cake.

Icing

½ cup butter or margarine,
  softened
1 16-ounce box powdered sugar

1 8-ounce package cream cheese
1 cup chopped pecans

Combine butter and cream cheese; cream until light and fluffy. Add sugar, mixing well. Stir in pecans.

Linda McDougal
Killen

Carrot Cake

3 cups cake flour
2 cups sugar
2 teaspoons soda
1 teaspoon cinnamon
½ teaspoon salt
2 cups grated carrots

1½ cups vegetable oil
3 large eggs
1 small can crushed pineapple
2 teaspoons vanilla
½ cup coconut
½ cup chopped pecans

Mix all dry ingredients together. Add carrots, oil, eggs, pineapple and vanilla. Then add coconut and nuts. Bake in a greased and floured layer pans at 350 degrees. Frost with orange icing.

Orange Icing

½ cup cornstarch or flour
2 cups sugar
2 cups orange juice
1 teaspoon lemon juice

2 teaspoons grated orange peel
2 tablespoons butter
½ teaspoon salt

Combine sugar, cornstarch, and juice (adding it slowly). Stir until smooth. Add remaining ingredients and heat, stirring constantly until thick. Let cool and spread on Carrot Cake, on top of and between layers.

Elsie Pierce
Sheffield

Carrot Cake

1½ cup cooking oil
2 cups sugar
4 whole eggs, beaten
2 cups plain flour

3 teaspoons cinnamon
2 teaspoons soda
1 teaspoon salt
3 cups grated carrots

Mix oil and sugar; beat well. Add eggs. Sift flour, cinnamon, soda and salt 2 or 3 times. Add to creamed mixture. Add carrots, a small amount at a time. Bake in 8x12-inch pan at 325 degrees for 30 to 40 minutes or until done.

Icing

1 (8 ounce) package cream
  cheese, softened
1 stick oleo, softened

1 box powdered sugar
1 teaspoon vanilla
1 cup chopped pecans

Beat all ingredients well. Spread on cake after it cools.

Mrs. Judy McKelvey
Tuscumbia

Strawberry Shortcake

1 quart fresh strawberries
1 cup sugar
2 cups all-pourpose flour
2 tablespoons sugar
3 teaspoons baking powder
1 teaspoon salt

⅓ cup shortening
1 cup milk
Butter or margarine
Light cream or sweetened
  whipped cream

Slice strawberries; sprinkle with 1 cup sugar and let stand 1 hour. Heat oven to 450 degrees. Grease round layer pan, 8 by 1½ inches. Measure flour, 2 tablespoons sugar, baking powder and salt into bowl. Cut in shortening thoroughly until mixture looks like meal.

Stir in milk just until blended. Pat into pan. Bake 15 to 20 minutes or until golden brown. Split shortcake while warm. Spread with butter; fill and top with berries. Serve warm with whipped cream.

Mrs. Jerry Turbyfill
Florence

Strawberry Cake

1 cup miniature
  marshmallows
2 cups (2 10-ounce packages)
  frozen sliced
  strawberries
1 package strawberry gelatin
½ teaspoon salt

2¼ cups flour (plain)
1¼ cups sugar
½ cup shortening
3 teaspoons baking powder
1 cup milk
1 teaspoon vanilla
3 eggs

Preheat oven at 350 degrees. Generously grease bottom only of a 13x9 inch pan. Sprinkle marshmallows evenly over bottom of pan. Thoroughly combine completely thawed berries and sugar with dry gelatin; set aside. In large mixing bowl, combine remaining ingredients. Blend at low speed until moistened; beat 3 minutes at medium speed, scraping sides of bowl occasionally. Pour batter evenly over marshmallows in prepared pan. Spoon berry mixture over batter. Bake in 350 degree oven for 45-50 minutes or until golden brown. Serve warm with ice cream or whipped cream.

Mrs. Martha Abernathy
Cloverdale

Cranberry Sauce Cake

1 1-pound can cranberry
   sauce
3 cups all-purpose flour
1 cup sugar
2 teaspoons salt

1 cup chopped pecans
1 cup mayonnaise or salad
   dressing
Grated rind of one orange
½ cup orange juice

Reserve ¼ cup cranberry sauce for frosting. Sift together dry ingredients. Add remaining cranberry sauce, nuts, mayonnaise and orange rind. Mix well. Stir in orange juice. Grease 9x3½-inch tube pan. Line bottom with waxed paper. Bake at 350 degrees for 1¼ hours.

Cranberry Frosting

3 tablespoons margarine
2 cups unsifted confectioners'
   sugar

¼ cup reserved cranberry
   sauce

Beat all ingredients until smooth. Spread over cake. This is an unusually good cake, and also a pretty one.

Mrs. Walter Shaff
Florence

Cranberry Spice Cake

½ cup shortening
1 cup light brown sugar
2 eggs
1 cup jellied cranberry sauce
1 cup chopped nuts
1 cup seedless raisins

2¾ cups sifted enriched flour
1 teaspoon soda
1 teaspoon salt
1 teaspoon cinnamon
1 teaspoon nutmeg
¾ cup buttermilk

Blend shortening, sugar and eggs. Stir in cranberry sauce, nuts and raisins. Add mixed dry ingredients alternately with milk. Place in greased 9-inch tube pan. Bake at 350 degrees about 1 hour. Cool; remove from pan. Ice with Creamy Lemon Icing.

Creamy Lemon Icing

2⅓ cups sifted confectioners'
   sugar
¼ teaspoon salt
1 egg

2 tablespoons lemon juice
¼ cup granulated sugar
½ cup shortening
1 tablespoon grated lemon rind

Mix confectioners' sugar, salt and egg. Boil lemon juice and granulated sugar together for 1 minute. Add shortening and lemon rind. Beat all ingredients together until creamy.

Mrs. James A. Gafford
Florence

Williamsburg Orange Cake

2¾ cups cake flour
½ cup sugar
1½ teaspoons soda
¾ teaspoon salt
1½ cups buttermilk
½ cup butter, softened
¼ cup shortening

3 eggs
1½ teaspoons vanilla
1 cup golden raisins, cut up
½ cup finely chopped nuts
1 tablespoon grated
   orange peel

Preheat oven to 350 degrees. Grease and flour cake pans. Measure all ingredients into a large bowl. Blend ½ minute on low speed, scraping the bowl constantly. Beat 3 minutes on high speed, scraping the bowl occasionally. Bake an oblong cake for 45 to 50 minutes and a layered cake for 30 to 35 minutes.

Williamsburg Butter Frosting
For Oblong Cake or Two 9-Inch Layers

⅓ cup butter or margarine,
   softened
3 cups confectioners' sugar

3 to 4 tablespoons orange-flavored
   liqueur or orange juice
2 teaspoons grated
   orange peel

For Three 8-Inch Layers

½ cup butter or margarine,
   softened
4½ cups confectioners' sugar

4 to 5 tablespoons orange-flavored
   liqueur or orange juice
1 tablespoon grated
   orange peel

Blend butter and sugar. Stir in liqueur and orange peel; beat until smooth.

Mrs. Jerry Turbyfill
Florence

Twelfth Night Cake

1 cup butter or margarine
3 tablespoons frozen concentrated
   orange juice, thawed
2 teaspoons grated orange rind
½ teaspoon vanilla extract
¼ teaspoon salt

4 eggs, at room
   temperature
1 cup sugar
1½ cups sifted all purpose
   flour
¼ cup sifted cornstarch
Confectioners' sugar

Combine butter, undiluted orange concentrate juice and rind, vanilla and salt in small saucepan; cook over low heat, stirring until butter is melted. Remove from heat; cool to lukewarm. Place eggs and sugar in large warm bowl; beat until tripled in bulk. Sprinkle flour and cornstarch over eggs gently. Add orange mixture; fold in very gently until there is no trace of butter. Pour into greased 9-inch tube pan. Bake in preheated 350 degree oven for about 50 minutes or until cake starts to come away from side of pan. Cool; remove from pan. Sprinkle top of cake with confectioners' sugar; garnish side with orange slices, if desired. Yield: about 12 servings.

Mrs. Joan Pugh
Florence

Candied Orange Slice Cake

1 cup butter or oleo
2 cups sugar
4 whole eggs
½ cup buttermilk
1 teaspoon soda
3½ cups flour

1 pound chopped dates
1 pound chopped candied orange
  slices
2 cups chopped pecans or walnuts
1 cup flaked coconut

Add all flour to chopped dates, orange slices, nuts and coconut. Let stand in large bowl. Cream shortening, add sugar, eggs one at a time. Stir soda into buttermilk then add to sugar, egg, shortening mixture. Add above mixture to the nuts, date, candy and flour mixture. Stir with a spoon until mixed. Pack into a 10-inch or larger greased tube pan lined with waxed paper. Bake at 250 degrees for 2½-3 hours. Remove from oven when done and while it is still hot add glaze consisting of one cup orange juice stirred into 2 cups powdered sugar. Let stand in pan overnite.

Mrs. Esther Burnett
Florence

Fresh Orange Oatmeal Cake

1½ cups orange juice
1 cup quick cooking rolled oats
½ cup butter or margarine
1 cup granulated sugar
½ cup finely packed brown
  sugar
2 eggs
1 teaspoon vanilla

1¾ cups sifted flour
1 teaspoon baking powder
1 teaspoon soda
½ teaspoon salt
¼ teaspoon cinnamon
1 tablespoon grated orange
  rind
½ cup chopped nuts

Bring orange juice to a boil; pour over oats and set aside. Cream butter until fluffy; add sugars gradually, creaming well. Add eggs and vanilla; beat until thoroughly blended. Sift together dry ingredients. Add alternately with oats to creamed mixture beating until smooth after each addition. Stir in orange peel and nuts. Pour into greased 13x9x2 inch baking pan. Bake at 350 degrees for 40 minutes. Remove from oven and spread immediately with orange delight topping. Place three to five inches from source of heat in cold broiler; broil about one minute or until bubbly. Watch closely to avoid scorching.

Orange Delight Topping

½ cup firmly packed brown sugar
¼ cup butter or margarine
1 tablespoon grated orange peel

1 tablespoon orange juice
1 cup flaked coconut
½ cup chopped nuts

Combine sugar, butter, orange peel and juice in small saucepan. Bring to a boil and cook one minute, stirring constantly. Blend in remaining ingredients.

Mrs. Orville O. Sharp
Florence

Scriptural Cake

4½ cups I Kings 4:22
  (flour)
1 cup Judges 5:25 (butter)
2 cups Jeremiah 6:20
  (sugar)
2 cups I Samuel 30:12
  (raisins)
2 cups Nahum 3:12 (figs)
1 tablespoon Numbers 17:8
  (almonds)

1 tablespoon I Samuel 14:25
  (honey)
1 tablespoon Ecclesiastes 10:19
  (wine)
Season to taste with II
  Chronicles 9:9 (spices)
6 Jeremiah 17:11 (eggs)
1 pinch Leviticus 2:13 (salt)
1 cup Genesis 24:20 (water)
2 tablespoons Amos 4:5 (leaven)

Follow Solomon's prescription for making a good boy: Proverbs 23:14, and you will have a good cake.

Pearlene Angel Creasy
Florence

1-2-3-4 Cake

1 cup shortening
2 cups sugar
3 cups cake flour
4 eggs
3 teaspoons baking powder

½ teaspoon salt
1 cup milk
1 teaspoon vanilla
½ teaspoon almond extract

Cream butter and sugar until fluffy; add eggs and blend well. Add baking powder and salt to flour and sift. Add flavorings to milk. Add flour mixture alternately with the milk to the creamed mixture, beating after each addition until smooth. Pour into three 9-inch layer pans that have been greased and floured. Bake for 25 minutes at 350 degrees. Cool in pans for 10 minutes and then turn out onto racks. Cover with your favorite frosting, topping with finely chopped English walnuts and coconut.

Mrs. Darrell A. Russel
Florence

Dump Cake

1 can cherry pie filling or
  orange pie filling
¼ tall can pineapple tidbits
  with juice

1 package yellow cake mix
2 sticks melted margarine
1 cup chopped nuts
1 cup flaked coconut

Dump all ingredients into a 9 by 13-inch ungreased cake pan. Never mix ingredients. Put ingredients in pan in order given for best results. Bake at 350 degrees for 45 minutes or until nicely brown.

Mrs. A. W. Nelson
Guin

"Sock It To Me" Cake

1 package Golden Butter cake
  mix
½ cup sugar

¾ cup cooking oil
1 teaspoon vanilla

Mix together the above ingredients. Add one at a time, beating between each addition. Blend in 4 eggs and beat until smooth. Stir in 8 ounces of sour cream. Pour one-half of the batter into a greased tube pan. Add one teaspoon cinnamon and two tablespoons brown sugar and sprinkle over batter. Pour remaining batter into pan. Bake at 350 degrees for one hour.

Mrs. F.A. Wallace
Killen

Watergate Cake

1 box of white cake mix
1 cup oil
1 cup 7-Up
1 box pistaschio pudding

3 eggs
½ cup nuts
5 drops green food coloring

Mix all ingredients together and bake 350 degrees in a bundt pan, approximately 45 minutes.

Frosting

3 drops green food coloring
1 box pistachio pudding

1 large container (13½ ounces)
  refrigerated whipped topping

Mix all ingredients thoroughly and spread on cooled cake. For a festive look, dot with maraschino cherries.

Jerri Patterson
Florence

Pea-Picking Cake

1 box butter cake mix
1 stick oleo, softened
4 eggs

1 can mandarin oranges,
  chopped

Mix cake mix, oleo and juice from oranges in mixer. Add eggs one at a time and beat well. Fold in chopped oranges. Bake in three layers at 350 degrees until center of cakes spring back when lightly touched.

Icing

2 large cartons frozen
  whipped topping
1 package instant vanilla
  pudding

1 large can crushed pineapple

undrained

Mix ingredients thoroughly. Spread on cake. Top each layer with flaked coconut mixed with chopped pecans if desired.

Mrs. Todd O'Flynn
Philpot, Kentucky

Diplomat Cake

1⅓ cup orange marmalade
⅔ cup dark rum
3 packages (3 ounce size)
  ladyfingers

1 cup heavy cream, whipped
Chocolate curls (instructions
  below)

Line a 1½ quart decorative mold with plastic film. In small bowl, combine orange marmalade with one-third cup rum; mix well. Set aside ¼ cup of mixture, and refrigerate for later use. Split ladyfingers; brush cut sides with one-third cup rum. In bottom of mold, arrange two layers of lady-fingers, cut side up. Spread with 2 tablespoons marmalade mixture. Repeat layer. Around side of mold, arrange a row of split ladyfingers vertically, rounded side against mold. Continue layering ladyfingers and marmalade mixture to fill center of mold, ending with ladyfingers. Cover top with plastic film, refrigerate several hours or overnight. To unmold, remove plastic film from top; invert mold onto serving plate; gently remove mold and film. Spoon reserved ¼ cup marmalade-rum mixture over top of cake, letting it drizzle down sides. Using pastry tube with number five star tip, make ro-settes of whipped cream around base of cake and on top; arrange chocolate curls on top of rosettes. Refrigerate. Makes 8 servings.

To make chocolate curls: Let squares of unsweetened chocolate or a chocolate bar soften slightly. Pare with vegetable parer, forming curls.

Mrs. Charles Willis
Tuscumbia

Whacky Cake

1½ cups flour
1 cup sugar
3 teaspoons cocoa
1 cup cold water

6 tablespoons cooking oil
1 tablespoon vinegar
1 teaspoon vanilla

Sift together dry ingredients. Put into an 8 x 8 pan. Make one large hole, one medium hole and one small hole in dry ingredients. Pour oil into large hole, vinegar into medium hole and vanilla into small hole. Pour water over all and mix well with fork.

Bake in same pan in 350 degree oven for 25 minutes. If desired, frost in baking pan after cake is cool.

Whacky Cake Frosting

Melt 3 tablespoons butter in saucepan. Stir in 2 tablespoons cocoa until dissolved. Add 1½ cups confectioners' sugar to 2 tablespoons milk and 1 teaspoon vanilla. Stir until smooth.

James Coburn
Florence

Moon Rocks

1 (6 ounce) package semisweet
   chocolate pieces
2 cups all-purpose flour
1½ teaspoons soda
½ teaspoon salt
½ cup softened butter

1½ cups packed brown sugar
3 eggs
1 teaspoon vanilla flavoring
1 cup water
2 cups miniature marshmallows

Melt chocolate in top of double boiler. Remove from heat, and set aside to cool. Combine flour, soda, and salt; set aside. Cream butter and sugar until fluffy. Add eggs, one at a time, beating well. Add vanilla, flour mixture, water and melted chocolate. Beat at low speed until blended, scraping sides of bowl often. Stir in marshmallows. Fill paper-lined cupcake pans half full; bake at 350 degrees for 20 minutes. Cool on cake rack. Yield: 24.

H.M. Mitchell
Florence

Funnel Cake

1⅓ cups flour
¼ teaspoon salt
½ teaspoon soda
2 tablespoons sugar

¾ tablespoons baking powder
1 egg, beaten
⅔ cup milk (or more if batter
   is too thick)

Sift together dry ingredients. Mix egg and milk together and add to dry ingredients. Beat until smooth.

Hold finger over the bottom of a funnel, pour in some batter, remove finger and let batter drop in a spiral motion into pan filled with 1 inch of hot oil (375 degrees). Fry until golden brown, turning once. Remove from pan and drain on a paper towel. Sprinkle with powdered sugar and serve hot.

Mrs. Dorothy Clement
Russellville

Out Of This World Cake

13½ ounce box graham cracker
   crumbs
4 eggs
1 can flake coconut
2 cups sugar

1 cup pecans, cut in pieces
2 sticks margarine, melted
1 cup milk
2 teaspoons baking powder

Mix well and bake in a 9 x 13 pan. Bake 35-45 minutes in a 350 degree oven. Remove cake from oven and immediately spoon medium-size can crushed pineapple over top (juice, too). Let cool before icing.

Icing

1 stick margarine, softened
1 box powdered sugar

1 8-ounce package cream cheese
1 teaspoon vanilla

Mix all ingredients together until soft. Ice cake.

Mrs. Nona Sandusky
Iron City, Tennessee

Puerto Rican Coconut Cake

2¾ cups flour
4 teaspoons baking powder
½ teaspoon salt
¾ cup butter or oleo

1½ cups sugar
1 cup coconut milk or milk
1 teaspoon vanilla
4 large egg whites

Sift together flour, baking powder, and salt; set aside. Cream butter, add 1 cup sugar and cream well. Combine coconut milk or milk and vanilla flavoring. Add dry ingredients to creamed mixture alternately with milk, beginning and ending with dry ingredients. In a small bowl, beat egg whites until foamy. Gradually add the remaining half cup sugar and beat until stiff and glossy. Fold beaten whites into the batter carefully. Bake in 2 9-inch layer pans at 350 degrees for 25-30 minutes. Frost with favorite seven-minute frosting and sprinkle with coconut.

Mrs. L.C. Jones
Florence

Halekulani Coconut Cake

2 cups sifted flour
1½ cups sugar
¼ teaspoon salt
1 tablespoon baking powder
7 egg yolks

½ cup cooking oil
½ cup water
¾ teaspoon vanilla
7 egg whites

Sift together dry ingredients and set aside. Beat together egg yolks, cooking oil, water, and vanilla with wire whip. Mix the egg mixture into dry ingredients and blend well; beat egg whites until stiff and in peaks, fold into other mixture. Line cake pans with paper and turn batter into cake pans and bake 325 degrees to 350 degrees 25-30 minutes. Do not over cook. Use whipped cream for filling and frosting, sprinkle coconut between and on top and sides of cake.

Filling for Halekulani Coconut Cake

1 pint whipped cream
Fresh grated coconut

4 tablespoons sugar (more if you like sweeter)

Whip the cream and add the sugar. Fill between layers and sprinkle with coconut. Frost top and sides and sprinkle with coconut. Keep in refrigerator.

Mrs. Price Counts, Jr.
Tuscumbia

Peanut Butter Icing

½ cup brown sugar, packed
¼ cup peanut butter
½ cup powdered sugar (sifted)

¼ cup margarine
¼ cup milk
Few grains salt
1 teaspoon vanilla

Mix margarine, milk and brown sugar, add salt. Cook over low heat until well mixed. Bring to a boil and boil for 1 minutes. Cool to luke warm—do not stir. When cool, add powdered sugar and vanilla. Beat until a spreading consistency is maintained. Spread over a favorite cake recipe.

Ethel Rutherford
Cherokee

Fresh Apple Cake

1 cup cooking oil
2 cups self-rising flour
2 cups sugar
3 cups very finely chopped
   raw apple
3 eggs

½ cup raisins
½ cup chopped pecans
1 teaspoon cinnamon
1 teaspoon nutmeg
1 teaspoon vanilla

Mix well and bake at 350 degrees in bundt pan for 40 to 45 minutes.

Billy Townsend
Florence

Applesauce Cake

2 cups applesauce
1 cup sugar
1 tablespoon cornstarch
1 egg
2 teaspoons soda
½ teaspoon nutmeg
2 teaspoons cinnamon
½ teaspoon cloves

1 cup raisins
2 cups flour
2 tablespoons cocoa
1 cup nuts (walnuts or
   pecans)
½ cup melted butter (put
   in last)

Mix all ingredients together with a spoon (not an electric mixer) and bake at 350 degrees for one hour.

Mrs. Martha Winter
Florence

Apple Dapple Cake

3 eggs
1½ cups salad oil
2 cups sugar
3 cups all-purpose flour
1 teaspoon salt

1 teaspoon soda
2 teaspoons vanilla extract
3 cups chopped apples
1½ cups chopped pecans

Mix eggs, oil and sugar and blend well. Combine flour, salt and soda; add to egg mixture. Add vanilla, apples and nuts. Pour into greased 8 or 9-inch tube pan. Bake at 350 degrees for 1 hour. While cake is warm, pour hot topping over it in the pan. When completely cool, remove cake from pan.

Topping:

1 cup firmly packed brown
   sugar

¼ cup milk
½ cup margarine

Combinate all ingredients and cook for 2½ minutes. Pour immediately over cake in pan.

Beth West
Florence

Orange-Nut Cake

1 18¾ ounce package orange
   cake mix
2 cups ricotta cheese
2 tablespoons milk
½ cups confectioners' sugar
¼ cup candied lemon peel
¼ cup cut-up candied citron

¼ cup finely chopped fresh orange
   peel
1 envelope unflavored gelatin
¼ cup rum (optional)
¼ cup cold water
2 cups heavy or whipping cream
1 cup very coarsely chopped
   hazelnuts

Make 2 8-inch layers of orange cake as directed on package. Cool. Meanwhile, in medium-size bowl, beat cheese and milk until smooth using medium speed of electric mixer. Gradually beat in 1½ cups confectioners' sugar. Fold in citron, lemon peel and orange peel. With sharp knife, carefully split each layer into 2 layers, making 4 layers in all. Sprinkle each layer and spread with ⅓ cheese mixture; top with final cake layer.

To make frosting: in measuring cup, sprinkle gelatin over cold water, set cup into pan of hot water and stir until dissolved; cool slightly. In medium size bowl, beat heavy cream with half-cup confectioners' sugar until fairly stiff. Add cooled gelatin slowly; beating enough to hold stiff peaks. Frost cake. Sprinkle hazelnuts on top of cake. Refrigerate until serving time. Makes 10 servings.

Doris Chenault
Sheffield

Angel Food Supreme

1 cup cake flour
12 egg whites
¾ cup plus 2 tablespoons
   sugar
1½ teaspoons cream of tartar

¼ teaspoon salt
¾ cup sugar
1½ teaspoon vanilla
½ teaspoon almond extract

Heat oven to 375 degrees. Stir together flour and first amount of sugar; set aside. In a large mixer bowl, beat egg whites, cream of tartar and salt until foamy. Add second amount of sugar, 2 tablespoons at a time, beating on high speed until meringue holds stiff peaks. Gently fold in flavorings. Sprinkle flour-sugar mixture, ¼ cup at a time, over meringue, folding in gently just until flour-sugar mixture disappears. Push batter into an ungreased tube pan, 10 by 4 inches. Gently cut through batter. Bake 30 to 35 minutes or until top springs back when touched lightly with finger. Invert tube pan on funnel ; let hang until cake is completely cool.

Mrs. Jerry Turbyfill
Florence

German Chocolate Cake

1 package German sweet
  chocolate
½ cup boiling water
1 cup butter
2 cups sugar
4 egg yolks, unbeaten

1 teaspoon vanilla
½ teaspoon salt
1 teaspoon soda
2½ cups sifted flour, plain
1 cup buttermilk
4 egg whites

Melt chocolate in boiling water. Cream butter and sugar until light and fluffy. Add egg yolks, one at a time, beating after each. Add chocolate and vanilla. Sift together salt, soda and flour. Add buttermilk. Beat until smooth. Beat egg whites until stiff peaks form. Fold into batter. Pour into three eight inch layer pans. Bake in moderate oven 350 degrees for 35-40 minutes. Cool. Frost tops only.

Coconut-Pecan Frosting

Combine one cup of evaporated milk, one cup sugar, three egg yolks, one-fourth pound margarine, and one teaspoon vanilla in a saucepan. Cook and stir over medium heat until mixture thickens (about 12 minutes). Add 1⅓ cups of canned coconut and one cup of chopped nuts. Beat until frosting is cool and thick enough to spread. Makes enough to cover the tops of three nine inch cake layers.

Mrs. F.E. Hooks
Florence

Bavarian-Style Chocolate Cake

2 cups sifted cake flour
1⅔ cup sugar
1½ teaspoons soda
1 teaspoon salt
½ teaspoon baking powder
½ cup shortening

3 squares (1 ounce each) semisweet
  chocolate, melted
⅔ cup milk
3 eggs
⅔ cup milk
1 teaspoon vanilla

Pre-heat oven to 350 degrees. Combine dry ingredients in mixing bowl; add shortening, melted chocolate, and ⅔ cup milk. Blend 30 seconds and beat with mixer at medium speed for 2 minutes. Add eggs, the additional milk, and vanilla. Beat 2 minutes. Spread batter in two well-greased and floured 9 x 1½ inch layer cake pans. Bake 30-35 minutes. Cool 10-20 minutes. Remove from pans and spread tops of layers with coconut pecan frosting.

Coconut Pecan Frosting

⅔ cup sugar
⅔ cup evaporated mlk
2 egg yolks
⅓ cup shortening

½ teaspoon vanilla
1⅓ cups flaked coconut
⅔ cup chopped pecans

In saucepan, combine sugar, milk, egg yolks, shortening, and vanilla. Cook and stir over medium heat until mixture comes to a boil. Remove from heat, add coconut and pecans. Beat until frosting is thick. Cool 15 minutes and spread on tops of layers.

Mable Allison
Tuscumbia

Kentucky Wonder Cake

2 cups sugar
1½ cups wesson oil
4 egg yolks
3¾ tablespoons hot water
1 small can crushed pineapple (drained)
1½ teaspoons cinnamon
1⅓ teaspoons nutmeg
1½ teaspoons soda
½ teaspoon salt
1 cup chopped nuts
4 egg whites
2½ cups cake flour

Mix sugar, oil, yolks. Sift flour, salt, soda, cinnamon and nutmeg. Add flour mix to sugar, egg and oil along with hot water and pineapple. Roll nuts in flour and add to mixture. Beat egg whites to a stiff peak and fold in gently. Bake in greased and floured tube pan at 325 degrees for 1½ hours.

Mrs. Kay Staggs
Florence

Georgia Cake

1 box yellow cake mix
4 eggs
1 can mandarin oranges
and juice
½ cup salad oil

Mix thoroughly and bake at 325 degrees for 20-25 minutes. Makes 3 9-inch layers.

Icing:

1 large container refrigerated
whipped topping
1 box instant vanilla pudding
1 large can crushed pineapple
and juice

Mix pudding with pineapple. Fold in and mix thoroughly, whipped topping. Frost cake and store in refrigerator.

Mrs. Jack Thomason
Muscle Shoals

Mississippi Mud Cake

2 cups sugar
⅓ cup cocoa
4 eggs
1 cup nuts
1 cup shortening
1½ cups flour
3 teaspoons vanilla
1 package miniature
marshmallows

Cream sugar and shortening. Add eggs and beat. Stir in flour and cocoa; add vanilla and nuts. Pour into greased and floured oblong pan. Bake at 300 degrees for 30 minutes. Remove from oven and spread with marshmallows. Return to oven and melt marshmallows for about 10 minutes. Cool cake before frosting.

Icing:

½ stick oleo, melted
⅓ cup cocoa
1 box confectioners' sugar
½ cup evaporated milk
1 teaspoon vanilla
1 cup nuts

Sift sugar and cocoa together. Mix well with melted oleo. Add milk, vanilla and nuts. Spread over cake mixture. Let stand before serving.

Miss Patricia Collier
Huntsville

Mother's Cake

(For Brides and Birthdays)

"Come sit ye under yonder trees
Where merry as the maids we'll be
And talk of brides, and who shall make
That wedding smock, the bridal cake."

1 cup butter
2 cups sugar
1 cup milk
3½ cups flour
1 teaspoon vanilla

1 teaspoon baking powder
5 egg yolks
3 egg whites
1 cup walnut meats, chopped fine

Cream butter and sugar, add yolks of eggs. Beat well. Sift flour twice, measure, add baking powder and sift into cake mixture alternately with milk. Beat egg whites until they stand in peaks, fold into cake mixture. Bake in tubular pan 1 hour and 20 minutes at 350 degrees. Frost with white icing.

Mrs. Charles M. Smith
Sheffield

Old-Fashioned Appalachian Mountain Stack Cake

2½ cups flour
1 cup sugar
2 teaspoons baking powder
½ teaspoon salt
½ teaspoon soda

½ cup shortening
2 eggs
¾ cup molasses
Spice (ginger, etc.)

Cream shortening and sugar. Add eggs and molasses. Sift together flour, baking powder, salt, soda, and spices. Add to creamed mixture. Pour out on floured board and knead until dough is stiff. Roll out in five small balls and place in five 8-inch cake pans. Layers will be thin. Bake 350 degrees for 10-12 minutes. Put together with dried sweetened apples to which spice has been added.

This recipe came from the old Appalachian mountain women in Kentucky.

Mrs. M.C. Kiel
Tuscumbia

Harvest Hand Cake

¾ cup butter or margarine
1 cup corn syrup
½ cup sugar
1 teaspoon vanilla
3 teaspoons baking powder
¾ teaspoon salt

3 cups sifted cake flour
1 cup milk
3 eggs
10 ounces semi-sweet
    chocolate bits

Into a big bowl, put butter or margarine (softened), sugar, syrup, salt, flour, milk, vanilla. Beat 8 minutes by hand or 5 minutes with mixer at low speed. When smooth, beat in eggs, one at a time, then fold in baking powder. Bake in a large pan 10 x 14 at 375 degrees, 30 minutes.

Cool 5 minutes. Sprinkle with the 10 ounces semi-sweet chocolate bits. Return to oven at 350 degrees for 2 minutes. Spread out softened chocolate bits. Makes 24 large servings.

Las Cruces, New Mexico

Italian Creme Cake

1 stick butter
½ cup shortening
2 cups sugar
5 egg yolks
2 cups flour
1 teaspoon soda

1 cup buttermilk
5 egg whites, beaten
1 cup nuts
1 cup coconut
1½ teaspoons vanilla

Cream butter, shortening, and sugar well. Add slightly beaten egg yolks. Add flour alternately with buttermilk and vanilla into which soda has been dissolved. Fold in beaten egg whites and add coconut and nuts. Bake in three 9-inch layers on one 13x9 inch pan at 350 degrees for approximately 45 minutes.

Icing

8 ounces cream cheese
1 box confectioners' sugar

½ stick butter (room
    temperature)
1 teaspoon vanilla

Cream cheese and butter. Add sugar and vanilla and beat until right consistency to spread.

Mrs. R.N. Hudson
Tuscumbia

Alabama Delight

1 cup flour (not self-rising)
½ cup margarine

½ cup pecans (chopped)

Melt margarine, mix all ingredients. Pat into a 9x13 inch pan, bake for 15 minutes at 350 degrees, then chill and set aside.

1 8 ounce package cream cheese
    at room temperature
1 cup powdered sugar

1 cup whipped cream
1 teaspoon vanilla

Mix all ingredients with electric mixer. Spread on chilled crust and chill again.

2 packages chocolate pudding
    mix

3 cups milk
1 teaspoon vanilla

Cook until thick, let cool before pouring it on other layers. Spread whipped cream on top. This desert is best if chilled overnight.

Mrs. Robert Lindsey
Florence

Mountain Dew Cake

1 box orange supreme cake
  mix
1 box coconut cream pie
  filling (not instant)
¾ cup cooking oil
1 bottle Mountain Dew
4 eggs

Mix all ingredients and bake in 3 layers (or 9 x 13-inch pan) at 350 degrees for 30 to 40 minutes.

Icing

1½ cups sugar
4 tablespoons flour
1 stick butter
1 large can crushed
  pineapple
1 cup coconut

Cook sugar, flour, butter, and pineapple until thick. Add coconut when icing is cooled and spread on cake.

Mrs. George Barnett
Florence

Orange Mountain Dew Cake

1 box orange cake mix
½ cup oil
1 box coconut pudding mix (not
  instant)
4 eggs
1 10-ounce Mountain Dew
  drink (cold)

Mix together cake mix and pudding mix. Add oil, mix well. Add one egg at a time, mixing well after each addition. Pour in cold drink, beat well (two or three minutes.) Pour into three layer pans. Bake in pre-heated oven at 325 degrees for 30 to 35 minutes. *Topping For Cake:*

1 cup sugar
3 tablespoons cornstarch
1 large can crushed pineapple
½ stick butter or margarine
1 cup flaked coconut

Mix sugar and cornstarch together, add pineapple. Cook over medium heat until thick. Remove from heat, add butter and coconut. Mix until butter is melted. Spread between cake layers on top and sides.

Mrs. Cecil L. Clark
Tuscumbia

Seven-Up Cake

1 lemon supreme cake mix
1 package instant pineapple
  pudding mix
1 Seven-Up drink (10-ounce)
  bottle
¾ cup cooking oil
4 eggs

Empty cake mix into large mixing bowl and mix the instant pudding into the cake mix and stir until well blended. Form a deep well in the center of the cake mixture and add cooking oil, eggs and gradually add Seven-Up and mix quickly. Pour this into a 11 x 15-inch greased and lightly floured cake pan. Bake for 40 minutes in a preheated 350 degree oven. Let cake cool and add icing.

1½ cups sugar
1 stick margarine
1 can coconut
1 small can crushed pineapple
2 eggs, beaten

Combine all ingredients in a 2-quart saucepan, stirring constantly over low heat. Cook until thick and creamy and spread on cake while hot.

Virta Virginia Cook
Florence

Banana Crunch Cake

5 tablespoons butter or
   margarine
1 package coconut pecan or
   coconut almond frosting
   mix

1 cup rolled oats
1 cup dairy sour cream
4 eggs
2 large bananas
1 package yellow cake mix

Preheat oven to 350 degrees. Grease and flour 10-inch tube pan. In saucepan, melt butter, stir in frosting mix and rolled oats until crumbly; set aside. In large bowl, blend sour cream, eggs and bananas until smooth. Blend in cake mix; beat 2 minutes at medium speed. (High speed with portable mixer.) Pour ⅓ of batter (2 cups) into prepared pan. Sprinkle with ⅓ of crumb mixture. Bake 50 to 60 minutes until toothpick inserted in center comes out clean. Cool upright in pan 15 minutes. Remove from pan, turn cake so crumb mixture is on top. Makes a 10-inch tube cake. High altitude: 5200 feet; add 2 tablespoons flour to cake mix. Bake at 375 degrees for 50 to 60 minutes.

Mrs. Ken Hewlett
Muscle Shoals

Banana Cake

1 cup shortening
1½ cups sugar
2 eggs, beaten
1 cup mashed banana
1 cup pecans, chopped
2 cups sifted flour

1 teaspoon soda
1 teaspoon baking powder
½ teaspoon salt
¾ cup sour milk
1 teaspoon vanilla

Cream sugar and shortening, add eggs and mix well. Add banana pulp and pecans. Sift dry ingredients and add to banana mixture alternately with sour milk. Add vanilla and bake in tube pan or 2 layer pans. Bake 30 minutes in 350 degree oven.

Adele C. Frazier
Florence

Banana Split Cake

3 cups vanilla wafers, 1 box
2 sticks margarine
2 cups confectioners' sugar
2 eggs
4 bananas

1 large can crushed
   pineapple, drained
1 carton refrigerated whipped
   topping
Chopped nuts

In a 9 x 13-inch pan, spread crushed vanilla wafers that have been mixed with one stick of margarine.

Beat with mixer 5 minutes; 2 cups sugar, 1 stick margarine and eggs. Spread over wafers. Slice the bananas over mixture. Mix drained pineapple into the whipped topping and spread over bananas. Sprinkle with nuts. Place in refrigerator overnight to chill.

Opalene Litral
Anderson

Pinapple Upside Down Cake

⅓ cup margarine
15¼ ounce can sliced pineapple, drained
1½ cups sifted cake flour
½ teaspoon salt
⅓ cup softened margarine
⅔ cup milk
½ cup brown sugar, packed
7 or 8 cherries
2 teaspoons baking powder
1 cup sugar
1 teaspoon vanilla
1 eggs

In 10-inch skillet or 9x9x2-inch pan, melt the ⅓ cup margarine over low heat. Remove from fire and sprinkle brown sugar evenly over. Arrange pineapple slices (about 7) on top and place a cherry in center of each slice and in between slices. Sift flour, baking powder, salt and sugar. Add the ⅓ cup margarine, vanilla and milk. Beat 2 minutes. Add egg, beat 2 minutes. Pour over pineapple. Bake 35-40 minutes at about 350 degrees. Serve warm as is or with whipped cream.

Mrs. Howard Kirdkpatrick
Florence

Plum Cake

2 cups flour, sifted
2 cups sugar
1 cup cooking oil
1 cup nuts, chopped
3 eggs
1 teaspoon cinnamon
1 teaspoon cloves
2 small jars strained plums (baby food)

Cook one hour and 15 minutes at 350 degrees in tube pan.

Mrs. Virgie Greer
Killen

Prune Cake

1½ cups sugar
1 cup cooking oil
3 eggs
1 cup buttermilk
2 cups flour
½ teaspoon salt
1 teaspoon soda
1 teaspoon cinnamon
1 teaspoon nutmeg
1 cup prunes
1 cup nuts

Mix and beat sugar and cooking oil. Mix with remaining ingredients and bake at 350 degrees for 40 minutes.

Icing

½ cup buttermilk
1 cup sugar
½ teaspoon soda
1 tablespoon corn syrup
½ stick butter
½ teaspoon vanilla

To egg, oil and sugar add dry ingredients alternating with buttermilk; mix well. Add prunes, nuts and pour in greased and floured oblong pan. Bake at 350 degrees for 30 to 40 minutes. Cook on top of stove until soft boil. Pour over cake.

Mrs. Claire S. Pitts
Sheffield

243

$1,000 Cake

2½ cups sugar
1 cup shortening
5 eggs, separated
1 cup buttermilk
5 tablespoons coffee
3 cups flour, plain
4 teaspoons cocoa

¼ teaspoon salt
1 teaspoon soda
2 teaspoons vanilla
1 can pineapple (small)
1 cup nuts
1 can small cherries

Sift flour, soda and cocoa together. Cream shortening and sugar together until well blended; add beaten egg yolks. Add sifted dry ingredients alternating with milk. Stir in coffee and vanilla, fold in stiffly beaten egg whites. Pour batter into 3 well-greased, 9-inch round cake pans. Bake at 350 degrees for 25 to 30 minutes.

Icing For $1,000 Cake

½ cup butter
1 egg yolk
2 teaspoons cocoa

3 tablespoons coffee
1 box powdered sugar

Sift sugar and cocoa together. Cream butter and egg yolks together with coffee and vanilla until light and fluffy. Mix together.

Evalyn Parker
Killen

Scotch Cake

2 cups sifted all-purpose flour
2 cups sugar
½ teaspoon salt
½ cup butter
½ cup shortening
¼ cup cocoa

2 beaten eggs
½ cup buttermilk
1 teaspoon soda
1 teaspoon cinnamon
1 teaspoon vanilla

Preheat oven to 350 degrees. Sift flour with sugar and salt. Set aside. Grease a 13x9x2 inch pan. In a saucepan, combine butter, shortening, cocoa and 1 cup water. Bring to a boil. Pour over flour mixture. Add eggs, buttermilk, soda, cinnamon and vanilla and beat with mixer until smooth. Immeditely pour into prepared pan. Bake 40 minutes or until done.

Icing for Scotch Cake

½ cup butter
¼ cup cocoa
6 tablespoons milk
1 box powdered sugar

1 teaspoon vanilla
2 cups coconut
1 cup nuts

In saucepan combine butter, cocoa and milk; bring just to boil. Remove from heat. Add powdered sugar and vanilla; with spoon, beat until smooth. Stir in coconut and nuts. Spread over hot cake.

Mrs. Brenda Heupel
Florence

Tropical Spice Cake

2½ cups sifted flour
1 cup granulated sugar
¾ cups brown sugar, packed
1 teaspoon salt
¾ teaspoon soda
1 teaspoon cinnamon

1 teaspoon nutmeg
½ teaspoon allspice
½ cup shortening
1 cup buttermilk
3 eggs

Preheat oven to 350 degrees. Grease and lightly flour 2 9-inch layer pans. Sift flour, sugar, salt, baking powder, soda and spices in a bowl. Add brown sugar, shortening and buttermilk. Beat 2 minutes. Add eggs. Beat 2 minutes more. Pour batter into prepared pans. Bake for 35 to 40 minutes. Frost with Spice Coconut Frosting.

Spice Coconut Frosting

1 package fluffy white frosting
    mix (or your favorite
    recipe)
½ teaspoon cinnamon

¼ teaspoon nutmeg
¼ teaspoon cloves
1 cup coconut

Follow the directions on the package for frosting mix and add cinnamon, nutmeg and cloves. Fold in coconut. Frost the top and sides of Tropical Spice Cake.

Mrs. Eddie Ross
Florence

Mississippi Pecan Cake

½ cup butter
2 cups sugar
1 teaspoon vanilla
4 egg yolks
3 cups sifted all-purpose flour

3 teaspoons baking powder
¾ teaspoon salt
1 cup water
1 egg white
Pecan mixture (recipe below)

Cream butter and sugar together, add vanilla. Add yolks one at a time, beating thoroughly after each addition. Mix and sift dry ingredients together and add to creamed mixture alternately with water. Fold in stiffly beaten egg white. Grease and line bottom only (not sides) of a 10-inch tube pan. Pour half the batter into pan. Spoon pecan mixture a little at a time over batter and cover with remaining batter. Bake in moderate oven (325 degrees) for about 1 hour and 25 minutes. Allow cake to cool right side up in pan on rack.

Pecan Mixture

3 egg whites
¼ teaspoon salt
¼ cup water

½ cup sugar
1 teaspoon baking powder
1 pound shelled pecans, ground

Combine salted egg whites with water; beat until stiff but not dry. Beat in sugar and baking powder mixed together. Add ground nuts.

Mrs. C.E. Martin
Florence

245

Old-Fashioned Nut Cake

2 cups brown sugar
½ cup melted butter
2 beaten eggs
½ cup sour milk
½ cup boiling water
1 teaspoon soda

2 teaspoons cocoa
2 cups plain flour
½ teaspoon baking powder
1 tablespoon vanilla
½ cup English walnuts

Mix eggs, sugar, milk, salt, baking powder. Dissolve soda in ¼ cup boiling water, add cocoa in the rest of water. Add flour, mix well. Bake 35 to 45 minutes in 350 degree oven.

Mrs. Ben Allen
Florence

Black Walnut Cake

½ cup butter
2 cups brown sugar
3 egg yolks, beaten
3 teaspoons baking powder
2 cups all-purpose flour

½ teaspoon salt
⅔ cup milk
1 teaspoon vanilla extract
1 cup black walnuts, chopped fine
3 egg whites, stiffly beaten

Combine butter and sugar and beat until smooth. Add beaten egg yolks and mix well. Combine dry ingredients and add to creamed mixture, alternately with milk. Add vanilla and walnuts and mix well. Fold in stiffly-beaten egg white.

Bake in greased 9 or 10-inch tube pan at 350 degrees or until cake is done.

Mrs. Ernest H. Moore
Florence

Pistachio Nut Cake

1 box white cake mix
1 box (3½ ounces) Pistachio
   instant pudding and pie
   filling
4 eggs

½ cup salad oil
½ cup orange juice
½ cup water
1 teaspoon almond extract
¾ cup chocolate syrup

Combine all ingredients, except chocolate syrup, mixing for 5 minutes at medium speed. Pour ⅔ of batter into a greased tube pan or bundt pan. Add chocolate syrup to remaining batter. Mix well and pour over batter in pan, zig-zagging a spatula through batter to marble. Bake at 350 degrees for 50 to 55 minutes.

Betty Pugh
Florence

Chocolate Oatmeal Cake

1⅓ cups boiling water
1 cup uncooked oatmeal
½ cup butter or margarine
1 cup granulated sugar
1 cup brown sugar
1 teaspoon vanilla

2 eggs
1½ cups sifted flour
½ teaspoon salt
1 teaspoon soda
3 tablespoons cocoa

Pour water over oats. Cover and let stand 10 minutes. Uncover, stir, and let stand 10 more minutes. Cream butter and sugars and vanilla. Add eggs and oats. Sift together flour, salt, soda and cocoa, and add to creamed mixture. Mix well and pour into 2 greased and floured 8-inch cake pans. Bake at 350 degrees for 30 minutes.

Mrs. Robert Walther
Tuscumbia

Mini Chip Cake

1 cup butter or margarine
2 cups sugar
1½ teaspoons vanilla
3 eggs
3 cups all-purpose flour
2 teaspoons baking powder

½ teaspoon salt
1 cup milk
2 cups mini semi-sweet chocolate
chips
Confectioners' sugar

Combine butter or margarine, sugar and vanilla in a large mixer bowl. Cream until light and fluffy. Add eggs one at a time, beating well. Combine flour, baking powder and salt; add alternately with milk, beating just until smooth. Stir in chocolate chips. Pour into a well-greased and floured Bundt pan or a 10-inch tube pan. Bake at 350 degrees for 1 hour and 10 to 15 minutes. Cool. Remove from pan, sprinkle with confectioners' sugar, just before serving.

Mrs. Orville O. Sharp
Florence

Twenty-Two Minute Cake

2 cups flour
2 cups sugar
1 stick oleo
1 cup water
½ cup shortening

3½ tablespoons cocoa
½ cup buttermilk
2 eggs
1 teaspoon soda
1 teaspoon vanilla

Do not use electric mixer. Sift flour and sugar together and combine in a large bowl. In a saucepan combine oleo, water, shortening, cocoa, and bring to a boil. Pour this over the flour and sugar mixture. Combine buttermilk, eggs, soda, and vanilla; add to the other mixture and blend. Grease a pan 12 x 18 and pour the mixture into the pan. Bake at 400 degrees for 18 minutes and while cake is baking, prepare topping.

1 stick oleo
3½ teaspoons cocoa
⅓ cup sweet milk

1 box confectioners' sugar
1 cup chopped nuts

Combine oleo, cocoa, and sweet milk; bring to a boil; add confectioners' sugar and chopped nuts. Pour this mixture over hot cake and return to oven to bake for 4 additional minutes. Serve in baking dish.

Mrs. Lucye Sherwood
Sheffield

One Bowl Cake

½ cup shortening
2½ cups sifted flour
3 teaspoons baking soda
1 teaspoon salt

1½ cups sugar
1 cup milk
2 eggs
1 teaspoon vanilla

Stir shortening just enough to soften. Sift dry ingredients together over shortening. Add about ¾ cup of milk and mix until all flour is dampened. Beat 2 minutes at low speed or 300 strokes by hand. Add unbeaten eggs and remaining milk; beat 1 minute longer or 150 strokes. Stir in vanilla. Turn batter into greased 8-inch pans. Bake in moderate oven (375 degrees) about 25 minutes for layers and 35 minutes for oblong pan. This makes 2 layers.

Mrs. Lee S. Broadfoot
Cloverdale

Elvis Cake

1 package yellow cake mix
½ cup cooking oil
1 package instant vanilla pudding
4 eggs

1 cup sour cream
½ cup water
2 tablespoons cinnamon

Mix all together in large mixing bowl and beat 10 minutes. Pour ½ of the mixture into large tube pan and sprinkle with 2 teaspoons of cinnamon. Pour in rest of batter. Bake one hour at 350 degrees. For topping, melt in a double boiler one six-ounce package of chocolate chips, one half cup sugar and 2 tablespoons butter. Dribble over cake. If topping is too thick, add 2 tablespoons of water.

Mrs. J.H. Mitchell
Florence

Poppy Seed Cake

1 box white cake mix
1 box vanilla pudding mix, instant
½ cup vegetable oil
4 eggs

1 cup hot tap water
2 tablespoons poppy seed
1 teaspoon almond flavoring

Mix cake mix and vanilla pudding mix. Add water and oil and mix well. Add eggs, 1 at a time, mixing well. Add flavoring and poppy seed. Pour into greased and floured tube pan. Bake at 350 degrees for 45 minutes.

Glaze

1 cup powdered sugar
Milk

1 teaspoon almond flavoring

Mix powdered sugar with milk and almond flavoring to make a soupy mixture. Punch holes in warm cake with ice pick to allow glaze to penetrate. Cover cake with glaze.

Mrs. J.E. Tease
Florence

Orange Surprise Cake

1 orange chiffon cake mix
   (prepared according to instructions
    and frozen)

Filling:

1 stick margarine
½ cup sugar
½ cup frozen orange juice
2 eggs
1 small can crushed pineapple

1 small can flaked coconut
½ cup pecans
1 box whipping cream with
   5 tablespoons sugar

Slice cake 2 times to make 3 layers. Melt margarine and add to other ingredients. Place filling between layers. Frost with whipped cream.

Brenda Kennedy
Sheffield

Cherry Nut Cake

1 scant cup shortening
1½ cups sugar
⅔ cup milk
1 cup finely chopped pecans
½ teaspoon salt
1 bottle maraschino cherries,
   drained and chopped fine
⅓ cup water

1 teaspoon vanilla
3 cups cake flour (sift before
   measuring)
2 teaspoons baking powder
5 tablespoons cherry juice
5 egg whites, beaten stiff with
   ½ cup of the sugar

Reserve a small amount of the sifted flour for dredging nuts and cherries. Add salt and baking powder to remainder and sift three times. Cream shortening and 1 cup sugar until light and fluffy. Add flour alternately with milk in small amounts, beating well after each addition. Add water, vanilla and cherry juice. Fold in nuts and cherries. Gently fold in beaten egg whites. Bake in three greased and floured 8 inch cake pans for 35 minutes at 375 degrees. Frost with 7 minute or boiled white frosting to which maraschino cherries and nuts may be added.

Christmas Cake Icing

2 cups raisins
2 cups coconut
8 egg yolks

2 cups walnuts
1 cup butter
1 cup sugar

Mix and cook in double boiler for 30 minutes.

Mrs. James A. Gafford
Florence

Coconut Cake with Sour Cream Icing

Cake

¾ cup shortening
1½ cups sugar
2 egg whites, unbeaten
2½ cups flour
5 teaspoons baking powder

1 teaspoon salt
1 teaspoon vanilla
1¼ cups milk
3 eggs whites, beaten

Cream shortening and sugar well. Beat in unbeaten egg whites. Then gradually add dry ingredients alternately with milk and vanilla, mixing well with each addition. Fold in the beaten egg whites. Pour mixture into three 8-inch cake pans greased and lined with wax paper. Bake at 350 degrees about 30 minutes or until done.

Sour Cream Icing

½ pint sour cream
2 cups sugar

2 grated coconuts

Blend sugar and sour cream, let stand 10 minutes. Add grated coconut using just enough to make thick spreading mixture and reserving small amount to sprinkle over top. Spread between layers and on top. Leave sides unfrosted. Refrigerate.

Mrs. John E. Higginbotham

Mandarin Orange Coffee Cake

1½ cups all-purpose flour
½ teaspoon salt
½ cup wheat germ
1 cup milk
1 egg
1 (11 ounce) can mandarin
 orange sections (drained)

3 teaspoons baking powder
½ cup sugar
⅓ cup cooking oil or
 melted shortening
1 teaspoon vanilla extract
Topping

Measure dry ingredients into mixing bowl; stir to blend. Combine milk, oil, egg, and vanilla in small bowl. Beat well with rotary beater or electric mixer. Add liquid ingredients to dry ingredients. Stir with fork only until all ingredients are moistened. Spread in a well-greased 8-inch square cake pan. Arrange mandarin orange sections over batter. Sprinkle topping over orange sections. Bake at 375 degrees for 40 to 45 minutes. Serve warm. Yield: One 8-inch square coffee cake.

Topping

¼ cup wheat germ
¼ cup all-purpose flour
¼ teaspoon ground cinnamon

¼ cup firmly packed
 brown sugar
¼ cup butter or margarine

Combine dry ingredients. Cut in butter until mixture is crumbly. Yield: topping for 8-inch square coffee cake.

Paula Doggett
Florence

Kentucky Feud Cake

6 eggs, separated
1½ cups sugar
1 teaspoon vanilla
2½ tablespoons flour

1 teaspoon baking powder
3 cups ground pecans (or
   blender-chopped)

Beat by hand the six egg yolks for 15 minutes or beat at low speed on mixer for 8 minutes, gradually adding sugar and vanilla. Add flour, sifted with baking powder to egg and sugar mixture. Add ground pecans. Mixture will be very stiff. Beat the six egg whites until very stiff. Fold into batter.

Bake in two buttered square layer cake pans, lined with oiled paper. Bake at 350 degrees for 30 minutes. Cake is done when it feels lightly firm and leaves the edge of pan. Frost with sweetened whipped cream. Can be served immediately or frozen and served directly from freezer. (Does not freeze hard.)

Mrs. Gene Hayes
Florence

Norwegian Cake

1 cup butter
1 cup sugar
2 eggs, beaten
1 teaspoon vanilla
1 teaspoon soda
2½ cups sifted flour
1 teaspoon baking powder

1 cup sour milk
1 cup chopped nuts
½ cup chopped dates
¼ cup raisins
Grated rind of 2
   oranges and 1 lemon

Cream butter and gradually add sugar, beating after each addition until light and fluffy. Add beaten eggs and vanilla; mix. Sift dry ingredients together. Blend about one-third of the dry ingredients with egg mixture. Now add about one-half of the sour milk and stir until smooth. Continue adding ingredients and milk alternately until all are blended. Fold in nuts, dates, raisins, and grated rind. Grease loaf pan and line with wax paper; grease again. Pour batter into pan and bake at 350 degrees for 35 to 45 minutes. While cake bakes, combine juice of 2 oranges and 1 lemon with ¾ cup sugar and boil 3 minutes. When cake is done, remove pan from oven and pour juice mixture over the top. Let cake stand in pan for two hours before cutting.

Mrs. Tracy Gargis
Sheffield

Apple Sauce Cake

½ cup shortening
1½ cups sugar
2 eggs
1 cup applesauce
2 cups flour

¼ teaspoon salt
1 teaspoon baking powder
½ teaspoon soda
1 teaspoon cinnamon
1 cup raisins

Cream shortening and sugar well. Add eggs and beat well. Add applesauce and dry ingredients which have been sifted together; beat until smooth. Fold in raisins. Pour into greased loaf pan lined with wax paper. Bake for 60 minutes at 350 degrees.

Mrs. Marshall Pennington
Tuscumbia

Western Cake

1 cup shortening
1 cup sweet milk
2 teaspoons lemon flavoring
1 teaspoons baking powder

3 cups sugar
5 large eggs
1 teaspoon vanilla
3 cups flour

Cream shortening and sugar; add eggs one at a time. Add milk, vanilla, lemon and vanilla flavorings. Sift flour and measure. Add baking powder. Add to creamed mixture. Bake in tube pan at 325 degrees for 1 hour; then reduce heat to 300 degrees and cook approximately 30 minutes. Do not open oven door until time to remove from oven. Cool. Do not use frosting.

Mrs. Howard Kirkpatrick
Florence

Mom's Old-Fashioned Molasses Cake

1 cup molasses
1 cup sugar
2 eggs
1 teaspoon vanilla

½ cup shortening
1 cup buttermilk
2½ cups all-purpose flour
½ teasoon soda

Beat eggs; add molasses, sugar and milk. Melt shortening. Beat well by hand. Add rest of ingredients. Place in large greased pan and bake in preheated oven at 325 degrees for 35 minutes. Cool and leave in pan.

Icing For Molasses Cake

½ cup buttermilk
1 cup sugar

½ cup chopped pecans
1 cup coconut

Cook milk and sugar in skillet until it begins to thicken. Add nuts and pour over cake while hot. Sprinkle coconut over top.

Dorothy Tucker
Lexington

Aunt Dinah Cake

3 eggs
1 cup sugar
1 cup molasses
4 cups flour
1½ teaspoons baking powder

1 teaspoon salt
1 tablespoon ginger
1 teaspoon nutmeg
1 teaspoon cinnamon
1 cup shortening

Cream sugar and shortening, add eggs and molasses, beat well. Then mix flour-sugar mixture with dry ingredients. Beat well and pour into deep pan. Bake for one hour in moderate oven or until done.

Mary M. Hayes
Sheffield

Babka

2 cups unsifted flour	¼ cup (½ stick) margarine
¼ cup sugar	3 eggs (at room temperature)
1 package active dry yeast	¼ cup mixed candied fruits
½ cup milk	¼ cup seedless raisins

In a large bowl thoroughly mix ¾ cup flour, sugar and undissolved active dry yeast.

Combine milk and margarine in a saucepan. Heat over low heat until liquid is very warm (120 to 130 degrees). Margarine does not need to melt. Gradually add to dry ingredients and beat 2 minutes at medium speed of electric mixer, scraping bowl occasionally. Add eggs and ½ cup flour, or enough flour to make a thick batter. Beat at high speed 2 minutes, scraping bowl occasionally. Add remaining flour and beat 2 minutes at high speed. Cover; let rise in a warm place, free from draft, until bubbly, about 1 hour.

Stir in candied fruits and raisins. Turn into greased and floured 2-quart Turk's Head pan or tube pan. Let rise, uncovered, in warm place, free from draft, for 30 minutes.

Bake in moderate oven (350 degrees) about 40 minutes, or until done.

Before removing from pan, immediately prick surface with fork. Pour Rum Syrup (below) over cake. After syrup is absorbed, remove from pan and cool on wire rack. When cool, if desired, frost with confectioners' sugar frosting. Makes 1 cake.

RUM SYRUP: Combine ½ cup sugar, ⅓ cup water and 2 teaspoons rum extract in a saucepan; bring to a boil.

Elizabeth Medaris
Vicenzia, Italy

Sour Cream Coconut Cake
Filling Mix (Prepare This First)

2 packages (6 ounces each) frozen coconut	1 cup sour cream
	1½ cups granulated sugar

Mix and set aside while preparing cake.

Cake

1 package deluxe yellow cake mix	1 package instant vanilla pudding
4 eggs	¼ cup oil
	1 cup water

Mix together. Bake at 350 degrees for 30 minutes. After cake has cooled completely, split and fill with filling mix.

Topping (Cook in double boiler)

2 egg whites	2 tablespoons water
¾ cup sugar	¼ teaspoon cream of tartar
⅓ cup white syrup	¼ teaspoon salt

Cook five minutes, beating at high speed. Remove from heat; add 1 teaspoon vanilla. Spread on top and side of cake. Sprinkle on shredded coconut.

Mrs. Jack Thomason
Muscle Shoals

Caramel Icing

½ cup sugar
1 stick oleo
½ cup milk

2 cups sugar
1 egg
Vanilla flavoring

Melt ½ cup sugar in heavy skillet. Combine the 2 cups sugar, oleo, egg and milk and vanilla and cook over low heat, stiffing constantly, until melted. Add the melted sugar and bring to a boil. Cook till soft ball stage. Beat until creamy.

Mrs. Howard Kirkpatrick
Florence

Maple Frosting

⅓ cup milk
1 tablespoon margarine
3¼ cups sifted powdered sugar

¼ cup packed brown sugar
¼ teaspoon maple flavoring
Nuts

Bring to boil, milk, brown, sugar and margarine, stirring constantly. Stir in maple flavoring and powdered sugar. Beat until well mixed. Cover cake and sprinkle with chopped nuts.

Mrs. Howard Kirkpatrick
Florence

Whipped Cream Frosting

Combine 1 cup heavy cream with ¼ cup sugar. Chill in refrigerator at least two hours then beat with a rotary or electric beater until stiff. Flavor with vanilla, almond, or orange extract.

Mrs. W.M. Barnett
Sheffield

Butter Cream Frosting

1 pound box plus 2 cups powdered
 sugar, sifted before
 measuring
¼ teaspoon salt

1 teaspoon vanilla
1 cup shortening
⅓ cup water (room
 temperature)

Place first four ingredients into a mixing bowl. Pour water over sugar mixture. Mix at low speed until all sugar is combined. Scrape the bowl often. Mix at high speed for 7 minutes, scraping the bowl often. Mix 1 minute longer. Place in an air tight container until rady to use. Will keep 3 weeks at room temperature.

Betty Pugh
Florence

Butter Frosting

1 stick butter
2 tablespoons evaporated
 milk

½ teaspoon salt
1 cup dark brown sugar

Heat butter, brown sugar, salt and milk in a saucepan, stirring constatnly until sugar dissolves. Add enough confectioners' sugar until of spreading consistency.

Mrs. Irene Parker
Muscle Shoals

Confectioners Sugar Icing

⅓ cup shortening
1 pound confectioners sugar
⅓ cup milk

1 teaspoon flavoring, either lemon,
vanilla, almond, etc.

Blend shortening and sugar together. Add milk and flavoring, beat until smooth. Thin milk if necessary. More sugar may be added if too thin. This is a good cake icing. It may be used for decorating by adding more sugar to make it stiff.

Mrs. Sandra Hollis
Florence

Never Fail Icing

2 cups sugar
¼ teaspoon cream of tartar
¾ cup hot water

2 tablespoons cold water
2 egg whites
¼ teaspoon flavoring

Put 1¾ cups sugar in a saucepan with the cream of tartar. Then put in ¾ cup hot water. Boil rapidly until it will spin a thread 10 inches long when dropped from the prongs of a fork. When the syrup begins to boil, begin beating egg whites and add to them gradually the cold water. When very stiff, beat in the remaining ¼ cup sugar. Add it gradually. When the syrup is done, allow it to stop boiling. Then pour it on the egg mixture in a fine stream. Beating constantly, add flavoring and spread on cake.

Mary M. Hayes
Sheffield

Sea Foam Frosting

⅓ cup sugar
⅓ cup brown sugar
⅓ cup water
1 egg white

¼ teaspoon cream of
tartar
1 tablespoon corn syrup

Cook until syrup forms a soft ball, 236 degrees. Beat egg white with cream of tartar until stiff peaks form. Add syrup to beaten egg white in slow stream, beating until thick.

Note: Whipped cream can be used in place of Sea Foam Frosting when your time is limited.

Mrs. Brenda Heupel
Florence

Fluffy White Icing

Beat 2 egg whites, 1½ cups sugar, ½ cup water, 1 tablespoon corn syrup and a dash of salt in double boiler for 1 minute. Then beat over boiling water at high speed for 7 minutes or until frosting will stand in stiff peaks. Remove from water and beat in 1¼ teaspoons vanilla and beat until thick.

Nancy Dickerson
Killen

Cream Cheese Frosting

1 package (8 ounces) cream
cheese, softened
1 teaspoon vanilla

1 tablespoons butter or oleo,
softened
1 pound Confectioners'
sugar

In a medium bowl, beat cream cheese, butter and vanilla until light and creamy. Add confectioners' sugar, beat until of spreading consistency. Fill and frost Fresh Apple Cake. Press remaining 1 cup nuts on sides of cake. The cake usually tastes better if it is allowed to sit on the counter and mellow for 2 to 4 days.

Mrs. Irene M. Parker
Muscle Shoals

Chocolate Cream Cheese Frosting

3 ounces cream cheese
(one small package)
¼ cup milk
3½ cups confectioners
sugar

3 squares bitter chocolate,
melted
1 teaspoon vanilla
½ teaspoon salt

Soften cream cheese with half the milk, beat until smooth, add sugar and remainder of milk. Beat thoroughly. Add chocolate, vanilla, and salt. Beat until creamy. Frost 9 inch cake.

Mrs. W.M. Barnett
Sheffield

Double Boiler (7 Minute) Frosting

2 egg whites (¼ cup)
1½ cups sugar
⅓ cup water
1 teaspoon vanilla

¼ teaspoon cream of tartar
or 1 tablespoons light
corn syrup

Combine egg whites, sugar, cream of tartar and water in top of a double boiler. Beat on high speed 1 minute with electric mixer. Place over boiling water; beat on high speed 7 minutes. Remove from pan boiling water; add vanilla., beat 2 minutes longer on high speed.

Mrs. Jerry Turbyfill
Florence

Waldorf Icing

¼ cup flour
1 cup milk
1 stick margarine

½ cup shortening
1 cup sugar

Cook flour and milk together till the pudding stage, set aside to cool. Cream margarine, shortening, add sugar, cream well. Add cooked mixture, beat until fluffy. Will look like whipped cream, add a few drops green food coloring. Ice cooled cake.

Vickie Rikard
Tuscumbia

Chocolate Fudge

2 squares baking chocolate
  or 3 tablespoons cocoa
2 cups sugar
1 cup milk
1 tablespoon white corn syrup
¼ teaspoon salt
2 tablespoons peanut butter
1 teaspoon vanilla
1 cup chopped nuts

Cut or break chocolate into small pieces; put into 3 quart saucepan with sugar, milk, corn syrup, salt and butter, over direct heat. Cook with occasional stirring to a soft ball stage, being sure to remove the pan from the heat while making the test in cold water. Beat fudge vigorously until it begins to stiffen and loses its shine. Add vanilla and nuts, turn out onto a buttered 8-inch square pan. Cool and cut into squares.

Darlene Smith
Tuscumbia

Chocolate Prize Fudge

3 cups sugar
6 tablespoons cocoa (or
  peanut butter)
1 cup evaporated milk,
  undiluted
1 cup white corn syrup
1 cup chopped black
  walnuts (optional)
½ stick margarine or butter
1 teaspoon vanilla

Measure and mix the cocoa and sugar together until smooth. Add milk, corn syrup and mix. Cook on medium heat and bring to a boil. Boil for about 10 minutes or until hard ball will form. Remove from heat and add nuts, margarine and vanilla. Beat until hard enough to pour. Pour into buttered pan and cool. Cut into squares. (Stir while cooking to prevent burning).

Verna Parson
Chattanooga, Tennessee

Mamie Eisenhower's Favorite Fudge

1 tall can (1⅔ cups) evaporated
  milk
4 cups sugar
2 tablespoons butter
1 package (12 ounce size, 2 cups)
  semisweet chocolate pieces
3 bars (4 ounces each) sweet
  cooking chocolate
1 pint marshmallow creme
2 cups chopped pecans
1 teaspoon vanilla

Combine milk, butter, sugar, and salt. Bring to a vigrorous boil, stirring often; then reduce heat and simmer 6 minutes. Meanwhile place remaining ingredients (except pecans) in a large bowl. Gradually pour boiling syrup over the chocolate-marshmallow mixture and beat until chocolate is melted. Stir in nuts. Pour into buttered pans and store in a cool place several hours to harden before cutting in squares.

Donna M. Hayes
Florence

Chocolate Fudge

1½ cups chocolate chips
1 tablespoon margarine
2 cups sugar
¾ cup evaporated milk

1 teaspoon vanilla
10 marshmallows
1 cup chopped pecans

Place marshmallows in double boiler, add 1 tablespoon water. Let melt. Combine sugar and milk, bring to a boil, slowly boil for 6 minutes. Place chips, margarine, nuts and vanilla in large bowl. Pour hot mixture and marshmallows over chip mixture, beat until melted. Pour in greased square pan. Chill.

Virginia Daily
Florence

Frying Pan Fudge

1⅔ cups granulated sugar
2 tablespoons butter
½ teaspoon salt
⅔ cup evaporated milk, undiluted
1 cup chocolate chips

½ teaspoon butterscotch chips
2 cups miniature marshmallows
¾ cup chopped nuts
1¼ teaspoons vanilla

Mix together sugar, butter, salt, and milk in an electric fry pan. Set temperature control at 280 degrees. Bring to boil, stirring constantly, and cook approximately 3-4 minutes. Turn temperature control off, add marshmallows and chocolate chips, butterscotch chips, nuts and vanilla. Stir until marshmallows are melted. Pour in 8-inch pan. Cool. Makes 36 pieces.

Mrs. Robert Walther
Tuscumbia

Mary Ball Chocolate Candy

5 cups sugar
½ teaspoon salt
Tall can evaporated milk
Tall jar marshmallow whip

2 cups chopped nuts
2 teaspoons vanilla
3 bags chocolate chips
2 sticks margarine

Combine chocolate chips and marshmallow whip in bowl. Set aside. Pour milk over sugar, add margarine and boil 8 minutes. While still boiling, pour over chocolate chips and marshmallow whip. Add vanilla, nuts and spread on platter.

Evelyn Parker
Killen

Fudge

1 small can evaporated milk
1 stick oleo

1 package (6 ounces) semi-sweet
    chocolate chips
2¼ cups sugar

Grease pan with oleo. Add milk, sugar and oleo. When it begins to boil, turn heat down to low and let boil 5 minutes. Take off heat then, add chocolate chips and beat until chips are melted. Pour into greased pan and let cool. Cut into squares.

Mrs. Martha Winter
Florence

Joyce's Fudge

2 cups sugar
1 cup milk
3 tablespoons cocoa

1 tablespoon butter
Vanilla
Nuts, if desired

Cook to soft ball stage. Beat a little at a time in a plate. A very creamy, delicate fudge.

Elizabeth Medaris
Vicenza, Italy

Remarkable Fudge

4 cups sugar
1⅓ cups evaporated milk

1 stick margarine
¼ teaspoon salt

Boil these ingredients to the soft ball stage, then remove from heat. Add the following ingredients:

1 pint marshmallow creme
2 cups chocolate bits

1 teaspoon vanilla
1 cup chopped nuts

Beat until mixture begins to thicken. Pour into buttered pans.

Evelyn Pless
Cherokee

Five Minute Fudge

2 tablespoons butter
⅔ cup undiluted milk
1⅔ cups sugar
½ teaspoon salt

2 cups miniature marshmallows
1½ cups semi-sweet chocolate pieces
1 teaspoon vanilla
½ cup chopped nuts

Combine butter, milk, sugar, and salt in a saucepan over medium heat. Bring to a boil and cook 4 to 5 minutes, stirring constantly. (Start timing when mixture starts to bubble around edges of pan.) Remove from heat and stir in marshmallows, chocolate pieces and vanilla. Also add chopped nuts. Stir vigorously for one minute (until marshmallows melt and blend). Pour into 8-inch square buttered pan. Cool. Cut in squares.

Linda McDougal
Killen

Magic Fudge

2 cups sugar
½ cup water
1 can Eagle Brand milk

3 squares unsweetened chocolate
1 cup chopped nuts

Mix sugar, water and milk in large saucepan. Cook, stirring constantly, over medium heat to 237 degrees or until soft ball forms in cold water. Remove from heat. Add cut up chocolate and nuts. Beat until thick. Pour into buttered pan.

Mrs. Bailey Anderson
Florence

Merry Ball Fudge

4½ cups sugar
1 cup fresh milk
1½ sticks oleo

Mix in pan; let come to boil and slowly boil for exactly 8 minutes. No more cooking. Do NOT beat at any time. Add 3 small packages of chocolate chips (I like the minichips as they melt faster) and 1 pint marshmallow cream and a pinch of salt (must work quickly). Stir till smooth. Add 2 cups chopped pecans and stir until fairly stiff. Pour into buttered oblong pan.

Claire S. Pitts
Sheffield

Fudge

2 sticks butter or margarine
3 blocks unsweetened chocolate
½ cup evaporated milk
3 boxes confectioners' sugar
2½ cups pecans, chopped

Melt butter, and chocolate slowly, remove from heat. Add milk, sugar, and pecans. Stir continuously until mixture is smooth and creamy. Add 1 tablespoon of vanilla extract. Butter three plates and fill.

Mrs. Charles Walker
Cherokee

Golden Nugget Fudge

3 cups sugar
1½ cups milk
¾ teaspoon salt
3 tablespoons butter or margarine
2 teaspoons vanilla extract
½ cup chopped dried apricots
½ cup marshmallow creme
⅓ cup chopped walnuts

Butter sides of 3-quart saucepan. Mix sugar, milk and salt in saucepan. Stir and heat until sugar dissolves and mixture boils. Cook, without stirring, to soft ball stage, 238 degrees. Stir in butter and vanilla. Place in pan of cold water and cool to lukewarm without stirring. Add apricots and beat until mixture holds shape (about 15 minutes). Stir in marshmallow creme and walnuts; beat until candy loses its gloss (about 5 minutes). Spread fudge in buttered 9-inch square pan; refrigerate. When fudge sets, cut into 32 bars. Fudge will be soft and creamy! Makes 32 bars.

Orange Fudge

3 cups sugar
1 cup evaporated milk
¼ cup orange juice
¼ teaspoon salt
Rind of 2 oranges, grated
1 cup pecans
2 tablespoons margarine

Heat milk in double boiler; caramelize 1 cup sugar in deep heavy saucepan. Stir in orange juice and the hot milk. Stir in remaining sugar and orange rind. Cook, stirring often, to a soft ball stage. Remove from heat and add margarine. When cool, beat until creamy and stir in nuts. Pour out on greased platter and cut into squares.

Mrs. Walter Shaff
Florence

Divinity

2⅔ cups sugar
½ cup water
1 teaspoon vanilla

⅔ cup light corn syrup
2 egg whites
⅔ cup broken nuts

Stir sugar, corn syrup and water over low heat until sugar is dissolved. Cook, without stirring, to 260 degrees on a candy thermometer until very cold, water forms a hard ball.

In a mixer bowl, beat egg whites until stiff peaks form. Continue beating while pouring hot syrup in a thin stream into egg whites. Add vanilla; beat until mixture holds its shape and becomes slightly dull. (Mixture may become too stiff for mixer). Fold in nuts. Drop mixture from top of a butter spoon onto waxed paper.

Makes about 4 dozen. On humid days use 1 tablespoon less water.

Mrs. Jerry Turbyfill
Florence

Bill Gray's Divinity

3 cups sugar
½ cup water
½ cup white syrup

2 egg whites
1 teaspoon vanilla
1 cup chopped nuts

Cook sugar, water and syrup slowly until it forms a soft ball in cold water. Beat egg whites. Pour ½ sugar mixture slowly over whites, beating all the time while the rest of the syrup cooks on low heat until almost brittle stage. Then pour slowly over egg mixture, still beating. Add vanilla and nuts. Drop from spoon on waxed paper.

Mrs. Bailey Anderson
Florence

No-Cook Divinity

1 package (7.2 ounces) fluffy
  white frosting mix
⅓ cup light corn syrup
1 teaspoon vanilla

½ cup boiling water
1 package (one pound)
  confectioners' sugar
1 cup chopped nuts

Combine frosting mix (dry), corn syrup, vanilla and boiling water in small mixer bowl. Beat on highest speed until stiff peaks form, about five minutes. Transfer to larger mixer bowl; on low speed, gradually blend in confectioners' sugar. Stir in nuts. Drop mixture by teaspoonsful onto waxed paper. When outside of candy feels firm, turn over and allow to dry at least 12 hours. Store candy in airtight container.

Linda Elledge
Leighton

Creamy Pralines

1 cup brown sugar
1 cup white sugar
1 cup milk
1 cup chopped pecans

⅛ teaspoon salt
3 tablespoons butter
1 teaspoon vanilla

Mix sugars, milk, nuts, and salt in a heavy saucepan. Cook over low heat stirring until sugar is thoroughly dissolved. Continue cooking until mixture forms a soft ball when dropped in cold water. Remove from heat; add butter and vanilla. Beat until it begins losing its gloss and becomes creamy. Drop by teaspoon onto waxed paper or oiled surface. If mixture becomes too stiff to drop, add a few drops of boiling water and stir to the right consistency.

Mrs. Tracy Gargis
Sheffield

Caramel Candy

1 cup black walnuts
2 cups brown sugar
1 cup white sugar

Milk sufficient to make thick syrup

Cook slowly, testing as you stir slightly. When a soft ball forms, remove from stove. Pour in walnuts and stir gently, until candy thickens slightly, then pour into buttered plate. Cut in squares and pack in tin box overnight, so black walnuts permeate all through candy.

Birdie Grubbs
Florence

Penuché

2 pounds light brown sugar
1 cup evaporated milk

½ cup butter
¼ teaspoon salt

Mix above ingredients. Cook, stirring until sugar is dissolved. Cook without stirring until a small amount of mixture forms a soft ball in cold water (238 degrees on a candy thermometer.)

Remove from heat and cool to lukewarm. Add 1 teaspoon vanilla, 1½ cups chopped nuts and ¾ cups chopped candied cherries. Beat until thick. Pour into buttered 9-inch square pan. When firm, cut into squares. Makes 3 pounds.

Mrs. E.B. Anderson, Sr.
Florence

Creamy Pralines New Orleans Style

2 cups sugar
1 teaspoon soda
1 cup buttermilk

2 teaspoons vanilla
2 cups pecan halves

Combine sugar, soda and buttermilk in heavy saucepan and cook over medium heat until small amount forms a soft ball in cold water. Remove from flame and add vanilla and pecans. Begin beating immediately. Beat until candy thickens slightly. Drop from teaspoons on waxed paper or greased baking sheet. Cool. Makes 30 pralines.

Peanut Butter Fudge

1 cup white sugar
1 cup brown sugar
½ cup canned milk
2 tablespoons butter

Few grains salt
1 cup miniature marshmallows
½ cup peanut butter
1 teaspoon vanilla

Cook sugar, milk, butter, and salt to soft ball stage. When taking from stove add the marshmallows, peanut butter and vanilla. Beat until thick. Pour into buttered pan and cut into squares.

Mrs. Walter Shaff
Florence

Jane's Peanut Butter Fudge

2 cups sugar
1 tablespoon cocoa

1 cup milk
2 teaspoons white syrup

Cook until forms soft ball in cold water. Cool until pan bottom is touchable. Add 3 or 4 heaping tablespoons of peanut butter, a big tablespoon of butter and 1 teaspoon vanilla. Beat until thickened. Pour into buttered pan.

Mrs. Bailey Anderson
Florence

Crunchy Peanut Butter Fudge

2 cups sugar
1 cup milk
2 cups marshmallow cream

1 jar (12 ounces) crunchy
  peanut butter
1 teaspoon vanilla

Combine sugar and milk. Bring to a boil; stir and cook over medium heat to soft ball stage. Remove from heat. Stir in marshmallow cream, peanut butter and vanilla. Beat until well blended and spread into a greased 9-inch square pan. Cool and cut into squares.

Mrs. Ray Rikard
Florence

Uncooked Peanut Butter Roll

1 stick margarine
1 teaspoon vanilla flavoring

Powdered sugar
Peanut butter

Cream margarine. Add enough powdered sugar to make a stiff dough. Add 1 teaspoon vanilla. Roll out on a board sprinkled with powdered sugar, until thin. Spread with peanut butter and roll up. Keep in refrigerator 24 hours before slicing.

Mrs. Howard Kirkpatrick
Florence

Peanut Brittle

3 cups sugar
1 cup syrup
1 tablespoon margarine
½ cup water

1 teaspoon salt
5 cups peanuts
3 tablespoons soda

Combine sugar, syrup, margarine, water and salt and cook to 250 degrees. Add peanuts and cook to 300 degrees. Add soda and stir quickly and thoroughly, then spread mixture about ⅜-inch thick on buttered pans. Let cool and break in pieces and store.

Mrs. Dwight Allen
Leighton

Peanut Brittle

1 cup granulated sugar
½ cup dark corn syrup
¼ cup water

1½ cups peanuts
1 teaspoon vanilla
1 level teaspoon soda

Boil sugar, syrup and water until it spins a thread when poured from a spoon. Add butter and vanilla. Then add peanuts. Cook until peanuts start to pop. Test to see if they are parched enough; if not, cook a bit longer. Add soda. Remove from heat and stir well. Pour into greased pans. Let cool after spreading; break into pieces.

Rev. Richard Lenz
Leighton

Jimmy Carter's Peanut Brittle

3 cups sugar
1½ cups water
1 cup light corn syrup
3 cups raw, unblanched peanuts

1 teaspoon baking soda
¼ cup butter
1 teaspoon vanilla

In a three quart saucepan, stir together sugar, water and corn syrup. Cook, stirring constantly, until mixture comes to a boil. Continue cooking until mixture reaches 232 degrees on candy thermometer, or until it spins a two-inch thread when the spoon is raised. Stir in peanuts, continue boiling, stirring occasionally, until mixture reaches 300 degrees or until small amount of mixture, when dropped into very cold water, separates into threads which are hard and brittle. Remove from heat; stir in baking soda, butter and vanilla. Quickly pour into two (15½ x 1 inch) greased jelly roll pans. As mixture begins to harden, pull until thin.

Walnut Bourbon Balls

2½ cups finely crushed vanilla
wafers
2 tablespoons cocoa
1 cup confectioners' sugar

1 cup finely chopped walnuts
3 tablespoons corn syrup
¼ cup bourbon
Confectioners' sugar

Combine wafer crumbs, cocoa, 1 cup sugar, nuts, and mix well. Add syrup, bourbon and mix well. Form into 1-inch balls and roll in confectioners' sugar. Store in covered container a day to ripen. These keep very well. Makes 3½ dozen.

Mrs. Linda J. McDougal
Killen

Bourbon Balls

3 cups crushed vanilla wafers
3 tablespoons white syrup
1 cup chopped nuts

½ cup bourbon
1 cup sifted confectioners' sugar

Mix ingredients except sugar; chill 1 hour. Form into small balls; roll in sugar. Chill 24 hours and roll again in sugar.

Mrs. Tracy Gargis
Sheffield

Pecan Roll

2 cups sugar
¼ cup corn syrup
1 cup milk

1 cup brown sugar
2 tablespoons butter
Pecans

Cook all ingredients together except butter and pecans until mixture forms a soft ball when dropped in cold water. Remove from heat, add butter and cool. Beat until creamy. Turn onto a pastry board dusted with powdered sugar. Knead until firm. Shape into a roll about 2 inches thick. Dip in corn syrup and roll in chopped pecans. Keep in cold place until firm enough to slice. Yield: about 1 pound.

Mrs. Earl Keeton
Cherokee

Irish Potato Candy

Boil a very small potato until tender. Peel off skin and mash. Add powdered sugar until a stiff dough. Roll out on a sugared board until thin. Spread with peanut butter to cover the potato dough. Roll up like a jelly roll. Chill and cut in thin slices.

Lou Ware
Tuscumbia

Heavenly Hash

3 6-ounce packages semi-sweet
  chocolate pieces
2 tablespoons butter

1 6½ ounce package (4 cups)
  miniature marshmallows
1 cup broken walnuts

In double boiler, over hot, not boiling, water, partially melt chocolate pieces and butter. Remove from heat and stir until smooth. Blend in marshmallows and nuts until coated with chocolate. Spread in buttered 8x8x2 inch pan. Refrigerate until firm and cut into 16x2 inch squares. Makes 1¾ pounds.

Mrs. Linda J. McDougal
Killen

Rocky Road Squares

1 package (12 ounces) semi-sweet
  chocolate morsels
1 can (14 ounces) sweetened
  condensed milk

2 tablespoons butter or margarine
2 cups dry roasted peanuts
1 package (10½ ounces) miniature
  white marshmallows

In top of double boiler, over boiling water, melt morsels with sweetened condensed milk and butter; remove from heat. In large bowl, combine nuts and marshmallows; fold in chocolate mixture. Spread in wax paper-filled 13 by 9-inch pan. Chill two hours or until firm. Remove from pan, peel off wax paper; cut into squares. Cover and store at room temperature.

Mrs. Jack Thomason
Muscle Shoals

Carnival Pistachio Balls

1 box (1 pound) confectioners'
  sugar
1 package (3½ ounce) instant
  pistachio pudding

⅓ cup light cream
¼ cup (½ stick) margarine,
  softened

Combine confectioners' sugar and pistachio pudding. Add cream and margarine. Knead until ingredients are thoroughly mixed. Shape mixture into 1-inch balls. Roll in chopped nuts, jimmies, or colored sugar as desired. Store in refrigerator. Makes 2½ dozen.

Trisha Chesnut
Greeneville, Tennessee

Eggnog Candy

1 cup eggnog
2 cups sugar

2 tablespoons white corn syrup
¼ teaspoon salt

Combine ingredients in two quart pan, stir. Cook to 235 degrees according to candy thermometer. Cool to lukewarm and add:

2 tablespoons butter
½ cup cut-up candied cherries

½ cup toasted almonds

Spread in buttered plate and cut when cool.

Mrs. Robert Walther
Tuscumbia

Opera Creams

3 cups white sugar   1 cup milk or cream
Scant cup coffee

Cook very slowly over low heat burner, stirring thin syrup almost continuously, so it does not get scorched or burned. Try by testing soft ball in water, care taken at last to keep syrup from burning or scorching. This candy is difficult to make. Beat as you do for fudge taking care not to let it get hard in pan. It should be soft until poured and cut in squares.

Birdie Grubbs
Florence

Coconut Candy Balls With Chocolate Coating
Filling

2 boxes confectioners' sugar   1 cup butter or margarine
1 can sweetened condensed milk   2 cups chopped nuts
1 tablespoon vanilla   1 can coconut

Cream butter and milk together, add vanilla, nuts and coconut. Drop by teaspoonsful onto waxed paper. Place in refrigerator until firm.

Chocolate Coating

4 cups semi-sweet chocolate chips   1 tablespoon vanilla
¼ pound paraffin

Place chocolate chips and paraffin on top of double boiler until melted. Add vanilla. Dip filling in chocolate by toothpicks until covered. Place back on paper until dry. Can be frozen to use later.

Mrs. R.W. Weaver
Florence

Mints

1 box (minus ¼ cup)   7 drops of desired coloring
   confectioners' sugar   7 drops of oil or peppermint
¼ cup melted margarine or butter   2½ to 3 tablespoons milk

Combine together sugar, margarine, coloring and oil of peppermint, mixing until moist. Add milk. Mix with hand until workable. Don't get mixture too moist. Place into mint molds and remove immediately.

Ethel Rutherford
Cherokee

Candied Pecans

1 cup sugar
½ cup cold water
¾ teaspoon salt

1 teaspoon vanilla
1 teaspoon ground cinnamon
1 pound shelled pecans

Combine all ingredients in a skillet except pecans. Simmer for 4 minutes or until mixture spins small thread from spoon. Remove from heat and stir in pecans. Continue stirring until syrup forms a sugar coating over the pecans. Gently separate nuts while cooling. Yields 1 pound.

Ruth Gobbell
Florence

Candied Peanuts

1 cup sugar
½ cup water

2 cups shelled peanuts

Bring sugar and water to a boil. Add peanuts and boil until sugar crystalizes (about 10 minutes). Place on a cookie sheet and bake at 350 degrees for about 8 minutes. Sprinkle salt over peanuts when finished.

Mrs. Jimmy Black
Sheffield

Butterscotch Kisses

1 can Chinese noodles
1 package butterscotch morsels

⅓ cup salted peanuts

Melt morsels in saucepan on medium heat. Pour melted morsels over noodles and add peanuts. Mix until noodles are coated. Drop by spoonfuls on waxed cookie sheet. Allow to cool and serve. Makes about 24 kisses.

Barbara D. Ayers
Phil Campbell

Glazed Popcorn

2 gallons popped corn, salted
2 sticks oleo
2 cups brown sugar
2 tablespoons white vinegar

½ cup white syrup
1 teaspoon vanilla
½ teaspoon soda

In a saucepan mix together oleo, brown sugar, white vinegar and white syrup. Boil 5 minutes, stirring constantly. Add vanilla and soda. While foaming pour over corn. After stirring well, pour into sheet cake pans and bake at 250 degrees for 1 hour, stirring every 15 minutes.

Jane Sherrell
Muscle Shoals

Vanilla Wafer Crust

1½ cups vanilla wafer crumbs   2 tablespoons sugar
1 teaspoon grated lemon rind   ⅓ cup melted butter

Combine all ingredients. Press firmly onto sides and bottom of a well buttered, round 9-inch layer cake pan.

Mrs. Tracy Gargis
Sheffield

Pie Crust

1 cup corn flakes, crushed   ¼ cup butter, melted
¼ cup sugar

Mix ingredients thoroughly and press into 9-inch pie pan. Bake 8 or 10 minutes at 350 degrees. Cool and fill with favorite pie filling.

Mrs. Donna Hayes
Florence

Potato Chip Pie Crust

1½ cups finely crushed   ½ cup melted margarine
  potato chips

Mix the potato chip crumbs with margarine. Press firmly into an ungreased nine-inch pie pan or plate. Bake in a moderate oven 375 degrees for seven minutes. Cool. This is delicious filled with any creamed seafood, creamed chicken or creamed vegetables. Top with potato chip crumbs.

Graham Cracker Pie Crust
(352 Calories)

10 graham crackers, finely   ¼ teaspoon Sweet'N Low
  crushed   (1 package)
2 tablespoons butter, melted

Combine all ingredients and press into 8-inch or 9-inch pie pan. Chill before adding filling.

Donna M. Hayes
Florence

Old Time Blackberry Pie

Line an 8x12 inch oblong baking dish with pastry. Mash 4 cups blackberries with 1½ cups sugar, 3 tablespoons cornstarch and ¼ teaspoon salt. Fill pastry-lined pan with fruit mixture. Dot with 3 tablespoons butter or margarine. Cover with top crust. Seal edges and make small slits in top. Bake at 350 degrees for 45 minutes. Serve with cream.

Donna M. Hayes
Florence

Blueberry Pie

2 cups berries cooked (add
 water to cook all
 to pieces)

3 tablespoons cornstarch
1 cup sugar
1 tablespoon butter

Cook until thick, add 1 teaspoon vanilla or almond extract. Pour into cooked crust. Cool—chill in refrigerator. Top with 3 ounces of whipped cream cheese or 1 package whipped cream.

Mrs. Raymond Bowles
Greenhill

Blueberry Pie Supreme

9 inch unbaked pie shell
1 can blueberry pie filling
8 ounces soft cream cheese
½ cup sugar

2 eggs
½ tablespoon vanilla
1 cup dairy sour cream

Preheat oven to 425 degrees. Prepare pie shell. Spread half of blueberry pie filling in bottom. Set rest of filling aside. Bake shell 15 minutes or just until crust is golden. Remove from oven. Reduce oven temperature to 350 degrees. In small bowl, use mixer to beat cheese with sugar, eggs and vanilla until smooth. Pour over hot blueberry pie filling. Bake 25 minutes. Filling will be slightly soft in center. Cool completely on wire rack. To serve, spoon sour cream around edge of pie. Fill center with remaining blueberry pie filling. Makes 8 servings.

Mrs. Marshall Pennington
Tuscumbia

Cherry Pie

1 can unsweetened cherries
1 cup sugar

½ stick butter or margarine

Cook ingredients together. Remove from heat and add ½ teaspoon almond extract and ½ teaspoon red food coloring.

Crust

1 cup flour
½ teaspoon salt
1 teaspoon baking powder

2 tablespoons sugar
2 tablespoons shortening
⅓ cup milk

Mix all dry ingredients well. Add shortening and milk and mix until thoroughly moistened. Drop with spoon on cherries. Bake till golden brown 20 to 30 minutes at 400 degrees. Serve with whipped cream or ice cream topping.

Mrs. W.C. Sumner
Florence

Cracker Pie

1½ cups water
1½ cups sugar
1 teaspoon cinnamon

¼ tablespoon vinegar
3 tablespoons butter
¼ teaspoon cream of tartar

Bring to boil and pour over crumbled white crackers in a pie crust. Bake at 350 degrees for 30 minutes.

Mrs. Raymond Bowles
Greenhill

Macaroon Pie

14 crushed soda crackers
½ cup nuts, finely chopped
12 dates, finely chopped
1 cup sugar

¼ teaspoon salt
1 teaspoon almond extract
3 egg whites, beaten stiff

Combine all ingredients and bake in a greased pan at 300 degrees for 45 minutes. Top with unsweetened whipped cream.

Gladys Hickman
Florence

Torte Pie

1 cup sugar
1 cup chopped pecans
1 cup coconut
1 cup graham cracker crumbs

4 egg whites
¼ teaspoon salt
1 teaspoon vanilla

Beat egg whites with vanilla and salt until stiff and gradually adding sugar. Fold in crumbs, coconut, nuts. Bake in an 8 or 9-inch buttered pie plate or 30 minutes at 25 degrees. Remove and cool. Top with unsweetened whipped cream. Leave in the refrigerator overnight before serving.

Gladys Hickman
Florence

Eggnog Pie

1 package (4½ ounces) egg
 custard mix
1½ teaspoons unflavored gelatin
2¼ cups milk
¼ teaspoon nutmeg

1½ cups thawed non-dairy whipped
 topping
2 tablespoons dark rum or 2 teaspoons
 rum extract
1 9-inch baked pie shell

Combine custard mix and gelatin in saucepan, blend in milk. Bring quickly to a boil, stirring constantly. Chill until thickened, then beat until smooth; add nutmeg and rum. Fold in whipped topping. Pour in pie shell. Chill until firm. Sprinkle with additional nutmeg, if desired.

Mrs. Robert Walther
Tuscumbia

Peanut Butter Pie

1 baked pie shell
1 cup powdered sugar
½ cup peanut butter
¼ cup cornstarch
⅔ cup sugar

2 cups scalded milk
3 egg yolks, beaten
2 tablespoons butter
¼ teaspoon vanilla
3 egg whites for meringue

Combine powdered sugar and peanut butter. Blend until like biscuit meal. Spread ¾ of this on baked shell. Combine sugar and cornstarch. Add a little of scalded milk. Mix and add beaten egg yolk. Mix and pour in scalded milk. Cook in top of double boiler until mixture is thick. Add butter and vanilla. Pour over prepared shell. Top with meringue. Sprinkle rest of peanut butter mixture over meringue and brown.

Mrs. Judy McKelvey
Tuscumbia

Peanutty-Crunch Pie

⅓ cup peanut butter
⅓ cup corn syrup

Mix until thoroughly combined. Add 2 cups rice crispies. Mix until well coated. Press mixture evenly and firmly around sides and bottom of 9-inch pie pan. Chill until firm. Spread 1 quart of vanilla ice cream softened in pie shell. Freeze until firm. Cut into wedges. Top with peach slices.

Mrs. J.P. Poe
Florence

Frozen Peanut Butter Pie

4 ounces cream cheese
1 cup confectioners' sugar
1 to 3 cups peanut butter
½ cup milk

1 container (8 ounces) heavy
cream, whipped
9-inch thin graham cracker
crust, baked and
cooled

Beat cheese until soft and fluffy. Beat in sugar and peanut butter. Slowly add milk, blending thoroughly into mixture. Fold in whipped cream. Pour into graham cracker crust. Freeze until firm. After pie is frozen, wrap in transparent plastic wrap. To serve, while frozen cut into medium-small pieces; return any remaining pie to freezer. Let cut pieces stand 5 to 8 minutes before serving. Pie stays creamy-smooth even when kept frozen for a week.

Lois Henderson
Florence

Crunchy Ice Cream Pie

⅔ cup brown sugar, packed
⅓ cup margarine
2 cups corn flakes

½ cup chopped nuts
½ cup flaked coconut
1 quart vanilla ice cream

Mix the first five ingredients. Reserve ¼ for topping. Press remaining into a 9-inch pan and chill. Spread the softened ice cream into the crust. Sprinkle the reserved mixture over the top. Freeze for 3 hours or more.

Evelyn Pless
Cherokee

Impossible Pie

4 eggs
½ stick margarine
2 cups sweet milk
¾ cup sugar

½ cup biscuit mix or self-
   rising flour
¾ teaspoon baking powder
⅛ teaspoon salt
½ cup coconut, optional

Mix all ingredients in a blender for 30 seconds. Pour into a greased and floured 10-inch pie pan. Bake at 350 degrees for 45 minutes or until brown. Nutmeg may be added.

Mrs. J.G. Sesler
Florence

Impossible Pie

3 eggs, slightly beaten
½ cup honey
3 tablespoons melted oleo
1½ cups milk
¾ teaspoon vanilla

¾ cup coconut
¼ cup and 2 tablespoons
   pancake mix
⅛ teaspoon salt

Mix together eggs, honey, oleo, milk, vanilla and coconut. Add pancake mix and salt. Pour into an 8-inch buttered pie pan. Bake at 350 degrees for 35-40 minutes.

Mrs. J.B. Malone
Tuscumbia

Kentucky Pie

3 cups brown sugar
5 eggs
½ cup butter

½ cup cream
1 teaspoon vanilla
1 pinch salt

Cream butter, eggs and sugar together. Then add the other ingredients. Pour into an uncooked 9-inch pastry shell. Bake in 450 degree oven for 5 minutes; reduce the temperature to 325 degrees and bake another 25-38 minutes or until filling is firm. Cool on a cake rack.

Mrs. Odessa Smith
Tuscumbia

Missouri-Walnut Rum Pie

3 eggs
½ cup sugar
¼ teaspoon salt
1 cup dark corn syrup

3 tablespoons rum
Coarsely broken walnuts
Unbaked pie shell
Whipped cream

Beat eggs slightly. Add remaining ingredients, except for pie shell and whipped cream. Mix well. Pour into pie shell. Bake in preheated 325 degree oven for 45 minutes. Cool and top with whipped cream.

Mary Ellen Priest
Tuscumbia

Old Fashioned Pumpkin Pie

1 stick of ½ packet pie crust
  mix
2 eggs
1 16-ounce can pumpkin
¾ cup sugar
½ teaspoon salt

1 teaspoon cinnamon
½ teaspoon ginger
¼ teaspoon cloves
1 13-ounce can evaporated whole
  or skim milk or
  light cream

Heat oven to 425 degrees. Prepare pastry for 9-inch, one-crust pie as directed on package. Beat eggs slightly with rotary beater; beat in remaining ingredients. Pour into pastry-lined pie pan. Bake 15 minutes. Reduce oven temperature to 350 degrees. Bake 45 minutes longer or until knife inserted center and edge comes out clean. Cool. Serve with Honey-Ginger Cream: In chilled bowl, beat 2 cups chilled whipping cream until stiff, gradually adding ¼ cup honey and ½ teaspoon ginger. Chill 1 to 2 hours before serving. Yield: 4 cups.

Sandra Goforth
Waterloo

Pumpkin Pie

¾ cup sugar (can be mixed
  with dark brown sugar)
2 cups pumpkin, well cooked
1 cup evaporated mlk
2 eggs, well beaten
1 tablespoon flour

¼ teaspoon ginger
½ teaspoon nutmeg
¼ teaspoon salt
1½ teaspoons grated orange
  rind

Mix all ingredients and cook over low heat until mixture is bubbly. Pour into unbaked pie shell and bake at 350 degrees until done. Recipe has been in my family for several generations.

Mrs. Mary Lou Fowler
St. Joseph, Tennessee

Pumpkin Chiffon Pie

1 envelope unflavored gelatin
1 cup sugar (divided)
½ teaspoon cinnamon, ginger
  and nutmeg
½ teaspoon salt

3 eggs, separated
¾ cup canned milk
1½ cups canned pumpkin
Baked 9-inch pie shell

In top part of double boiler, mix gelatin, ½ cup sugar, spices and salt. Stir in egg yolks, milk, pumpkin. Put over simmering water and cook, stirring, 10 minutes or until mixture begins to stiffen. Beat egg whites until almost stiff. Then gradually add remaining sugar and beat until stiff. Fold into pumpkin mixture and pour into shell. Chill overnight or until firm.

Lou Ware
Tuscumbia

Pie-In-The-Sky

8 ounce package cream
  cheese
¼ cup sugar
½ teaspoon vanilla
3 eggs
1 cup evaporated milk

1¼ cups canned or cooked
  pumpkin
½ cup sugar
1 teaspoon cinnamon
¼ teaspoon each ginger and nutmeg
Dash of salt

Combine cream cheese, sugar, and vanilla. Add 1 egg, mix well. Spread mixture on bottom of unbaked pie shell. Combine pumpkin, sugar, cinnamon, ginger and nutmeg, and salt. Mix well. Blend 2 slightly beaten eggs, 1 cup evaporated milk, and carefully pour over cheese mixture. Bake at 350 degrees 65-70 minutes or until done. Cool.

Mrs. Sam Pendleton, Jr.
Florence

Pumpkin Pie

1 unbaked 9 inch pie shell
1½ cups sugar
Dash of salt
½ teaspoon nutmeg
½ teaspoon allspice

½ teaspoon ground cloves
1½ cups cooked pumpkin
¼ stick butter
2 eggs, well beaten

Mix sugar, butter, salt, spices and add to eggs. Stir until smooth. Pour into shell and bake 10 minutes at 400 degrees, then lower to 375 degrees for 40 minutes.

Mrs. W.A. Jones
Florence

Pumpkin Pie

1 box vanilla instant pudding mix
1 cup milk

1 cup prepared whipping cream
1 cup cooked pumpkin (mashed)

Mix instant pudding mix and milk, fold in whipped cream and mashed pumpkin. Pour in baked pie shell and chill. Serve with whipped cream.

Mrs. Otis Bolton
Tuscumbia

Tawny Pumpkin Pie

1½ cups mashed cooked pumpkin
2 eggs, well beaten
1 small can evaporated milk
1 cup sugar
½ stick butter
1 tablespoon flour
1 tablespoon vanilla

¼ teaspoon mace
¼ teaspoon ginger
½ teaspoon cinnamon
¼ teaspoon allspice
½ teaspoon nutmeg
1 unbaked pastry shell

In medium sized mixing bowl on medium speed of mixer, mix pumpkin, eggs, milk, butter and vanilla. Beat until smooth. Add other ingredients. Pour into pie shell. Bake in preheated oven at 350 degrees until knife inserted in middle comes out clean.

Mrs. Brenda Heupel
Florence

Innkeeper's Pie

1 cup sifted all-purpose flour	1 teaspoon baking powder
½ teaspoon salt	⅓ cup shortening

Combine flour, salt, and baking powder in bowl; mix well. Cut in shortening until particles are pea sized. Add 2 tablespoons cold water, tossing with fork until moistened. Roll into circle slightly larger than 9-inch pie plate. Fit into pie plate, building a high rim. Set aside.

Filling

1½ squares unsweetened chocolate	1 teaspoon baking powder
1½ cups water	½ teaspoon salt
Sugar	¼ cup soft shortening
¼ cup butter or margarine	½ cup milk
2 teaspoons vanilla flavoring	1 egg
1 cup sifted all-purpose flour	½ cup chopped walnuts

Melt chocolate in water in saucepan; add ⅔ cup sugar. Bring to a boil, stirring constantly. Add butter and 1½ teaspoons vanilla. Remove from heat. Combine flour, ⅔ cup sugar, baking powder, and salt in bowl; add shortening, milk and remaining vanilla. Beat at medium speed for 2 minutes. Add egg; beat for 2 minutes longer. Pour into prepared pie shell. Stir chocolate mixture; pour over batter slowly. Sprinkle with walnuts.

Bake at 350 degrees for 55 to 60 minutes or until toothpick inserted in center comes out clean. Cool until slightly warm.

Topping

1 cup whipping cream	1 teaspoon vanilla
2 tablespoons sugar	

Whip cream, adding sugar, 1 tablespoon at a time. Add vanilla, beat until fluffy. Pile cream around edge of pie. Garnish with additional chopped walnuts. Serve immediately.

(Miss) Mildred Mason
Cherokee

German Chocolate Pie

1 (4 ounce) package German sweet chocolate	1 (10-inch) unbaked pie shell
¼ cup butter	1⅓ cups flaked coconut
1⅔ cups evaporated milk	⅛ teaspoon salt
1½ cups sugar	1 teaspoon vanilla
2 eggs	½ cup pecans, chopped
	3 tablespoons cornstarch

Melt chocolate with butter over low heat; stir until blended. Remove from heat and gradually blend in milk. Mix sugar, cornstarch, salt; beat in eggs and vanilla. Gradually blend in chocolate mixture. Pour into pie shell. Mix coconut and pecans and sprinkle over filling. Bake at 375 degrees for 45 minutes or until top is puffed. (Filling will be soft, but will set while cooling.) Cool at least 4 hours before serving. This is rich—serve small portions.

Mrs. Pat Peck
Florence

Chocolate Fudge Pie

2 squares unsweetened chocolate   Water
1 can sweetened condensed milk

Melt chocolate squares in double boiler. Add sweetened, condensed milk, and water as needed.

Stir over medium heat until thick. Pour into baked pie shell. Top with whipped topping.

Bill Musgrove
Florence

Chocolate Fudge Pie

1 stick butter or
  margarine
¼ cup cocoa
2 eggs, beaten
1 cup sugar

¼ cup flour, sifted
½ teaspoon vanilla
1 cup pecans, chopped
1 (10-inch) unbaked pie shell

Blend cocoa into melted butter. Add remaining ingredients; mix well. Pour into pie shell. Bake 25 minutes at 350 degrees. Cool. Serve with ice cream or whipped cream with chocolate on top. Serves 6.

Mrs. Robert Burdine
Florence

"Philly" Velvet Cream Pie

1½ cups finely crushed
  chocolate wafers

⅓ cup melted margarine

Combine and press onto bottom of 9-inch spring pan. Bake at 325 degrees for 10 minutes.

Filling

1 8-ounce package cream
  cheese, softened
¼ cup sugar
1 teaspoon vanilla
2 beaten egg yolks
1 6-ounce package chocolate
  chips, melted

2 egg whites, beaten
  until soft peaks form
¼ cup sugar
1 cup heavy cream,
  whipped
⅓ cup chopped pecans

Combine and blend the cheese, sugar and vanilla. Stir in beaten egg yolks and melted chips. Add sugar to beaten egg whites and fold into chocolate mixture. Fold in whipped cream and pecans. Pour over crumbs. Freeze until ready to use. Serves 8 to 10.

Mrs. Bailey Anderson
Florence

Creamy Chocolate Pie

1 package (4½ ounces) instant
   chocolate pudding
1 cup milk

1½ cups whipped topping
¼ cup chopped nuts

Prepare chocolate pudding according to directions on package, using only 1 cup of milk. Blend in whipped topping and chopped nuts. Pour into baked pie shell. Garnish with more whipped topping and sprinkle with nuts if desired. Chill at least 1 hour.

Ethel Rutherford
Cherokee

Chocolate Angel Pie

2 egg whites
½ teaspoon vinegar
¼ teaspoon salt

¼ teaspoon cinnamon (if
   desired)
½ cup sugar

Beat egg whites with vinegar, salt and cinnamon until soft mounds form. Add sugar gradually, beating until meringue stands in stiff, glossy peaks. Spread on bottom and sides of baked pie shell. Bake at 325 degrees for 15-18 minutes until lightly browned. Cool.

Chocolate Whipped Cream Filling

2 slightly beaten egg yolks
¼ cup water
1 cup melted semi-sweet
   chocolate pieces

¼ cup sugar
¼ teaspoon cinnamon
1 cup whipping cream

Add egg yolks and water to chocolate pieces. Spread three tablespoons over cooled meringue. Chill remainder. Combine sugar, cinnamon and whipping cream; beat until thick. Spread half over chocolate in pie shell. Combine remaining whipped cream with the chocolate mixture. Spread over whipped cream in pie shell. Chill four hours.

Mrs. Wayne C. Wells
Florence

Self Crust Chocolate Pie

1 stick margarine, plus 1
   tablespoon
1 cup sugar
¾ cup flour

1 teaspoon vanilla
2 eggs
¼ cup cocoa

Melt the margarine in a 9-inch pie pan. Pour margarine over other ingredients, mixing well. Pour this mixture back into pie pan. Bake at 325 degrees for 25 minutes.

Nancy Dickerson
Killen

278

Derby Pie

3 eggs
1 stick butter
1 cup pecans, chopped
½ cup flour

1 unbaked pie shell
1 cup chocolate chips
1 teaspoon vanilla

Combine eggs, sugar, butter, pecans, chips and vanilla and mix well. Add flour and mix well again. Put in pie shell and bake in 350 degree oven for about 30 minutes.

Dana DeVoss
Florence

Bourbon Pie

1 unbaked 9-inch pie shell
2 eggs
1 cup sugar
½ cup oleo, melted
3 to 4 tablespoons bourbon

¼ cup cornstarch
1 cup finely chopped pecans
1 cup semi-sweet chocolate
 chips (6 ounces)

In small bowl, beat eggs slightly; slowly add sugar; add melted oleo and bourbon mix. Blend in cornstarch; stir in chips and pecans. Pour into pie shell and bake about 50 minutes at 350 degrees. Serve warm with bourbon flavored whipped cream.

Mrs. Ruth Stribling Eads
Florence

French Silk Chocolate Pie

Cream ½ cup butter plus 2 tablespoons. Gradually add ¾ cup sugar. Cream well. Blend in ½ cup and 1 teaspoon vanilla. Add 2 eggs, one at the time, beating 5 minutes after each egg. Add 6 ounces melted chocolate chips, beating slowly. Turn into a graham cracker crust. Let set until firm.

Nancy Dickerson
Killen

No-Milk Chocolate Pie

1¼ cups sugar
½ cup self-rising flour
2 cups water
1 teaspoon vanilla

3 tablespoons cocoa
½ stick butter
3 eggs, separated
Dash of salt

Mix sugar, flour and cocoa. Add enough water to make a paste. (About ½ cup).

Beat in egg yolks well. Heat remaining water and add with butter and salt. Cook until thick. Remove from heat and add vanilla. Cool and pour into baked pie shell. Cover with meringue and brown.

Roger Moore
Cherokee

279

Perfect Lemon Meringue Pie

1 9-inch frozen ready-to-bake
  pie crust
⅓ cup cornstarch
⅛ teaspoon salt
1½ cups sugar
Grated peel of 1 lemon
½ cup lemon juice
4 eggs, separated
1 tablespoon butter or
  margarine
¼ teaspoon cream of
  tartar

About six hour before serving bake the pie crust as label directs. In a saucepan stir cornstarch, salt and 1 cup sugar. Stir in 1½ cups water, lemon peel and juice; cook over medium heat, stirring constantly, until lemon mixture is thickened and boils; remove from heat.

In a small bowl with wire whisk, beat yolks; stir in small amount of hot mixture. Slowly pour yolk mixture back into lemon mixture, stirring rapidly to prevent lumping. Return to heat; cook, stirring constantly, until lemon filling is thickened; do not boil. Stir in butter, pour into pie crust. Let cool 10 minutes.

Preheat the oven to 400 degrees. In a small bowl, with mixer at high speed, beat egg whites and cream of tartar until soft peaks form. Gradually sprinkle in ½ cup sugar. Whites should stand in stiff glossy peaks. With spatula, spread meringue over filling to edge of crust. Swirl meringue with back of spoon to make attractive top. Bake 10 minutes or until golden. Cool on wire rack away from draft. Refrigerate. Makes 6 servings.

Lois Henderson
Florence

Lemon Ice Box Pie

1 can Eagle Brand milk
Juice from 2 lemons
2 egg yolks

Beat eggs, lemon juice and milk together. Pour into graham cracker crumb pie shell. Top with meringue; brown and refrigerate.

Thelma Batey
Russellville

Lemon Pie

1½ cups sugar
3 tablespoons flour
4 tablespoons vinegar
3 eggs yolks, well beaten
Butter, the size of a
  hickory nut
1½ cups of boiling water
1½ tablespoons lemon
  flavoring

Stir together sugar, flour, vinegar, egg yolks, butter and boiling water and cook until thick. Remove from heat and add lemon flavoring. Pour in precooked pie shell. Top with meringue. Makes one large pie. To make 2 average pies, add ½ more of the ingredients.

Mrs. Dock L. Springer
St. Joseph, Tennessee

Shaker Lemon Pie

2 lemons cut paper thin,
    rind included
2 cups sugar

4 eggs
Pie crust

Remove seeds from lemons and soak in sugar for at least 2 hours. Pour in beaten eggs. Put in pie crust, top with crust and seal. Cook in 425 degrees oven for 15 minutes. Lower heat to 350 degrees and cook 30 to 40 minutes. Serves 8.

Mrs. Nancy Gonce
Florence

Lemon Chiffon Pie

1 9-inch Sweet 'N Low
    graham cracker pie crust
4 egg yolks, beaten
1½ tablespoons Sweet 'N Low
    (21 packages)
½ teaspoon salt
3 tablespoons lemon juice

1 teaspoon lemon rind
    (grated)
1 tablespoon unflavored
    gelatin
¼ cup cold water
4 egg whites

Combine egg yolks, Sweet 'N Low, salt, lemon juice, and rind, in top of double boiler. Cook, beating with rotary beater, until thick, about 5 minutes. Soften gelatin in the cold water and dissolve in hot mixture. Cool, beat egg whites until stiff, but not dry, and fold into lemon mixture. Pour into pie shell and chill until firm. Total calories 757, ⅛ of pie 94 calories.

Donna M. Hayes
Florence

Old Fashion Lemon Pie

1¼ cups sugar
½ cup all-purpose flour
Dash of salt
1¼ cups water
3 eggs, separated

1 tablespoon butter
½ cup lemon juice
Grated rind of 1 lemon
1 pie shell, cooked and
    cooled

Combine sugar, flour and salt in top of a double broiler. Add water and slightly beaten egg yolks, stir until mixed. Place over hot water and cook 10 minutes, stirring constantly. Cover and cook 5 minutes longer. Remove from heat and stir in lemon juice, rind and butter, stirring well. Spoon into pie shell. Frost.

Betty Pugh
Florence

Lemonade Pie

1 can (6 ounces) frozen
    lemonade
1 envelope whipped topping

1 can sweetened condensed
    milk

Put milk, lemonade and whipped topping in a bowl. Whip until it stands in peaks. Put in a graham cracker crut. Cool in the refrigerator for 24 hours.

Mrs. Elizabeth Burns
Florence

Buttermilk Pie

½ cup butter
1½ cups sugar
1 tablespoon flour

3 well-beaten eggs
1 teaspoon vanilla
3 cups buttermilk

Cream butter and sugar together, add flour, eggs, vanilla, and buttermilk. Pour into uncooked pie shell and place in 450 degree oven. Reduce heat to 350 degrees at once and cook about 35 minutes.

Mrs. . Raymond Bowles
Greenhill

Buttermilk Pie

3 eggs, beaten well
1¼ cups sugar
1½ tablespoons flour
½ cup buttermilk

¼ cup melted oleo
1 teaspoon each vanilla and lemon
extract

Mix together and pour into a 9-inch unbaked pie shell. Bake 45 minutes at 350 degrees.

Mrs. Ralph Hall
Florence

Buttermilk Pie

1 cup sugar
3 tablespoons flour
2 eggs, beaten
½ cup margarine, melted

1 cup buttermilk
1 teaspoon lemon flavoring
2 teaspoons vanilla
1 unbaked pastry shell

Combine sugar and flour in a bowl, add eggs, margarine, buttermilk and flavorings; mix well. Turn into a pastry shell. Bake in preheated 425 degree oven for 10 minutes. Reduce heat to 350 degrees; bake 30 minutes longer. Yields 6 to 8 servings.

Mrs. Floyd Stephenson
Tuscumbia

School Teacher's Pie

2 egg whites
¼ teaspoon cream of tartar
¾ cup sugar
1 teaspoon almond flavoring
1 package flaked coconut (frozen)

18 soda crackers, crushed
1 cup finely chopped pecans
½ pint whipping cream
1 12-ounce jar pineapple or peach
preserves

To make pie shell, beat egg whites with cream of tartar until stiff. Gradually add sugar as you beat. Add flavoring. Fold in crackers and pecans. Pour into greased pie pan (one large or two 9-inch pan). Bake for 25 minutes in 350 degree oven. Cool. Whip cream and fold in preserves. Pile on top of cooled pie shell. Sprinkle heavily with flaked coconut. Chill before serving. Freezes well.

Mrs. J.P. Poe
Florence

Pineapple Pie

1 cup pecans, chopped
1 can evaporated milk
2 lemons (juice)

1 pint whipping cream
1 can crushed, drained pineapple
1 cup sugar

Cream sugar and milk. Add lemon juice, crushed pineapple, and pecans. Whp the cream and add to mixture. Pour into cold cooked pie shells. Makes 2 9-inch pies.

Mary V. Cooper
Tuscumbia

Orange Pineapple Pie

1 15-ounce can condensed milk
¼ cup lemon juice
1 4½-ounce whipped topping
1 11-ounce can mandarin oranges, drained

1 1-pound 4 ounce can crushed pineapple, drained
1 baked pie shell or graham cracker crust

Cream milk and lemon juice until thick. Add pineapple and mix well. Add oranges and mix well. Add whipped topping and mix. Pour into shell and chill.

Mrs. Howard Kirkpatrick
Florence

Million Dollar Pie

3 pie shells, baked and cooled
2 cans sweetened, condensed milk
Juice of 4 lemons
1 large can crushed pineapple, drained

1 large can sliced peaches, drained
2 small cans mandarin oranges, drained
1 large container whipped topping

Mix condensed milk and lemon juice. Fold pineapple, peaches and oranges into lemon mixture with whipped topping. Pour into pie shells and refrigerate 2 to 3 hours before servings. Makes 3 pies.

Mrs. Louis Copeland
Florence

Pineapple Chiffon Pie

2 baked pie shells
1½ cups sugar
1 can (small) crushed pineapple

Vanilla wafer crumbs
2 eggs, well beaten
1 box lemon gelatin

Mix together crushed pineapple, sugar, and egg. Cook until egg is done. Add one box lemon gelatin. Chill mixing bowl, beaters and one large can of evaporated milk for a few minutes. Whip milk until stiff; then put all other ingredients into milk and mix. Pour into cooked pie shell and cover with vanilla wafer crumbs. Makes 2 large pies.

Mrs. Harlon McMurtry
Killen

Barbara Rush's Ice Box Pie

1 can condensed milk
½ cup fresh lime juice
1 small can pineapple
  (drained)
Few drops green food coloring
Whipped cream for topping
1 baked 9-inch pie shell

Mix first four ingredients in a bowl. Mix well, pour into baked pie shell and chill three hours until set. Before serving pour on whipped cream and sprinkle with chocolate.

Mrs. Martha Winter
Florence

Ice Box Pineapple-Pecan Pie

½ pound butter
2 cups sugar
2 eggs
2 cups pecans, chopped
1 can crushed pineapple,
  drained
1 teaspoon vanilla
1 box vanilla wafers

Have butter at room temperature. Cream with sugar until very light and creamy. Add eggs and mix. Add chopped pecans, pineapple and vanilla and mix. Arrange layer of whole vanilla wafers on bottom and around sides of pie pan, add layer of pie mixture. Add another layer of wafers and mixture, etc. until all the mixture is used. Chill overnight. Top with whipped cream if desired.

Monteen Stanley
Sheffield

Pineapple Pecan Pie

¼ cup butter or margarine
½ cup brown sugar, firmly packed
2 tablespoons flour
1 teaspoon vanilla
½ teaspoon salt
3 eggs, beaten
1 cup dark corn syrup
1 can (1 pound, 4 ounce) pineapple
  tidbits, well drained
1 unbaked 9 inch pie shell

Cream thoroughly butter, sugar, flour, vanilla and salt; blend in eggs and corn syrup. Fold in pecans and pineapple. Pour into pastry shell. Bake in 350 degree oven one hour or until firm.

Mrs. Eddie Ross
Florence

Summer Time Pies

Vanilla wafers
1 large container whipped
  topping
1½ cups pecans, chopped
1 can coconut
1 large can crushed pineapple,
  with juice
1 can sweetened condensed
  milk
1 No. 2½ can peaches,
  drained and cut up
1 teaspoon vanilla

Line 2 large or 3 small pie pans with vanilla wafers for the crust. Mix remaining ingredients together, blending together well. Pour into prepared pie pans and refrigerate overight before cutting. (May be frozen.)

Elsie Pierce
Sheffield

Mama's Old Time Fruit Pies

2 cups sugar
3 tablespoons flour
Dash of salt
½ to ¾ teaspoon each:
  allspice, nutmeg, cloves

½ stick margarine, melted
5 eggs
2 cups cooked unsweetened
  mashed fruit

Mix sugar, flour, salt and spices well. Add 4 egg yolks plus 1 whole egg and margarine. Then add fruit and blend well. Pour into 2 unbaked pie shells and bake at 400 degrees until pie is set (will not shake). Beat egg whites until stiff and add dash of salt and 4 scant tablespoons of sugar. Beat until stands in peaks. Add 1 tablespoon lemon flavoring, mix and place on baked pies. Return to oven and brown.

Louise Quigley
Iron City, Tennessee

Fruit Pie

1 cup sugar
2 heaping tablespoons flour
2 eggs
Juice of one lemon

5 tablespoons butter or
  margarine
1 teaspoon vanilla

Line pie shell with peach halves seed side up.

Sauce

1 large pie shell

1 29-ounce can of peach halves

Mix in mixer and pour over peaches. Bake 1 hour at 325 degrees.

Mrs. Russell Jeffreys
Town Creek

Hawaiian Pie

1 9 inch graham cracker
  crust, baked
2 bananas, sliced
1 (15 ounce) can sweetened
  condensed milk
½ cup freshly squeezed lemon juice
1 (20 ounce) can crushed pineapple,
  drained

½ pint whipping cream
¼ cup sugar
¼ cup flaked coconut
¼ cup chopped nuts
¼ cup chopped maraschino
  cherries

In baked graham cracker crust, put a layer of banana slices. Top with a layer of sweetened condensed milk which has been mixed with lemon juice. Add a layer of crushed pineapple, topped with a layer of cream, whipped with sugar. Repeat layers until all have been used. Garnish with coconut, nuts and chopped cherries. Chill before serving (3 to 4 hours.) Makes one 9 inch pie.

Mrs. J.R. Gobbell
Florence

Japanese Fruit Pie

2 unbaked pie shells
  Mix together:
2 cups sugar
1 cup margarine, melted
1 cup coconut

1 cup pecans
2 teaspoons vanilla
  Add four beaten eggs.

Topping
½ pint heavy cream, whipped

After mixing the ingredients together, place in two pastry shells and bake in 300 degree oven for 50-55 minutes. Top with heavy cream that has been whipped. This makes 2 9-inch pies or half recipe for 1 9-inch pie.

Jackie Smith
Leighton

Grandma's Raisin Pie

9-inch unbaked pie shell
4 eggs, separated
2 tablespoon soft butter
1½ cups sugar

1 cup chopped nuts (preferably pecans)
½ cup dark raisins
1 tablespoon cider vinegar
1 teaspoon vanilla extract

Preheat oven to 325 degrees. In medium bowl, slightly beat egg yolks. Beat in butter until blended. Add sugar, beat until light and fluffy. Add pecans, raisins, vinegar and vanilla. Mix well. In medium bowl, beat egg whites until foamy. Add to nut mixture, stir until well blended. Pour into pie shell. Bake 50 minutes.

Brenda Heupel
Florence

Raisin Pie

2 cups raisins
1½ cups water
½ cup sugar
2 tablespoons flour, all purpose

½ cup chopped walnuts
1 teaspoon grated lemon peel
3 tablespoons lemon juice
Pastry for 2 crust pie

In saucepan combine raisins and water; cook covered for 10 minutes or until raisins are plumped. Combine sugar and flour, stir into raisins. Cook over low heat, stirring constantly, till mixture thickens and bubbles. Cook one minute more. Remove from heat, stir in nuts, lemon peel and juice. Line 9-inch pie plate with pastry, add hot raisin mixture. Adjust top crust; cut slits to allow steam to escape. Bake in 350 degree oven 30-45 minutes until brown.

Mrs. F.E. Hooks
Florence

Strawberry Pie

½ pound fresh strawberries
6 teaspoons cornstarch
4 tablespoons strawberry gelatin
1 cup sugar

1 cup water
1 pie shell
Whipped cream

Mix cornstarch and sugar. Stir in 1 cup water and cook until thickened. Add gelatin to mixture. Place fresh strawberries in baked pie shell and pour gelatin mixture over strawberries. Cover with whipped cream.

Marie Powell
Russellville

Fresh Strawberry Pie

1 pie crust
1 pint strawberries
3 tablespoons cornstarch

3 tablespoons strawberry
  gelatin
1 cup sugar
1 cup boiling water

Bake pie crust until half done. Put strawberries in the bottom of the pie crust. Put cornstarch, gelatin and sugar in boiling water. Cook until thick. Pour over strawberries when cool and top with whipped cream.

Mrs. Troy Trousdale
Sheffield

Shoney's Pie

1 cup sugar
1 cup water
2½ teaspoons cornstarch
1 large package strawberry gelatin

1 quart strawberries
1 baked pie shell
Whipped topping

Combine sugar, water, and cornstarch in saucepan. Cook until thick. Cool for 8 minutes. Add gelatin. Stir well. Pour over strawberries. Pour into pie shell; place in refrigerator to chill. Serve with whipped topping.

Mrs. Joe Puckett Sr.
Muscle Shoals

Strawberry Chiffon Pie

1 package frozen strawberries
1 package strawberry gelatin
1 cup sugar
1 large can evaporated milk

1 stick margarine
Graham crackers for crust (about
  ½ box for two
  pies)

Prepare crust first by following directions given on box. Have milk, large mixing bowl and beaters chilled. Have strawberries thawed. Empty gelatin in small bowl; take ½ of juice from thawed strawberries, bring to boil and mix with gelatin until dissolved. Put chilled milk in large mixing bowl and beat until stiff, beat in sugar well, then add strawberries and beat again. Add gelatin mixed with the juice and beat again. Pour into pie pans. Set in refrigerator for several hours to congeal.

Mrs. B.C. Harvey
Cherokee

Banana Split Pie

1 baked (9-inch) pie shell
1½ cups powdered sugar
2 eggs, beaten
1 stick of margarine, softened
   to room temperature

1 ounce sweetened chocolate,
   grated
3 bananas

Combine powdered sugar, eggs, and margarine; beat with an electric mixer about 5 minutes until fluffy. Add grated chocolate and mix well. Dip bananas in lemon or pineapple juice to prevent darkening. Then thinly slice 2 bananas and arrange in cooled, baked pie shell. Pour sugar mixture over bananas. Top with one sliced banana arranged around the rim of the pie to form border. Chill 2 hours. Just before serving top with whipped dessert topping and chopped nuts.

Mrs. Frances M. Holt
Florence

Banana Gingersnap Pie

1⅓ cups gingersnap cookie
   crumbs
¼ cup brown sugar, firmly
   packed
¼ cup melted butter

1 cup whipping cream
¼ cup sugar
1 teaspoon vanilla
4 to 5 medium bananas
Lemon juice

Reserve 1 tablespoon crumbs. Combine remaining crumbs and brown sugar. Add butter and mix well. Press firmly onto bottom and sides of buttered 9 inch pie plate. Chill well. Add sugar and vanilla to cream and whip. Slice bananas, dip in lemon juice and fold into whipped cream. Place mixture in pie shell and sprinkle with remaining crumbs. Chill.

Mrs. James A. Gafford
Florence

Peach Pie

2 tablespoons cornstarch
1 cup water
1 cup sugar

Canned peaches
1 box peach gelatin
1 9-inch pie shell, browned

Combine sugar and cornstach; then add cold water slowly. Cook till thick and clear. Remove from heat. Add gelatin and mix well. Let cool. Pour in pie crust over peaches. Top with whipped cream. Cool.

Jane Sherrell
Muscle Shoals

Mom's Apple Pie
(Use Skinny Piecrust)

6 cups thinly sliced apples
½ cup sugar or sugar substitute
   to equal ½ cup sugar
1 tablespoon cornstarch
¼ teaspoon salt
½ teaspoon ground cinnamon
¼ teaspoon ground nutmeg

Prepare pastry; roll out to an 11-inch round on a lightly floured board. Fit into 8-inch pie plate; turn edge under; flute. Sprinkle apples with sugar or sugar substitute, cornstarch, salt, cinnamon and nutmeg and turn into pastry-lined pie plate. Cut a piece of foil into round to cover the apples, but not pastry. The foil will keep the apple filling juicy and flavorful, just as in a conventional pie crust. Bake in a moderate oven (375 degrees) 1 hour, or until apples are tender.

Roll out pastry trimmings; cut into leaves or other fancy shapes with cooky cutter; place on cooky sheet. Bake cutouts with pie, or after pie is out of oven and you have room just until golden brown. Then arrange on top of the pie. Makes 8 servings at 151 calories each.

Mrs. Joan Allen
Florence

All-Time Favorite Apple Pie

½ cup sugar
3 tablespoons flour
¼ teaspoon nutmeg
¼ teaspoon cinnamon
Dash salt
5 cups thinly sliced pared
   tart apples
1 tablespoon butter or
   margarine

Heat oven to 425 degrees. Prepare pastry. Stir together sugar, flour, nutmeg, cinnamon, and salt; mix with apples. Turn into pastry-lined pie pan; dot with butter. Cover with top crust which has slits cut in it; seal and flute. Cover edge with 2 to 3-inch strip of aluminum foil to prevent excessive browning; remove foil last 5 minutes of baking. Bake 40 to 50 minutes or until crust is brown and juice begins to bubble through slits in crusts.

Mrs. Jerry Turbyfill
Florence

Kleem's Apple Pie

1 tablespoon flour
4 tablespoons butter, melted
½ teaspoon nutmeg
¾ cup orange juice
1 cup sugar
3 medium-sized very tart
   apples, finely chopped
1 unbaked pie crust

Stir flour into melted butter. To this, add nutmeg, orange juice, sugar, and mix together. Place chopped apples in pastry shell and pour above ingredients over them. Put strips of pastry over top and bake for 15 minutes in 400 degree oven. Reduce heat to 300 and bake until done 25 to 30 minutes. Use well-greased 9 inch pie pan.

Mrs. Gene Hayes
Florence

Ozark Apple Pie

Beat one egg well. Add ¾ cup sugar. Again beat well. Then add ⅓ cup flour, 1¼ teaspoons baking powder (double action), ⅛ teaspoon salt, again beat well. Peel and dice 1 cup of tart apples, ½ cup chopped pecans and 1 teaspoon vanilla. Put into a greased 8-inch square pan and bake at 325 degrees for 30 minutes

Mrs. Gene Hayes
Florence

Apple Pie

4 to 6 apples, cored and
  sliced
¾ cup sugar
2 tablespoons flour
½ teaspoon cinnamon
½ teaspoon nutmeg
1 tablespoon butter

Fill pastry-lined pie pan with sliced apples. Combine sugar, flour, cinnamon and nutmeg. Sprinkle over apples. Dot with butter. Cover wih top crust. Bake at 425 degrees for 40-50 minutes or until crust is brown and apples are tender.

Mrs. Marjorie Y. Fisher
Sheffield

Crazy Crust Apple Pie

1 cup all-purpose flour
1 teaspoon baking powder
½ teaspoon salt
1 tablespoon sugar
1 egg
⅔ cup shortening
¾ cup water
1 can apple pie filling
1 tablespoon lemon juice

Mix all ingredients together except apple pie filling, in a small bowl. Pour in a pie dish. Pour pie filling over flour mixture, do not stir. Bake at 450 degrees for 45 to 50 minutes.

Betty Pugh
Florence

Peanut Crunch Apple Pie

5½ cups apple slices
1 9-inch unbaked pie shell
¼ cup water
1 cup sugar
¾ cup graham cracker crumbs
¾ cup chopped peanuts
½ cup all-purpose flour
1 teaspoon cinnamon
¼ teaspoon salt
½ cup melted butter or margarine

Arrange apple slices in bottom of shell, sprinkle water over apples. Combine remaining ingredients except butter and sprinkle over apples. Drizzle butter over all. Bake at 350 degrees for 1 hour.

Lela Hall
Leighton

Crunchy Caramel Apple Pie

1 20-ounce can sliced
  apples (for pies)
30 soft caramel candies
2 tablespoons water
2 pie shells in aluminum pans
¾ cup flour

⅓ cup sugar
½ teaspoon cinnamon
1 stick (⅓ cup) whipped margarine
½ cup chopped nuts (pecans or
  walnuts)

Melt caramels with water in top of double boiler until smooth. Add apples (which have been cut in small pieces to melted caramel. Pour in partially baked (about 5 minutes) pie shells. Combine flour, cinnamon, and sugar; cut in whipped margarine, until mixture is crumbly; stir in nuts and sprinkle over top of pies. Bake at 375 degrees for 35 minutes or until golden brown.

Mrs. Horace Mitchell
Florence

Mincemeat Cranberry Pie

1 cup of sugar
2 tablespoons all-purpose flour
2 cups ready to use mincemeat
2 cups whole cranberries

Pastry for one 9 inch double
  crust pie
Butter or margarine

Combine sugar and flour. Mix with mincemeat and cranberries. Put into pastry lined pan. Dot with butter. Cover with top crust and seal edge by folding upper crust over lower crust. Bake at 45 degrees for 35 minutes.

Mrs. E.H. Moore
Florence

Cranberry Orange Pie

2½ cups fresh ground cranberries
1 small unpeeled orange, ground
2 unpeeled apples, ground
1½ cups sugar
3 tablespoons flour

3 tablespoons cinnamon
½ teaspoon nutmeg
1 unbaked 9-inch pie shell
3 tablespoons butter

Preheat oven to 425. Mix cranberries, orange, and apples. Add sugar, flour, cinnamon and nutmeg. Stir to blend and pour into pie shell. Spread evenly and dot with butter. Bake 40 to 50 minutes or until brown. Cool before serving.

Mrs. J.P. Poe
Florence

Fresh Coconut Pie

1 cup sugar
1 tablespoon flour
2 eggs
1 cup milk (sweet)

½ stick margarine, melted
1 teaspoon vanilla
1 can coconut (3½ ounces)
 or fresh coconut

Mix sugar with flour. Combine with slightly beaten whole eggs, milk and melted butter. Add dash of salt, vanilla and coconut. Pour into unbaked pie shell and place in pre-heated 400 degree oven. Reduce to 350 degrees after 10 minutes and bake for 30 minutes or until filling is well set and nicely brown.

Mrs. F. E. Hooks
Florence

Coconut Cream Pie

4 tablespoons sugar
5 tablespoons flour
¼ teaspoon salt
2 cups milk
3 egg yolks, slightly beaten
1 cup shredded coconut

2 teaspoons vanilla
1 baked 9 inch pie shell
2 egg whites
4 tablespoons sugar
½ cup shredded coconut

Combine sguar, flour, and salt and add milk and egg yolks, mixing thoroughly. Cook until thickened, add 1 cup coconut and vanilla. Cool slightly, then turn into pie shell. Beat egg whites until foamy throughout. Add sugar, 2 tablespoons at a time, beating after each addition until sugar is blended. Then continue beating until mixture will stand in peaks. Pile lightly on filling; sprinkle with ½ cup coconut. Bake in moderate oven 15 minutes or until browned.

Mrs. Hattie K. Bailey
Rogersville

One Step Coconut Custard Pie

1 (15.4 ounces) vanilla
 frosting mix
¼ teaspoon salt
½ cup milk
2 tablespoons butter or margarine,
 melted

1 teaspoon vanilla
3 eggs
1½ cups flaked coconut
2 tablespoons chopped
 maraschino cherries

Lightly grease and flour bottom and sides of 10 inch pie pan or 13 by 9 inch baking pan. In a large mixing bowl combine all ingredients except coconut and cherries. Beat at medium speed for 2 minutes. Then stir the cherries and coconut in. Pour into prepared pan. Bake at 350 degrees for 30 to 35 minutes or until golden brown and center is almost set. Cover with foil the last 5 to 10 minutes if crust becomes too dark. Best served warm.

Mrs. Neca Allgood
Lexington

Old-Fashioned Coconut Pie

1 stick margarine or butter
1½ cups sugar
3 eggs
3 tablespoons vinegar

1 cup coconut
1 teaspoon vanilla or lemon
  flavoring
Unbaked pie shell

Blend sugar and butter, add eggs and blend well. Add flavoring, vinegar and coconut and bake for 1 hour at 325 degrees.

Ethel Rutherford
Cherokee

Coconut Pie

1 cup sugar
1 teaspoon vanilla
Hunk butter
1 package coconut

½ cup milk
1½ cups water
2 egg yolks
3 tablespoons flour

Mix ingredients in a blender. Cook over low heat until thick. Pour into a baked pie crust and frost.

Pie Frosting

Egg whites
4 tablespoons powdered sugar

1 teaspoon vanilla

Beat desired amount of egg whites until stiff. Add 4 tablespoons powdered sugar and vanilla.

Betty Pugh
Florence

Cream Chill
Crust

2 cups flour
½ cup brown sugar

1 cup chopped nuts
1 cup butter

Mix like pie crust and pat into pan. Bake at 400 degrees for 15 minutes. Crumble while still warm, and pat back into pan (long pyrex dish is better).

Filling

(Chill 12 hours)
1 8 ounce package cream
  cheese
1 cup powdered sugar

1 tablespoon sugar
2 packages whipped cream
1 can fruit pie filling
  (cherry, blueberry, etc.)

Mix cheese, sugar and vanilla together. Beat whipped cream and mix into cheese mixture. Pour into pie crust; spread top with pie filling.

Mrs. Johnnie Turner
Brea, California

293

Pie Custards

3 egg yolks
⅔ cup sugar
2 tablespoons cornstarch

¼ teaspoon salt
2 cups milk
1 teaspoon vanilla

Heat milk; beat yolks very light; add sugar and cornstarch. Beat again, mix with a little hot milk, and add mixture into rest of milk. Cook until thick, stirring all the time. Line pan with pastry and bake crust until set. Pour in custard and bake until brown.

For Banana Cream Pie

Slice bananas; add to custard; add meringue and bake for 15 minutes at 300 degrees.

For Coconut Cream Pie

Add one cup of grated coconut to custard, top with meringue and brown.

For Chocolate Cream Pie

Add one-fourth pound of bitter chocolate or three tablespoons cocoa; then add two tablespoons butter to custard recipe. Top with meringue and brown.

Mrs. Jack B. Freeman
Tuscumbia

Buttermilk Custard Pie

1 unbaked 9 inch pie crust
3 tablespoons butter
3 egg yolks
⅔ cup sugar
2 tablespoons flour

⅛ teaspoon salt
1⅔ cup buttermilk
2 teaspoons vanilla
3 egg whites

Prepare pastry crust according to your favorite recipe. Melt butter; cool. Beat egg yolks slightly; stir in sugar, flour and salt. Add butter, buttermilk and vanilla. Beat egg whites till soft peaks form. Fold into buttermilk mixture. Pour into pastry crust.

Bake at 400 degrees for 10 minutes. Reduce heat to 350 degrees; bake 15-20 minutes or till thin bladed knift inserted in pie halfway between center and edge comes out clean and pie is golden brown. Allow to cool on rack. Chill.

Note: This filling is too much for a bought pastry. However, you can thaw pastry for 10 minutes and can transfer it to a larger pie pan or other container with higher sides. If it is glass, remember not to start at 400 degrees because that is too hot.

Mrs. Orville O. Sharp
Florence

Egg Custard Pie Which Makes Its Own Crust

1½ cups sugar
½ cup plain flour
2 cups milk
4 eggs

2 tablespoons oleo, melted
1 teaspoon vanilla
Pinch of salt

Mix sugar and flour. Add milk, eggs and other ingredients. Start baking in 400 degree oven for about 10 minutes. Cut oven back to 350 degrees and bake for 50 minutes.

Mrs. Gene Hamby, Jr.
Sheffield

Meredith's Pecan Pie

1 stick margarine
1 cup sugar
4 eggs
1 cup Karo syrup (red)

1 cup pecans
Several dashes of
  cinnamon

Melt oleo and pour over sugar. Let set for at least 20 minutes. Add eggs one at a time, beating after each. Add Karo, pecans and cinnamon. Pour in unbaked pie crust and bake at 350 degrees for 30 to 45 minutes. This will make two small pies—perfect for the frozen pie crust.

Mrs. R.E. Brown
Florence

Pecan Pie

1½ cups white sugar
2 cups dark corn syrup
6 eggs

1 stick margarine
2 teaspoons vanilla
2 cups pecans

Boil sugar and syrup together for two minutes. Pour slowly over slightly beaten eggs and continue beating. Add melted butter and vanilla. Pour into unbaked pie crusts and sprinkle pecans on top. Bake at 350 degrees for 55-60 minutes. Makes two pies.

Mrs. Ron Chesnut
Greeneville, Tennessee

Pecan Pie

1 cup sugar
1 cup red syrup

1 cup shelled pecans
3 whole eggs

Beat eggs and sugar, add syrup and pecans. Pour in uncooked pie shell and bake until firm.

Lou Ware
Tuscumbia

'Pride Of Dixie' Pecan Pie

1 9 inch pastry crust
3 tablespoons butter or
  margarine
2 teaspoons vanilla extract
¾ cup sugar

3 eggs, well beaten
½ cup chopped pecans
1 cup maple syrup
⅛ teaspoon salt
½ cup pecan halves

Line pie pan with pastry; flute edges and set aside. Cream butter with vanilla. Gradually add sugar, creaming well after each addition. Add beaten eggs in thirds, blending well after each addition. Thoroughly blend in chopped pecans along with syrup and salt. Turn into pastry shell. Bake at 450 degrees for ten minutes; reduce heat to 350 degrees. Arrange pecan halves over top of filling. Continue baking 30-35 minutes or until set. Cool on rack.

Mrs. Alfred Craft
Sheffield

Granny's Original Southern Pecan Pie

3 eggs
½ box brown sugar
½ stick butter or oleo
1 cup chopped pecans
1 tablespoon vanilla
1 9-inch unbaked pastry
   shell

Beat eggs, add sugar, dash of salt, melted butter. Add vanilla and pecans. Pour into pastry shell. Decorate top with pecan halves, cook at 350 degrees for about 50 minutes or until toothpick comes out clean when sticking into center of pie. Cool to serve.

Mrs. Walton O. Thompson
Killen

Jello Pudding Pecan Pie

1 package Jello vanilla pudding
   and pie filling
1 cup corn syrup
¾ cup evaporated milk
1 egg, slightly beaten
1 cup chopped pecans
1 unbaked pie shell

Blend pudding mix with syrup. Gradually add evaporated milk and egg, stirring. Add pecans. Pour into pie shell. Bake at 375 degrees till firm—about 40 minutes. Cool 3 hours.

Mrs. Raymond Bowles
Greenhill

Pecan Crunch Pie

3 eggs whites
½ teaspoon baking powder
Pinch of salt
1 cup sugar
¾ cup graham cracker
   crumbs
1 cup chopped pecans

Sprinkle baking powder and salt over egg whites. Beat until stiff; beat in sugar. Fold in graham cracker crumbs and then pecans. Pour into greased pie plate and bake at 350 degrees for 30 minutes. Serve with vanilla ice cream or cover with whipped cream and chill for 4 hours before serving.

Mrs. Joe Patterson
Florence

Maple Pecan Pie

1 baked 9-inch pastry shell
1⅓ cups (15 ounce can)
   sweetened condensed milk
⅔ cup maple syrup
⅛ teaspoon salt
½ cup chopped pecans
1 tablespoon confectioners' sugar

Blend sweetened condensed milk, maple syrup and salt in heavy saucepan; mix well. Cook over low heat, stirring occasionally, until mixture thickens, about 4 minutes. Cool. Add about half the pecans to cooked mixture, saving rest for the top. Put into cooled, baked pastry shell. Sprinkle top with remaining pecans. Whip cream until stiff and fold in sugar. Pile cream lightly on pie filling. Garnish with whole pecans or toasted coconut, if desired. Chill.

Doris Chenault

Blender Pecan Pie

Unbaked pie shell
2 eggs
⅔ cup sugar
¼ teaspoon salt
¼ cup pancake syrup

2 tablespoons butter or margarine,
  melted
1 teaspoon vanilla
1 cup pecans
12 pecan halves

Place eggs, sugar, salt, syrup, butter, and vanilla in blender bowl and blend well. Add 1 cup pecans and blend just enough to chop pecans coarsely. Pour into pie shell. Place pecan halves on top. Bake in hot oven (425 degrees) for 15 minutes. Reduce heat to 350 degrees and continue baking until top is lightly browned, about 30 minutes.

Mrs. Linda J. McDougal
Killen

Pecan Pie

1 tablespoon flour
3 eggs
½ cup sugar
1 cup dark corn syrup (or white)
¼ teaspoon salt

1 teaspoon vanilla
¼ cup melted tablefat
1 cup pecan meats
1 unbaked nine inch pastry
  shell

Mix eggs, sugar, syrup, flour, salt, vanilla and fat. Then spread nuts in bottom of shell, pour in the filling and bake at 350 degrees.

Mrs. Eunice McMeans
Rogersville

Mock Pecan Pie

¾ cup quick oats
¾ cup dark corn syrup
¾ cup milk
½ cup white sugar

½ cup brown sugar
½ cup butter
1 cup coconut
2 eggs, well beaten

Mix all ingredients together and pour into an unbaked pie crust and bake in 375 degree oven for about 40 to 45 minutes or until a deep golden brown.

Mrs. Lester King
Tuscumbia

Osgood Pie

3 eggs, separated
½ stick butter
1 tablespoon vinegar

1 cup sugar
½ cup raisins
½ cup nuts

Beat whites and fold in last. Bake as you would a pecan pie.

Doris Simmons
Muscle Shoals

Chess Pie

½ stick margarine, melted
½ stick butter, melted
2 cups sugar

3 egg yolks
1 whole egg
2 tablespoons flour

Cream all above ingredients together. Add 1 teaspoon vanilla. Heat one cup milk and add. Pour into unbaked deep dish pie shell. Bake at 450 degrees for 13 minutes. Bake at 350 degrees until it shakes.

To make a chocolate chess pie, mix two tablespoons cocoa with the flour. Make a meringue of the 3 egg whites and add 6 tablespoons sugar.

Mrs. Ruby McCormick
Earlington, Kentucky

B.D.'s Chess Pie

1 stick butter
4 eggs
2 cups sugar
½ cup milk
1 tablespoon corn meal

1 tablespoon white corn
    syrup
1 tablespoon vinegar
1 teaspoon vanilla
¼ teaspoon salt

Cream butter and sugar. Add meal, then 4 beaten eggs, milk, syrup, vinegar, vanilla and salt. Beat well. Pour into unbaked pie shell. Bake at 350 degrees until set. Then top with meringue of 3 egg whites and 6 tablespoons sugar.

B.D. Nisbet
Madisonville, Kentucky

Chess Pie

1 stick oleo
2 cups sugar
5 eggs
1 cup milk

1 teaspoon vanilla
1 tablespoon flour
1 tablespoon meal

Melt oleo. Stir in sugar. Add eggs (slightly beaten) in 2 additions. Stir until smooth. Add milk, vanilla, flour and meal. Pour ino an unbaked 9⅝-inch pie shell. Bake at 350 degrees 45 minutes to 1 hour until filling sets and pastry is slightly browned.

Mrs. Rachel Holt
Florence

Mother's Chess Pie

1½ cup sugar
½ cup butter or oleo
3 eggs
1 tablespoon vinegar

1 teaspoon vanilla
2 tablespoons corn meal
    (plain)

Cream together sugar and butter. Add eggs and beat well. Add to this vinegar and vanilla. Add corn meal last and pour into unbaked pie shell and bake slowly until almost solid in a 275 degree oven.

Ruth Latham
Florence

Chess Pie

3 eggs
1 cup sugar
1 stick butter or margarine
1 tablespoon corn meal
1 tablespoon flour
2 tablespoons lemon juice
1 teaspoon lemon extract
½ cup whole milk

Mix sugar, meal, and flour together. Beat eggs lightly and add to mixture. Add lemon juice, extract, and milk. Pour into a partially baked pie shell and bake for 45 minutes at 350 degrees.

Mrs. E.E. Hargett
Muscle Shoals

Chess Pie

3 eggs, beaten
2 cups sugar
½ cup butter
1 tablespoon vinegar
2 tablespoons meal
¼ cup milk
1 tablespoon vanilla
Unbaked pie shell

Put in oven 425 degrees five minutes and then turn back to 350 degrees. Let bake for 30 minutes.

Mrs. E.S. Couch
Florence

Lemon Chess Pie

2 sticks butter
2 cups sugar
1 tablespoon corn meal
1 tablespoon flour
5 eggs, beaten
1 teaspoon vanilla
¼ cup fresh lemon juice
2 unbaked 8-inch pie shells

Cream butter and sugar. Add other ingredients. Pour into pie shells. Bake in 300 degree oven for one hour. Makes two 8-inch pies.

Evie Boyles
Russellville

Chocolate Chess Pie

1 can evaporated milk
1½ cups sugar
2 eggs
3 tablespoons cocoa
½ stick butter
1 teaspoon vanilla
1 unbaked pie shell

Mix ingredients together and pour into an unbaked pie shell. Bake for 30 to 35 minutes in a 350 degree oven.

Mrs. Selma Wallace
Killen

Corn Meal Pie

1½ cups sugar
3 eggs
1 tablespoon vinegar
1 stick oleo
5 tablespoons meal
1 teaspoon vanilla

Cream eggs and oleo. Add sugar and cream well. Add meal, vinegar and vanilla. Pour in unbaked pie shell and bake slowly until golden brown. Cook very slowly, around 275 to 300 degrees the last few minutes.

Mrs. Neca Allgood
Lexington

Caramel Pie

1 cup brown sugar	3 heaping tablespoons
1 cup white sugar	flour
2 cups milk	1 teaspoon vanilla
⅛ stick margarine	4 eggs, beaten

Mix well and pour into browned pie shell and top with whipped cream.

Jane Sherrell
Muscle Shoals

Burnt Carmel Pie

2 cups sugar	1 cup hot water
4 egg yolks	1 teaspoon vanilla
4 tablespoons flour	2 cups sweet milk
½ stick butter	

Take ½ cup of sugar and brown it in an iron skillet, then pour hot water into it, let stand while you beat the egg yolks. Add 1½ cups of sugar, flour, sweet milk. Mix well and pour into the skillet with sugar and water and cook until it thickens, stirring constantly. Add butter and vanilla. Pour into a baked pie crust, then add meringue, and bake until brown. This will make 2 pies.

Meringue

4 egg whites	8 tablespoons sugar
Pinch of salt	Vanilla
Cold water	

Beat until stiff the egg whites, a pinch of salt and a few drops of cold water. Add sugar and a few drops of vanilla and mix well.

Lillian Clemons
Killen

Caramel Pie

2 cups sugar	2 cups hot milk
3 tablespoons cornstarch	4 eggs, separated
(or 4 tablespoons plain flour)	1 teaspoon vanilla
½ stick margarine	¼ teaspoon salt

Caramelize 2 cup sugar and add to hot milk. Mix cornstarch, remainder of sugar and salt with the milk mixture. Cook in thick pot over medium heat, stirring constantly until thick. Separate eggs and beat yolks slightly; add small amount of hot mixture and beat; then stir into hot mixture and stir until thick. Add margarine and 1 teaspoon vanilla. Pour into two 8-inch pastry shells, already baked and cooked.

To caramelize sugar: Put sugar in heavy skillet or sauce pan; put on medium high heat, keep stirring through the lumpy stage until all starts turning brown. Remove from heat and stir until all is brown. Pour immediately into hot milk.

Mrs. Murphy Thorne
Barton

Butterscotch Pies

Put 2 cups sugar, 9 tablespoons milk, 1 cup butter in skillet. Brown as much as you like. Beat 3 egg yolks, 2 cups milk and 9 tablespoons flour (or cornstarch). Put into skillet and cook until thick. Pour into baked pie shells; top with egg whites with 1 teaspoon vanilla flavoring.

Ernestine Hannah
Rogersville

Butterscotch Pie

3 boxes butterscotch pie
and pudding mix
(do not use instant)

4 cups sweet milk
4 egg yolks, saving whites
for icing

Mix all three ingredients together in the top of a double boiler. Beat with a hand mixer until well mixed. Cook over boiling water until thick. Pour into 2 baked pie shells. Let stand for about ten minutes before spreading icing. The pie will look shiny and have a glazed look.

Icing

4 egg whites
¼ teaspoon cream of tartar
½ cup sugar

1 teaspoon vanilla, butternut
flavor

Whip egg whites until light and fluffy. Add sugar, cream of tartar and flavoring and beat until well mixed. Spread on pies and bake to a golden brown.

Racine Pace
Leighton

Whipped Angel Food Pie

1 3 ounce package lemon
gelatin
½ cup sugar
⅔ cup hot water
⅓ cup hot lemon juice

1 teaspoon grated lemon rind
1 cup undiluted evaporated milk
2 tablespoons lemon juice
9-inch crumb crust

Dissolve gelatin and sugar in hot water and ⅓ cup hot lemon juice. Chill to consistency of unbeaten egg white. Add lemon rind. Chill milk in refrigerator tray until soft ice crystals form around edges of tray (15-20 minutes). Whip until stiff (about 1 minute). Add 2 tablespoons lemon juice and whip very stiff (about 2 minutes longer). Fold whipped milk into gelatin mixture. Spoon into cool pie shell. Chill until firm (1-3 hours).

For 9 inch crumb crust, mix 1½ cups graham cracker crumbs with 2 tablespoons sugar and ¼ cup melted butter. Line sides and bottom of 9 inch pie plate. Bake in moderate oven (325 degrees) 7-8 minutes.

Mrs. Sandra Hollis
Florence

Christmas Pie or Mixed Fruit Pie

1 large can red sour cherries,
 drained (pitted)
1 large can crushed pineapple
 with juice
¼ cup self-rising flour
1½ cups sugar

1 package cherry gelatin
4 large or 6 small bananas,
 sliced
1 cup chopped pecans
2 baked pie shells

Cook cherries, pineapple, flour and sugar till thick about 8 minutes. Remove from heat, add gelatin, mix well. Cool, add nuts and bananas, pour into pie shell and add this topping:

1 can sweetened condensed
 milk
⅓ cup lemon juice

1 large tub prepared
 whipped topping
1 can fruit cocktail, drained

Mix milk, lemon juice, fruit cocktail, and whipped topping. For Christmas garnish dye 2 slices pineapple green for wreath, circle with cherries.

Jane Sherrell
Muscle Shoals

Christmas Pie

1½ cups finely ground Brazil nuts
 (about ¾ pound
 unshelled)
3 tablespoons sugar
1 envelope unflavored gelatin
¼ cup cold water
1½ cups scalded milk
3 eggs, separated

¼ cup sugar
⅛ teaspoon salt
½ cup sliced candied cherries
2 tablespoons white rum
¼ cup sugar
½ pint whipping cream
¼ cup Brazil nut meats

Combine one and a half cups ground Brazil nut meats (use food grinder) with 3 tablespoons sugar. With a spoon, press to bottom and sides of 9 inch pie pan up to rim. Bake at 400 degrees for 8 minutes or until lightly brown. Meanwhile dissolve gelatin in cold water for five minutes. Scald milk in a double boiler over very hot water until it coats a spoon. Remove at once from heat and stir gelatin in thoroughly. Cool and chill until it mounds when dropped from a spoon. Beat smooth with egg beater and add cherries and rum.

Beat egg whites until they form peaks, add slowly one-fourth cup sugar and add to custard. Pour into cool pie shell and chill. Whip cream and cover pie. Shave or grind one-fourth cup of nuts and sprinkle over pie.

Mrs. Virginia Ray
Florence

Golden Delight

1 cup ginger ale
1 cup orange juice
1 pound marshmallows
1 pint heavy cream, whipped

1 orange chiffon cake, broken
   into small pieces
2 cups flaked coconut

Place ginger ale, orange juice and marshmallows in double boiler; heat until marshmallows dissolve. Chill for one hour and thirty minutes; fold in whipped cream. Place half the cake in a glass baking dish. Pour half the marshmallow mixture over cake. Add remaining cake, pour remaining marshmallow mixture over top. Sprinkle with coconut. Chill overnight. Yield: 12 servings.

Mrs. Glen Stewart
Tuscumbia

Grandma's Pink Stuff

1 large can crushed pineapple
1 package (3 ounce) strawberry
   gelatin
2 cups tiny marshmallows
1 small package cream cheese

½ pint whipping cream or 9 ounces
   whipped topping
1 cup cottage cheese
½ cup chopped nuts (optional)

Dissolve gelatin in one pint of hot water. Add marshmallows and cream cheese, stir until melted. Add cottage cheese and pineapple. Pour into a flat dish. Chill until slightly set, then add whipped cream and ½ cup chopped nuts. Let set until firm.

Jeannie Malone
Tuscumbia

Heath Bar Dessert

7 egg whites, stiffly beaten
1¾ cups sugar
9 Heath Bars

1 pint whipping cream
Vanilla

Add sugar to beaten egg whites for meringue. Place on two well-greased paper-lined cake pans. Bake at 300 degrees for one hour. Grind or crush Heath bars; whip the cream and flavor with sugar and vanilla. Place one cooled meringue on large plate, then cover with whipped cream and sprinkle Heath bars over it. Repeat. Refrigerate several hours before serving. Makes 12 servings.

Mrs. E.B. Anderson Sr.
Florence

Velvet Supreme

1½ cups plain flour
1½ sticks margarine

1 cup pecans, chopped

Melt margarine and combine it with flour and pecans. Pat into a crust in a large oblong pan. Bake at 350 degrees for 20 minutes. Be sure not to let brown. Let cool completely.

Filling

1 package (8 ounces) cream cheese, softened
1 cup confectioners' sugar
1 cup whipped topping

1 small package instant vanilla pudding
1 small package instant chocolate pudding
3 cups milk

Mix together cream cheese, confectioners' sugar and whipped topping. Spread over cooled crust. Mix together vanilla pudding, chocolate pudding and milk and spread over cream cheese mixture. Top both layers with more whipped topping. Place shavings of a chocolate bar on whipped topping.

Joni James Gardner
Augsburg, Germany

Fat Man's Misery

14 chocolate wafers, crushed
1 stick butter
1 cup confectioners' sugar
1 egg
Few drops almond flavoring

½ pint whipped cream
½ tablespoon sugar
1 teaspoon vanilla
1 cup chopped pecans

Line pie pan with wafers; cream butter and sugar. Add eggs and cream again. Add almond flavoring. Spread this on the crumbs. Whip cream with sugar; add vanilla, then pecans. Fold until well blended. Spread over first mixture. Cover with more crushed wafers. Let stand in refrigerator 12 to 24 hours. Yields six to eight servings.

Mildred Anderson
Florence

Fudge Scotch Ring

1 6-ounce package semi-sweet chocolate morsels
1 6-ounce package butterscotch morsels

1 cup condensed milk
1 cup coarsely chopped walnuts
1 teaspoon vanilla
1 cup walnut halves

METHOD: Melt morsels and milk in double boiler (over hot *not* boiling water). Stir until mixture begins to thicken. Remove from heat, add nuts and vanilla. Blend well. Chill for 1 hour. Line 9" Pie Pan with 12 inch square foil. Place ¾ cup nuts in bottom of pan; forming a 2 inch wide flat ring. Spoon chocolate mixture in small mounds on top of nuts. Add cherries if desired. Chill until firm enough to slice. Cut into ½ inch slices. (Makes about 36 slices.)

Mary Doris Cain
Florence

Chocolate Cream Cups
(8 Servings)

2 cups bottled or canned
  eggnog
1 package (6 ounces) semi-sweet
  chocolate pieces

1 envelope unflavored gelatin
1 cup cream for whipping

Combine eggnog and chocolate pieces in a medium-size saucepan; sprinkle gelatin over top; let stand several minutes to soften gelatin.

Heat very slowly, stirring constantly, until gelatin dissolves and chocolate melts completely. Chill one hour or until mixture mounds lightly on spoon. Beat cream until stiff in a medium-size bowl; fold into chocolate mixture; spoon into custard cups. Chill at least 2 hours or until firm. Garnish with more whipped cream if desired.

Doris Chenault
Sheffield

Graham Cracker Delight

2 eggs
½ cup butter
1 cup sugar
1 can crushed pineapple

1 package orange gelatin
20 graham crackers
½ cup pecans
½ pint whipping cream

Beat eggs, mix with butter and sugar, cook in double boiler until thickened. Cool; meanwhile, prepare gelatin. Whip gelatin as it begins to thicken. Place 10 whole graham crackers on bottom of pan. Pour on cooled egg mixture, scatter on broken pecans. Add another layer of ten whole crackers. Pour on whipped gelatin. Chill. To serve, cut in squares and top with whipped cream.

Mrs. Walter Shaff
Florence

Heavenly Hash

1 bag large marshmallows
1 medium size jar red
  maraschino cherries

1 large can crushed pineapple
1 medium size container
  of whipped topping

Cut marshmallows into pieces. Drain pineapple juice and add to marshmallows and let stand overnight. Cut cherries in small pieces and add to whipped topping. Fold cherries and whipped topping into marshmallow mixture. Mix thoroughly and serve on sliced angel food cake.

Addie C. Montgomery
Tuscumbia

Orange Bavarian Cream

½ cup evaporated skimmed milk
1 envelope unflavored gelatin
¼ cup cold water
¾ cup orange juice
2 tablespoons lemon juice
½ teaspoon grated orange rind

Sugar substitute equal to
  ⅓ cup sugar
¼ teaspoon salt
1 egg white
1 tablespoon sugar

Use a bowl large enough for whipping. Place milk in freezer until almost frozen, then whip. Sprinkle gelatin in water and soak a few minutes. Heat fruit juices and rind with sugar substitute and dissolve gelatin in the hot fruit juice. Chill until partially set. Salt egg white and beat until glossy. Fold egg white into whipped milk and combine with gelatin. Pour into individual dessert dishes and chill. This does not keep well, so make just what you will need for the day. Makes six servings and each portion has 50 calories.

Donna M. Hayes
Florence

Gingerbread

½ cup shortening
½ cup molasses
2½ cups sifted all-purpose
  flour
1 teaspoon baking powder
½ teaspoon cloves
½ teaspoon nutmeg

1 cup sugar
2 eggs
½ teaspoon salt
½ teaspoon soda
1 teaspoon ginger
1½ teaspoons cinnamon

Cream together shortening, sugar, molasses; add eggs and mix well. Sift together flour, salt, soda, baking powder and spices. Add to molasses mixture and mix well. Chill in refrigerator 1½ hours; roll out on lightly floured board and cut with any size cookie cutter. Press in raisins. Place on ungreased cookie sheet. Bake in moderate oven at 350 degrees. Cool and frost if desired. (Recipe has been in family for three generations.)

Addie C. Montgomery
Tuscumbia

Meringue Shells

6 egg whites
1 teaspoon vanilla

2 cups sifted sugar
½ teaspoon cream of tartar

Preheat oven to 225 degrees. Beat egg whites until foamy, add cream of tartar and beat until stiff but not dry. Add sifted sugar gradually, then add flavoring. Beat 10 to 15 minutes on high speed with electric mixer. Shape meringue on a sheet of brown paper on a cookie sheet. Bake for 15 minutes and leave in oven overnight to cool.

Lemon Filling For Meringue Shells

6 egg yolks, well beaten
½ cup lemon juice
1 teaspoon lemon rind, grated

¼ teaspoon salt
1 cup plus 2 tablespoons sugar
2 cups heavy cream, whipped

Mix egg yolks, lemon juice, lemon rind, salt and sugar in a medium saucepan. Cook until thick. Cool, fold in heavy whipped cream. Refrigerate.

Mrs. Galen Shinkle
Russellville

Fruit Cobbler

1 cup sugar
¾ cup flour

¾ cup milk
2 teaspoons baking powder

Melt one stick of butter in bottom of pan. Pour mix over melted butter then pour fruit over this. Cook about 45 minutes in 400 degree oven.

Mrs. John M. Gargis
Leighton

Krazy Krust Kobbler

1 stick oleo
1 cup sugar
1 cup self-rising flour

1⅓ cups sweet milk
1 layer vanilla wafers
3 cups fruit

In oblong baking dish place oleo and melt. Place fruit into pan; place one layer of vanilla wafers on top of fruit. Mix sugar, flour and milk together and beat with mixer until all lumps have dissolved. Pour this mixture over oleo, fruit and wafers. Bake at 350 degrees. Wafers will come to top for crust. Serve with ice cream.

Mrs. Racene Pace
Leighton

Canned Fruit Cobbler

2½ to 3 cups canned fruit
  and juice (about ¾ cup)
½ teaspoon cinnamon
2 tablespoons prepared biscuit
  mix

½ to 1 cup sugar (according to
  sweetness of fruit)
1 teaspoon-1 tablespoon
  lemon juice

Heat oven to 425 degrees. Mix ingredients in oblong baking dish. Top with "Short pie dough." Bake 25 minutes.

Short Pie Dough

Add 3 teaspoons boiling water to 1 cup prepared biscuit mix and add one-fourth cup soft butter. Stir vigoruosly with fork until dough forms a ball and cleans the bowl. Dough will be puffy and soft. Drop on top of fruit by spoonsful.

Billy Townsend

Peach Crisp

4-5 sliced, peeled fresh peaches
1 tablespoon lemon juice
½ cup sugar
½ cup graham cracker crumbs

½ cup slivered almonds or pecans
2 tablespoons butter
1 teaspoon cinnamon

Preheat oven to 350 degrees. Spread peaches in 9 inch pie pan; sprinkle with the lemon juice; mix sugar, crumbs, nuts, and cinnamon. Sprinkle over peaches; dot with butter. Bake 30 minutes in 350 degree oven. Serve warm or cold with whipped cream or ice cream.

Mrs. Walter Shaff
Florence

Peach Cobbler

1 cup sugar
2 tablespoons cornstarch
½ teaspoon cinnamon
1 cup water

2 tablespoons butter or
    margarine
5 cups sliced pared fresh peaches

Biscuit Topping

1½ cups biscuit mix
4 tablespoons sugar
⅔ cup light cream

2 tablespoons grated lemon
    peel

Set oven at 450 degrees. Blend 1 cup sugar, cornstarch and cinnamon in a 2 quart saucepan; add water. Bring to a boil, stirring constantly. Remove from heat; add butter and peaches. Pour into a shallow baking dish. Combine biscuit mix and 2 tablespoons sugar; blend in cream with a fork, drop dough in 6 mounds around edge of baking dish. Combine 2 remaining tablespoons sugar and lemon peel; sprinkle on dough. Bake 25 minutes or until peaches are tender and biscuits golden brown. Serve warm with whipped cream or plain.

Mrs. Joan Pugh
Florence

Easy Peach Cobbler

1 large can (No. 12) peaches,
    sliced or halved
1½ cups sugar

1 stick margarine
1 cup flour
1 cup sweet milk

Mash peaches and mix with ½ cup sugar and margarine. Heat until butter is melted. Mix flour, remaining sugar and milk; stir well. Add peaches mixture and stir all together. Bake at 350 degrees until crust is brown and crisp.

Mrs. Larry W. Hester
Muscle Shoals

Quick Peach Cobbler

½ cup butter or
    margarine
1 cup self-rising flour

2 cups sugar, divided
1 cup milk
4 cups sliced peaches

Melt butter in a 13 by 9 by 2-inch pan. Combine flour, 1 cup sugar and milk, mixing well. Pour over melted butter, do not stir. Combine peaches and remaining 1 cup sugar in a saucepan and bring to a boil. Pour over batter, do not stir. Bake at 375 degrees for 30 minutes or until brown.

Lela Hall
Leighton

Honey-Baked Apple Slices

3 large apples
⅔ cup honey
1 tablespoon sugar

2 tablespoons water
1½ teaspoons cinnamon
3 tablespoons butter

Core apples; do not pare. Cut each in four slices. Arrange in shallow baking pan (buttered). Combine honey, cinnamon and sugar. Pour over apples. Dot with butter. Bake at 350 degrees for 30 to 40 minutes, basting occasionally.

Mrs. James A. Gafford
Florence

Glazed Cinnamon Apples

6 medium apples
2 cups water
1 cup sugar

1 small package cinnamon
candies

Heat sugar, water and candies over low heat until dissolved. Pare and core apples. Place in syrup. Cover and cook until tender, turning apples occasionally. Remove apples from syrup and place in serving dish. Cook syrup until it will congeal. Glaze the apples with syrup. If desired, fill the center of apples with hard sauce or top with coconut.

Mrs. James A. Gafford
Florence

Baked Apricots

2 extra large cans peeled
apricots (drained)
2 boxes light brown sugar

1 large box Ritz crackers
Lots of butter

In a greased baking dish, put a layer of peeled apricot halves. Cover with brown sugar, then a layer of crumbled Ritz crackers; dot thickly with lumps of butter. Repeat layers and top dish with lumps of butter. Bake slowly in 300 degree oven about an hour. It should be thick and crusty on top. Serves 10.

Sherry McKenzie
Florence

Baked Fruit

In a slightly buttered casserole dish, cut in ½ inch chunks, one large or two small bananas. Add 12 to 15 halves, dried apricots cut in quarters. Add one can of chunk pineapple, drained. Cover this fruit with one medium size can applesauce. Bake in 275 degree oven for four hours. The fruit will all blend and turn a pale pink. Good served hot or cold with meats or fowl or as a topping for cake squares or to fill peach or pear halves. May be served in other various ways. If served from a casserole after taking from oven, sprinkle lightly with light brown sugar so fruit will not brown.

Mrs. Elizabeth McDonald
Florence

Cherry Delight

Crust

1½ cups flour, sifted
½ cup finely chopped nuts

1½ sticks margarine, softened
to room temperature

Combine flour, butter and nuts. Knead well and press flat into buttered oblong pan. Cook 20 minutes at 325 degrees. Crust won't brown. Cool as long as possible.

Filling

1 cup cherry pie filling, (2 cans)
1 package (8 ounce) cream
cheese, softened to
room temperature

3 cups sifted, powdered
confectioners' sugar
2 packages whipped topping

Mix whipped topping as directed on package. Combine with cream cheese and sugar. Pour into cooled crust. Top with cherry pie filling. Let set overnight if possible.

Mrs. Ken Hewlett
Muscle Shoals

Strawberry Dessert Mold

2 packages (3 ounces each)
strawberry gelatin
¼ cup sugar
1 cup boiling water
1 pint strawberries, sliced
1 can (1 pound, 4½ ounces)
crushed pineapple with
juice

1 cup dairy sour cream or
1 cup vanilla or strawberry
ice cream
½ cup toasted coconut
¼ cup chopped pecans
Strawberries for garnish

In bowl, blend gelatin and sugar. Pour boiling water over gelatin and stir until dissolved. In chilled bowl with chilled beaters, whip ice cream until doubled in volume, five minutes with an electric mixer at high speed. Add coconut and nuts to gelatin mix and fold in ice cream. Pour into 8 cup mold. Chill until firm. Unmold onto chilled plates and garnish with strawberries. Yields six to eight servings.

Mrs. John A. (Daryl) Thompson
Florence

Frozen Dessert
(Low Calorie)

Juice of 1 orange
Juice of 1 lemon

1 small can crushed pineapple
1 pint milk

Mix together in ice cube tray and freeze.

Donna M. Hayes
Florence

310

Ambrosia I

3 oranges, peeled and thinly
  sliced
½ cup powdered sugar
2 cups shredded coconut

Arrange a layer of orange slices in serving dish and sprinkle with sugar and coconut. Repeat layers until all ingredients are used, ending with coconut. Chill. Makes six servings.

Mrs. J.R. Gobbell
Florence

Ambrosia II

½ pint sour cream
½ cup shredded coconut
1 cup mandarin oranges
1 cup pineapple chunks
1 cup miniature marshmallows

Mix all ingredients together and chill. Serves four.

Mrs. Roy P. Johnson
Cherokee

Yogurt Ambrosia

2 large ripe bananas, sliced
1 red apple, unpeeled and
  diced
1 pear, peeled and diced
Lemon juice
2 navel oranges, sectioned
1⅓ cups flaked coconut
1 cup pineapple yogurt

Dip sliced bananas, diced apples and pears in lemon juice; drain. In glass bowl, combine mixed fruit and orange sections. Chill about one hour. Mix in coconut and yogurt. Serves 6.

Mrs. J.H. Mitchell
Florence

Peach Ambrosia

2 cups sliced peaches
1 banana, sliced
2 tablespoons sugar
1 tablespoon lemon juice
⅓ cup flaked or shredded
  coconut

Combine first four ingredients and chill at least 30 minutes. Just before serving, add coconut and spoon into sherbet glasses.

Mrs. Ernest H. Moore
Florence

Banana Smoothie

Beat four peeled ripe bananas until smooth. Add three cups cold milk, half cup heavy cream, two teaspoons vanilla extract; beat until well mixed. Pour into four glasses. Float one scoop of vanilla ice cream on each. Place banana slice on edge of each glass. Makes four servings.

Rhonda Rickard
Florence

Blueberry -Yum-Yum

1 cup graham crackers, ground
½ cup margarine, melted
½ cup sugar
1½ cup powdered sugar

1 package whipped topping
  mix
8 ounces cream cheese
1 can blueberry filling

Mix first three ingredients thoroughly for crust. Make in square pan. Mix whipped topping mix by package directions. Add next two ingredients and mix until creamy. Pour alternate layers of cheese mixture and filling into crust beginning and ending with cheese mixture. Sprinkle crushed graham squares. Serve hot with vanilla ice cream.

Jean Bowling
Florence

Blueberry Delight

Use one envelope of Dream Whip and follow directions on package; add half cup extra milk. Stir in half cup sugar and one package (8 ounces) softened cream cheese.

Butter an 8x8 inch square pan and cover bottom with generous layer of graham cracker crumbs. Cover crumbs with cream cheese mixture.

Spoon in one can blueberry pie filling. Cover with remaining cream cheese mixture and top generously with cracker crumbs. Chill several hours or overnight. Cut in squares to serve. Makes 8 or 9 servings.

Mrs. Walter Shaff
Florence

Raspberry Dessert

1 box frozen raspberries
1 stick oleo
2 eggs
1 pint cream, whipped

1 pound box vanilla wafers
1 cup powdered sugar
1 cup chopped nuts

Thaw frozen raspberries in a colander. Then add ½ cup sugar to the juice and cook gently several minutes for a thick syrup; not too long. Add about one-third box of raspberry gelatin. While this cools: Crush vanilla wafers and put ½ of them in bottom of pan. Cream the stick of oleo with one cup powdered sugar and beat in 2 egg yolks, one at a time. Whip well.

Now whip egg whites until fluffy and fold this into egg yolk mixture. Then, spread all this over top of crumbs in your dish. Add raspberries to syrup mixture and pour on top of egg mixture. Now sprinkle with ½ cup of nuts, chopped. Whip cream and put on top of all. Add remainder of crumbs. Leave in refrigerator overnight or longer. Pan size 8 x 8 x 2.

Mrs. James M. Hopper
Florence

312

Bread Pudding

4 slices bread
4 tablespoons margarine
1 cup sugar

2 eggs
1 cup milk
Flavor preferred

Cut each slice bread in four pieces and place in baking dish. Beat eggs thoroughly, add milk, and flavor and pour over bread and bake 30 minutes at 350 degrees.

Alpha Jeffreys
Town Creek

Holiday Treats

1 cup sugar
1 tablespoon corn syrup
½ cup water
⅛ teaspoon salt

6 large marshmallows
½ teaspoon peppermint extract
3 cups pecan halves

Cook sugar, water, syrup, and salt, removing before it reaches soft boil stage. Add marshmallows and stir until melted. Add peppermint and pecan halves, stirring in circular motion until each pecan is covered and mixture hardens. Turn onto waxed paper and separate pecans with fork. Let dry. Seal in tightly covered jar.

Mrs. Hollis Kitchen
Leighton

Christmas Tree

3 tablespoons regular margarine
½ cup light corn syrup
½ teaspoon green food coloring
3 tablespoons sugar

3½ cups corn flakes
Colored candies
Chocolate candy bar

Measure all ingredients, except corn flakes, in medium size sauce pan. Cook over medium heat, stirring constantly, until sugar dissolves and mixture boils. Boil slowly for 5 minutes stirring frequently; remove from heat. Add corn flakes and stir until well coated. Pour on waxed paper. With well-buttered hands, shape to resemble a Christmas tree. Decorate with small colored candies; place a chocolate candy bar at the base to resemble trunk. To serve, let guests break off desired portions, or miniature trees may be made in the same way.

Mrs. Hollis Kitchen
Leighton

Old-Fashioned Boiled Custard

1 quart sweet milk
4 eggs
2 tablespoons flour

¾ cup to 1 cup sugar
1 teaspoon vanilla

Scald milk. Mix flour with sugar—dry. Beat eggs and add to sugar and flour. Pour into hot milk, stirring constantly over low heat until thickened. Add vanilla. Do not let come to boil as this will curdle. Good to freeze or serve as custard topped with whipped cream. This is a very sweet custard.

Mrs. John Gargis
Leighton

Grandmother's Boiled Custard

9 eggs, separated
1 gallon milk

2 cups sugar

Separate eggs. Heat 1 gallon milk to a hot scald. Add a little hot milk to beaten egg yolks, then add to rest of hot milk. Keep this on a low boil. Add 2 cups sugar. Beat egg whites until fluffy and add to hot milk. Put in refrigerator and chill for several hours. This is truly old fashioned goodness. I got this recipe from my grandmother, Vertie Bevis, and it was handed down to her from her mother, Molly Darby.

Nancy Dickerson
Killen

Old-Fashioned Egg Custard

5 eggs (save 3 whites for meringue)
1 level tablespoon flour
1 cup sugar

1 cup milk
Nutmeg or any flavor preferred

Beat eggs and flour until smooth. Add sugar, milk, and flavor. Mix well. Pour into unbaked pie crust. Bake at 400 degrees until crust begins to brown (about 10 minutes). Reduce heat to 325 degrees and bake 40-45 minutes or until firm. Beat egg whites with ¼ teaspoon cream of tartar until stiff. Gradually add 6 level tablespoons sugar. Spread over pie sealing edges to prevent shrinking. Bake at 425 degrees until lightly browned.

Alpha H. Jeffreys
Town Creek

Egg Custard

4 eggs
2 cups sugar
1 cup milk
2 tablespoons melted butter

¼ teaspoon salt
2 teaspoons lemon flavoring
¼ teaspoon nutmeg, (optional)
4 tablespoons flour

Beat eggs slightly. Add other ingredients. Bake 45 minutes in a 300 degree oven.

Mrs. W.D. Allen
Tuscumbia

Dobos Torte

Slice frozen pound cake horizontally into six thin layers. Melt one package (12 ounces) semi-sweet chocolate chips. Add 1 cup sour cream. Spread between layers of pound cake and freeze. Let thaw slightly, slice and serve.

Mrs. W.M. Barnett
Sheffield

Broken Glass Torte

3 boxes flavored gelatin
  (2 cherry, 1 lime)
1 envelope plain gelatin in
  ¼ cup cold water
1 cup pineapple juice

1 pint whipping cream
½ cup sugar
1 teaspoon vanilla
24 crushed graham crackers
½ cup sugar

Make flavored gelatin using 1½ cups hot water only to each box. Put in three separate pans. Let set. Cut in small cubes. Heat pineapple juice; add gelatin, let cool. Whip cream. Add sugar and vanilla. Fold in pineapple juice; then the gelatin cubes. Mix graham cracker crubs with sugar and butter. Use about 1 tablespoon melted butter. Use ½ this mixture to line bottom of pan. Pour in cream mixture and cover with the rest of cracker crumbs. Let set in refrigerator 1 hour.

Mrs. Marty Nunnelly
Florence

Tortoni

1 egg white
1 tablespoon instant coffee
⅛ teaspoon salt
2 tablespoons sugar
1 cup whipped cream

¼ cup sugar
1 teaspoon vanilla
⅛ teaspoon almond
  extract (optional)
¼ cup toasted chopped almonds

Combine egg white with coffee and salt; beat until stiff. Add 2 tablespoons sugar and beat until stiff and satiny. Beat cream, ¼ cup sugar, and vanilla until stiff. Fold with ½ cup toasted, chopped almonds. Freeze in paper cups and top with remaining nuts. Yield: 8 portions.

Mrs. Bert Haltom
Florence

English Trifle

2 packages lady fingers or
  1 loaf pound cake, sliced
1 package vanilla pudding
  or your favorite cream
  pie recipe

1 cup sherry
1 package raspberries or
  strawberries
1 large carton whipped topping

Mix pudding according to package directions (or make favorite cream pie recipe.) Cool. Add 1 cup sherry. Line bowl with lady fingers or pound cake. Cover with raspberries or strawberries. Pour pudding mix over raspberries. Chill. Just before serving cover with whipped topping.

Mrs. Robert Burdine
Florence

Fruit Slush

1½ cups sugar
2 cups hot water
2 small cans prepared frozen
   orange juice
1 No. 2 can crushed pineapple
   not drained

6 ripe bananas, mashed
1 large jar maraschino
   cherries
1-10 ounce box frozen
   strawberries

Dissolve sugar in hot water. Mix with other ingredients. Place in small containers and freeze solid. Allow to stand 1½ hours at room temperature before serving.

Sherry McKenzie
Florence

Fruit Cup

1 large cantaloupe
1 can (11 ounces) mandarin
   oranges
1 can (20 ounces) pineapple
   chunks, drained

3 or 4 peaches
½ cup sugar
Juice of 2 lemons

Peel cantaloupe and cut into medium-sized chunks. Combine with remaining ingredients and lightly toss together. Chill. Will keep in the refrigerator for four or five days.

Lela Hall
Leighton

Cranberry Crunch

1 cup quick oats
¾ cup brown sugar
½ cup flour
⅓ cup oleo

1 pound can cranberry sauce
½ cup chopped nuts
1 tablespoon lemon juice

Mix oats, brown sugar, flour, nuts and oleo. Place half in greased dish. Combine cranberry sauce and lemon juice. Place on top of mix in baking dish. Top with remaining crumbs. Bake 40 minutes at 350 degrees. Cut into squares. Serve hot with vanilla. ice cream.

Mrs. Tracy Gargis
Sheffield

Sherbet

6 tablespoons cottage cheese
1 cup buttermilk
1 teaspoon almond flavoring
1 envelope unflavored gelatin

¼ cup cold water
¾ cup hot water
Fresh fruit

Put cheese through sieve or blender. Blend with buttermilk and almond flavoring. Soften gelatin in cold water and stir until gelatin is dissolved. Place in pan of ice cubes and stir steadily until water begins to thicken. Combine gelatin and cheese mixture and chill in individual dessert cups. Garnish with a little fresh fruit or dribble some non-calorie fruit-flavored soda on it.

Mrs. Donna M. Hayes
Florence

Ice Cream Nut Roll

1 cup sifted self-rising flour
¼ teaspoon mace
6 eggs, separated
1 cup sugar
½ teaspoon vanilla

½ cup chopped walnuts or
  pecans
1 to 2 pints soft chocolate
  ice cream

Sift together flour and mace. Beat egg whites until foamy; gradually add sugar, beating until shiny peaks form. Set aside. Beat yolks until thick and lemon colored; blend in vanilla and nuts. Fold into beaten egg whites. Sift flour mixture, ¼ cup at a time, over egg mixture, folding in gently, but thoroughly after each addition. Pour into waxed paper lined pan (jelly roll). Bake in preheated oven at 350 degrees for 15-17 minutes. Turn onto a towel sprinkled with powdered sugar. Remove waxed paper. Trim crusts. Starting with narrow edge, roll up cake and towel jelly roll fashion. Cool completely. Unroll; remove towel and spread with soft ice cream. Reroll and freeze. Before serving decorate with whipped cream.

Mrs. Brenda Heupel
Florence

Pecan Roll

1 pound vanilla wafers
1 pound seedless raisins

1 can sweetened condensed milk
1½ cups chopped pecans

Roll vanilla wafers with rolling pin to make fine crumbs. Put raisins through food chopper. Use large bowl (this makes a heap) and mix all ingredients together well; shape into two rolls. Wrap in waxed paper and chill.

Mrs. Walter Shaff
Florence

Peach Freeze

1 cup fresh crushed peaches
1 cup crushed pineapple

1 cup orange juice
1 cup sugar

Place all ingredients into bowl, stir well until sugar is dissolved. Pour into ice tray, freeze. Remove from freezer several minutes before serving. Canned peaches may be used instead of fresh peaches. Makes 6 servings.

Mrs. Roisell Miller
Tuscumbia

Peachy Delight

1 large or 2 small boxes of
  peach gelatin
1 22-ounce can peach pie filling
1 8-ounce package cream cheese

1 cup (8 ounce) dairy sour cream
½ cup sugar
1 teaspoon vanilla flavoring
Finely chopped pecans

Make gelatin using 2 cups of boiling water to dissolve, then add 1 cup of cold water and pie filling and mix well. Place in the refrigerator until set. When firm, combine softened cream cheese, sour cream, sugar and vanilla and spread on top of gelatin mixture. Sprinkle with finely chopped pecans. Variations: Use blackberry gelatin and blueberry pie filling, or strawberry gelatin and strawberry pie filling.

Mrs. Dwight Allen
Leighton

Cream Puff Batter and Fillings

1 cup water
1 stick butter
1 cup sifted all purpose flour
¼ teaspoon salt

4 eggs
Vanilla ice cream
Chocolate fudge sauce

Heat water and butter to boiling in medium heavy saucepan. Add flour and salt, stir vigorously with wooden spoon till batter forms a thick, smooth ball that follows spoon around pan. Remove from heat at once. Beat in eggs, 1 at a time until batter is shiny-smooth. Spoon batter in mounds of one teaspoon (rounded) 2 inches apart. Bake at 400 degrees 25 minutes, till puffs are puffed, crisp and golden. Remove carefully and cool on wire rack. Split puffs and add a tablespoon ice cream; press tops back in place. Place in shallow serving pan and drizzle with fudge sauce. You can also use whipped cream and jelly or your favorite filling.

Mrs. Earl Keeton
Cherokee

Cream Lemon Filling For Tarts

½ cup butter
1 cup sugar
2 whole eggs

2 egg yolks
2 lemons, juice and rind (you
 can use bottled lemon juice)

Put whole eggs and yolks in top of double boiler. Beat gently until whites and yolks are mixed. Add rest of ingredients. Stir with wooden spoon and cook over gently boiling water until thick. Store in covered jar in refrigerator. Will keep for weeks. This recipe is easily doubled.

Mrs. Howell Heflin
Tuscumbia

Hot Fudge Sauce

1 square semi-sweet chocolate
1½ cups confectioners' sugar
⅔ cup evaporated milk

¼ cup butter
¼ teaspoon vanilla

Mix all ingredients, except vanilla, in top of double boiler. Cover and heat over boiling water. When chocolate melts, stir mixture with an electric mixer until well blended. Cook 30 minutes, stirring occasionally. Add vanilla. Delicious served over plain cake or ice cream. Can be refrigerated and reheated.

Mrs. Don White
Florence

Apple Crisp

6 to 7 cups sliced, and peeled
  apples or 2 1-pound,
  4-ounce cans

¾ to 1 cup of sugar (depending
  on tartness of apples)
2 tablespoons flour
½ teaspoon cinnamon

Mix flour, sugar and cinnamon together. Fold in apples. Place in a large baking dish.

Topping

1 cup oats
1 cup brown sugar (packed)
1 cup flour

¼ teaspoon soda
Margarine, softened

Use enough margarine softened to hold dry ingredients together. Crumble heavily on top of apples. Bake at 325 to 350 degrees until golden brown and apples are done. May be served plain with cheese slice or ice cream.

Ethel Rutherford
Cherokee

Bavarian Apple Torte

Pastry

⅓ cup sugar
⅓ cup butter
1 tablespoon shortening

¼ teaspoon vanilla
⅛ teaspoon salt
1 cup sifted, all-purpose flour

Filling

4 to 5 apples
1 (8 ounce) package cream
  cheese, softened
¼ cup sugar
1 egg

½ teaspoon grated lemon peel
¼ teaspoon vanilla
⅛ teaspon salt
Cinnamon sugar
¼ cup sliced almonds

To prepare pastry: Cream together sugar and butter, shortening, vanilla and salt. Blend in flour. Pat into bottom and 1½ inches up sides of lightly-greased 9-inch spring form pan. Pare, core and slice apples to measure 4 cups. Turn apples into a shallow pan, cover with foil and place in a hot oven (400 degrees) for 15 minutes while preparing filling. Beat cheese with sugar. Beat in egg, lemon peel, vanilla and salt until smooth. Turn into pastry-lined pan. Top with warm, partially cooked apple slices. Sprinkle with cinnamon sugar (blend ⅓ cup sugar with ½ teaspoon cinnamon) and almonds. Set pan on baking sheet. Bake in 400 degree oven about 40 minutes, until crust is nicely browned and apples cooked. Cool before cutting. Makes 8 to 10 servings.

Mrs. Braxton W. Ashe
Sheffield

Apple-Cranberry Dumplings

Syrup

2 cups water
2 cups sugar

½ teaspoon cinnamon
½ cup butter

Combine first three ingredients and boil together five minutes. Remove from heat and add butter.

Biscuit Dough

2 cups sifted flour
1 tablespoon baking powder
1 teaspoon salt

2 tablespoons sugar
½ cup shortening
¾ cup milk

Sift together dry ingredients and cut in shortening. Gradually add milk, tossing dry ingredients to make a soft dough. Roll out on floured board to rectangle 18 x 12 inch.

Filling

4 cups grated peeled apples
1 can whole cranberry sauce

½ cup black walnuts, chopped

Spread apples, cranberries and nuts on top of rolled dough. Roll up into jelly roll. Cut in one inch slices and place in lightly buttered 13x9x2 inch pan. Pour hot syrup over all and bake in hot oven for 40 minutes at 425 degrees. Serve warm, 12 servings.

Mrs. L. O. Kimbrough
Tuscumbia

Apple Porcupine

½ teaspoon cinnamon
Blanched almonds
2½ cups water

1½ cups sugar
6 medium-sized apples
1 tablespoon butter, fat or oil

Cook the sugar and water for three minutes. Pare and core the apples and cook them in the syrup until tender, but not broken, turning them frequently. Then drain them and place in a baking dish. To the syrup add the fat and cinnamon and continue to cook until quite thick. Fill the cores of the apples and the surrounding space with the syrup and stick the apples with the blanched almonds lengthwise. Place in a 450 degree oven just long enough to brown the nut tips. Cool and serve with whipped cream. Yields six servings.

Mrs. Joan Pugh
Florence

Ozark Pudding

¾ cup sugar
⅓ cup flour
1¼ teaspoon baking powder
Pinch of salt
Cinnamon

Nutmeg
½ cup nuts
1 cup chopped apples
1 egg
Vanilla

Mix all ingredients. Bake for 30 minutes at 350 degrees.

Mrs. E.B. Anderson, Sr.
Florence

Chocolate Fudge Pudding

1 cup sifted flour
2 teaspoons baking powder
1 teaspoon salt
⅔ cup granulated sugar
6 tablespoons cocoa

½ cup milk
2 tablespoons melted shortening
1 teaspoon vanilla
½ cup chopped pecans
1 cup brown sugar, packed

Sift flour, baking powder, salt, granulated sugar, and 2 tablespoons cocoa. Add milk, shortening, and vanilla; mix only until smooth. Add pecans. Put in greased, shallow one quart baking dish. Mix brown sugar and remaining 4 tablespoons cocoa; sprinkle over mixture in baking dish. Pour 1½ cups boiling water over the top. This pudding, when baked, has a chocolate sauce on bottom and cake on top. Bake in moderate oven (350) for 40 minutes. Serve warm or cold, topped with ice cream if desired.

Mrs. Craig H. Groce
Muscle Shoals

Winter Mince Pudding

1 egg, slightly beaten
¼ cup molasses
1 cup minced pie filling

1 roll (18 ounces) refrigerated
oatmeal raisin cookies,
softened to room temperature

Grease bottom and sides of 8 or 9 inch square pan or 1½ quart pudding mold. In large mixing bowl, combine egg, molasses and pie filling. Crumble in cookie dough and mix well. Pour into prepared pan and bake at 375 degrees for 35-40 minutes until center is firm. Serve warm with Fluffy Sauce.

Fluffy Sauce

½ cup butter, softened
2 cups sifted powdered sugar

2 tablespoons brandy extract

Cream butter until light. Gradually add sugar and extract; beat until fluffy. Serve with warm pudding.

Mrs. R.A. Fonseca
Florence

Date Pudding

½ cup firmly packed brown sugar
2 eggs, well beaten
2 tablespoons flour
1 teaspoon baking powder

1 cup pitted dates , cut in
pieces
1 cup nuts, coarsely chopped

Beat the brown sugar into the eggs. Stir in a mixture of flour and baking powder. Stir in the dates and nuts. Turn mixture into a shallow 1½ quart baking dish. Bake at 325 degrees about 30 minutes. Serve with cream. About 8 servings.

Mrs. Tracy Gargis
Sheffield

323

Norwgian Rice Pudding

4 cups water
2 cups milk
½ teaspoon salt

1 cup rice
½ cup sugar

Bring water, milk and salt to a boil and add rice and sugar. Cook over low heat ½ hour or until rice is soft and fluffy. Stir gently once or twice. Chill.

Whip ¾ cup heavy cream, add 1 teaspoon vanilla and mix with rice just before serving. Put saran wrap over rice when cooling so rice does not crust.

Serve strawberries, peaches, or any fruit on top of each serving of rice. Crushed pineapple may be added to rice mixture, if desired.

Mrs. Elliot Bergsagel

Indian Pudding

1½ quarts milk
½ cup regular yellow cornmeal
¾ cup molasses
6 tablespoons sugar

¾ teaspoon salt
1½ teaspoons ginger
Vanilla ice cream, cream or
    whipped cream

Scald 1 quart milk in top part of double boiler. Mix cornmeal with ½ cup milk and slowly stir into scalded milk. Cook, uncovered, stirring occasionally, 20 minutes. Add next 4 ingredients and mix well. Pour into buttered shallow 1½ quart baking dish and bake in slow oven (325 degrees) 1 hour. Stir in remaining milk and bake about 1½ hours longer. Serve warm with ice cream. Makes 8 servings. This is a favorite in New England.

Danish Pudding

1 cup shortening
1¾ cups sugar
3 eggs, beaten
1 tablespoon orange juice
1 tablespoon grated orange
    rind
1 cup buttermilk

3 cups sifted flour
1½ teaspoons soda
1 teaspoon salt
8 ounces dates, chopped and
    rolled in flour
1 cup chopped pecans

Cream together sugar and shortening; add eggs well beaten, orange juice and rind. Sift together all other dry ingredients and add to creamed mixture alternately with the buttermilk. Fold in dates and pecans. Pour into well-greased and floured large tube pan. Bake in preheated oven 350 degrees for one hour. Have ready one cup orange juice, grated rind of one orange and one cup sugar. Combine, stir until all sugar is dissolved. When cake is done, pour the sauce over and allow cake to cool before removing from pan.

Mrs. Emmett Abramson
Cloverdale

Old Tennessee Woodford Pudding

1 cup flour (sifted)
1 teaspoon soda
1 cup sugar
½ cup butter
3 egg yolks
1 cup blackberry jam

Cream sugar, butter, egg yolks, and jam together. Add dry ingredients to creamed mixture. Add milk and stir until smooth. Fold in stiff beaten egg whites and pour into greased 8x8x2 inch pan. Bake in 350 degree oven for 30 to 35 minutes. Serve with whipped cream. Makes 6 to 8 servings.

Mrs. Donna M. Hayes
Florence

Raw Apple Pudding

½ cup butter
1 cup sugar
1 egg
1 teaspoon soda
1 teaspoon cinnamon
½ cup chopped nuts
1 cup flour, sifted
½ teaspoon salt
1½ cups raw apples, diced

Cream butter and sugar well; add egg, beating until fluffy. Add all dry ingredients; add apple and nuts. Bake in a greased baking dish for 45 minutes at 350 degrees.

Mrs. Tracy Gargis
Sheffield

Custard Bread Pudding

¼ cup raisins
1 tablespoons Kirsch, or other
   liquor or lemon juice
2 cups milk
2 eggs
2 egg yolks (or 1 egg)
½ cup light corn syrup
1 teaspoon vanilla
2¾ cups soft, medium-fine
   enriched bread crumbs
   (6 slices)
1 tablespoon margarine, melted
2 tablespoons sugar

When preheating oven, set a pan of water in oven to serve as water bath for pudding. Soak raisins in warm water to plump. Drain. Discard water. Pour liquor over raisins and set aside. Scald milk and let cool slightly. Beat eggs and yolks slightly. Gradually stir in light corn syrup and vanilla, then milk. Strain. Stir in raisins and liquor, then ¾ or the bread crumbs. Pour into 1½ quart baking dish. Toss remaining crumbs with melted butter and place lightly on top of baking dish. Sprinkle sugar over crumbs. Place in hot water in pan in oven. Bake at 350 degrees oven 50 to 60 minutes, or until a knife inserted into center comes out clean. Makes 6 to 8 servings.

Donna M. Hayes
Florence

Harriet's Cherry Pudding

2 cups cherries
(juice too)
1 cup chopped nuts
2 cups sugar
2 cups flour

2 teaspoons soda
½ teaspoon salt
2 tablespoons butter
2 eggs, well-beaten

Sift flour, sugar, salt and soda. Add cherries, juice, nuts, eggs and butter. Bake at 350 degrees for 45 minutes.

Sauce

2 cups brown sugar
1 tablespoon corn starch

2 cups hot water

Cook together until like syrup. Pour over baked pudding. Cool and refrigerate. Top with whipped cream.

Mrs. Bailey Anderson
Florence

Old Fashioned Rice Pudding
"My Mother's Own Recipe"

¾ cup rice
4½ cups hot water

1½ teaspoons salt

Cook in top of double boiler until tender. Makes 4 cups cooked rice.

Pudding

4 eggs—beat thoroughly
Add:
½ cup plain flour
2 cups skimmed milk
1 can Carnation milk (large
size)

2½ cups sugar
2 teaspoons vanilla flavoring
1 teaspoon lemon extract
4 cups cooked rice
1 stick oleo (melted)

Beat eggs, and add flour, skimmed milk, and carnation milk. Beat well. Add sugar, vanilla, lemon extract, rice, and oleo, and mix thoroughly. Bake in a well greased baking dish or pudding pan at 350 degrees for 50 minutes.

Mrs. Leroy Kennum
Tuscumbia

Sweet Potato Pudding

2 eggs
¾ cup sugar
1½ cups milk
½ cup butter

1 teaspoon vanilla flavoring
¼ teaspoon salt
2 cups grated potatoes

Mix ingredients together and bake in slow oven.

Monteen Stanley
Sheffield

The highlight of any meal is dessert. Smooth and creamy. . . cool and refreshing. . . sweet and rich. . . an elegant dessert makes any meal a special occasion.

Lindy's Famous Cheesecake
Crust:

1 cup sifted all-purpose flour	1 teaspoon lemon peel, grated
¼ cup sugar	1 egg yolk
½ teaspoon vanilla extract	¼ cup soft butter or margarine

Filling:

5 8-ounce packages cream cheese (2½ pounds) at room temperature	1½ teaspoons grated orange peel
	¼ teaspoon vanilla
	5 eggs
1¾ cups sugar	2 egg yolks
3 tablespoons all-purpose flour	¼ cup heavy cream
1½ teaspoons grated lemon peel	

Make crust: In small bowl, combine flour, sugar, lemon peel and vanilla. Make a well in center. Add egg yolks and butter. With fingertips, mix until dough leaves side of bowl. Form into a ball; wrap in waxed paper. Refrigerate one hour.

Meanwhile, preheat oven to 400 degrees. Lightly grease bottom and side of a 9-inch springform pan; remove side.

Remove ⅓ of dough from refrigerator. Roll out directly on bottom of springform pan; trim dough even with edge. Bake 8-10 minutes, or until golden. Cool.

Divide remaining dough into three parts. On lightly floured surface, roll each part into a strip 2½ inches wide. Press strips to side of springform pan, joining ends of strips, to line outside completely. Trim dough so it comes only ¾ cup side. Refrigerate until ready to fill.

Preheat oven to 500 degrees. Make filling: In large bowl of electric mixer, combine cheese with sugar, flour, lemon peel, orange peel and vanilla. Add eggs and yolks, one at a time, beating after each addition. Beat only until mixture is well combined. Add cream, beating until well combined. Assemble springform pan with baked crust on bottom and unbaked pastry around side. Pour filling; bake 10 minutes.

Reduce oven temperature to 250 degrees. Bake one hour. Cool in pan, on wire rack. Then refrigerate three hours, or overnight.

To serve: Remove side of springform pan. Serve cheesecake plain or topped with a glaze.

Frank Johnson
Sheffield

No-Cook Cheese Cake

1 package lemon flavored
   gelatin
1 cup boiling water
1 8-ounce or three 3-ounce
   packages of cream
   cheese

½ cup sugar
1 teaspoon vanilla
1 tall can evaporated milk
3 cups graham cracker crumbs
½ cup butter or margarine, melted

Dissolve gelatin in boiling water. Chill until slightly thickened. Cream together cheese, sugar and vanilla; add gelatin and blend well. Fold in stiffly whipped milk. (This can be done with electric mixer). Mix graham cracker crumbs and melted butter together; pack ⅔ of mixture on bottom and sides of 9x13x2 inch pan (or larger). Add filling and sprinkle with remaining crumbs. Chill several hours (or overnight). Serves 12-16.

Lemon Cheesecake

1½ cups graham cracker crumbs
3 tablespoons sugar
¼ cup butter or margarine,
   melted
1 package (6.5 ounces) lemon
   fluff frosting mix

1 package (8 ounces) cream
   cheese, softened
1½ cups dairy sour cream
1 package (10 ounces) frozen
   strawberries, thawed

Heat oven to 300 degrees. Mix thoroughly graham cracker crumbs, sugar and butter, reserving ⅓ cup crumb mixture. Press crumb mixture evenly in bottom of a square pan, 9-by-9-by-2-inches. Prepare frosting mix as directed on package. Blend cream cheese and sour cream in a large mixing bowl. Gradually beat in frosting. Pour cream cheese mixture over crumb mixture. Sprinkle with reserved crumbs. Bake for 45 minutes. Cool slightly and chill. Serve with strawberries.

Mrs. Jerry Turbyfill
Florence

Pumpkin Cheesecake

⅓ cup margarine
⅓ cup sugar
1 egg
1¼ cups flour
2 8-ounce packages cream cheese
¾ cup sugar

1 16-ounce can pumpkin
1 teaspoon cinnamon
¼ teaspoon ginger
¼ teaspoon nutmeg
Dash of salt
2 eggs

Cream margarine and sugar until light and fluffy; blend in egg. Add flour; mix well. Spread dough with spatula on bottom and 2 inches high around sides of 9-inch springform pan. Bake at 400 degrees for five minutes. Reduce oven temperature to 350 degrees.

Combine softened cream cheese and sugar, mixing at medium speed on electric mixer until well blended. Blend in pumpkin, spices and salt; mix well. Add eggs, one at a time, mixing well after each addition. Pour mixture into pastry lined pan; smooth surface to edge of crust. Bake at 350 degrees, 50 minutes. Loosen cake from rim of pan; cool before removing rim of pan. Chill. Garnish with whipped cream just before serving.

Table of Measurements and Equivalents in U.S. and Metric

U.S.	EQUIVALENTS	METRIC *volume-milliliters*
Dash	Less than 1/8 teaspoon	
1 teaspoon	60 drops	5 ml.
1 tablespoon	3 teaspoons	15 ml.
2 tablespoons	1 fluid ounce	30 ml.
4 tablespoons	1/4 cup	60 ml.
5 1/3 tablespoons	1/3 cup	80 ml.
6 tablespoons	3/8 cup	90 ml.
8 tablespoons	1/2 cup	120 ml.
10 2/3 tablespoons	2/3 cup	160 ml.
12 tablespoons	3/4 cup	180 ml.
16 tablespoons	1 cup or 8 ounces	240 ml.
1 cup	1/2 pint or 8 fluid ounces	240 ml.
2 cups	1 pint	480 ml.
1 pint	16 ounces	480 ml. or .473 liter
1 quart	2 pints	960 ml. or .95 liter
2.1 pints	1.05 quarts or .26 gallons	1 liter
2 quarts	1/2 gallon	
4 quarts	1 gallon	3.8 liters
		weight-grams
1 ounce	16 drams	28 grams
1 pound	16 ounces	454 grams
1 pound	2 cups liquid	
1 kilo	2.20 pounds	

Temperature Conversion from Fahrenheit to Celsius

FAHRENHEIT	200	225	250	275	300	325	350	375
CELSIUS	93	106	121	135	149	163	176	191

FAHRENHEIT	400	425	450	475	500	550
CELSIUS	205	218	231	246	260	288

Index

Pork (See Meats)

POULTRY

Chicken

Other Poultry

Dove or Quail. Roast. 99
Duckling. Rotisserie. 99

Turkey

Sandwich Dressing. 101
Sandwich. Kentucky Hot Brown. 101
Sandwich. Lucky Seven. 101
Turkey Drumsticks. Grilled. 100
Turkey. Grilled Outdoor. 100

Rice (See Grains)

SALADS

Apple-Tuna Salad. 42
Avocado Bacon Boats. 40
Buffet Taco Salad. 53
Celery Salad. 44
Chicken Salad. 50
Chicken Salad with Fruit. 50
Chinese Chicken Salad. 50
Congealed Salad. 58
Copenhagen Salad. 52
Cranberry Horseradish Salad. 40
Cucumbers in Sour Cream. 39
Cucumber Salad. 39
Dressing. Low Calorie. 49
Dressing. Fruit Salad. 47
Dressing. Hidden Valley. 47
Dressing. Lemon Honey. 48
Dressing. Lime Honey. 48
Dressing. Low Calorie French. 49
Dressing. Oil-less French. 48
Dressing. Papa's Italian. 47
Dressing. Roquefort Cheese. 48
Dressing. Sweet Fruit. 47
Dressing. Thousand Island. 47
Fruit Salad. 56
Fruit Salad. Alaskan. 61
Fruit Salad. Angel Flake. 56
Fruit Salad. Blueberry. 64
Fruit Salad. Buttermilk. 59
Fruit Salad. Cherry. 62
Fruit Salad. Cola Congealed. 59
Fruit Salad. Cottage Cheese. 54
Fruit Salad. Dry Gelatin. 56
Fruit Salad. Easy Bavarian. 64
Fruit Salad. Easy Summer. 56
Fruit Salad. Fresh Cranberry. 63
Fruit Salad. Frosted. 63
Fruit Salad. Frozen. 54
Fruit Salad. Gingerale. 57
Fruit Salad. Gelatin. 60
Fruit Salad. Green. 57
Fruit Salad. Heavenly. 54
Fruit Salad. Heavenly Hash. 55
Fruit Salad. Holiday. 65
Fruit Salad. Jellied Pineapple. 58
Fruit Salad. Lemon. 61
Fruit Salad. Lime. 60
Fruit Salad. Lime Congealed. 60
Fruit Salad. Lime Gelatin. 60
Fruit Salad. Magnolia. 54

Fruit Salad. Marshmellow. 63
Fruit Salad. Orange Sherbert. 64
Fruit Salad. Paradise. 55
Fruit Salad. Pineapple. 58
Fruit Salad. Pineapple Lime. 58
Fruit Salad. Pink Gelatin. 59
Fruit Salad. Raspberry. 62
Fruit Salad. Ribbon. 57
Fruit Salad. Sawdust. 65
Fruit Salad. Seven-Up. 61
Fruit Salad. Sherbert. 64
Fruit Salad. Sour Cream. 55
Fruit Salad. Sprinkle. 55
Fruit Salad. Strawberry-Nut. 62
Fruit Salad. Summer. 59
Fruit Salad. Sunset. 62
Fruit Salad. Sunshine. 57
Fruit Salad. Yuletide. 65
Green Bean Salad. 43
Green Pea Salad. 40
Hot Buttons and Bows. 51
Hot Lettuce. 43
Low Calorie Salad. 49
Macaroni Salad. 53
Macaroni Supper Salad. 53
Peanut Salad. 46
Pimiento Cheese Mold. 51
Potato Salad Cheese. 39
Potato Salad. German. 44
Potato Salad. Meaty. 39
Rice Salad. 52
Salmon Salad. 41
Shrimp Luncheon Salad. Diabetic. 49
Shrimp Salad. 41
Shrimp Salad Mold. 41
Shrimp Tomato Stars. 41
Slaw. 45
Slaw. Cabbage. 46
Slaw. Creamy Corn. 46
Slaw. Refrigerator. 45
Slaw. Refrigerator Cole. 45
Slaw. Vegetable. 45
Slaw. 24-Hour. 46
Spinach Salad. 44
Spinach Salad. Dutch. 44
Spinach Salad. Molded. 42
The Salad. 40
Tomato Aspic. Mom's. 52
Tuna Salad. 42
Vegetable Salad. Overnight. 43
Waldorf Salad. 51
Waldorf Salad. Jellied. 51

Salad Dressings (See Salads)

Salmon (See Seafood)

SAUCES and DRESSINGS

Barbecue Lover's Sauce. 152
Barbecue Sauce. 89, 127, 129
Clam Sauce. 180
Fluffy Sauce. 324
Fondue Sauces. 119

SEAFOOD

Shrimp (See Seafood)

SOUPS

Tuna (See Seafood)

Turkey (See Poultry)

Veal (See Meats)

VEGETABLES